INDIA IN THE SECOND WORLD WAR

DIYA GUPTA

India in the Second World War

An Emotional History

OXFORD

UNIVERSITY PRESS

OXFORD
UNIVERSITY PRESS

Oxford University Press is a department of the
University of Oxford. It furthers the University's objective
of excellence in research, scholarship, and education
by publishing worldwide.

Oxford   New York
Auckland   Cape Town   Dar es Salaam   Hong Kong   Karachi
Kuala Lumpur   Madrid   Melbourne   Mexico City   Nairobi
New Delhi   Shanghai   Taipei   Toronto

With offices in
Argentina   Austria   Brazil   Chile   Czech Republic   France   Greece
Guatemala   Hungary   Italy   Japan   Poland   Portugal   Singapore
South Korea   Switzerland   Thailand   Turkey   Ukraine   Vietnam

Oxford is a registered trade mark of Oxford University Press
in the UK and certain other countries.

Published in the United States of America by
Oxford University Press
198 Madison Avenue, New York, NY 10016

Library of Congress Cataloging-in-Publication Data is available
Diya Gupta.
India in the
Second World War: An Emotional History.
ISBN: 9780197694701

Printed in the United Kingdom

Ujjalendu Gupta (11 April 1952–12 October 2021)
To Baba, the luminous moon, without whom, nothing

CONTENTS

LIST OF ILLUSTRATIONS

Embedded images

ACKNOWLEDGEMENTS

In writing about the history of emotions in India during a global war, I would like to start with my own. Most acknowledgements will let you know how books were born; this one will tell you how a book came nearly not to exist.

On 12 October 2021, I lost my father to Covid. Apart from medical staff, I was the last person to see him alive; he never returned home from the emergency ward. Living with that knowledge was like falling, slowly but surely, into an abyss. To use a war analogy, it felt as though an incendiary bomb had dropped on my world; as I lay helpless, I could only see the tatters of what had been a rich, whole and happy life. My old life, now unrecognisable. I did not think I would be writing again soon.

I returned to the UK from India at the end of November that year. My father travelled with me. I saw him everywhere—in my flat, on the Tube, on the train, walking next to me on the street. He had always liked London. One of my most vivid memories is of looking up from my desk at Senate House Library and seeing him smiling down at me. I was trying to take up the threads of work again, and felt happiness radiate from him. I could have reached out and touched him that day. He felt intimately, viscerally real.

Every darkness has its cradles of light, and so did mine. I remain particularly grateful to my friends Bárbara, Gary, Hannah, Faten and Sinéad in the UK, and to Ushasi, Haimanti and Mahua in India for the love they showed me in those terrible days. I can recall a conversation I had with another friend, Mim, about the mysterious connections between us all—in life, death and beyond—and some wonderful email exchanges about loss with Philip Carter at the Royal Historical Society. All manner of people—friends and strangers alike—were in touch, talking of experiencing similar sorrow or sharing the love they bore for my father. It was both a painful and extraordinary outpouring.

Thanks also to my bereavement counsellor who understood how much I was averse to the language of 'healing' or 'being cured' from grief. Losing my father is a wound that I will carry forever. In retrospect, acknowledging this was one of the first steps in being able to take up work on the book again. And, with this realisation, in turning once more to the craft of writing, there came a strange joy.

I cannot express enough regard for my postdoctoral mentor Matthew Hilton, my former PhD supervisor Santanu Das and the Royal Historical Society's Race, Ethnicity and Equality Working Group co-chairs Sadiah Qureshi and Jonathan Saha for their unstinting support during this time. This book would not be published today without them. My thanks also to the readers of my chapters—Suzanne Bardgett, Anna Maguire, Mrinalini Sinha, Daniel Morse, Daniel Todman, Jonathan Saha, Supriya Chaudhuri, Santanu Das and Matthew Hilton—for their thoughtful and considered feedback, and to the two anonymous peer reviewers who so warmly advocated for this book's publication with Hurst and Oxford University Press. Suchetana Chattopadhyay sent me wonderful reading suggestions, while Margot Finn looked through my book proposal in its draft stages and offered sage advice. I am very grateful to both.

It was at King's College London that my doctoral research, on which this book is based, took shape, and I have fond memories of the collegiality and conviviality I enjoyed there. Thanks also to my external examiners Yasmin Khan and Elleke Boehmer for their careful consideration of my thesis and productive suggestions for transforming the PhD into a book. It is no exaggeration to say that they helped me find my scholarly voice. And working on the Imperial War Museum's AHRC-funded 'Provisional Semantics' project on colonial war photography in India during the Second World War enabled me to refine my thinking further. The project helped me to slow my scholarship down, to examine closely the presence of Indian men framed by the colonial lens. I found myself questioning—could visual culture tell us something that textual material could not?

This book is founded upon transnational archival work, which can be rewarding but also demanding and frustrating, even in pre-

ACKNOWLEDGEMENTS

Covid times, and I am grateful to everyone who made this process smoother—Sugata Bose for facilitating access to the Netaji Research Bureau in Kolkata, Jawhar Sircar for his networks and contacts, Sitanshu Kar and Nitin Wakankar for access to the Indian Ministry of Defence archives in Delhi, and archivists in the Private Papers section at the National Archives of India, Delhi. Staff at the British Library, Imperial War Museum, National Army Museum and the National Archives at Kew, as well as the Tagore Centre in London, have been incredibly generous with their time, and I thank them all.

Thanks are also due to all those engaged readers of my journalistic pieces on India and the Second World War, published online and in both India and the UK. I would particularly like to mention Arnab Bardhan Paul from Bangladesh, who sent me copies of the memoir *Arakan Fronte* and Baren Basu's war novel *Rangrut*, revealing to me that cultural memories of this war in modern South Asia are far from forgotten. I would also like to thank Priyanka Basu and Farha Noor for their help in securing a wonderful translator for a Punjabi poem that I discuss in the Introduction. Ajmal Kamal did a nuanced English rendering of this challenging work, for which many thanks. I am grateful to Ghee Bowman for sharing this poem with me.

I have been extraordinarily fortunate in being able to interview Indian veterans of the war during the course of my research. Thanks to Air Commodore S.P. Singh in Delhi, and Pratapaditya Dasgupta, Jyotindra Mohun Nag and Helenia Daniel (the latter now sadly no more) in Kolkata for allowing me to speak to them about their wartime lives. Geshe Graham Woodhouse, Kabir Saxena, Dipankar and Debanuj Dasgupta, Boudhayan Nag and Priyanka Biswas were enthusiastic organisers of these interviews—thank you!

A special thanks also to Aniket Mitra for telling me about his grandfather, Ajit Kumar Mitra, and his Second World War story right at the start of my research journey. This was truly an inspirational encounter. For all those in India and the UK who sent me photographs and private papers of their loved ones at war, and filled out my research questionnaire, many grateful thanks—these include Ujjal Maitra; Ritwick Mukherjee; Muhammad Abul Hay; Harish, Jayati and Parmanand Bhambhani; and Tehseen Gulzar.

Thanks are due to the Royal Historical Society and the Institute of Historical Research, both of which served as my intellectual home between 2020 and 2022, during the writing of this book, and to *Past and Present* for financially supporting my research. I am very grateful to Michael Dwyer at Hurst for responding to my book proposal with an acceptance in what seemed like record time! Lara Weisweiller-Wu has been a wonderfully patient and encouraging editor and Daisy Leitch efficient and resourceful in taking the book through the production process. Thanks also to Alice Clarke and Mei Jayne Yew for their help with everything book-related.

To my sister Poopsie and her husband Shobhit, thank you for all the encouragement and support in my writing journey. I fully trust that you will read this book from cover to cover! To Ma at home in Kolkata, I know how happy the publication of this book will make you. And to our pug Leo, thank you for all the playfulness and laughter you have brought us. I firmly believe that dog cuddles are an indispensable part of the academic writing journey, and this book is the better for all the dog hairs you have shed on me.

To my partner Shaun, thank you for everything, but most of all the music. I could not have written anything without your curated soundtracks to accompany my words. Sorry for going on about the war for nearly eight years now.

Finishing my first book has made me think of how my father had wanted to write his own. A very different one to this, but we had discussed book proposals and writing tips. He was hugely supportive of my research, and very pleased indeed when my work was accepted for publication. Nothing suited him better than to ring me in the afternoon, to ask me how it was going and why I was taking so very long over each chapter. After all, didn't writing just mean one word after another? This book is dedicated to him.

INTRODUCTION

'V' FOR VICTORY?

Fig. 0.1: 'He gives the "V" sign from the porthole of a ship as he arrives at Singapore—and his "V" is backed by a million Indian troops and the rest of the Empire as well.' © Imperial War Museum.[1]

This photograph of an Indian soldier on board a troop ship to Singapore in the 1940s confronts us with a familiar gesture. The soldier thrusts his head and arm through the ship's porthole and appropriates Winston Churchill's well-recognised 'V for Victory' symbol with the fore and middle fingers of his right hand, although his palm faces inwards.[2] This physical gesture punctures our Euro-

1

and US-centric memory of the Second World War with a non-white colonial presence. The soldier's smiling, youthful face attests to the two-and-a-half million men from undivided India,[3] the largest volunteer army in the world at the time,[4] which served as the British Empire's 'greatest reservoir of military manpower'.[5] This photograph belongs to a colonial archive, part of the British Ministry of Information's collection at the Imperial War Museum, used for propaganda purposes in Britain and abroad. As its caption highlights, the photograph was taken to demonstrate the 'loyalty' and participation in the war of not just Indians but well over half-a-million Africans and several thousand West Indians, who served alongside men from the white Dominions—Australia, New Zealand, Canada and South Africa.[6] These were imperial forces represented as fighting under a united flag, or symbol, in this case.[7] But what does recreating the 'V for Victory' symbol mean to this Indian soldier in this photograph, particularly when there is no name provided in the caption—the soldier is simply referred to as 'he'? How does he stake a claim to his own presence in, and emotions of, the Second World War? And is the soldier playing with this Churchillian symbol by deliberately inverting the 'V' sign as an obscene hand gesture, with his palm facing inward? Is it an ironic response to the colonial photographer's demands, or performed as an anti-imperialist symbol?

This photograph shares similarities with another image, also related to Empire and war, although from a different context. In his famous essay 'Myth Today' (1957), Roland Barthes illustrates the layers of myth-making contained in the object of his study, a photograph displayed on the cover of the magazine *Paris Match* portraying a young black soldier gazing upwards, saluting the French flag. Barthes's analysis draws our attention to visual signifiers similar to those in the Indian 'V for Victory' photograph. He writes:

> I see very well what it [the photograph] signifies to me: that France is a great Empire, that all her sons, without any colour discrimination, faithfully serve under her flag, and that there is no better answer to the detractors of an alleged colonialism than the zeal shown by this Negro [translator's word] in serving his so-called oppressors.[8]

Fig. 0.2: Cover of *Paris Match* commented on by Barthes in *Mythologies*.[9]

Barthes recognises how French imperialism seeks to reduce the saluting black soldier to 'nothing more than an instrumental signifier',[10] yet the very 'naturalness' of this implied meaning is suspect. The photograph, rather literally in this case, gestures us instead towards the constructed, '*fabricated* quality of colonialism'.[11] Barthes also notes why the saluting black soldier cannot simply function as an instrument of empire in the photograph—'he has too much presence'.[12] It is this overflow of 'presence', in all its tangled and complicated forms, that I recover and analyse in this emotional history of undivided India in the Second World War.

While the 'V for Victory' symbol dominated the Indian political landscape during the war years, the Indian Army grew ever more corpulent, swelling to two-and-a-half million men. In October 1939, the Indian Army comprised 194,373 troops, and by August

1945, its size had increased to 2,065,554.[13] The numbers peaked in May 1944 at 2,668,470.[14] In parallel, the Royal Indian Air Force grew from 285 officers and men to 29,201 officers and men, with nine squadrons, while the Royal Indian Navy expanded from 1,846 men to comprising 30,748.[15] Of the 2,499,909 men serving in the Indian Army between 3 September 1939 and 31 August 1945, 2,038,001 were classified as combatants.[16] By the end of hostilities in August 1945, an estimated 74,992 had been killed, 64,354 were injured, 11,754 were missing and 79,489 had been taken prisoners of war.[17] And, during these war years, India became a wartime industrial production house and suffered acute shortages in grain, kerosene, cloth and other essential items.[18] But did the people of India believe this war to be their own? Contested feelings pushed against one another, particularly after Japan's rapid military take-over of British-occupied territories in Southeast Asia by May 1942. Songs composed by the Indian People's Theatre Association (IPTA), established by the Communist Party of India in 1943, proved extremely popular among impoverished peasants from Bengal, particularly sharecroppers, as a response to their plight caused by global war:

> O kishan, tor ghore agun, baire je toofan.
> Bideshi sarkar ghore, duare Japaan (p. 223).

> O farmer, your home is on fire, and outside a typhoon rages.
> A foreign government occupies your home, and on your doorstep is Japan.[19]

While British colonialism is symbolised here by fire—a theme I take up in this book—the ferocious threat of external invasion from the east is represented by the imminent typhoon. Both colonialism within India and imperialism without are seen as ravaging, destructive forces, as anticolonial and anti-capitalist emotion here surges against anti-Japanese sentiment.

Yet another folk song highlights a community of lamentation formed among Bengali women left behind at home while their men join the imperial war effort:

> Chatignaye ranga go mati,
> O tor bhaiyer kachhe likhchhi chitthi.
> Guner nanad go, tor bhai gelo boideshe,

Aar ailo na deshe.
Militaryte je jon chakri go kore,
Shejon keno biya kore go? Tor bhai gelo boideshe,
Aar ailo na deshe.

The earth of Chittagong is red!
O, I am writing a letter to your brother.
My talented sister-in-law, your brother left for foreign lands,
And never returned to his own land.
Those who take up work in the military,
Why do they choose to get married? Your brother left for foreign
lands,
And never returned to his own land.[20]

Composed by unknown rural poets, the song foregrounds the act of
letter-writing—another significant theme in this book—but there
is a sense of hopelessness and despair in having to undertake such a
task. Instead of letter-writing becoming a tool of communication,
connecting remote villages to international battlefronts where
Indian soldiers were stationed, it transforms into a poignant
reminder of physical absence. Are these letters ever answered by
the soldier-husband? The refrain—'Your brother left for foreign
lands, / And never returned to his own land'—suggests not. They
certainly do not lure him back home. The tone of abandonment and
pathos is underscored by the reference to the redness of Chittagong's
earth, to which the soldier's wife is rooted. But is the redness also
a suggestion of warfare in the 'foreign lands' where the soldier
serves, with bloodshed and violence that the soldier's wife can only
guess at but never fully know?

And then there is poetic composition by the itinerant soldier
himself in these 'foreign lands'. In *Jangi Safarnama* (*Journey Through
War*, c.1944), Nawazish Ali, using the *takhallus* Mushtaq, writes of
his battlefront experiences in Burma in the Punjabi language,
employing the Shahmukhi script.[21] The poem draws upon the infor-
mal *qissa* or storytelling style and the *masnavi* form, where two lines
of each couplet rhyme with each other, and declares:

Come, O my pen, fill your mouth with ink and write of the
sorrows;
Cry your heart out and give full account of the distress.

First bow your head in the *durbar* of your readers;
Prostrate in supplication and tell of the heart's sufferings.

[...]

People of that country were so unnerved
That they fled to the jungles, leaving their treasures and wealth
behind.

We saw them walking on the roads, crying and panting;
Their feet were full of boils due to walking, but they continued to
walk.

[...]

They had no idea what the world outside home felt like;
O my God! Why did the people of this country have to suffer so?[22]

The personified pen here is seen as weeping its story through ink, metaphorically aligning itself to the human heart and tears of suffering. Nawazish Ali self-consciously gives his pen agency, projecting its humble acknowledgment of the presence of a *durbar* or court of readers to whom 'the heart's sufferings' must be narrated. Here, Nawazish represents witnessing the exodus of Burmese civilians from their homeland in 1942, and in doing so highlights several themes that are important in my book: the pain endured by the body; the emotions associated with home and the anxieties surrounding its loss; and the role of testimony in the empathic portrayal of another's suffering.

In these three compositions, the impoverished male farmer, the Bengali soldier's wife and the imperial soldier from north India locate themselves within wartime subjectivities in particular ways, negotiating their class, caste, religious and gendered experiential realities. The farmer is made aware of the dangers of imperial conflict on his livelihood; the deserted wife sings of war-induced marital absence and loneliness; the colonial soldier in Burma writes in horror of others losing their home even as he fondly remembers his own. But there were other perspectives too. In her book *The Raj at War* (2015), Yasmin Khan observes:

Politicians struggled to articulate a response to an international war which was meaningful for their followers. Some *dalit* leaders thought of their own community's share of military jobs. Some

Sikhs wanted to protect their historic advantages in the army. Jailed communists protested by hunger striking. For peasants, with less contact with the state, the war was even more obscure—a quarrel with Europeans not rooted in Indian conditions—but they were also on the march, campaigning for their own freedoms.[23]

If the IPTA song about the *kisan* or farmer discussed above highlights a conscious political and personal awakening among peasant communities, exacerbated by war, the conflict was also an opportunity for new employment and transnational mobility, a means of protecting entitled access to jobs, and a battleground for securing community rights. To most civilians, however, it appeared remote and removed from their lived experiences, even though the war brought the physical threat of Axis invasion—in the form of imperial Japan's conquests in Southeast Asia—uncomfortably close to India. To others, the war continued to be viewed as enforced and unnecessary. Between 1939 and 1941, communist groups challenged the British Raj and its allies in India. The *kisan sabhas* or farmers' assemblies had protestors shouting: '*Na ek pai, na ek bhai*' (Not one paisa to the war effort, not one man to the army)![24] They also opposed the demands of the *zamindars* or landlords and their extortions, campaigned for more security for tenants and mobilised jute cultivators to insist on government protection when jute prices fell during wartime.[25] On the one hand, Indian men were signing up to an imperial conflict; on the other, insurgent politics—to use Priyamvada Gopal's evocative adjective[26]—that resisted both this war and oppressive measures within India made itself felt.

The Second World War comes to India

This book investigates a knotted emotional history produced by combatants and non-combatants, civilians and prisoners-of-war, poets and intellectuals, men and women in response to Indian involvement in the Second World War as a British colony. The contested social and political history of 1930s and 1940s India provides the foundation of my analysis of a complex range of wartime emotions. Indian political responses to the hostilities that marked the start of the Second World War grew from the hinterland of the previous global war, when the British Empire faced its worst crisis

7

to date between the years 1919 and 1922.[27] This was a markedly different political situation from the beginning of the First World War, which saw even M.K. Gandhi raise an Indian ambulance corps to assist the Red Cross in 1914 and later support the British colonial government's resolution in 1918 to enlist half-a-million Indian troops.[28] In the spring of 1919, protests against the draconian measures of the Rowlatt Act in India led to the infamous Amritsar Massacre. Soldiers from the Indian Army, under the command of Colonel Reginald Dyer, fired their rifles into hundreds of unarmed Indians, who, breaking curfew, had gathered in Jallianwala Bagh in Punjab.[29] This imperial attempt to suppress resistance transformed, instead, into a catalyst for the outpouring of staunch anticolonial feeling. Indian poet, philosopher and intellectual Rabindranath Tagore famously renounced his knighthood in protest against 'treatment [which] has been meted out to a population, disarmed and resourceless, by a power which has the most terribly efficient organisation for destruction of human lives'.[30]

Amritsar did not remain an isolated incident. The British used 'extreme and widespread violence'[31] to subdue rebellions across the Empire, including Ireland, Iraq and India, just as the French undertook similar techniques of suppression in their expanding territories in the Levant and Indochina, as did the Japanese in the Korean Peninsula. Reading the First World War as a product of expansionist imperial ambitions rather than a conflict between nation-states, Robert Gerwarth and Erez Manela argue that the violence generated by the war was far from over in 1918. Instead, 'the entire edifice of the imperial world order was convulsing violently in the aftermath of the Armistice even as it reached its greatest territorial extent. The organised mass violence of the war had not ended; it had only shifted its modes and focal points.'[32]

When the Second World War reached India, then, the subcontinent was already witnessing war within its borders, now compounded by the war outside with Hitler's invasion of Poland in September 1939.[33] The British Raj was divided into two, threatened abroad by imperialist ambitions of the Axis powers and in India by rising nationalist forces. The external war brought in its wake internal foment: India was declared a belligerent state in the Second World War in September 1939 by the Viceroy, Lord Linlithgow, who failed to consult the burgeoning Indian political leadership on this decision. As Srinath Raghavan notes, even before Britain had formally entered into war with Germany, nearly 10,000 Indian troops had been sent off to Egypt, Aden, Singapore, Kenya and Iraq.[34] The Quit India movement, beginning as protests against this undemocratic inclusion in the Second World War, evolved into mass agitations against 200 years of British colonial rule, suppressed in turn by an occupation-style use of force. The Empire needed men and resources for the war; it would not be quitting India just yet. The Sunday newspaper in Britain, *Reynold's News*, carrying an article by journalist H.N. Brailsford on 22 October 1939 on India and the Second World War, recognised the crucial role that the subcontinent needed to play in its headline, which read: 'India—the Path to Victory'.[35] Indeed, fifty-seven infantry battalions of the Indian Army were moved inward, within India, to restrain the August *kranti*.[36]

While nationalism contested colonialism and therefore challenged participation in an imperial war, other political discourses jostled against each other in the subcontinent. India could not be partitioned into those who supported and those who opposed the war; neither did such political positions remain fixed for the duration of the war. Communism intersected with anti-fascism—revolutionary communist factions, to whom the war became 'The People's War' after Hitler invaded the Soviet Union on 22 June 1941, supported their former imperialist adversaries in a transnational ideological battle against fascism.[37] In 1942, the communist intellectual Manabendra Nath Roy believed that Hitler's victory would be far more disastrous than further British rule over India, which would soon be overthrown, and he 'viciously attacked the most prominent Congress leaders such as Nehru and Gandhi for their "Quit India" politics in the context of the Second World War.' For this, Roy was considered to be a 'British spy' and a 'traitor', and even thought by some to have gone mad.[38]

Political radical and Indian revolutionary Subhas Chandra Bose's military intervention strategies, on the other hand, opposed Gandhian non-violent forms of protest with the single-minded aim of securing Indian independence, using the opportunities for new political alliances generated by the war. Indians became targets for a 'pincer movement' of Axis propaganda—from Germany in the west and Japan in the east.[39] This fused itself with the militaristic independence movement spearheaded by Bose, resulting in the creation of the Indian Legion in Germany in 1942 and a resurrected Indian National Army (INA) in 1943 in Southeast Asia, both formed from Indian PoWs and civilian expatriates to fight the British Empire alongside Axis forces.[40] In the cities of Imphal and Kohima at the Indo-Burmese border between March and July 1944, some 84,000 Japanese troops of the 31st, 33rd and 15th divisions and 12,000 INA troops faced 155,000 British, British Indian, British West African and American troops of the Fourteenth Army.[41] These became decisive confrontations in the Burmese theatre of war, with Japanese and Indian forces finally being defeated by Allied troops. Consequently, instead of marching westwards onto Delhi as they had hoped, INA soldiers had to retreat further inward into Burma, where they eventually surrendered to the British.[42] The INA also included a women's Rani of Jhansi Regiment. Bose's naming of this regiment established a mythological and historical thread, starting from the legendary Rani of Jhansi, who had fought the British during the Sepoy Uprising of 1857, to Bengal's women revolutionaries of the 1930s, and these young volunteers.[43] Meanwhile, in Europe, another war narrative was unfolding, with Indian resistance agent Noor Inayat Khan being recruited into the British Special Operations Executive and sent to occupied France, where she was captured and executed at the Dachau concentration camp in 1944.[44]

Such asymmetrical, and often conflicting, entanglements between political positions and 'causes' shaped the turbulence of Indian discourse during the Second World War years. It was, however, opposition to the war by the established Indian political leadership which rapidly became the most intractable problem for British colonial authorities, even before the launch of the Quit India movement in August 1942. The Marquess of Zetland, Lawrence John Lumley Dundas, Secretary of State for India, writing to the Home Department of the Government of India on 12 November 1939, was sharp in his dismissal of the Indian National Congress, castigating their objections as 'impertinent efforts to squeeze advantages out of the Government at a time when the Empire is waging war against the greatest enemy of freedom that has yet arisen in the world'.[45] Yet, colonial participation complicated the Second World

War's fight against fascism, its 'moral righteousness',[46] this very notion of freedom. Tracing his family's history of involvement in the Second World War in the semi-fictional, semi-biographical book *Farthest Field* (2015), Raghu Karnad discusses the ideological shifts in the meaning of this word:

> Indians, who had spent two decades entering the river of nationalist sentiment, now found its flow violently reversed or eddying in confusion. The freedom struggle was a diversion from the fight against fascism, or vice versa. The word 'freedom' pulled one way and then the other. It meant freedom for the men of Europe. It meant freedom *from* the men of Europe. Likewise 'victory': frowning black Vs appeared amidst the newsprint and on walls, everywhere, demanding that the populace believe the war their own.[47]

Despite its own opposition to fascism, India's political elite in the Indian National Congress widely regarded the war as one where the country was forcibly made to participate as a British colony.[48] On 25 November 1939, in the newspaper *Harijan*, Gandhi objected in uncompromising terms to war service without a guarantee of Indian independence, presenting it as an ethical issue:

> The issue [...] becomes purely moral for, owing to her material and military control over India, Britain is able to regulate the Indian and British garrison and drain India's wealth at her will. Eight provinces out of eleven have said in emphatic language that they cannot participate in the war, if it does not mean, among other things, India's complete freedom. All other issues are subordinate.[49]

Gandhi's feelings received a sympathetic echo in the colonial metropole by Clement Attlee, Leader of the British Labour Party, in an article published in *The Times* in the same year. Attlee observed: 'At the beginning of a great struggle of liberty and democracy against dictatorship and domination we realise the depth of feeling of the Indian people in support of the principles of freedom and self-government.'[50] And the *Manchester Guardian* carried an opinion piece on 4 October 1939 that reinforced the same point:

> In the struggle which lies before us, the whole-hearted support of the people of India may well be of vital assistance both materially, through men, money and materials, and morally, by proving to the

world that England is not fighting oppression with bondage in her own house.[51]

The question of obtaining freedom, then, could not be contained within combating fascism alone; it became implicated in the struggle against colonialism, brought to a head by the return of global war. Freedom's complicated nuances were recognised both within India and in sections of British political discourse.

That Indian independence occupied a central role in the consideration of world freedom, where fascism and imperialism were conjoined, was emphasised by Jawaharlal Nehru in his reworking of the Quit India Resolution of 7 and 8 August 1942. Nehru states:

> [B]y the freedom of India will Britain and the United Nations be judged, and the peoples of Asia and Africa be filled with hope and enthusiasm [...] A free India will assure this success by throwing all her great resources in the struggle for freedom and against the aggression of Nazism, Fascism and Imperialism.[52]

The question of whether to fight fascism, then, was not moot—it became, instead, a matter of being able to exercise choice. Yet this was no narrow or parochially nationalist perspective. Manu Bhagavan argues that the Nehruvian and Gandhian philosophy outlined in the Quit India Resolution is, in fact, a world vision, and that both Nehru and Gandhi realised the need for 'an external democratic authority, world government' with the capacity to 'check the power of the state'.[53] The resolution goes on to declare:

> [T]he future peace, security and ordered progress of the world demand a world federation of free nations, and on no other basis can the problems of the world be solved. Such a world federation would ensure the freedom of its constituent nations, the prevention of aggression and exploitation of one nation over another, the protection of national minorities, the advancement of all backward areas and peoples, and the pooling of the world's resources for the common good of all.[54]

In Bhagavan's reading, for Nehru and Gandhi, the idea of this 'one world' was woven into the vision of a democratic and independent India. In August 1942, however, these views were seen as seditious by colonial authorities. Gandhi, Nehru and other members of the Indian National Congress leadership were sent off to prison, where they remained for the duration of the war. And for most civilians in India, wartime life posed significant challenges. While certain monopolising businesses expanded their profit margins—such as the jute, aluminium and tea industries, coal mining and cotton textiles—industrial urban workers had to endure long hours of work in poor conditions and for low wages. It was an impoverished time for peasants in the countryside too, especially in Bengal.[55] These crucial material conditions also affected writers in India, who had to contend with considerable postal delays, paper shortages and lack of printer's ink.[56] The Indian home-front was altering in drastic and, in the case of Bengal in 1943, horrific ways.[57]

The charged word 'freedom', as noted earlier, made a powerful return to Indian political discourse in the immediate aftermath of the war, when the victorious Allied nations held much-publicised trials for war crimes, the most well-known of these being at Nuremberg between November 1945 and October 1946.[58] The Indian equivalent, however, taking on a staunchly nationalist hue, blurred the boundary between 'treason' and protest against antico-lonial rule. The most famous of these Red Fort trials, conducted between November 1945 and May 1946, saw three high-ranking INA officers, of different faiths—Prem Kumar Saigal (Hindu), Gurbaksh Singh Dhillon (Sikh) and Shah Nawaz Khan (Muslim)—being court-martialled for 'waging war against the King' and murder, and sentenced to deportation for life.[59] Ultimately, however, the sentences against these three INA officers were commuted by Commander-in-Chief of the Indian Army, Claude Auchinleck, because of tremendous public pressure. The INA might have lost its war against Allied forces, but it gained incredible political significance in India in 1946, immediately after the war.[60] Defended by a committee of lawyers, including future Indian Prime Minister Jawaharlal Nehru, these INA men became the heroes of the moment.[61] The INA Red Fort trials established the trajectory of post-war anticolonial resistance: soon afterwards in the same year, over 20,000 members of the Royal Indian Navy mutinied against the British Empire.[62] The next year, in 1947, the British finally quit India.

Enlisting for war

Why did Indian men sign up to this war? Did fighting fascism mean anything to them? A British civil servant from the Moradabad district of the United Provinces in 1941 notes in exasperation the 'ignorance' of Indian village recruits: 'I asked one chap, if he had ever heard of Hitler *Budmash* [the villainous Hitler] and he said he supposed it must be the new *Patwari* [village accountant].'[63] It is the economics of Indian rural life that this villager understands and prioritises. And yet, as Auchinleck observed, British people 'wouldn't have come through both wars if they hadn't had the Indian Army'.[64]

Indian soldiers were posted in nearly every single theatre during this war—Persia, Iraq, Palestine, Egypt, East Africa and Abyssinia, Syria, Aden, Greece, Italy, Burma and Malaya.[65] Out of these, the Middle Eastern and North African battlefronts proved particularly significant, as Indian troops were crucial in the Battle of Tobruk in Libya in 1941 and the breaking of the Mareth Line held by German and Italian forces in 1943, before contributing to the liberation of Greece and Italy.[66] Some 31,000 Indian troops started arriving in the Middle East in 1941 to fight the Italians in North Africa, of which the Fourth and Fifth Indian Infantry Divisions became especially well known for their battlefield successes.[67] The Fourth Indian Division became the first formation of the Indian Army to serve on the frontline.[68] The Fourth and then Fifth Indian Divisions formed part of the British and Empire forces comprising the Eighth Army, which in late 1942 under the command of General Montgomery fought and defeated Rommel's *Panzerarmee Afrika*, comprising German and Italian troops, at the Second Battle of El Alamein.[69] Again, out of a total of one million men sent to Burma under the British-controlled South East Asia Command (SEAC) to fight Japanese forces as part of the Fourteenth Army, about 700,000 were Indians.[70]

At the start of the Second World War, new Indian recruits were ostensibly granted the power of choice. Unlike in Britain, conscription was never introduced in India, and enlisting was therefore voluntary. But, as Indivar Kamtekar explains, 'In a strictly legal sense, the men were indeed volunteers who enlisted of their own will; but most of them, desperate for jobs, were forced to join up through necessity.'[71] The British Empire needed men urgently, and requirements for entry were considerably relaxed, including the acceptance of underweight and anaemic applicants—those most 'desperate for jobs'. A study conducted by the Indian Council of Medical Research in 1961 on nutrition standards in the Indian Army during the Second World War notes:

> It has been the general impression among the Army circles that an Indian Army recruit who, as a rule, is poorly nourished at the time of enlistment undergoes a marked physical improvement thereafter. The factors considered to be responsible for this are (a) the more nutritious army rations, (b) physical training and (c) control of infectious diseases.[72]

Joining the army meant access to food, medicine and better health, and this is why 'volunteers' enlisted. New recruits to the army were granted a similar social status to urban workers, who had been given access to subsidised food and cloth, fuel and medicines to keep war-time industries in India in production. Further benefits followed: court proceedings in India against a soldier would be dropped if he was stationed abroad, and children studying up to Grade 8 in Punjabi schools had their tuition fees waived if their father was on active service overseas.[73] Indian soldiers were also allowed to send up to three quarters of their monthly wages back home.[74]

The military recruitment drive in 1940s India took place in a significantly altered political climate to that of the First World War, where Indian leaders such as M.K. Gandhi had become recruitment agents for the colonial state.[75] In the Second World War, as we have seen, Indian National Congress provincial ministries resigned in 1939 at the declaration of war made by the Viceroy of India, Lord Linlithgow, while Gandhi, Nehru and others were imprisoned because of their opposition to India's forced participation in the war. At the same time, colonial tactics to build support for the war were in full swing, buttressed by legislation in the form of a series of military ordinances, such as subjecting all civilians serving in the army to military law, and sanctioning the compulsory retention of civilians in certain types of employment. Passing this legislation, as Anirudh Deshpande argues, authorised the colonial state to retain control so that it could combat the mounting nationalist and anti-war feeling in India.[76] Furthermore, as a foil to anti-British propaganda generated abroad,[77] new and bespoke colonial governmental publicity messages targeted Indian military servicemen right until the end of the war. These imperial publicity measures promoted allowances for Indian soldiers and their families during the war years to highly priced goods in short supply.

Colonial propaganda also advertised the war as a training opportunity to learn crucial skills and become employable in a post-war, newly industrialised India.[78] A propaganda booklet published in 1943, entitled *Mutu Joins Up*, outlines how a young recruit in the 3rd Madras Regiment becomes an exemplary soldier, while in 1941 and 1942, an exhibition train showcasing tools used by soldiers journeyed 1,500 miles through central and southern India to generate publicity for the armed services.[79] Benjamin Zachariah writes about how these material benefits countered the perceived threat from a vastly expanded Indian Army. He draws attention to a colonial assessment made in June 1942, which revealed that 33 per cent of the infantry and cavalry were from the 'educated' middle classes. Such new recruits were seen as being more 'politically conscious', and Zachariah highlights the decision taken to replace 'the old loyalty' based on the allegedly superior martial capabilities of certain Indian communities with a new 'sense of purpose'.[80]

The pressures of these recruitment measures appear to have worked to some extent. Men from Punjab, following a well-established military tradition, comprised the highest numbers of recruits at 18.33 per cent with the neighbouring North West Frontier Province providing 2.7 per cent, and 'Mussalmans' or Muslim men making up the largest group in the army, nearly 35 per cent of the total number of combatants in February 1942, followed by the Sikh community at just over 10 per cent.[81] The idealised Punjabi peasant recruit of the colonial 'martial races' theory,[82] much vaunted in imperial military discourse, was outnumbered this time by tenants, labourers and artisans from Punjab—effectively, the 'lower castes' from the region, who had until now been denied entry into the army. No more than 30 or 40 per cent of Punjabi recruits in the Second World War owned land.[83]

Southern India also broke new ground by closely following Punjab in recruitment numbers (17.87 per cent), compared to its contribution of a mere 3 per cent of soldiers before the war.[84] Most of such men were labourers, and served as non-combatants—drivers, carpenters, cooks, clerks and electricians—in the war. The Lingayats from southern India, for instance, comprised an entire garrison battalion in the Maratha Light Infantry.[85] Bengal, another new enlistment ground for men in the Second World War, ranked fourth, supplying 3.7 per cent of new recruits.[86] Nearly 100,000 soldiers from Bengal mostly came from towns, with about 30,000 belonging to technical professions, and a large number also enrolled in labour units. Of the 42,000 Bengali men whose professions had been officially classified by 1944, nearly 12,000 served as cooks, clerks, fitters and drivers.[87] Again, tribal communities from Bihar—the Hos, Oraons, Mundas and Santals—which had been linked to uprisings in the nineteenth century and denied access to the army, were allowed to enlist this time, as were the 'untouchable' Chamars, who were recruited in enough numbers to form, temporarily, a Chamar Regiment.[88]

This opening up of the army's carefully preserved gated community to men not considered inherently militaristic resulted in a collapse of colonial fantasies about Indian military 'types'.[89] Before the Second World War, men from the Madras and Bengal provinces were seen as particularly effeminate and unwarlike, underpinning pervasive stereotypes of colonial masculinity, which we shall find reflected in the book.[90] In the Second World War, the fact that unfamiliar men in such numbers formed the bulk of the army was perceived by commanding officers as a threat, undermining the very fabric of a hitherto stratified and selective imperial army. The War Office observed that 'the great expansion of the Indian Army makes its loyalty much less certain than it was and affords the enemy, external or internal, a far better target for propaganda than the carefully selected and trained pre-war army'.[91] Churchill himself feared in January 1943 that this army would turn against the British and should therefore be reduced in size by as many as 500,000 men—a reduction that never, in the end, took place.[92] And military intelligence represented new recruits as sharing deep emotional bonds with the vicissitudes of fortunes affecting their homes—famine and revolution, for example—rather than alignment to any ideological 'cause'. A British commanding officer complained: 'I feel sometimes that I do not command this Battalion; it is commanded by forces in the Punjab.'[93]

The traditional power structures of the army were also disrupted by the rise of the educated, aspirational Indian elite. After the First World War, in response to the growing pressures of nationalism, the British government reluctantly conceded to a limited Indianisation of officers in the army, rupturing the long and carefully established imperial hierarchies of Indians serving under British officers; by 1930, seventy-seven King's Commissioned Indian Officers (KCIOs) were in service.[94] Once more, the Empire's need for men at the onset of war exacerbated the situation: from 396 Indian officers serving in 1939, there were 8,340 by 1945.[95] Srinath Raghavan, however, states that the army was 'unable to attract the best talent', particularly with regard to its officer corps, with nearly 75 per cent of proposed candidates being rejected by the military selection committee. He argues that the pull of the nationalist movement was very strong, and this affected the quality of the new officer recruits.[96] Indeed, out of 108 Indian Commissioned Officers surveyed before or during the war, a fifth had friends or family involved in nationalist politics.[97]

The Indian soldier, then, entered into the discourse of the Second World War in competing, and often conflicting, ways. He was a carefully crafted tool for imperial defence but was also unknown and threatening to colonial powers. He was seen as vital in defeating Axis forces but considered vulnerable to their propaganda. He served in the Indian Army and fought alongside other Allied troops—and in many cases such military employment was a source of considerable masculine, ethnic and familial pride and prestige, as we shall discover through an analysis of wartime letters—but this did not guarantee his immunity from anticolonial, nationalistic feeling or despair at the tribulations of his homeland. As Anirudh Deshpande notes: 'The war came as an employment opportunity to millions of Indians but their willingness to serve the colonial armed forces should not be taken as their consent to colonial rule.'[98] And, in some cases, the Indian soldier enlisted to obtain basic daily army rations—'20 oz. of cereals, 2.5 oz. of *dal* [lentils], 2.0 oz. of meat, 6.0 oz. of vegetables and fruits, and 2.5 oz. of ghee or oil'.[99] He simply needed to eat.

INTRODUCTION

Why write an emotional history?

India in the Second World War: An Emotional History responds to an extraordinary silence regarding the scope and depth of Indian emotional representations during this war, in which two-and-a-half million men—regarded as the largest volunteer army in the world—served, and over three million people died as a result of a man-made, war-induced famine. A recent publication such as Lucy Noakes, Claire Langhamer and Claudia Siebrecht's *Total War: An Emotional History* (2020) breaks new ground in exploring European emotions in the two world wars, but does not include the British Empire, while the three volumes of *The Cambridge History of the Second World War* (2015) contain little on the themes of gender or race, ideas of home or emotional lives.[100] There has, however, been a recent surge of academic interest in the social, political and military history of India and the Second World War, which my book complements. This includes Yasmin Khan's social analysis of the impact of war on India in *The Raj at War: A People's History of India's Second World War* (2015) and Srinath Raghavan's detailed military history of the Indian Army in *India's War: The Making of Modern South Asia, 1939–1945* (2016). Journalist Raghu Karnad has also re-imagined his family history during the war years in *Farthest Field: An Indian Story of the Second World War* (2015), which I have found extraordinarily inspiring.[101]

My book offers an interdisciplinary and multilingual literary and cultural history of wartime India—working across English and Indian languages, principally Bengali, my mother tongue—where I study, for the first time, how our understanding of the Second World War is transformed through a recovery of this emotional history. In the case of 1940s undivided India, the relationship between revolutionary and nationalistic ideology on the one hand and being colonial subjects fighting for an imperial war on the other created a rich and contested social and political history, which in turn generated a complex history of emotions, and it is this little-studied history that I examine. In terms of methodology, scope and analysis, my book shares its closest affinities with Santanu Das's *India, Empire, and First World War Culture: Writings, Images, and Songs* (2018), although there are important points of departure. Principally, the political conditions under which undivided India took part in the Second World War were significantly different from those of the First World War. My book pays close attention to this evolving historical context, providing insights into how Indian wartime writing was produced and circulated in the 'stormy decades' of the 1940s—or '*uttal challish*, as Amalendu Sengupta put it'[102]—and continued after the end of the war. In this way, by using visual, literary and life-writing sources, the book also contributes to broader debates on the role of South Asia and emotions, such as Amélie Blom and Stéphanie Lama-Rewal's *Emotions, Mobilisations and South Asian Politics* (2020), which reconsiders the emotional dynamics of political mobilisation in modern South Asia.

Emotions reveal how we communicate with ourselves and the external world. They can, of course, be predictable, but they can also take us by surprise, forging affinities between strangers, undercutting political and nationalist divides. I begin my chapters by considering the relationship between emotions and visual culture. As anthropologist Elizabeth Edwards argues, photographs have the potential to enact history in ways we might not expect, when they are used not simply as evidence but as tools with which to think through how historical experience is constituted. I use photographs, both colonial and Indian, to question how we can conceptually open up the archive. If photographs are 'raw histories', they need to be 'articulated, digested and made active' in relation to textual sources.[103]

At the heart of my book, then, are analyses of Indian sepoy and officer emotions gleaned from both textual and visual forms. I read these representations against their political and historical context, focusing on how colonial and military authorities, along with civilian networks, framed Indian soldiers within contemporary discourse. From these histories, my research then radiates outwards: I move from an understanding of war as 'combat' to 'conflict',[104] from battlefronts across the world to the Indian home-front, from life-writing to literary and intellectual responses by Indian combatants, non-combatants and civilian writers, women and men. I have deliberately chosen not to include European writers' perspectives on India and their emotional legacy, giving primacy instead to Indian voices and feelings. Again, moving away from studying well-researched political leaders such as M.K. Gandhi and Jawaharlal Nehru during the 1940s, my book foregrounds little-known writers and offers fresh perspectives on recognised political philosophers, poets and novelists. These figures include intellectual Rabindranath Tagore (1861–1941), novelist Mulk Raj Anand (1905–2004), and diasporic Tamil poet M.J. Tambimuttu (1915–1983), alongside novelist Bibhutibhushan Bandyopadhyay (1894–1950), communist poets Sukanta Bhattacharya (1926–1947) and Samar Sen (1916–1987), social reformer and female poet Tara Ali Baig (1916–1989), educationist and female poet Muriel Wasi (1912–1995) and soldier-novelist Baren Basu (exact dates unknown). In some cases, the texts under consideration were written during the war years but published after the war, once censorship measures in India were lifted.[105] For others, like Anand's novel *The Sword and the Sickle*, publication was possible in England in 1942 but not in India. Tambimuttu's Blitz poem *Out of This War* (1941) too was published in London for an English readership, as was Muriel Wasi's and Tara Ali Baig's English-language poetry in 1945.

I have recovered much of my material for scholarly analysis from a wide range of archives—the India Office Records at the British Library; photographs and private papers from the Imperial War Museum; INA records from the Netaji Research Bureau in Kolkata, India; memoirs, private papers and newspaper records from the National Archives of India in Delhi and the National Library in Kolkata. Some of these sources, such as letters exchanged between Indian soldiers and their loved ones at home, are beginning to receive attention by historians; others are fresh and assessed in my book for the first time. The process of recovering this archival material revealed to me the necessity for adopting an interdisciplinary methodology, straddling historical, cultural and literary analysis, as well as a multilingual approach—combining English and Indian languages, in particular Bengali—to unravel Indian emotional responses to the Second World War.

My book reveals a complex Indian emotional terrain, inflected by differences in military rank, political belief, race, class, caste and gender—where recovery becomes a challenging scholarly endeavour. To tackle this challenge, in five thematic chapters, I have brought the visual, experiential, literary and intellectual into conversation with one another. This draws attention to the depth and scale of emotions depicted, and allows for fresh layers of meaning to emerge from such a comparatist approach. Here I focus, as Sara Ahmed argues in *The Cultural Politics of Emotion* (2004), not on what emotions are, but what they do in enabling us to uncover, even only partially, what war might have meant for Indian men and women living and writing in the 1940s.[106] My book analyses how visual and textual cultures transform into repositories for such emotions, which become activated as they are read and responded to, especially in relation to one another.

The book's thematic structure comprises five chapters—on home; hunger; male communities; witnessing the Indian home-front; and reading poetic writing as testimony. These themes have been carefully selected to enable a variety of texts and visual sources to engage with each other, allowing me to examine their emotional particularities and differences as well as points of intersection. I establish, for instance, unexpected connections between the new and the familiar by examining how Indian recruits, the principal characters in a rare anticolonial and anti-war novel, internalise Rabindranath Tagore's metaphor of the *danob* or demon of war with its terrifying mechanistic capabilities and voracious appetite for destruction. And I propose that it is by making image and text, life-writing and literature, 'speak' to each other that we can disentangle the troubled yet transformative emotional legacy of the Second World War in the Indian subcontinent.

But how does the nature of historical evidence differ from literary sources? Do the methodologies required by the latter produce a different understanding, or cast a different historiographic light, on this excavation of the past? And what is the heuristic yield of the literary, both methodologically through close reading practices and as material for analysis, in the work of recovering an emotional history?[107] Travelling across geographic and generic boundaries, and sometimes chronological order, in framing its chapters, this book deliberately draws together letters from the Middle Eastern and North African fronts with the Bengali novel and modernist poetry, or women poets writing in English from the Indian home-front with Mulk Raj Anand's English-language realist novel charting the radicalisation of the returned Punjabi soldier Lal Singh. By using such a comparatist approach, I highlight the multiplicity of narratives, perspectives and contexts—from the sepoy on the battlefront anxious to hear from his family, to civilians in India who write about food shortages; from the doctor on the Burma front for whom home increasingly merges with the anticolonial nation, to the utopian imaginings of freedom by the INA men, physically realised through contact with the body of their leader, Subhas Chandra Bose. This multiplicity suggests not only how profoundly the Second World War altered the lives of the writers under discussion, but also how much it transformed Indian writing itself in both Bengali and English. The letters and memoirs I consider in this book bring our attention to writers who draw upon their own experiences, although the emotional registers they employ are often mediated through memory, particularly in the case of memoirs written later in life. In the case of literary narratives—the novel and the poem—the authors are mostly working at a remove. They are witnesses to war and famine, but seldom its direct victims. And the one case of a Bengali novel written by a soldier assessed in the book shows us the possibilities of fantasy in employing this literary form.

The complicated nuances of home as a site of feeling become evident when I interpret soldier and civilian letters alongside an INA officer's memoir of loss, written in English, and an Indian doctor's increasing distaste towards war on the Indo-Burma frontline, written in Bengali. Although divided by military allegiance— one serving with Japanese forces and the other with the British— the two men surprisingly occupy similar emotional worlds. On the other hand, in their experiments with Bengali modernist poetry, Samar Sen and Sukanta Bhattacharya only obliquely reference the war. For writers based in the Indian home-front, it is witnessing the atrocity of the 1943 Bengal Famine through which the violence of war enters language. This is also the case in Bibhutibhushan Bandyopadhyay's realist and humanist novel *Ashani Sanket* (*Intimations of Thunder*, 1944–1946), examined in the book. Composing poetry and writing novels on the famine takes us away from historical distance and the abstraction of statistics into the immediate, viscerally felt, subjectivity of the suffering body. Literature has a particular relationship with atrocity and emotion here—it is invested in forms of representation that foreground in complex and nuanced ways how others' experience is imagined, and empathy registered. The Bengali poem and the novel become a means of alerting us to the emotional legacy of a historical event which did not end with the removal of corpses from the streets of Calcutta in 1943. Instead, it left enduring and intimate traces in writing.

Such self-conscious modes of emotional representation in the book continue with the poet Tara Ali Baig showcasing her experimentation with modernist practices in English, while fellow poet Muriel Wasi, in contrast, relies upon the older, plangent Victorian lyric form to highlight a gendered mode of suffering for India in the aftermath of war. Through my practice of literary close reading, I also foreground in the book how the mobile identities generated by war push against normative conceptions of masculinity, creating unpredictable, and often unpermitted, emotional alliances. Male connections forged with fellow PoWs and Japanese prison guards in New Guinea, off the coast of Australia, keep John Baptist Crasta alive during three-and-a-half years of captivity under extreme physical duress, as he highlights in his memoir. Again, a burgeoning homosocial friendship between Indian officer and escaped PoW R.G. Salvi with the Italian soldier Romano, detailed in another memoir, reveals the tremendous charge of personal relationships that undercuts boundaries enforced by race and nation.

While analysing the Bengali realist novel *Rangrut* (*The Recruit*, 1950), I foreground how the Burmese border with India becomes the place where abjection in witnessing pain leads to the fantasy of overthrowing colonial military authority, felt by the men from Bengal who have signed up to this war. Significantly, by engaging in a dialogue between different forms of writing—memoirs, letters and literature—I propose that this Bengali wartime novel allows for a more imaginative resistance to political authority to be developed, much as the Indian novel in English does in the case of Anand. Furthermore, my recovery and examination of this history of emotions also underscores the global nature of the Second World War—New Guinea, Italy and the Indo-Burmese border become important sites of feeling in these texts.

My book considers the ways the war itself is understood and responded to as a particular moment of historical crisis. Does civilisational critique count as war testimony, and, if so, what is the nature of this witnessing? Through the poetic and philosophical writings of Rabindranath Tagore and the Blitz poetry of Tamil poet M.J. Tambimuttu, I examine how the Second World War can be read as a form of 'savagery' that attacks the heart of 'civilisation', Europe. If for Tambimuttu, wartime exposes and normalises this 'savagery' in European metropolitan life, for a disheartened and disillusioned Tagore, such 'savagery' goes beyond Europe, to include the brutalising subjugation of China by imperial Japan in Asia. It is not simply Europe but humanity itself that has let Tagore down, making this civilisational crisis into a personal one. As he realises so profoundly, the personal is the political.

In recovering this emotional history of India in the Second World War, I foreground an important shift necessary in our understanding of this conflict. By drawing upon photographs, letters and literature that re-conceptualise Indian emotional responses to war, I argue that colonialism and imperialism are as implicated as fascism, and therefore push us towards a more problematic understanding of this war. The literary, in my analysis here, does not merely reflect war experience but becomes a generative, interpretative force that opens up for us ways of understanding how Indian soldiers and civilians thought about and represented the war. Both life-writing and literature function in my book as frames of knowledge through which this war history is reconfigured. As Vasudha Dalmia argues in her analysis of urban north India through Hindi novels, the 'minute documentation of shifts in structures of feelings' that literature contains itself signifies a unique record of social history.[108] In enabling us to inhabit a form of imaginative, empathic knowing, the literary, then, transforms our understanding of Second World War emotional history.

Wartime and creativity

From considering the political background to India's conflicted involvement in the Second World War, tensions inherent within the colonial recruitment drive, and the new understanding revealed to us through the perspective of an emotional history, I now turn to consider the forms of writing that acquired fresh impetus with the outbreak of global war. Right from the 1920s and 1930s, literature in India was already responding to political and social turbulence, influenced by both international modernist techniques in the works of James Joyce, Virginia Woolf and D.H. Lawrence, among others, along with the social realism embedded in Soviet writers' movements and the independence struggle within India itself. *Angare* (*The Embers*, 1932), a collection of ten short stories by authors Sajjad Zahir, Rashid Jahan, Ahmed Ali and Mahmud-uz-Zafar, published in Lucknow, galvanised the Progressive Writers' Association, the most important Urdu literary movement of the twentieth century. *Angare* was strident in its criticism of conservative Islam and British colonialism—'it was a declaration of war by the youth of the middle class against the prevailing social, political and religious institutions'.[109] In 1935, at an initial meeting in Bloomsbury, Mulk Raj Anand—whose novel *The Sword and the Sickle* (1942) is analysed in Chapter 4—was elected President of the Progressive Writers' Association with a similar social and realist mandate; in 1936, the Progressive Writers' Association in Hindi was inaugurated in Lucknow by the well-known writer Premchand.[110] And challenging both modernism and the romanticism of Rabindranath Tagore, the All Bengal Progressive Writers' Association published its own collected volume, *Pragati* (*Progress*), in 1937.[111]

Hitler's invasion of Russia on 22 June 1941 significantly altered the cultural and literary contexts within which Indian writing was being produced. As Amit Kumar Gupta observes, 'If Britain had become a "friend" in the "just" war, should the colonised Indians, and the toilers among them, actively support the British authorities and their war efforts, even to the extent of abandoning the national liberation struggle and all other forms of resistance against their immediate exploiters?'[112] This was a position taken up by the Communist Party of India, considered illegitimate by colonial authorities since 1934, whose members suffered routine imprisonment at the hands of the British.[113] The ban on the party was lifted on 23 July 1942, when the slogan '*Japaanke rukhte hobe*' ('Japan must be stopped') became popular in Bengal.[114] Communist poet Sukanta Bhattacharya, whose famine poetry we will consider in Chapter 2, called for a popular alliance against Japan, while in July 1942 the Anti-Fascist Writers' and Artists' Association (AFWAA) published *Jana Juddher Gaan* (*Songs of the People's War*), a compilation of thirty songs on the 'people's resistance', brought out by Bengali poet

Subhas Mukhopadhyay.[115] Other AFWAA publications included *Fascibad O Nazibad* (*Fascism and Nazism*) by Rahul Sankrityan and a collection of poems called *Baishe June* (*22 June*) by Bengali poet Bishnu De, highlighting how significant Hitler's occupation of Russia had become to 1940s Indian cultural discourse.[116]

The 1943 Bengal Famine signalled yet another important shift in Indian contemporary artistic and creative production. Moving away from the fraught Quit India politics of 1942, the Communist Party of India now discovered both its political footing, through organising famine relief work, as well as an intense creative impetus. As Sanjukta Sunderason notes, 'by late 1943, hunger and destitution became shared content in the palpable cultural production that emerged around the famine, the image of the starving rural migrant appearing in literature, plays, painting and sculpture'.[117] The Indian People's Theatre Association (IPTA), emerging in 1943 as a response to witnessing the atrocity of famine, is one such example; *People's War*, the Communist Party of India's weekly publication, where 'a new genre of famine reportage was being generated',[118] is another, as we shall see in an examination of photojournalist Sunil Janah's images in Chapter 2.

Against the backdrop of such fertile cultural production, this book uses the lens of the Second World War to examine writing, in principally English and Bengali languages, both before Hitler's invasion of the Soviet Union in June 1941, and afterwards. It argues for the importance of foregrounding Indian soldiers' emotions as well as those of civilians and intellectuals, as well as affirms the significance of poetry and essays written and published in the early years of the war, such as that of Tamil poet Tambimuttu and Indian philosopher Rabindranath Tagore, as a testimonial act. The book also pays close attention to how famine in 1943 registers in language as a form of mutated war violence in Chapters 2 and 4.

Throughout the book, I have realised the significance of moving beyond English-language representations.[119] For Indian writing from the Second World War, the use of English does not necessarily signify privilege, nor does the use of Indian languages indicate non-elite perspectives. Colonial sources and their modes of survival into the twenty-first century have been shaped, among other factors, by the language in which they are accessible today. As discussed in

Chapters 1 and 2, extracts from Indian soldiers' letters in British military censorship reports—offering to us arguably our most sustained insights into a vast range of subaltern emotions during wartime—have evolved into English as their final translated form from the Indian languages in which they were initially written. The modernist Bengali poetry on famine that I analyse in Chapter 2, on the other hand, is composed by middle-class, educated and highly literary young men from Calcutta responding to the dominance of a particular romantic aesthetic in Bengali literature. Yet a PoW memoir studied in Chapter 3, outlining the nearly unbearable conditions of life under Japanese control, is written in English by a non-commissioned Indian officer (NCO) from an Indian Christian background, closer in terms of military rank to a sepoy than an elite commissioned officer. The need to look beyond the English language, then, for this book, demonstrates the scope and range of Indian testimonial, literary and intellectual responses to war rather than reinforcing a binary division between English-language sources representing a privileged minority and Indian languages those of non-elite voices.

Chapter outlines

Extracts from thousands of letters, written and received between August 1942 and March 1945 by Indian soldiers stationed along the Middle Eastern and North African fronts, are archived in the British Library as part of military colonial censorship reports from the Second World War. In Chapter 1, analysing colonial photographs, letters and memoirs, I tease out how these letters reconstitute meanings of 'home', and how the family unit—mothers and wives, fathers and brothers—regulates ideas of colonial 'duty' for Indian soldiers serving abroad. From the diverse perspectives of home revealed here, I move on to two memoirs. The first, *Arakan Fronte* (*On the Frontlines at Arakan*, 1946) was written in Bengali by an Indian doctor, Shantilal Ray, serving in the British-led Fourteenth Army in Burma in 1944; the second, *The Men from Imphal* (1970) by Indian officer Abid Hasan Safrani, was written in English from the perspective of Japanese and INA defeat at the hands of the same Fourteenth Army in 1945. In *Arakan Fronte*, I consider a more philosophical understanding of home and its relationship with the earth, while *The Men from Imphal*, I argue, establishes the most overtly political narrative in this chapter, where home is equated to the expansive, decolonised nation. These two little-known memoirs work as a productive foil to the letters: they reveal how ideas of 'home' expand, from reinforcing forms of martial masculinity to including the personal and the intimate, and ultimately encompass both nationalist and utopian ideas of freedom.

From imaginings of home, I move on to emotions associated with hunger arising from the Bengal Famine of 1943 in Chapter 2. The Bengal Famine was the culmination of large-scale hardship and suffering in regions of the Indian subcontinent during the Second World War, compounded by colonial policies of resource extraction. The lines between battlefront and home-front became increasingly blurred, with tremendous loss of civilian life: over three million people died. In this chapter, I read photographs and soldiers' letters alongside Bibhutibhushan Bandyopadhyay's well-known Bengali novel *Ashani Sanket* (*Intimations of Thunder*, 1944–1946), and an analysis of famine-related Bengali modernist poetry by Sukanta Bhattacharya and Samar Sen. The chapter focuses on how starvation is imagined, witnessed and represented, and argues that letter-writing and literary texts read alongside each other yield new depths of meaning to the emotions of hunger in the homeland. These include highlighting the role played by the body in famine writing, and how this enables us to inhabit the subjective experiences of a soldier on an international battlefront hearing about famine, a Bengali village character represented as experiencing famine in a novel, and a civilian poet and emergency relief provider on the streets of Calcutta witnessing famine. Middle Eastern and North African battlefronts, Bengal's rural spaces and the streets of Calcutta, then, form new connections in this reading. If Bibhutibhushan in his novel highlights the everyday violence of famine inflicted upon a small Indian village, where the Bengali verb '*jwala*' ('burn') acts as a refrain, how is hunger registered in the novel, and how is Bengali poetry remade by the use of new imagery? This chapter concludes by discussing how, in the midst of catastrophic death, communities of knowledge and bonds of empathy are formed.

In Chapter 3, I turn my attention to another form of remaking in the creation of alternative male communities of feeling beyond political and military divides. Along with colonial photographs, I consider two Indian PoW memoirs written in English in this chapter, contrasted against a politicised, revolutionary Indian novel of war service. In the first memoir, *Eaten by the Japanese* (written in the post-war years; published in 1997), by rank-and-file Indian soldier John Crasta, who was incarcerated by Japanese forces in Singapore, I examine unexpected moments of male connection which illuminate Crasta's PoW years with the material and emotional sustenance he needs to keep living. In the second, entitled *Whom Enemies Sheltered* (1983), by Indian officer R.G. Salvi, I explore Salvi's friendship with a lapsed enemy, an Italian soldier named Romano. The chapter highlights how male connections in two PoW memoirs draw upon established Indian traditions of martial comradeship and fellow-feeling, as well as reveal long-standing anxieties regarding the nature of colonial masculinity. I read these memoirs alongside the highly politicised Bengali novel, Baren Basu's *Rangrut* (*The Recruit*, 1950), to reveal the pressures that war places on the history of Indian masculinity and male relationships, and argue that unpermitted, transcultural acts of male bonding during the war become a means of subverting established political structures, even across enemy lines.

The fourth chapter considers elite Indian intellectual responses to the war, written in English and focusing on the Indian homefront. Here, I bring together the well-known writer Mulk Raj Anand with little-studied women writers Muriel Wasi and Tara Ali Baig to examine how staunch anti-fascist feeling in all three rubs against equally intensely realised anticolonial emotion. Anand's novel *The Sword and the Sickle* (1942) highlights the journey of Lalu, the Indian soldier coming home after serving in Europe during the First World War, who begins to find his political voice in the 1920s. Why does the soldier's return after the first global war become so important to Anand during the second? And how does communism function here as anticolonial feeling? Again, the rare poetry of the two women writers Wasi and Baig points to a growing articulation of female political and civic authority, blurring the boundaries between gendered experiences of war: both Wasi and Baig accepted opportunities opening up for women in the Indian public sphere during the war years. The chapter concludes by analysing how all three writers—men and women—reconfigure ideas of anti-fascism, colonisation and nationhood as well as wartime trauma and suffering endured in the Indian home-front.

The final, fifth chapter considers interpretations of the Second World War as a moment of profound historical crisis by two colonial intellectuals—diasporic author M. J. Tambimuttu experiencing the London Blitz and poet-philosopher Rabindranath Tagore in India, writing his final essays. The long poem *Out of This War* (1941) traces Tambimuttu's arrival in London and the aerial bombing of the city, and establishes causal links between the two world wars while interrogating the purpose of Western violent action. The poem culminates in an examination of 'savagery' and 'barbarism', and mourns a global brotherhood of suffering created by war. The chapter forges fresh connections between this little-known poem and Tagore's philosophical response to the Second World War, which becomes to him a means of interrogating the heart of 'civilisation' and its implications for the future of humanity. Here, I read Tagore's exchange of letters with Japanese poet Yone Noguchi in 1938—after the start of the second Sino-Japanese war, where Tagore thoroughly repudiates the rise of a militant, nationalist and aggressive Japan—alongside his last essay *Crisis in Civilisation* (1941). The chapter concludes by assessing how the resurgent violence of the Second World War is seen by Tambimuttu and Tagore as a civilisational crisis in the 1940s.

India in the Second World War: An Emotional History highlights how colonial emotions undercut the myth of the Second World War as the 'good' war. It reveals to us how the 'freedom' that men and women thought they were fighting for itself becomes fractured and complex. By viewing the war through Indian eyes, we understand that the political ideologies of anti-fascism, anticolonialism, communism and nationalism rubbed against one another in the 1940s, often contesting each other. The book makes the case that it is through an emotional history that we can home in on the particularities of Indian war lives, their relationship to political ideologies, and their dramatisation in textual and visual forms. If colonial photographs foreground an aesthetic of emotion that is often undercut in the very creation of the image, with the agency of those being photographed penetrating through, what can Indian texts from the war years tell us about the act of writing and its relationship with our emotional worlds? Reading these texts over eighty years afterwards, in relationship with one another, enables us to challenge wartime stereotypes, uncover fresh nuances of meaning and forge unexpected connections.

1

'THE THING THAT WAS LOST'

RE-CONCEPTUALISING HOME IN INDIAN LIFE-WRITING

Fig. 1.1: 'Village hero: New recruit on his first leave. A new recruit to the Indian Army arrives in his village on his first leave'. © Imperial War Museum.[1]

A photograph of a stern-faced young Indian soldier back home on leave, surrounded by smiling village boys, in the Imperial War Museum archives arrests our attention. The soldier—tall, in a clean and smart Western military uniform—stands rather self-consciously upright. His uniformed posture contrasts with the typical Indian garments worn by the only adult villager in the image, who appears far more relaxed, as do the boys themselves. The colonial lens seeks to invest the spectacle of the soldier with status and prestige; the caption, most likely provided by the British Ministry of Information,[2] attempts to curtail the photograph's narrative within the frame of 'heroism' and the soldier's return home. Yet there is something both staged and playful about the image. While the soldier himself seems to revel in the status that the army has bestowed upon him, the children appear at once gleeful and curious. What emotions do they feel on seeing the return of this soldier? Is he their poster boy for the military, a model to aspire towards? Is this what they too can hope to become? Or is he someone they recognise, simply dressed up and rather entertaining? Again, the stripe on the soldier's right arm indicates that he is a Lance Naik—a non-commissioned officer in the Indian Army—and should have already had at least two or three years of military service. He is hardly, then, as the colonial caption would have us believe, a new recruit. And then, on the left, the photograph is framed by the cows sauntering off, seemingly unimpressed by the young military man. The cows' movement, captured by the colonial photographer's lens, is likely deliberate, part of 'exoticising' an image of an Indian village from which recruitment has taken place.

Hovering on the borderline between the serious and the jocular, the photograph also alerts us to another important aspect of the Indian war experience. The uniformed soldier on display to his village audience looks rather young and thin. These physical attributes reveal the enlistment practices of British colonial authorities: desperate for men from 1942 onwards, they accepted underage and underweight recruits.[3] Furthermore, this young soldier's performance of military masculinity is being observed by even younger boys in his village, and in turn, by the camera. How, then, is the war being constructed through the image of the upright, smart, purposeful soldier and being brought home here? What relationship does the colonial government seek to establish between military service and the Indian soldier's home?

Contrasted against the focus on a single soldier surrounded by villagers, yet another photograph captures a group of tall and well-built Indian volunteers gathered outside an army recruitment cen-

Fig. 1.2: 'Recruiting for the war in northern India: Punjabi volunteers crowding round the gates of an Army recruiting office'. © Imperial War Museum.[4]

tre, which sits within a collection of images in the Imperial War Museum archives covering military recruitment in India in 1942. The photograph's caption suggests that men from Punjab throng the gates of this army recruitment office. The war, therefore, is popular: Indians choose to volunteer, and they must feel it is 'their war'. Yet the men themselves appear strangely stationary. With legs slightly apart and arms by their sides—a 'stand-at-ease' position— many of the men in the first row look directly at the camera. They know they are being examined, and so instead of pushing their way forward, they respond by inviting inspection themselves, as though already on military display.

Colonial photographs such as the ones above target public, collective emotions during wartime in India. The camera's gaze is far from neutral: these photographs aim to impose a particular narrative on Indian participation in the war, circumscribing what the Second World War was supposed to mean and feel. It is significant that both photographs demonstrate military presence *within* the Indian home-front—the first through the reception of the young Lance Naik coming back to his village on leave, and the second with north Indian men surrounding the gates of an army recruitment office in Punjab. Yet there is a disconnect between the emotions sanctioned by colonial authorities—willingness to sign up, pride in wearing the colonial military uniform, 'heroism' symbolised in military service—and the subjective, intimate and often conflicted understanding of war experienced by soldiers and civilians themselves. The young boys' gleeful expressions in the first photograph and the Punjabi men's physical response to the camera's gaze in the second draw our attention to the limits of colonial narratives of war and the relationship it seeks to project with the Indian home-front. Despite the photographs' careful modes of construction, accentuated by the layer of meaning contained in the captions, there are details that the colonial photographer cannot control. The emotional agency of those being photographed, like Barthes' *punctum*, pierces through, recalibrating the connections between war service and home.

What brought millions of Indian men in the 1940s to the gates of army recruitment offices for inspection, measurement and enlistment? And how were the emotions associated with home repurposed by colonial censors as well as re-interpreted in the men's own narratives of war? Moving on from colonial photographs, this chapter investigates the meanings of home in different forms of Indian life-writing during the Second World War. Some forty years after this war, Salman Rushdie, based in London, tells us in his essay 'Imaginary Homelands' (1982) that it is his 'present that is foreign, and that the past is home'. He continues: '[O]ur physical alienation from India almost inevitably means that we will not be capable of reclaiming precisely the thing that was lost [...] we will, in short, create fictions [...] imaginary homelands, Indias of the mind.'[5] Such conceptions of a geographically distant home, with their attendant anxieties and desires, have accrued a critical energy in postcolonial contexts. In this chapter, however, I argue for the importance of studying the emotional resonances of home *within* the framework of colonialism and war. After all, Indian soldiers during the Second World War—and during the First—led itinerant, mobile lives long before questions of diaspora, exile and migration in post-independence years came to the forefront.

The different forms of Indian life-writing during the Second World War that this chapter studies reformulate perspectives of home from a variety of locations across the world—Middle Eastern and North African battlefronts; remote Indian villages; the city of Imphal; and the Arakan region on the Indo-Burma border known today as the Rakhine state, the homeland of the persecuted Rohingya community. My chapter reads these life-writing texts alongside each other to reveal the multiple layers of war memory that emerge, opening up political and emotional complexities and discrepancies. Writing or expressing feelings to communicate them, as Claudia Siebrecht notes, becomes more than subjective experience—it is a performance that can be analysed and interpreted.[6] Emotions, then, are a means of evaluating one's own role in relation to politics; the naming of emotions becomes a powerful act. I start with military censorship reports of Indian soldiers' letters during this war, using postcolonial insights to examine military and civilian emotional responses to home, and how the family unit—mothers and wives, fathers and brothers—regulates ideas of colonial 'duty' for Indian soldiers serving abroad. From the disparate, fragmented and partially realised perspectives of these letters, I move on to two memoirs: *Arakan Fronte (On the Frontlines at Arakan*, 1946), written in Bengali by a doctor, Shantilal Ray, serving in the British-led Fourteenth Army in Burma in 1944; and *The Men from Imphal* (1970), by INA officer Abid Hasan Safrani, written in English from the perspective of Japanese and INA defeat at the hands of the same Fourteenth Army in 1945.

In my reading of both memoirs, wartime Burma becomes a site of transformative possibility, establishing emotional connections with the Indian homeland in complex ways. There is, of course, a long pre-history to Indo-Burmese and, in particular, Bengali-Burmese relations. Devleena Ghosh has persuasively argued for the existence of a pre-colonial cosmopolitan world across the Bay of Bengal, and shown how these connections between Bengal and Burma were altered by the lived experience of British colonisation. From being known as the 'golden land' or '*suvarnabhumi*' in Bengali, Burma in the 1920s became the centre of radical political activities for militant Bengali revolutionaries. However, by the 1930s, Indo-Burmese connections, mediated through colonialism, were more contentious: Indians were seen by the Burmese as dominant in economic, cultural and political terms. Ghosh discusses how, in the Bengali imaginary during the nineteenth and early twentieth centuries, Burma continued to function as an 'elsewhere', a place of potential and change.[7] This chapter highlights how Indian memoirs of the Second World War push this imaginary of Burma in fresh emotional directions.

In *Arakan Fronte*, I explore the phenomenological aspects and spatial features of Shantilal Ray's making and remaking of home in the Burmese earth, analysing how living in a dug-out—as he has to do for extended periods of time—feels both enwombing and entombing for him. Assessing how the Arakan evolves from arduous geographical terrain into a liminal psychological space, I discuss how Ray confronts the ferocity of the Japanese forces but is also compelled to recognise their humanity. I then trace the growing politicised emotions associated with Ray's ideas of home that map onto notions of the Indian homeland. Moving on to Hasan's memoir, I argue that *The Men from Imphal* is the most overtly political narrative in this chapter, where home is equated to the independent nation. This is, however, no narrow espousal of nationalism. Instead, Hasan highlights how the emotions associated with home are generous and broad-ranging—the decolonised nation becomes one where all communities, religions and ethnic groups have a stake, as do expatriate Indians. These two little-known memoirs, then, work as a productive foil to the breadth of feeling suggested by the letters.

Studied together, the letter extracts and the memoirs reveal how ideas of home expand. In the letters, the relationship established between Indian soldiers stationed abroad and their home becomes a means of reinforcing martial masculinity and a sense of honour and prestige in signing up to colonial war service. However, soldiers also imagine the home they have left behind in more complex ways—through feelings of nostalgia and longing, anxiety and alienation. For Ray in *Arakan Fronte*, home becomes a way of connecting with the Burmese earth in which he shelters every night. It is also his route towards understanding and empathising with the enemy, by thinking of the Japanese as those who were once loved at home, leading peaceful lives. If Ray's ultimate realisation is that the home to which he seeks to return is the independent Indian nation, it is this anticolonial vision that Hasan's memoir overtly takes up, right from the beginning. Home, in Hasan's memoir, is indeed the political nation—but an all-inclusive, pluralistic one, where different ethnicities and religions can thrive.

'Letters mean half meetings': imaginings of home from the Middle East and North African fronts

> You assure me that you post me letters alright but I don't get them.
> I wish somebody who cares for our welfare to look into it. I get so
> miserable and don't want to do anything if I don't hear from you.
>
> — An Indian 'Other Rank' in Urdu, writing home from
> North Africa in 1943

Extracts from hundreds of letters, written between August 1942 and March 1945 by Indian soldiers stationed along the Middle Eastern and North African fronts—stretching from the Persian Gulf to Iraq, Transjordan (modern-day Jordan) and Palestine, and from Cyprus to Cyrenaica (eastern Libya), Tripolitania (western Libya), Egypt, Sudan and Somaliland[8]—are archived in the British Library as part of military colonial censorship reports from the Second World War. The letters also cover the time of the Fourth, Eighth and Tenth Indian Divisions' absorption into the Central Mediterranean Forces (CMF) after Axis troops were defeated in the Middle Eastern theatre by 1943. A selection of Indian troops was sent on to Cyprus and Greece,[9] and formed part of the CMF's invasion of Sicily in July 1943 and Allied landings in mainland Italy in September 1943.[10] The letters, then, become textual connectors between the farthest corners of the Empire and imperial strongholds requiring defence against the Axis alliance; they serve as agents of communication between remote villages spread across India and theatres of war thousands of miles away.

The original drafts have not been recovered and may be irretrievably lost, but we understand from the censorship reports that the letters were written in a variety of Indian languages—Hindustani, Gurmukhi, Urdu, Bengali, Malayalam, Tamil and others—and often dictated to scribes by Indian sepoys who were non-literate.[11] The letters were then translated for the censor, who compiled selected quotations into a report testifying to the spirit or 'morale' of the soldiers. These reports include British and Indian officers' epistolary writing, but the majority comprises that of Indian 'Other Ranks' or non-officers, as they were called in the army. The censor also monitored incoming mail—the news soldiers received from home—and selected extracts from these letters to produce the censorship reports.[12] This, then, was the British Empire's wartime project of surveillance, studying the range and scale of emotion exchanged between Indian men on international battlefronts and their friends and families at home.[13]

Colonial surveillance and censorship in India were particularly dominant during the Second World War years, relaxing only after the Japanese formally surrendered, as *The Times* noted in September 1945.[14] In her book *War over Words* (2019), Devika Sethi provides rich detail on these practices after the Defence of India Act and Rules were issued in September 1939. Sethi believes that military censorship was 'more influenced by political considerations than the other way round',[15] and observes how the role of the censor grew substantially during this period. While censorship operations came under the purview of the military Commander-in-Chief, it also resulted in another military official, the Chief Censor such as Lieutenant Colonel M.G.M. Mair,[16] to work in tandem with government departments in India, and to advise on ways of controlling the press during wartime. Newspaper articles on frontline operations, for instance, could not be published without securing his permission. Again, excising sections of letters Indian soldiers wrote and received on international battlefronts ensured that such letters could be delivered—but not published.

While Indian soldiers' letters from the First World War are now regularly drawn upon by a range of scholars,[17] the Second World War letters have only recently begun attracting academic attention in, for example, Yasmin Khan, Gajendra Singh and Srinath Raghavan's work on India during this war. My focus is more literary: while continuing to read these partial epistles as embedded in their social, historical and political contexts, I also interpret them as *texts*, analysing the ways in which language—translated, excerpted and censored—shapes the representation of war emotions. Forms of life-writing, as James Hinton believes, do not serve as 'transparent windows on the soul'.[18] Instead, they become sites where experiences are narrated and identities fashioned, with a private audience in mind. But these translated and truncated extracts do not enable us, as Hermione Lee notes in her influential work *Body Parts* (2005), to 'bring a whole life home'.[19] Instead, I argue that they exert pressure on the very scope of life-writing itself, making us question whether there must always be an individual as the focal point of the writing of lives. When a rich body of life-writing material is missing, it is these surviving extracts that we must turn to as archival trace.

The remains of these letters need to be read with an awareness of the protean quality of their textuality, shifting from the verbal to the transcribed, Indian vernaculars to the English language, and a reception that troubles the borders of the public and the private. We encounter here not only the voice of the original letter-writer but also the filters of a possible scribe, military translator and colonial censor in his institutional editorial role. As Santanu Das has argued in relation to the First World War, these epistolary pieces are 'incomplete, fragmentary', but also 'tantalising'.[20] Reading the extracts today makes us discover in them a curious disembodied quality: being anonymised, stripped of the names of places and individualised context, the fragments offer our only glimpse into a vast and complex spectrum of non-elite narratives. Hovering in the censorship reports like so many textual shards, these letters may not be able to provide the arc of a life but represent an enormous range of Indian subaltern wartime feelings that would have otherwise been lost.

Through their many mutated forms, these Second World War letters reveal a variety of influences on Indian soldiers' emotional worlds. In the hundreds of letter extracts documented in the censorship reports, there are fewer than twenty mentions of Hitler. The letters discuss, instead, travel and tourism, astonishment and pleasure on seeing Europe for the first time, the travails of life in the desert, the range of entertainment provided by mobile Indian cinemas, the joys of eating a *bada khana* or big feast, and the annoying lack of cigarettes. Few of them focus on political causes of the war or mention battlefield gains and losses, although some do mention victories in North Africa, consolidated with the fall of Tunis and Bizerte.[21] Others comment on the changes brought about by the Quit India movement in the country, the extreme difficulties in procuring leave from colonial authorities, and discuss hardships in India resulting from the 1943 Bengal Famine, which I examine fully in Chapter 2. Perhaps the awareness of the colonial censor's gaze created a form of self-censorship for Indian soldiers, leading to silences in their emotional response to combat experiences, political opinion or even expressing physical longing and sexual desire in letters home. Or perhaps they simply wanted loved ones at home not to worry.

In this section, I focus on how Indian soldiers maintained an intense and sustained emotional relationship with home as a site through which internalised imperial tropes and indigenous identities were interwoven. In the letters, home becomes a nostalgic space infused with longing but also a focus of anxiety, dejection, madness and even alienation. Such textures of feeling are underpinned by the awareness of irrevocable, often devastating, change, resulting from 'not only the passing of time but the experience of the journeying itself', as Elleke Boehmer terms it.[22] The home the soldiers will return to can never be the one they left.

Towards the end of 1942, letters sent from Indian villages and towns to soldiers abroad attest to soaring levels of army recruitment in north India. Punjab, with its long history of armed service for the British Empire, continued to provide the highest numbers of men—18.33 per cent out of 2.5 million soldiers, as noted previously—while the North West Frontier Province also supplied 2.7 per cent.[23] As Srinath Raghavan observes, 'the traditional bastion of the north-west continued to be mined intensively for military manpower'.[24] A letter from Punjab thus unsurprisingly reads: 'There is no young man now in Kharian. All have got themselves enrolled'; while 'Enlistment is going on with full speed. What can be done?' queries another from the United Provinces. There was, however, a shift in the type of recruits signing up—the highly prized 'martial class' of Jat Sikh recruits from Punjab, for instance, were performing so well agriculturally that they were reluctant to leave their land.[25] In the Second World War, as Indivar Kamtekar observes, only a small percentage of recruits from Punjab owned land: the majority comprised tenants, labourers and artisans.[26] The letters reflect this shift in profession and status among the recruits, along with its emotional undertones. 'Not a single man of military age and eligible for enlistment has been left behind, not even a potter [...] or a barber,' declares one,[27] while a sepoy's father from Mohri, Hazara, North West Frontier Province writes sorrowfully in Urdu: 'You want to know the names of the men who have joined the army from our village. They are too many to be mentioned.'[28] We discover through these letters a rural India from where less economically secure men have simply disappeared, leaving behind a great absence: even the potters and barbers have become part of the machinery of the imperial army.

Yet the letters do not simply reveal the scale of army recruitment and its effects on Indian rural life; they also foreground how emotions associated with home function as a political tool for military enlistment, how Indian soldiers become locked into the socio-economic realities of Empire. In her insightful analysis of the role of the Indian family in pre-colonial and colonial times, Indrani Chatterjee argues for the long history of domestic and imperial sites being closely interwoven. She asserts that political control over the private and the intimate had been well-established colonial policy right from the nineteenth century, and that state formation played an important role in moulding the family as a cultural unit.[29] In the Second World War letters, we discover these continuing entanglements between colonial power structures and the feelings evoked by home, inflected by caste and clan considerations along with preconceptions about 'martial races'.

A soldier's father, writing in Urdu from a village in Mardan district in the North West Frontier Province in April 1943, fully endorses his son's service in the Indian Army:

> Your encouraging letters and money-orders have helped us to enlist ten recruits to serve the Government. You should continue to discharge your duties faithfully and to the satisfaction of your officers. To do so is the virtuous tradition of a Rajput. All young men in our village have joined the army. Your eloquent letters have made all the young of Babri [in the United Provinces] go to field service.[30]

This remarkable letter shows us the interplay between paternal discipline reinforced by male members of the soldier's family and adherence to the codes of an imperial army. Heather Streets notes how the Rajputs from northern India had served as a popular recruiting group for the British because they 'came from long traditions of pre-colonial military service' and conceived of military service as 'both a respectable and an honourable means of employment'. Bolstered by such indigenous martial traditions, the British could depend on Rajput familial and village community connections for a regular supply of recruits from the nineteenth century onwards.[31] Serving in the colonial army during the war built on the qualities of valour, prowess and nobility already associated with Indian groups such as the Rajputs. In the letter, to 'discharge duties faithfully' metamorphoses, therefore, into the 'virtuous tradition of a Rajput'; the prospect of material benefit in the money-orders sent home provides an incentive for the soldier and his family to 'enlist ten recruits'; and ethnic identity and imperial subjecthood combine in paternal advice on a son's behaviour abroad. The son's enlistment here also makes him an ambassador for recruitment in his village— his father's words transform him into a clan leader, the embodiment of Rajput ideals of masculinity.

A letter sent to another Indian soldier in the Middle East, written in Urdu from Thall, Waziristan, in the North West Frontier Province, reveals similar structures of colonial control and familial reinforcement along with their emotional undertow. The letter notes how the soldier 'should not worry about [his] children as the families of men serving overseas are well looked after by the Government'. He should, instead, 'forget everybody for the present and work wholeheartedly for King and Country'.[32] The 'Government', a recurring motif in the letters, is ascribed here the qualities of benevolent paternalism, replacing the soldier's fatherly responsibilities at home and any anxieties he might have about them in his absence.[33]

Rajit Mazumdar has drawn attention to this nexus between material benefit and colonial army service when he discusses the impact of military incomes between 1880 and 1940 on the district of Amritsar in Punjab as a case study. Mazumdar examines how, out of three *tehsils* or sub-districts of Amritsar with similar geographical features, it is the one that has the highest rates of military service that performs best economically. He also observes that the highly desired 'martial race'—the Jat community—increased their holdings of cultivated land during the late nineteenth and early twentieth centuries in these *tehsils*, a factor that 'reinforc[es] the dominance of the recruited community in the district' by foregrounding how military pay and pensions benefited the area. He concludes: 'It was rational on their [the peasants'] part to aid a government which had strengthened their economic position and reinforced their social standing.'[34] This very same discourse of mutual benefit, under-pinned by emotional allegiance to the Raj, is highlighted by the Waziristan letter.

Moving on from the traditional enlistment areas, how do letters from other districts in India reveal the new recruits' relationship with home? Regions such as southern India, not considered 'martial' by colonial authorities and therefore not having developed a long and 'loyal' history of military service to the Empire like the Rajputs, had provided only three per cent of men for the pre-war army. During the Second World War, however, as we have already learnt, the Indian Army was compelled to broaden its recruiting pool, and southern India supplied the second highest numbers of men to the army—17.87 per cent.[35] Rather than reinforcing the emotions of clan identity and belonging or emphasising the mutual advantage of war service, letters from this region demonstrate the economic imperatives leading to enlistment. A Havildar Clerk, part of the Sappers and Miners unit, declares candidly in July 1943: 'I joined the Army in order that I may get rid of this accursed devil of unem-ployment so very prevalent in India', and then continues to provide counsel back home: 'Advise your brothers to join the Army as clerks so that they can draw at least Rs. 84/- to 300/- p.m. [per month]. Don't lose this golden opportunity.'[36]

Again, without a history of colonial military service, Bengal too, as we know, broke new ground during the war by supplying 3.7 per cent of new recruits. In July 1943, the same month as the Havildar Clerk's letter, a Bengali Assistant Surgeon in the Medical Corps expresses annoyance at a friend's lack of military initiative, underscoring mate-rial benefit once again: 'I am really very sorry to learn that Sunil has accepted a civilian job of Rs. 50/-. I wonder why he has not joined the Army. He can go for [a] King's Commission if he only tried for it.'[37] Such letters, then, enable us to recover how combatants and non-combatants across the ranks—from sepoys to Havildars and doc-tors—were not simply passive subjects upon whom colonial authority was exercised; rather, they exhibit emotional agency in actively responding to and engaging others in the demands of war.

Letters home also highlight a certain self-consciousness about the act of writing itself. This is particularly evident in an extract by an Indian sepoy from a Cattle Stock Company in Tunisia, dated 16 May 1943:

> I have written to you many times, but God alone knows why I don't get your letters. You say you write regularly. Letters mean half meetings and they are a great consolation to us.[38]

The sepoy links the impact of the letter (its 'consolation', assuaging loneliness, homesickness and longing) to its inherent materiality ('letters mean half meetings'). Recreating a spectral connection between the writer who is present, ghostlike, in the medium of the letter, and the physicality of it being read, he highlights how these exchanges become a substitute for seeing loved ones in the flesh; the letters turn into literal incarnations of the writer, even if penned by a scribe. In revealing such intricate imaginings of intimacy, such negotiations between distance and proximity, the extract opens up for us the textured emotional world of Indian soldiers, suffused with the desire to hear from families on the home-front.

But if letters themselves become material objects connecting the writer to the reader, carrying the home-front to the war, and bringing the war into millions of Indian households, they also bear witness to the anxiety brought about by silence. Writing back, however, especially for rural families, could be difficult: paying for postage was becoming harder, stamps were routinely stolen from letters and there were significant postal delays.[39] As Yasmin Khan observes, 'the cost of postage was a burden for families with sons overseas; in 1940 and 1941 so many letters were being posted without stamps that it became a government matter'.[40] An Indian sepoy in the Railways Conservation Company surmises:

> I have not received any letter either from you or from home since [sic] a long time. There are two possible explanations. Either all of you have forgotten me or due to expensiveness in India you cannot afford to pay for postage.[41]

A deep-seated anxiety regarding home becoming unrecognisable, evidenced in the suggestion of being forgotten, is intensified here by the frustration of waiting for a reply. In the absence of textual exchange, home also becomes a site where economic desperation, real or imagined, is projected. Other soldiers respond to similar epistolary silences by using the language of anguish and suffering. An Assistant Signal Master writes in Urdu, 'I have written several letters home, but I have not received a reply. It is making me miserable',[42] while a sepoy in the Indian Army Police Corps reveals, 'I have written to you so many letters, but no reply is being received. It is just enough to drive one mad. Perhaps something is wrong somewhere.'[43] For soldiers stationed abroad, their state of homelessness and mobile lives exacerbate the emotional force with which the idea of home is invested: it is at the same time joyful and poignant with memory, but also fraught at a rapidly changing, and hostile, time.

As appeals for the soldiers' return home become painfully acute in the letters they receive, the enforced separation takes its toll on their emotional resilience—the 'morale' that colonial censors were so concerned about. In late 1942, a sepoy observes to his family: 'You write and ask me why I don't come home on leave. In our country he who is a prisoner cannot go home until the term of imprisonment is over, no matter if he has troubles at home and has affairs to settle. Our position is exactly like this. We too cannot go home until our term of imprisonment is over (i.e. overseas service).'[44] This is a significantly different analogy to make, compared to the letter extracts from home highlighting masculine valour and pride in being an imperial warrior, with which our discussion began. The letter here, instead, sees international war service as physical and psychic incarceration—an utter powerlessness over the material conditions of life.

Again, a little over a year later, an Indian 'Other Rank', part of the Tenth Indian Division stationed in Palestine, Syria and Transjordan, writes in a deploring tone in January 1944:

> I am an ignorant sepoy. Who is there in this world to take care of me? After completing three years' service in this confounded wilderness, I am now lamenting my fate because all my hopes and attempts for a spot of leave in India were frustrated. [...] I do not know when I am going to meet you all. Please do not accuse me that I am not trying for leave. I shall go mad! I was crying when I read your letter.[45]

The language used here, even in its mutated and translated form, is far more despairing and dramatic than that of the previous letters.

Studying Italian peasant soldiers' references to tears in First World War letters, Vanda Wilcox argues that the experiences of war and the fear of violence and death were difficult to articulate, and that writing about crying became a means of verbalising such emotions.[46] In this Second World War letter by a sepoy, though, male tears are used to epitomise the emotions of pain rather than serving as a metonym for it. The language of suffering draws upon Indian modes of lamentation such as the Islamic *marsiya*[47] to work its way up, from evoking feelings of being alone and powerless to madness and despair, and culminating in tears. It is important for the sepoy to articulate this depth of feeling to his family, to demonstrate his love and longing in a textual display of emotion.

As a counterpoint to this expression of intense sorrow at being denied leave, a sepoy in the Frontier Force Rifles writing in Urdu on 15 May 1943 asks his family, in much more measured tones, not to be anxious about his physical return: 'I don't understand why you worry so much. I know I can't get leave so please don't worry unnecessarily. I am quite alright in my way. That is what you want.'[48] While letters here become a textual substitute for physical encounters, the act of writing cannot entirely replace the act of meeting one another—the letters remain 'half meetings', incomplete and partial. Dismissing familial concerns in this way, however, works as a form of reassurance to loved ones at home. It also becomes a rhetorical device for the sepoy, a mode of feeling by which he is able to examine the vulnerability of his own existence as an imperial subject abroad. Sentences such as 'I know I can't get leave' reflect his knowledge of the intransigence of the colonial will, even as soldiers extol the virtues of the King Emperor and pray for his long life in their letters. Writing from hospital in Hindustani after a landmark victory by the Fourth Indian Division over the *Panzerarmee* in North Africa in May 1943,[49] a sepoy comments:

> We have a lot of work to do out here but with the complete victory of our King and our forces we are happy and comfortable and pass our time nicely. Having finished this task we are now day and night thinking of what is going to happen next.[50]

Interwoven with expressing satisfaction at his present situation and praise for the King, the letter also reveals the sepoy's dilemma—

now that the campaign is over, what will happen next? Compared to soldiers' emotional agency discussed earlier in their endorsing and promoting imperial military service at home, we discover here how constrained and limited such agency really is. Will the soldier be sent home to India, as many of the troops yearn for, or will he be fighting yet another battle? Such questions are clearly on the sepoys' minds as they write home.

Moving between these emotions of ambivalence, dejection, anxiety and lamentation, Indian soldiers' letters about home become a layered repository of feeling. Writing about British soldiers' letters from the Second World War, of which substantially more survive,[51] Lucy Noakes observes how 'autobiographical writing is composed in both senses', becoming narratives that reflect a particular historicised and localised form of selfhood, but also represent attempts at psychological composure. Noakes alerts us to the pressures which this mode of expression faces because of war—'a particularly discomposing experience'.[52] How, then, does such discomposure register psychologically on Indian soldiers? It is in expressions of despair and weariness written to family in India that we understand the fragility of the Indian soldiers' self, cracking under the tremendous strains of war.

Certain letters, however, reveal that sepoys do not find a leave of absence as emotionally rewarding an experience as they initially might have envisioned. Such extracts highlight a growing sense of alienation from the homeland once soldiers return there temporarily. A Havildar in the Indian Army Police Corps, on leave in Amritsar in north India, writes to a fellow soldier in June 1943:

> When we reached India, then alone we realised the value of being
> in Egypt. What with shortages, expensiveness and political turmoil,
> India is not a liveable place these days. As soon as my leave is over,
> I shall come back to my unit. Moreover, I cannot sit at home like [a]
> Purdah woman, when the enemy is at our door. It is impossible.[53]

From longing, home has turned into 'an unliveable place these days' as the Havildar experiences the turbulent economic and political realities of the Indian home-front. In fact, through the simile of the 'Purdah woman', the idea of home here problematically becomes a feminised space associated with political escapism. Again, is the 'enemy' being 'at our door' a reference to Hitler, or a more direct threat to India from the Japanese? And is the zeal with which the Havildar wishes to return to military life used to mask his desire for the male-dominated space of the battlefront—itself a form of retreat from the difficulties of home?

Another, considerably more empathetic, letter from a Lance Naik highlights his meeting with soldiers returning to the frontline after their period of leave in India:

> Some men arrived here from India today. I asked them all about the situation. They informed us that when anybody goes to the bazaar to buy something he has to stand in a row in order to buy things and it is very hard to get things. Are there such difficulties prevailing in India? You let me know how people are passing their days [...] I have no knowledge of what is going on in India. I am extremely surprised to hear this news and don't understand how people in India can manage to live under such conditions.[54]

Astonishment, concern and desire to understand the lived realities of the home-front are fused in this Lance Naik's response. While Susheila Nasta observes that home 'is not necessarily where one *belongs* but where one *starts* from',[55] for the Lance Naik, his emotional connections with a home he has left behind are represented by deeply felt ties of belonging. The sentence 'I have no knowledge of what is going on in India' is self-admonitory: the Naik is alarmed by his ignorance of how loved ones are faring in an economic situation he finds impossible to comprehend.

From the haplessness felt by this soldier on hearing of a rapidly changing homeland, we also encounter a more troubling hopelessness—regret at enlisting in the army at all. A sepoy in a Transit Camp declares in Urdu in 1943:

> You write to me so often that things have become very expensive and you ask me to send you more money and more money. Where can I get money? Why doesn't your land which supplied us all before all this produce enough for you to eat something? Work hard on the land. I know what mistake I have committed. But it is too late. It was better if we had all worked on the land, at least we would have lived as before. Now I cannot earn even enough grain to last you two months.[56]

Here, the transition of roles and economic practices from sustenance farmer to salaried imperial soldier has been undermined
because the value of money itself decreased very sharply in India
during the war years. Indivar Kamtekar notes that the amount of
currency circulating in India multiplied six-and-a-half times during
the war years, resulting in extremely high rates of inflation. As a
point of comparison, he studies food prices in wartime Britain
against those of India. In Britain, prices were controlled by government subsidies and rose by 18 per cent; in India, the price of even
rationed food during the 1940s rose by an extraordinary 300 per
cent,[57] increasingly placing essential food items out of the reach of
ordinary people. Eventually, this lack of price control would be one
of the crucial factors leading to the 1943 Bengal Famine—which is
when this letter was written—accompanied by widespread economic hardship across many regions of India.[58]

In Chapter 2, I will explore the cultural, literary and emotional
legacies of the famine in detail; here, we receive only its intimations
with the peasant-farmer-turned-imperial-soldier finding his colonial
employment opportunity falling foul. In his desperation as an inad-
equate provider for his family, the soldier realises that his lived
experience undercuts colonial propaganda about the economic
opportunities presented by war. To him, the privileged status of
being in the army is meaningless if his family at home is unable to
eat. However, even though the sepoy confesses, 'I know what mis-
take I have committed. But it is too late', the letter is not a subver-
sive one. Rather than resisting colonial power structures, it shows
us the extent of the sepoy's emotional realisation: he recognises the
futility of his economic position and understands that both home-
front and battlefront are entangled within larger, often terrible
forces, over which he and his family have little control. It is this very
realisation that Shantilal Ray, the Bengali doctor on the Burma
front, experiences in his complex and changing relationship with the
idea of home, to which this chapter will now turn.

*'Janmabhumi bharatbhumi' ('My motherland, India'): home and the
radicalised Bengali doctor in Burma*

Today I came to know that soon I would be returning home to my
country, to my motherland. What an extraordinarily joyful feeling

that was! I was counting the days left one by one—time passed by so slowly! The closer the day of return came, the more I felt an ever-increasing pull at my heart.

— Shantilal Ray, *Arakan Fronte* (*On the Frontlines at Arakan*, 1946)

Arakan Fronte is a rare and out-of-print memoir by a Bengali doctor who journeys to Burma along with the British-led Fourteenth Army during the first six months of 1944, witnessing some of the final battles against Japanese forces.[59] The Pacific War brought a million British, Indian, Gurkha and African troops, under the aegis of Lord Mountbatten's Southeast Asia Command (SEAC) from November 1943 onwards, to fight the Imperial Japanese Army.[60] This war to reclaim Burma from the Japanese was painful and drawn out. The first Arakan campaign had taken place during the winter of 1942–1943, resulting in a Japanese victory. In February 1944, however, Japan lost its offensive here, followed by defeats in Imphal and Kohima.[61] Ray joins the Fourteenth Army for this second campaign in the Arakan, resulting in Allied victory. A long strip of land along Burma's western coast, the Arakan (now known as Rakhine state, home of the Rohingya people) is bordered by the Bay of Bengal to the west, undivided Bengal (now the Chittagong Division of Bangladesh) to the north-west, and the north-eastern region of India to the north. The Arakan Mountains, rising to over 3,000 metres and bisected by small, steep streams, separate the region from central Burma's lowlands.[62] It is within these mountainous jungles that the memoir is set, a landscape intimately woven into Ray's emotional world.

It has proved very difficult to recover biographical details of Shantilal Ray's life, but from the memoir we understand he had served in Malaya from 1940 to 1942 in peace stations, and came back to India as British-led forces retreated in the wake of Japanese victories in Southeast Asia. The Arakan in 1944 thus forms his first war experience on an international battlefront. Ray, the memoir tells us, is the only Bengali surgeon recruited to his unit. The crucial importance of medical services in Burma provided by doctors like Ray is recognised by Christopher Bayly and Tim Harper in their remarkable study of the 'forgotten' armies of Southeast Asia during the Second World War. Bayly and Harper note the importance of treating serious wounds on the frontline in 1944 so that the

Fourteenth Army could withstand Japanese forces and not retreat, as had disastrously occurred in 1942 during Japan's takeover of British-controlled territories—Hong Kong, Malaya, Singapore and Burma—in Southeast Asia.[63] Ray forms part of these 'armies of nurses and doctors—Indian, Chinese, Anglo-Indian and Anglo-Burmese—[who] provided aid and compassion in the midst of fighting which brought the brutalities of the Middle Ages face-to-face with modern mechanised killing'.[64]

As Bayly and Harper note, the Arakan was complicated fighting ground: trench warfare and guerilla tactics prevailed, mules had to be used for transporting essential supplies across rocky terrain, and Allied airpower proved vital in providing rations, medical provisions and other needs. It was a strange combination of old-school fighting techniques with industrialised warfare, and Ray acknowledges the simultaneous presence of both when he says in gratitude: 'There are the mules upon the earth, while in the sky the planes rain all necessary goods upon us tirelessly, like blessings from the gods' (38). The Arakan thus becomes militarily an in-between zone, and Ray starts to view it as a psychologically liminal space too, where he can shed the vestiges of his past life and acknowledge the growth of a new and fractured identity. 'I will not easily be able to take up my old flow of life again' (43), he thinks at one point. Functioning as a travelogue, the memoir dramatises the continuing development of the 'mobile new Indian identities'[65] that Elleke Boehmer highlights in her focus on British and Indian cultural encounters in Britain a little earlier, from the opening of the Suez Canal in 1870 up until the First World War.

In the foreword to the memoir, Ray's fellow war companion Nihar Ranjan Gupta notes how Ray continues to write amidst the 'golaguli' or 'flying bullets' of the frontline, privileging what James Campbell has called 'combat gnosticism' in relation to First World War poetry.[66] The implication, Campbell tells us, is that readers understand war poetry as documentary evidence rather than art. The same impulse, I argue, applies to life-writing in the Second World War. While Gupta encourages us to see the memoir as a direct transmission of battlefront life, we instead discover it to be a highly mediated narrative of Ray's emotions, fusing together memory, nostalgia, horror, empathy and a rising political consciousness.

Narrative tensions, then, pull *Arakan Fronte* in different directions, transforming it into an extraordinary piece of work that combines war writing and life-writing.[67] From the doctor's boredom on being stationed at a military hospital within India in 1943, and desire for the romance of travel, we are taken through the minutiae of military camp life on the Arakan frontline. Combining a documentary zeal with the style of an adventure story, the memoir evokes a world of makeshift hospitals, operations aborted under sudden Japanese assault, narrow escapes from death, journeys across dust-covered mountainous roads bordered by dense jungle and companions left behind—only to be found again. We learn of the still, dark nights when Ray lies awake in his only shelter—a hole dug in the earth—fully clothed and clutching a revolver, tense with the anticipation of an enemy attack. Undercutting this impulse for battlefield realism and the pace of a thriller, however, are times when the memoir turns inwards to reflect. It is at these moments that Ray's representations of landscape become evocations of feeling. *'Matir shonge ei bhabe nibir parichoy ei prothom'*,[68] he says. 'This was the first time I had known the earth in such an intimate way.'

This section interrogates how such intimacies with the earth are intertwined with Ray's shifting understanding of home. I examine here how home functions as an emotional site in two principal ways: it serves as a route towards empathy for all those who suffer and die in war, across enemy lines, and it enables the expansion of Ray's nostalgic memories of his childhood spent in a Bengali village to the vision of a liberated India. In interrogating these trajectories of meaning, I reveal how the Arakan becomes both a material and psychic landscape, where for Ray a new birth takes place. This is represented by Ray's investment in the richness of Indian—in this case, predominantly Bengali—literature. As the highly literary memoir weaves its 'tissue of quotations',[69] Ray calls the front a *'mrityur Kurukshetra'* (68) or a 'Kurukshetra of death', referring to the famous battlefield in the Indian epic of fraternal war, the *Mahabharata*. Again, its concluding quote is from Rabindranath Tagore's poem *'Sonar Tari'* ('The golden boat'):

Janani lahogo morey
Shaghano bandhan taba, bajuge dhore [...]
Amare loyia jao—rakhiyo na dure.

O Mother, take me to you,
Your bonds last ever so long, when you hold me in your arms [...]
Take me to you—don't keep me away.[70]

From his feelings on witnessing death on the battlefront to highlighting a deep longing for return to his motherland, Ray's literary references demonstrate to us his changing relationship with the earth. The prospect of actually returning home, then, which he learns about while on the Indo-Burmese border, on the brink of a global war ending, overflows into imagining a new and uncharted political world.

Ray's emotional relationship with the Arakan begins by his highlighting how inhospitable the landscape is, made habitable only by a *'chirantan garta khnora'* (31)—'an eternal hole-digging'—to form places of rest. In a mixture of affection and irony he calls these holes his *'bhugarba prashad'*—'subterranean palaces'—and declares: *'mati-i khnati'* (42)—'the earth is the real thing'. Living in these makeshift holes leads Ray to question the structures of his previous life and the purpose of modern civilisation itself, which the memoir later importantly connects with imperialism. Ray feels as though he now lives like *'adim juger manush'*—'primitive man', away from *'shabyatar chakchikya'*—the 'false glitter of civilisation'—and reflects how much his perspectives on earth have changed: 'Dwelling in the city, what appeared for so long to be dirty and best avoided, today became intensely, intimately my own' (47). He nonetheless worries that, at the end of the war, people's more wholesome selves would once again be hidden beneath the gilt-edged *'rangin ghomta'* (43) or 'colourful veil of civilisation', which 'clings to falsehood' and promotes selfishness (47). The notion of civilisation, to him, becomes a mask, which can slip to reveal *'adim barbarata'* (43) or 'primitive barbarity'. Ray's realisation that the heart of civilisation may contain its very opposite, barbarity—a truth that is exposed by war—powerfully echoes South Asian intellectual responses to the Second World War, which I examine in detail in Chapter 4.

If the earth becomes the site of Ray's re-making, where 'civilisation' drops away to connect him intimately to the natural world, it also generates feelings of terror. Walking through battlefield debris after a fierce clash between Allied and Japanese forces, Ray encounters corpses burnt by the sun's rays, rotting and swollen, and is drawn to a strange sight: two dead bodies, one Japanese and one Indian, co-mingled, sitting in a trench with a bayonet through them, locked in a '*drira alingan*' (59) or 'tight embrace'. Ray's choice of words here shows how easily the Arakan fluctuates between living and dying, where it becomes difficult to tell apart the intimate physicality of love from the rigor mortis of a sudden and violent death.

This merging of life and death, of shelter and terror, is also high-lighted in the first Japanese night-time attack, from which he escapes. Ray tells us how, caught unawares, men take refuge in '*trencher buke, matir gorte*' (14)—'in the heart of the trench, in the hole in the earth'. Male bodies are uncomfortably pressed up against each other, knees banging one another. Their faces have turned white; while some men become unconscious, others have lost control and even defecated in fear. Ray muses, almost as though he were a detached observer of this spectacle: 'Facing death head-on, they were clinging desperately to life' (14). But when he is alone, trying to rest at night, such detachment vanishes. Ray draws attention to how the mouth of his 'fox-hole' is closed with branches from wild trees and clumps of grass, so that bending his head and knees he can just about enter and lie down but has no place to move. Without light or air, it seems a '*jibanta shamadhi*'—a 'living tomb' (42). Feeling imprisoned, with nightmares crowding in on him, he wonders if the night would ever end. It is this sense of growing suffocation and primordial apprehension of being buried, of being entombed, that haunts him. The 'fox-hole', then, not only serves the function of being home and habitation through which Ray feels connected to the natural world; like Bachelard's cellar in a symbolic house of dreams, it also becomes 'buried madness', a darker, sub-terranean and irrational entity, from which he must break free.[71]

In a memoir where the emotions associated with making one's home in the earth are fraught, witnessing others' homelessness takes on a particular poignancy. Ray highlights how air raids transform Burmese villagers' huts into a '*dhwangshostup*' (28) or 'pile of rubble'. Thinking of these exiles from their '*janmabhumi*' or 'motherland', as homeless both in personal and political terms, his critique becomes pointed: 'What is their crime? Did they ever want war? Yet it is their peaceful lives which have to bear the brunt of the biggest transformation of the age— '*shabcheye bada jugantakari bibartan'* (28–29). But it is not simply displaced people who attract his attention; displaced objects have their own emotional resonance too. Ray provides us with a phantasmagoric account of wandering through a ravaged battlefield, where he sees the conjoined corpses of the Japanese and Indian soldiers mentioned earlier. Here, his gaze lingers on assorted wreckage—metal dishes, bullet-pierced steel helmets, discarded old clothes. Out of this haphazard array, he homes in on delicate Japanese pillowcases made by 'the beloved's tender hand' (57), where love-knots and forget-me-nots have been embroidered. All of these now roll about in the dust and debris, abandoned.

Why, out of all the flotsam and jetsam of the battlefield, is Ray's attention arrested by these pillowcases? Perhaps it is because, contrasted against military objects and their utilitarian benefits, it is these pillowcases that suggest a place of comfort and rest, transforming into a metonym for home. Re-enacting Freud's notion of '*Unheimliche*' or the uncanny, which literally translates into 'unhomely',[72] they became familiar objects in a strange and unsettling context—un-homed. Ray can only see them as objects of love, and it is this empathetic insight that begins to rupture for him the category of the enemy.

The funerary associations of the earth continue to provide Ray with insights into the enemy's psyche. On coming across the grave of a high-ranking Japanese official, he observes:

> As a mark of respect for the dead, the outer part of a tree trunk had been smoothed over, and all sorts of things were written on it in the Japanese script and placed on top of the grave. At the bottom, a few dried leaves inside two empty tin containers were arranged like *amro pallab*—mango leaves in a religious ceremony.

In the middle, an extinguished earthen lamp stood in place of a *mangal ghat*—a pitcher representing good fortune (60). Unable to understand the Japanese script, he nonetheless brings his knowledge of Hindu ritual to the placement of the leaves and earthen lamp, recognising them as accoutrements to the ceremony of mourning and loss. In doing so, he reveals his ability to penetrate with empathetic insight the emotional world of the Japanese. And, although Ray later acknowledges 'the poison of racial hatred' (70) that he feels towards Japanese PoWs who need his medical treatment, such emotions are short-lived. Instead, he thinks:

> [...] some time back, these very soldiers were living peacefully with their wives, sons, brothers, sisters in their homes, surrounded by love ('*bhalobashar snehonire*'), without causing anyone harm. They are but tiny insects, caught within the sudden onset of a cyclone. It is the machinations of the imperialists' greed and desire which created this sacrificial play of killing ('*maron yogner shoghar leela*'). (70–71)

Through such imaginings, Ray is able to conclude that all soldiers, including the enemy, are caught, like him, within the larger forces of history. Such feelings deepen on seeing graves rapidly multiply in the Arakan during a particularly intense few weeks of fighting during the Battle of the 'Admin Box' in February 1944, in which the Japanese were ultimately defeated.[73] Despite the final successful outcome for the Allies, as Ray looks upon the hasty burial of soldier after soldier from the Fourteenth Army, he recalls in sorrow this army's remarkable diversity:[74]

> I felt saddest thinking of the far-flung countries that formed their motherland—where are all their relatives, friends, loved ones? Not only were they unable to see their nearest and dearest for the very last time, but were also denied the tenderness of touch, the parting comfort of a few final words. One day the war will end. But then everything will have been swept away at tidal speed. The dead will remain asleep in the earth's shadowed lap, in a green corner of this forest. (67–68)

His elegiac tone imbues the earth with pastoral and maternal associations as it evolves into the soldiers' final resting place, a surrogate permanent home in the absence of human love and belonging. We also understand how Ray relates familial affection and the friendships of home with the 'motherland', an association which the memoir continues to build upon.

This 'rich earth', however, has more than 'a richer dust concealed'[75]—it transforms into the site where Ray brushes most closely against the enemy's daily life and confronts his primordial fears of falling prey to entombment. He recounts venturing underground into the heart of a deserted Japanese bunker—'*patalpurir gohobor*' (76) or an 'underground world of caves'.[76] Again, instead of people, he encounters Japanese household objects. Exploring the empty kitchen area, he sees symbols of ordinary domesticity such as a hearth and biscuit tins, while two shining wooden chopsticks with ivory handles, used for eating rice, attract his eye. However, the deeper Ray descends into this labyrinthine abandoned 'home', the more he is surrounded by death. He chances upon an enormous hole in which Japanese corpses have been buried in a hurry, their bodies now mangled by foxes and emanating a terrible stench. A nervous Ray begins to imagine the spectres of the dead all around him; it is as though the earth with its '*birat atankajanak nistobdhota*' (79)—'great and terrifying silence'—were his living grave. Rapidly starting his ascent and terrified of being lost underground, he succeeds in finding his way out. Nonetheless, he finds it impossible to rid himself of the trauma of this experience, and from this point onwards the earth of the Arakan contains only associations of death for him.

As Ray's feelings of dejection become more pronounced, the Arakan earth loses all sense of comfort, shelter and associations of home for him. When informed that he has been allocated night patrol duty, for instance, he feels only despair: 'How many more days will I spend living like a wild animal in forests, inside holes in the earth and within mountain caves?' (81), and then again: 'My heart became heavy and gloomy. I started to pray—"Now send me back"' (84). He imagines, and starts longing for, the return home. This is also the moment in the memoir when the idea of home incorporates the experiential warmth and closeness of human companionship, felt by Ray with his Bengali companions near the Ngakyedauk Pass, where they are stationed for two months at the start of the monsoon season. Once more, Ray's use of language is significant—he describes the '*sukher nir*' (88) or 'happy home' that he builds with these friends, especially Paritosh Ray, Uma Mukherjee and author Nihar Ranjan Gupta,[77] with whose encouragement he starts writing this memoir. Ray's Bengali identity is encouraged and affirmed by this association: he describes how Mukherjee manages to procure unripe mangoes and *kul* or jujube berries and makes pickle for them all, recreating the familiar, longed-for tastes of Ray's childhood.

This emphasis on Bengali identity as a marker of home is hinted early on in *Arakan Fronte*. When first signing up for war service, Ray notes how unusual it must be for a British officer to receive such a request from a '*bhiru, asamorik Bangali*' (2)—the 'cowardly, unmilitary Bengali'. He thus draws upon a legacy of colonial stereotypes about Bengali effeminacy that Mrinalini Sinha has insightfully explored in relation to the late nineteenth century, and which I mentioned earlier in this chapter.[78] But such insecurity about his identity is reversed when injured INA PoWs, whom he has to treat, are delighted on discovering that he is a Bengali, like their commander Subhas Chandra Bose, making Ray's 'heart swell with pride' (30). And, perhaps most significantly, Ray aligns his thinking to a dominant South Asian intellectual response to European imperialism: he associates modern urban civilisation with the West and links its materialism to what he believes to be the root cause of this global war: greed. Evoking metaphors of burning, Ray conveys to us the war's destructive power, 'in whose flames all of humanity burns today'—'*jar shikhaye samasta manabatwa aj jwale pure jacche*' (122).

In contrast to the metaphoric 'burning' associated with war and the physical reality of a charred and devastated Arakan landscape, Ray's idea of home in Bengal transforms into the nostalgic village of his childhood, invested this time with political significance. Enormously relieved to leave the Arakan mountains for the plainlands, Ray is finally billeted further east, by the River Naf, whose course marks Burma's border with Bengal. From across the river, he is able to see the outlines of Bengali villages with their characteristic leafy huts, lined by rows of coconut trees, where he imagines the *babui pakhi* or weaver bird to be building its nest. As he gazes upon this village, memory and desire suffuse him:

> Looking at the village path in the lush green Bengal that I had left very far behind, my heart grew agitated. Sitting in the lap of nature's beauty in the midst of the chaos of war, I could hear the forsaken village mother's call—'Leave it all behind, tear apart all your bonds.' A deep distaste for this nomadic life was born in me. (120)

He imagines what awaits him on his return home—'maternal love, affection from brothers and sisters, the loving warmth of friends, good wishes of neighbours, well-wishers and relatives, the blessings from elders' (123). The intimate space of home now glides into ideas of the political homeland; in the final paragraph of the memoir, he declares:

> Of all the places I have seen, and all the people I have encountered, no person and no place has attracted me with the pull of the motherland [...] so today I fervently call upon my mother [...] *Bande Mataram*—Hail, my motherland![79] (124)

'Mother', a metonym for home, has morphed into the motherland; the scenes of reunion fondly imagined by Ray now transform into the well-known revolutionary cry for Indian independence.

In what ways, then, do Ray's ideas of home map onto the politicised homeland? Earlier on in the memoir, the positivity Ray starts feeling about being Bengali is itself a political realisation, not only bolstered by his group of newly formed friends but also linked to a recognition of regional, linguistic and cultural affiliation with INA commander Subhas Chandra Bose. Ray reveals to us his support for securing Indian independence through military means under Bose's leadership—although he does not himself defect to the INA, and never says why. Nonetheless, his growing regional pride is fostered by a keen realisation of the injustice of white supremacist beliefs and racial discrimination during the war, an understanding that the '*kala admi*' (102) or 'black man' could never be good enough.

When a Japanese attack is feared and troops need to re-locate swiftly, Ray notes how it is the white British officers who are the first to leave their posts. Again, in a fight for 'world freedom' (102), he ironically observes how Indian soldiers in hospital receive lower-quality rations than their British counterparts; on requesting replacements for their dirty mattresses, he is informed that Indians never slept on mattresses before the war and should be grateful simply for receiving beds. He acerbically comments: 'Despite seeing all this, we still don't seem to lose our fascination for the coloniser' (108). In other words, he understands that the relationship between coloniser and colonised is not only predicated upon asymmetrical material benefit for the former but embeds itself in complex emotional and psychological ways into the minds of the colonised.[80] This fascination has, by the end of

the memoir, entirely dissipated for Ray. Radicalised by his experiences on the Arakan front, it is by linking himself to anticolonial,
nationalist politics that he can imagine his return. Home must be
to an independent Bengal—and by association, India—and it is
this return that he anticipates.

'This all-embracing India': Transnational imaginings of home in
The Men from Imphal

Fig. 1.3: 'The Ranis at target practice', c. 1943–5. © Netaji Research Bureau,
Kolkata, India.

A photograph in the Netaji Research Bureau archives in Kolkata
shows three South Asian women in military uniform, taking careful
aim to shoot. Their faces, set in frowning concentration while
wielding rifles on bended knees and aiming at targets, indicates a
steely resolution. The three women are from the Rani of Jhansi
Regiment, raised from expatriate Indian communities in Singapore
and Malaya by Bose in July 1943, discussed in the Introduction to
the book. If the two colonial photographs with which this chapter
started highlight Indian 'loyalty' to imperial war recruitment, the

third draws attention to the spectacle of women bearing arms for the nationalist cause, deliberately rupturing our pre-conceptions of gender and combat, and, most importantly, of home. Nationalist and imperialist visual propaganda, then, each drawing upon their contested histories, jostle against each other; the gendered domestic connotations of home are explicitly, even violently, linked by the image of women bearing arms to its more expansive political meanings of anticolonial independence and liberation.

By October 1943, the Rani of Jhansi Regiment comprised 156 women;[81] the rest of the INA consisted of men, mainly Indian PoWs in Southeast Asia who had defected from the Indian Army, along with civilians from the Indian expatriate community. In contemporary Indian war narratives, like Shantilal Ray's *Arakan Fronte*, Burma becomes the site of a strange meeting where the imperial logic underpinning the employment of colonial soldiers is subverted. Echoing the mythological internecine battlefield of Kurukshetra in the *Mahabharata* referenced by Ray in his literary memoir, in Burma, men from the Indian Army and the INA repeatedly face one another in combat.[82] While the Indian Army provided most of the Allied ground troops for Burma in what became the largest land campaign fought by the Japanese outside China,[83] the INA numbers were comparatively smaller. Only 12,000 out of approximately 40,000 PoWs who had defected in Southeast Asia served in Kohima and Imphal—key border towns targeted by the Japanese as entry points into India.[84] The fighting was fierce: the road to Imphal was later said by local residents to be a place of ghosts, created by what Sugata Bose, among others, has described as 'some of the bloodiest battles of the Second World War'.[85] The end of such encounters, however, saw the first death-knell to Indian militant nationalism. The British Empire had, for the moment, won.

In post-independence Indian memory, the myth of the INA has overtaken a recognition of the complex specifics of the soldiers' lived experiences. Yet even nationalist symbols are accorded their hierarchies: the narrative of armed resistance against the British Empire did not sit comfortably with Gandhian non-violence. Arjun Appadurai, whose father served as minister of publicity and propaganda in Bose's government-in-exile, the 'Provisional Government of Free India' established in Japanese-occupied Singapore in

1943,[86] remembers how, on returning to India in 1945, his father and friends became 'unwelcome heroes, poor cousins in the story of the nationalist struggle for Indian independence'. They remained 'pariah patriots, rogue nationalists'; their India 'with its Japanese connections and anti-Western ways, carried the nameless aroma of treason'.[87] Further examination into the lived experiences of INA soldiers has also been subsumed by the mythopoeic status of Bose within India and the controversies surrounding his death in August 1945;[88] much of the contemporary documentation on Bose and his involvement with the INA, written by his close companions and officers, tends towards the hyperbolic and the hagiographic.[89]

Out of this dense entanglement of contested allegiances, motivations and political discourses, the final section of this chapter focuses on a short memoir, entitled *The Men from Imphal* (1970), by INA officer and Bose's companion Abid Hasan Safrani. Initially delivered as an oration at the Netaji Bhavan, Calcutta, in January 1970, *The Men from Imphal* was published in December 1970 in *The Oracle*, the quarterly journal on Subhas Chandra Bose and the INA brought out by the Netaji Research Bureau until 1995. Hasan himself had formed part of Bose's 'Indian Legion' in Germany in 1942,[90] and had accompanied Bose on a remarkable secret journey by German and Japanese submarine from Kiel in north Germany to Tokyo and Japanese-controlled Singapore in 1943.[91] He then fought with the INA against the British-led Fourteenth Army at Imphal. The Japanese strategy in approaching Imphal and Kohima by land from their occupied Southeast Asian territories had been risky—their troops were instructed to travel light with limited supplies across a 200-mile difficult terrain over 'some of the world's worst country, breeding the world's worst diseases, and having for half a year the world's worst climate'.[92] Instead, while American air power provided supplies and reinforcements to Allied troops for three-and-half months during the siege at Imphal, Japanese forces and the INA were close to starvation and short of medical supplies.

The Men from Imphal begins at this point, with INA soldiers in straitened, desperate circumstances. Composed twenty-five years after this catastrophic military defeat, the memoir constitutes one of the few Indian accounts of the life of INA men after the Imphal loss, straddling the observational, the symbolic and the emotional. My focus here is on how Hasan uses the event of the Imphal defeat as a route in to uncover personal and cultural memory, and in doing so, how he is able to probe the emotions associated with home. To Hasan, home becomes synonymous with the homeland, but, building on Bose's own controversial anticolonial resistance formulated outside India, in Germany and Japan, it is re-conceptualised as a vision that includes the Indian expatriate community and expands into ideals of human freedom itself. Tapan Raychaudhuri draws attention to the fierce emotional current running through such anti-colonial nationalism when he talks in 1979—nine years after Hasan's memoir was published—of 'the hopes, passions and heartbreak of millions'[93] of Indians who had fought for political change under the British Empire. Raychaudhuri writes: '[O]nce, not so very long ago, to countless Indians nationalism was a fire in the blood'.[94] I argue that this 'fire' finds its fullest expression in Hasan's memoir in the body of the INA commander himself, Subhas Chandra Bose, or Netaji, as he was affectionately called.

Like Shantilal Ray's *Arakan Fronte*, Hasan's memoir focuses on the emotions aroused by the devastation of place and the wrecked bodies of the INA men. It starts at the moment of the realisation of defeat, with collective male bodies in ceaseless motion, retreating as they had been ordered to do:

> We kept on marching, if the trek we took could be called a march. Those among us who suffered from dysentery and malaria had long ceased to beseech that we slowed down our pace. There was no one left who could march faster than they.[95]

These are the ravaged and diseased men of the INA's Gandhi Brigade, whose route was meant to be a historic one towards Delhi and independence but here is dispiritingly back towards Burma, to the city of Moulmein and then Mandalay. The landscape is barren; the men's rations have been eaten a long time back. The absence of food turns into a metaphor for defeat, the bareness of the landscape a visual reminder of the field being lost. Hasan recalls: 'Food of any kind, even nourishing roots and leaves, was not available. The sick was [*sic*] with us and the weak. We had to struggle ourselves and help others to drag on' (4).

To complicate the situation further, the monsoons arrived earlier than expected in late May 1944, turning the Indo-Burma border into 'rivers of green mud',[96] much like the First World War 'slime-scapes', as Santanu Das terms it.[97] With all bridges being destroyed by the Allied forces, Hasan describes having to wade through small rivers soaked up to his chest, holding his weapon above his head and grasping the man in front, so as not to be carried away by 'the angry waters' (4). He observes how even 'the rats had left the villages forsaken by their inhabitants on this route to Moulmein, trodden [sic] already by our allies, the Japanese in their thousands, on their retreat from Burma' (1). He also reveals the rapacious nature of the Allied pursuit—the INA are now the hunted:

> And while we marched there was no one among us, however low his rank and limited his understanding, who did not realise that the war was lost and the tanks following us and the aeroplanes menacing us would chase us into the waves of the Pacific Ocean. (1)

Not everyone was able to cope with the intense physical demands of battlefront losses, lack of food and an arduous march back towards Burma. Hasan remembers how, on the Imphal battlefront, his appointment as second-in-command of the INA's Gandhi Brigade had taken place because his predecessor, Major Garewal, defected to the British after fierce fighting against the Scottish soldiers of the Seaforth Highlanders, and had taken with him details of the INA's strategic positions.[98] Peter Ward Fay believes that the question of procuring food rapidly became a vital one for the INA during the Imphal siege, and that 'there could be no question of living off the country': 'if rations failed, the men went hungry'. He also observes that Hasan 'believes that it was despair born from hunger' that made Major Garewal join British forces.[99] The siege at Imphal reveals how counter-defection threatens this newly formed national army; Imphal, to Hasan, is not simply a place or event but a fraught 'story written with our blood and more so with our sweat' (2). The memoir, then, foregrounds how the emotional trauma of place is understood through the human body: the disintegration of one is predicated upon the other.

Throughout Hasan's narrative of the march, starvation continues to threaten the retreating INA men. INA officer Shah Nawaz Khan notes in his own memoir how four men from Garhwal under his command had died of hunger on the retreat to Burma,[100] while Hasan writes of emotions serving as their only nourishment: 'An army, it is said, marches on its stomach but we marched sustained only by a great desire and a great longing' (1). When the men stopped for rest at the small town of Kalewa, Hasan recalls how the decimation of this town was reflected in the dying officer Cherian from Malaya. What remained of Kalewa was a 'sick bay' or accommodation for the ill 'with all its filth, stench and utter neglect'. Cherian, he remembers:

> stretched himself at the sick bay and nothing I could say would persuade him to rise. 'Mandalay?' he questioned and added 'How far off, how far away! There is no Kalewa here and should we even reach it will we find a Mandalay there?' He died the next day after we left. (5)

That Mandalay is perceived as an impossible goal recurs in Hasan's memory of Major Akbar Ali Khan, a Pathan from the North West Frontier Province and Chief Medical Officer, who, overcome by fever and dysentery, decides to make his way to a hospital in the city of Monewa in Burma. Before departing, he announced his own death to Hasan: '"This is the end of me," he said as we parted company. "I shall not see you again in Mandalay or elsewhere"' (6). Bearing witness to this suffering endured by his friends and fellow-soldiers in the INA infects Hasan's own emotions as he thinks of penetrating further eastwards into Burma, then Thailand, and ultimately re-uniting with their commander: 'Yes, we would reach Moulmein, we would reach Bangkok, we would be there at the roll-call,' he declares (7). The verbal repetition captures the recurrent monotony of the march, lending a hallucinatory edge to the sentence as Hasan stubbornly continues to imagine the INA men presenting themselves for inspection under Bose's watchful and approving eye, regardless of their actual physical condition.

The disintegration of place and the death of the INA men serve an important function in the memoir: they signify a shift in Hasan's focus from representing the terrible physical reality of the retreat to the liberating possibilities of imagining home. He writes:

> What I wondered, as we trodded [sic] along strange paths in that foreign place so far away from home, what I wondered was the

force that united us, we who were otherwise so different one from the other, individually and in smaller groups? (7)

The notion of home makes its first appearance in the memoir here, and in the very nature of its conceptualisation gains a powerful emotional appeal. Fusing 'home' with 'nation', Hasan continues to observe:

> What a group we were [...] Baluchis were there among us and Assamese, Kashmiris and Malayalis, Pathans and Sikhs and Gujeratis [sic], proud members of classes called the martial and those till then denied reputation for martial valour but who proved in battle that they could by their deeds claim equal honour [...] every religion and every caste, mixed inseparably together not only in bigger formations but even in small platoons and sections, each unit being a living tribute to the unity of India. (7)

Hasan here expands the imperialist 'martial races' theory into a broader, more inclusive military fraternity, transforming the INA into a microcosm of the nation itself. His words also foreground the structural differences between the Indian Army and the INA regarding the formation of their respective fighting units. Bose deliberately broke away from the British model of segregated units based on religion or ethnicity and promoted intermingling among his men.[101] Sugata Bose also notes how Bose encouraged Hindu, Muslim, Sikh and Christian soldiers to eat together—'a striking departure from the British custom of having separate mess halls'.[102] Hasan later tells us that Bose encouraged an equal distribution of food between himself and his men (14), while Sugata Bose observes that he frequently made unannounced visits to soldiers' barracks and shared meals with them.[103] These gestures of solidarity highlight how the INA soldiers come together not 'in spite of [their] differences' but 'through [their] differences'.[104] For the first time, this army becomes the realisation of an alternative emotional brotherhood that acknowledges variations across undivided India but remains aligned in its common anticolonial mission.[105]

Writing in the context of whether there can be any positive consequences to nationalist feeling, Amartya Sen explains how his answer depends upon the ends to which nationalist discourses are being used—what he terms as 'the contingent variability of the role of nationalism'.[106] In his essay 'Is Nationalism a Boon or a Curse?', Sen reminds us that Subhas Chandra Bose himself spoke of Japan as 'militant, aggressive and imperialist', and that cooperating with the Japanese to form the INA did not necessarily imply that Bose's perspectives on Japan itself had changed. Instead, Sen importantly argues, Bose chose to give 'conditional priority to the national identity' under a specific context.[107] Ceymil Aydin makes a similar point while examining the creation of pan-Asian discourses in the twentieth century. Aydin believes that 'Bose's nationalist agenda was the main motive for collaboration, rather than a vision of Asian regionalism under Japanese leadership'—in fact, 'the legitimacy of wartime pan-Asianism intimately depended on the idea of national self-determination'.[108]

Bose's version of nationalism, then, although problematic in its collaboration with fascist powers, can be read as a strategic response to colonial domination; exemplified by the INA, it worked 'against the divisiveness of communal distinctions'.[109] Again, following Amartya Sen's reasoning, nationality is but 'one identity among many that we all have, on the relative importance of which we have to decide, if only implicitly'.[110] Hasan's emotions as a member of the INA, and his view of the INA as a symbol of a diverse and complex but ultimately harmonious home, highlights the extent to which nationalism here is privileged, prioritised and even celebrated. And Hasan's is an inclusive, 'all-embracing' (8) national identity. He observes:

> [...] we found for ourselves a new identity, perhaps for the most of us an identity for the first time. Till then we were a part of the herd, now we became individuals, the interest of everyone among us being to securely establish this identity. (8)

To Hasan, the emotions underpinning this collective is nuanced: it is a military community conceived of as Indian, and practically realised by transcending social, ethnic, religious and even gender differences. But what is the history of this collective and why does it carry such emotional charge? In his thought-provoking work challenging Benedict Anderson's conception of the nation as simply an imagined community, Rajat Ray argues for the pre-existence of 'emotional collectivities' upon which the modern political nation-state is established. Ray believes that the cultural, social and linguistic commonalities that developed between people who shared the same land were not simply imagined or constructed but deeply *felt*. During Indian resistance to the British Empire, therefore, 'the mixture of cultures and the shared experience of subjection to alien rule provided a common emotional basis to the struggle(s) for freedom. Freedom in the subcontinent was in that sense one and many at the same time.'[111] It is this accommodating plurality embedded in India's historical social structure, transformed by a unifying anticolonial feeling, that Hasan draws upon.

Hasan's memoir, then, encourages a re-conception of home as India itself, but one in which the two-and-a-half-million-strong expatriate Indian community in Southeast Asia also has a stake and a reason to fight.[112] Sugata Bose notes that 18,000 civilians, coming from the Tamil community in South India but living in Southeast Asia in the 1940s, joined the INA—those that the traditional colonial 'martial races' theory would have rejected.[113] This inclusive vision of an anticolonial movement was promoted across these expatriate Indian communities. Again, Hasan's conversation with the eighteen-year-old Janaki Thevar also becomes revealing:

> I remember a walk I had once, not far from Rangoon, with Capt. Thevar of the Rani of Jhansi Regiment. We went to a hillock and sat there looking at the ground around us. 'Doesn't the country-side remind you of home?' I enquired, adding 'it looks so typically Indian.' 'I do not know,' she replied simply, 'I have never been to India.' (13)

To Janaki Thevar, raised in Malaya, there are no emotional investments in place, and yet the idea of resisting colonialism in this unseen and unknown 'home' of India makes her enlist in the INA. Perhaps it was because in Malaya too she had understood how it felt to live as a colonised subject. Sugata Bose also attempts to explain such support by noting how the charismatic Bose was incredibly well received by the expatriate Indian community in Malaya, Thailand and Burma.[114] This warm reception did not simply result in raising funds, although financial support was crucial to Bose's nationalist project. While wealthy financiers and bankers contributed to the INA, a much greater number of poor migrant labourers also signed up. The INA was their means of resisting oppression; it gave them 'their first taste of human dignity and a feeling of equal citizenship'.[115]

If the INA carried this emotional import in nation-building, and saw 'its role as that of a catalyst for a civilian uprising against British rule',[116] as the 1946 Red Fort trials later demonstrated, what—or rather, who—lends this symbol its significance? Hasan declares: 'He who was our banner and shield, he who gave us our identity and unity, he who gave meaning to our struggle and to our lives' (9). Subhas Chandra Bose, attaining a quasi-religious status in Hasan's memoir, becomes the ultimate signifier of home. Hasan notes a high-ranking INA officer telling British interrogators afterwards that his 'reward' for suffering all hardship was Bose's embrace (8). Bodily contact with Bose, then, transforms into the supreme gift, where the emotions felt towards nation, political liberation and human freedom powerfully collide.

Perhaps most significantly in relation to the hardships of the Imphal retreat, Hasan thinks of Bose's own arduous journey after escaping house arrest, undertaken by foot across the Afghan hills, which Bose endured while nearly blind without his glasses. At considerable personal risk, Bose also met the retreating INA soldiers in Mandalay, and Hasan describes the flurry of careful physical preparations amongst the men as they readied themselves for the occasion. We are told that Bose's words dispelled their tiredness and galvanised new blood in their veins. Hasan even says: 'So I thought, must miracles have been worked in the past of which we hear' (9). Is this the apotheosis of the dead, or the cherished memory of a beloved leader lost suddenly and tragically?[117] It is surely also the emotional reinforcement of an alternative and far more combative vision of freedom for the Indian homeland, contrasted against Gandhi and Nehru's policies of negotiation with the British. Yasmin Khan observes how, in 1946, it was this language of the body that carried enormous emotional charge: 'Gandhi was barely heeded by a new generation of protestors who were angry, strident and determined to achieve independence. Their hero was Subhas Chandra Bose and their battle cry was "Blood is calling to blood."'[118]

However, Sugata Bose notes how, after the war, Nehru, despite defending INA men at the Red Fort trial, would not assimilate them

71

into the army of independent India. None of the INA men got their old jobs back, although quite a few, like Hasan himself, were absorbed into diplomatic service in the post-war years. Nehru, then, in Sugata Bose's words, 'opted for postcolonial continuity over anticolonial rupture' while shaping a post-independence Indian Army.[119] In the memoir, to Hasan, the alternative, militant path to freedom symbolised by the INA movement has been elided by the mainstream Indian nationalist narrative. He thus concludes, bringing us back to his present, 'in these frustrating times [...] India again seems to be a house divided against itself' (18).

Conclusion

Establishing an Indian context to home, this chapter has examined the shifting, often volatile emotions generated when discourses on nationalism, anticolonialism and global war fiercely intersect and contest one another in the subcontinent. In the Second World War, for Indian soldiers stationed in the Middle East and North African fronts, doctor Shantilal Ray on the Arakan frontline and INA officer Abid Hasan Safrani marching wearily back to Moulmein and Mandalay in Burma, the present is always foreign, as Salman Rushdie puts it. All lead peripatetic lives, but it is the state of displacement, their very homelessness, that makes their imaginings of home so politically and emotionally febrile.

Yet, throughout such life-writing, we do not find an easy corelation between home and the nation. Soldiers' letters, as we have seen, foreground the nexus between home and colonial recruitment strategies. Home has also been revealed to be a site for a complex range of feeling expressed in these letters—love and lamentation, anxiety and despair, nostalgia and alienation, and even a questioning of why one should serve in the colonial army at all. Turning to the memoirs, we find a further broadening out of these emotions. For Shantilal Ray, the affective responses to home are tactile and embodied. His desire for the embrace of his motherland is a deeply felt physical yearning—'*Janani lahogo morey*', 'O Mother, take me to you'—strikingly similar to the meanings of Subhas Chandra Bose's embrace for the INA men, which becomes their ultimate 'reward'.

Home is also deeply gendered for Ray. Is he, in some ways, 'unmanned' by war? After all, the Burmese earth might enwomb

Ray but also, terrifyingly, entombs him. And yet, it is a philosophical understanding of home as the earth itself, with all the terror that
it evokes, that sends Ray on his journey towards empathy for all
those who suffer in war, including the Japanese. For Hasan, the
destruction of place and the death of his INA men coalesce. His
memoir expresses the political opportunities possible in exile,
despite military defeat. Such feelings, however, are inverted for
Ray. Burma, to him, is a growing site of loss, and the Indian nation
can only map onto the emotions of home when it is overtly anticolonial and racialised.

We have also seen how each genre of life-writing discussed in this
chapter has a different temporal relationship with the Second World
War, which reframes its understanding of home. Indian letters
exchanged between soldiers and civilians—although fragmented—
serve as the textual expressions of immediacy. Their circulation and
reception took place during the war years themselves. Shantilal
Ray's memoir *Arakan Fronte*, on the other hand, was published in
1946, just after the official end of hostilities in September 1945.
That year, 1946, was tumultuous in Indian politics, as the
Introduction to the book outlines—the year of the INA Red Fort
trials and the Royal Indian Navy revolt, when nationalist and anticolonial emotions were at their sharpest, and when imperial authorities realised that their control over the subcontinent was slipping
away. Perhaps this is why, towards the end of the memoir, Ray
wears his anticolonialism so stridently. He knows his time serving
in the Indian Army is over, and that the Bengal he gazes upon so
longingly from across the river in Burma has now become the motherland of the Indian nationalist dream, to which he must return.

Strangely enough, although Hasan serves with opposing forces in
Burma, with the INA and Japanese troops against the Indian Army,
his responses to home strongly resemble Ray's. The two men are
divided by military allegiance, but they occupy similar emotional
worlds. *The Men from Imphal*, published in December 1970, is the
memoir most inflected with the weight of memory and sorrow for
the INA's military loss. Yet, remembering how he was forced to
retreat away from the Burma front some thirty-five years previously, Hasan finds consolation in the enduring symbolism of the
INA. He conceives of home as an expression of the possibilities of

73

political and human freedom represented by the inclusive Indian nation, manifested by the depth of feeling the men shared for their commander, Subhas Chandra Bose. On the threshold of yet another homeland being violently created—the nation of Bangladesh in 1971—it becomes significant for him to remember and communicate this liberating potential of an all-encompassing home that transcends religious and ethnic difference.

As twenty-first-century readers of Indian life-writing from the Second World War, we realise that there is yet another accretion to these accumulated layers of emotion in relation to home. The Arakan province of Ray's memoir—now known as Rakhine state—has today become the site of genocidal violence inflicted upon the displaced Rohingya community, an ethnic and territorial conflict whose roots go back to the Second World War itself.[120] The emotional resonances of home and homeland, then, are as charged today as they were in the war years. There is still much to recover and reappraise regarding how the Second World War transformed colonised homelands, and it is to this theme that I will now turn.

2

'EVERY DAY I WITNESS NIGHTMARES'

HUNGER AND THE HOMELAND

Fig. 2.1: Sunil Janah, 'Women queuing for rice during the Bengal Famine, Lake Market, Calcutta, 1943'. © Estate of Sunil Janah, courtesy of Arjun Janah, suniljanah.org.

A serpentine row of women, some holding on to their children, horizontally bisects the photograph above. Where does the queue begin; where will it end? We do not know: the women and children spill over the frame of the camera, as though uncontainable within a single image. In the black-and-white photograph, the women's saris are indistinguishable from one other; under the ubiquitous *ghomta* or veil one gaunt face after another starts becoming less distinct too. Towards the left of the photograph bodily needs continue unabated as a child breastfeeds; in its centre, conjoined to their mother's body, another infant sleeps, with ribs protruding disturbingly. The women know they are being photographed: many of them directly observe the camera. Yet the woman who holds the sleeping child averts her gaze, looking downwards contemplatively. Stepping a little out of the queue, she stands, with legs apart and face sombre—a tableau of resignation.

If, as Susan Sontag says, narratives can make us understand but it is photographs that haunt us,[1] this chapter begins with the evocative force of images before analysing the emotions contained in texts that interrogate hunger and the homeland. I have deliberately chosen not to include here graphic visual horror from the Bengal Famine of 1943–1944. Such grim, but necessary, photographic documentation was published by the Calcutta editor of the British-owned English-language daily *The Statesman*, Ian Stephens, who defied wartime government censorship in India to highlight the scale of the famine.[2] Instead, moving on from the colonial photographs of Chapter 1, I examine here how the visual reframes the human at a time of crisis or 'emergency'.[3] By focusing on the collective physical presence of women and children, it is able to highlight their pathos, vulnerability and resilience, and invite our active and urgent response as spectators.

We began by considering the image of women queuing for rice in Calcutta during the famine in 1943, and how it inscribes the politics of gender, scarcity and endurance on civilian bodies. As a point of comparison, I now turn to the photograph below, which was taken during the following year in Bengal's neighbouring province of Orissa, where food shortages had also spread. The same photographer zooms in here on a field of crop stubble where twenty-odd children squat, waiting, their small, bony knees on display. The sky above them lowers menacingly. But the children do not look upwards at the sky—while some return the camera's gaze, others in the foreground, in various positions of scowling and shielding their eyes from the sun's glare, focus elsewhere. The image draws our attention to

Fig. 2.2: Sunil Janah, 'Orphans waiting for Food at a Famine-Relief Centre, Orissa famine, 1944'. © Estate of Sunil Janah, courtesy of Arjun Janah, suniljanah.org.

how diminutive the children are—they take up only about a third of the photograph. And yet this is an intimate close-up. The adult photographer has bent down to take his shot, so that we see the children at nearly the same height from which they now survey their world. It is a deeply affective and empathic technique.

Both of these photographs capture a sense of 'precarious life',[4] but nonetheless reinforce the presence of the women and children as visceral and tangible. As spectators, we are alerted to their fragility but also, importantly, to their humanity and ordinariness in the midst of catastrophe. Writing in the context of problematising Susan Sontag's concept of 'empathy fatigue' in viewing atrocity images, Ariella Azoulay powerfully argues for our role as spectators to be practised as a 'civic duty', rather than a passive response, when we meet those in photographs who have been dispossessed of their rights. Images such as the two under discussion here recalibrate encounters with the camera, the photographer, the photographed and the spectator; they speak to us, compellingly, in the present. If the image, then, forges a relationship between the photographer and the photographed, it is also a marker of a promise made by the former to the latter—the promise of bearing witness, of ensuring visibility and viewership. The people in these photographs, according to Azoulay, call on us 'to recognise and restore their citizenship' by our very act of seeing.[5]

The twenty-five-year-old Communist Party of India (CPI) member and photojournalist Sunil Janah would have agreed. In 1943, Janah was commissioned by P.C. Joshi, the head of the newly legalised CPI, to visit famine-afflicted areas and generate awareness of the unfolding catastrophe, which was being strenuously suppressed by British colonial authorities.[6] Janah's photographs, including the two images discussed here, were published as visual essays, accompanied by Joshi's first-hand textual accounts of witnessing famine, in the CPI's national weekly newspaper *People's War*.[7] Because of wartime censorship, the CPI could not directly criticise British colonial policy as the primary cause of the famine.[8] Janah's talent for photography, instead, was channelled primarily to a fundraising cause, in raising money for famine relief, particularly since, by 1943, the national circulation of *People's War* had grown to 25,000–30,000 copies across India.[9] As Emilia Terracciano insightfully observes in her writing on Sunil Janah, this reach enabled 'the impersonal cruelty of lived hunger [to become] a more intimate affair'.[10]

Historians such as James Vernon in *Hunger: A Modern History* (2007) have drawn attention to the long history of famine in colonised India and argued that it was in representing these famines that the effects of photography in news reports were felt within Britain. Journalists like F.H.S. Merewether, for instance, travelled through India during the 1896–1898 famine, which had spread to large parts of the country and caused the deaths of about one million people. Merewether took photographs of 'starving bodies and skeletal corpses',[11] which, Vernon notes, created a new style of visual reportage, making a spectacle out of suffering and transforming the viewer into voyeur. Nonetheless, Merewether's attempts tried to 'recalibrat[e] the civilising mission as one of assuming immediate humanitarian responsibility for those whose hungry cries had to be heard'.[12] And, dispensing with the civilising mission altogether, it

was the relentless recurrence of famine in India—twenty-six famines in the nineteenth century alone[13]—that became crucial to early
nationalists like Dadabhai Naoroji in articulating the failure of British
colonial rule in India.

The 1943–1944 Bengal Famine was the culmination of large-
scale hardship and suffering in regions of the Indian subcontinent
during the Second World War, compounded by colonial policies of
resource extraction. Instead of a Japanese invasion, as was feared in
1942, war reached the Bengal home-front in 1943 in the form of
dearth and slow death. Over three million people died, through a
combination of starvation and the associated diseases of cholera,
diarrhoea and dysentery.[14] The most affected regions were largely
in east Bengal, including the districts of Dacca, Faridpur, Noakhali,
Mymensingh, Pabna and Khulna, while the sub-divisions of Contai
and Tamluk in the district of Midnapur and Diamond Harbour in 24
Parganas, were the main regions affected in west Bengal.[15] Food
shortages stretched across the provinces of Orissa in the east and
Assam in the north-east, and also reached southern India, particularly the princely state of Travancore.

Those whose lives were most financially precarious in rural
Bengal suffered the most—the very young and the old, women,
artisans, labourers, landless farmers, wandering minstrels or 'bauls',
village artists and painters—some of whom would have best been
able to represent hunger in Bengal but became instead the worst
victims of famine. Along with the tremendous scale of death, the
famine 'caused irreparable damage to folk memory'.[16] Thousands
of villagers walked miles from rural heartlands to reach Calcutta in
the hope of obtaining food, begging for a little 'phyan' or rice-starch,
only to die on the streets. While free food supply centres were
eventually set up, those in desperate need to eat died searching for
leftovers on the pavements, near relief kitchens, shops and dustbins,
making 'a mockery of the government's food and famine policy and
all other attempts at relief'.[17] Indivar Kamtekar notes: 'In sheer
scale, the tragedy of the Bengal Famine bears comparison with any
other of the Second World War, and dwarfs other incidents in
India. The dead outnumbered the entire Indian industrial working
class.'[18] Political radical Subhas Chandra Bose, in fact, made an
announcement from Rangoon in September 1943 that his new

government-in-exile, the Provisional Government of Free India, was ready to buy and ship 100,000 tons of rice for the people of Bengal.[19] The offer, of course, was never taken up by colonial authorities; as the future Prime Minister of independent India, Jawaharlal Nehru, would say, the Bengal Famine eventually became 'the final judgment on British rule in India'.[20]

Lizzie Collingham has interpreted the 1943 Bengal Famine as a product of colonial outsourcing: 'Although Britain did not set out with the explicit intention of exporting wartime hunger to their empire, this is in fact what happened.'[21] She provides a wider context for such an occurrence:

> Throughout the empire those who bought their food on a daily basis were faced by inexorable rises in the price of food, which meant that every day they were able to buy a little less to eat. For some the price rises deprived them of their ability to buy even the most basic of subsistence diets. Uncontrolled inflation in effect robbed them of their entitlement to food.[22]

Collingham observes that severe malnourishment affected British island colonies such as Mauritius; famine came to northern Nigeria and Tanganyika; while the number of African subjects in the British Empire who died of hunger during the war still remains unknown. The Bengal Famine was the extreme manifestation of this world-wide wartime colonial export.[23] And, as Indivar Kamtekar notes, there is a reason why the numbers of the dead in Bengal are still disputed: 'Those who died in the Bengal Famine could not even be counted properly, because they counted for so little.'[24]

The most famous analysis of the Bengal Famine, provided by Amartya Sen's 1981 Nobel-prize winning *Poverty and Famines: An Essay on Entitlement and Deprivation*, argues that the famine was manufactured—a man-made product rather than a natural one. Later research has predominantly confirmed this importance of political entitlement to food rather than an overall shortage of its supply.[25] More recently, Iftekar Iqbal, by drawing attention to the long-term environmental contexts of a decline in food availability along with changes in land ownership and production, has mapped out an important 'ecological prehistory' of the famine too.[26] A sustained analysis of the Bengal Famine as a product of the socio-political conditions of wartime India is an emerging field of scholarship to which this chapter contributes. I interpret the famine through the lens of its emotional legacy in life-writing and literature,[27] and argue for the significance of colonial emotions associated with wartime hunger. A focus on both life-writing and literary texts, as Srimanjari has indicated, also reveals how the famine transforms into a means of interrogating the bankruptcy of late imperial rule as well as the violence of indigenous and localised power structures. Furthermore, I examine here whether representing hunger—or the empathic perception of another's hunger—can become a new form of physically imagined connection with the reader.

In this chapter, I advocate for the significance and place of the literary in historical knowledge. The chapter therefore considers a variety of textual material, from letters exchanged between Indian soldiers stationed in the Middle East and North African fronts and their loved ones, to the Bengali novel *Ashani Sanket* by Bibhutibhushan Bandyopadhyay and poems by two practitioners of Bengali literary modernism—Sukanta Bhattacharya and Samar Sen. Reading these letter extracts and literary texts alongside each other allows for fresh layers of meaning to emerge: we start to understand the diverse ways in which hunger in the homeland was experienced, imagined and represented. While the first section of the chapter focuses more on the cultural history of the Bengal Famine, recovered and assessed through the wartime letters, the second and third sections analyse how hunger and its contexts influence literary form. I relate the rapid transformation of Bengali literary form in the politically conscious poetry of Sukanta Bhattacharya and Samar Sen to imagery used in Bibhutibhushan's Bengali novel, which reveals the everyday violence brought into the lives of villagers when food suddenly vanishes from the marketplace.

Most significantly, through this comparatist approach, I trace the ways by which wartime communities of knowledge and bonds of empathy were being formed. How did Indian soldiers, fighting for the British and stationed in the Middle East and North African fronts, discover that there was widespread hunger in their homeland, despite the censorship of their letters? How did they conceive of the food they consumed as army rations while knowing that others at home remained hungry? In what ways do the formal aspects of letter-writing become testimonial narrative when used by Indian civilians who did not themselves starve, but witnessed the ravages of famine? And how do literary texts complement—and complicate—testimonial accounts? I argue that it is in literature that history becomes an affective charge; the literary, then, enables us to inhabit a form of imaginative, empathic knowing.

'We become crazy as lunatics': distress in response to hunger in Indian soldiers' letters

As discussed in Chapter 1, wartime letters written by Indian soldiers stationed abroad were not simply read by family and friends at home. Intercepted by colonial censors, these letters were translated from Indian languages into English, and extracts selected to comprise military censorship reports, which became official testaments testifying to the 'morale' of Indian soldiers. These censorship reports on epistolary exchanges in the Indian Army stationed in the Middle East and North Africa which survive in the India Office Records at the British Library include the Bengal Famine. The extracts of these letters provide us with multiple glimpses into the lived realities of the famine and its reception on international battlefronts, including emotional responses from Indian soldiers abroad, civilians on the Indian home-front, and even the colonial censor himself.

In his book *The Brutish Museums* (2020), a powerful polemic which reconsiders our understanding of the famously looted Benin Bronzes, Dan Hicks urges us to consider the suppressed narratives of loss and death when we think of the life histories of objects in museums. He calls such acts of excavation 'necrography' and the knowledge produced from them 'necrology'.[28] Applying Hicks's anthropological methodology to this emotional history of wartime India, particularly in relation to extracts from letters excavated from colonial archives on the Bengal Famine, is apposite. As we will see in the discussion that follows, in extract after extract, letter-writing and editorial censorship policies were employed to record dying—and barely living—during the famine. In that sense, foregrounding these letters is very much an exercise in necrography. Again, by the very mode of its construction and survival into the twenty-first century, this archive becomes testament to a history of loss and death. Partial and unremembered, it transforms, in Achille Mbembe's words, into 'a montage of fragments'.[29] We do not know the names of the letter writers, the particularities of their lives, or even if they survived the famine. This archive, however, remains evocative because it contains a first-hand witnessing of atrocity.

In Indian soldiers' letters, life is measured out in food prices. The letters become ledgers where the materiality of starvation is logged in excruciatingly granular detail; they serve as textual connectors that convey this despairing knowledge from home-front to the battlefront. Rising price lists are mentioned regularly, as a letter from Bengal to a Havildar Clerk notes: 'The prices are as follows— Rice Rs. 40 a *maund*; Atta Rs. 35 to 38 a *maund*; Coal Rs. 2½ a *maund*. Sugar is not procurable and the prices of other things are at least five times in comparison to pre-war prices.'[30] Such sharp rises in prices are mentioned to shock the soldier-reader into realising the writers' crippling lack of purchasing power at home, the fact that they are being priced out of essential items. Death rates form a grim counterpoint to these price lists. From Bombay a letter-writer observes in Marathi: 'In Bengal daily deaths by hunger are increased by 31';[31] from a Captain in the Indian Medical Service: 'I think half the population will be wiped off in near future';[32] from Malabar, in Malayalam: 'You will be astonished to see that ¼ of our neighbours have left for the better world—when you come back with anxiety to see them'; and from a village near Medha, in Marathi: 'People are dying of hunger and if this goes on for another two or three months, then you won't find a single soul alive in our village. God knows when this wretched war will end.'[33]

These metrics of death within families and communities are countered by repeated references to the inability of language to express the pain of witnessing, as though the task of narration has been passed on to numbers. 'The plight of our country is beyond description,' writes a family member from Bengal to a doctor in the Indian Medical Service, while another, addressed to a Captain in the Indian Medical Service, asks: 'What will happen if the war lasts longer? Can you imagine?'[34] Civilian letters reveal that, though the conditions of famine were at their severest in Bengal, other parts of India—such as Malabar and Travancore in southern India—experienced extreme food shortages too, a little-remembered fact which historian P. Priya has recently drawn our attention to.[35] A letter written in English from Travancore in south India by 'a Hindu' man on 21 April 1943, where he depicts starving people begging for alms, forms a valuable counterpoint to one by the wife of a doctor in the Indian Medical Division, who recalls reading about the abandoned children of famine in Bengal. The 'Hindu' man begins with the inability of language to express the intensity of his emotions:

> I cannot explain to you the extent of poverty in Travancore, but this form of misery is not anything peculiar to this place only; the whole of India is experiencing difficult days. On our way from Bombay we could see hundreds of men, women and children of all ages sitting on the sides of the roads and crying for alms. The sight of those naked and half naked wretches reduced to skeletons was too strong even for the most strong-hearted persons. They were begging from all indiscriminately and even soldiers of other nationalities took pity on them and gave them alms. These wretches had left their villages and were moving towards the towns in crowds.[36]

The passage reveals to us the physical markers of the violation of the human body during famine, 'naked and half-naked', visualised in the collective, with no individual contours or definitions. Humanity has depleted, shrunk, 'reduced to skeletons', and reduced too to pleading for help. Linguistic choices become illuminating here, particularly so since this letter was originally written in English. The word 'strong', for instance, is repeated in the sentence: 'The sight of those naked and half naked wretches reduced to skeletons was too strong even for the most strong-hearted persons.' If one remains 'strong-hearted' and emotionally unaffected even while witnessing terrible hunger and suffering, such strength is highly morally culpable, the writer suggests. As Shoshana Felman says in her analysis of the relationship between historical crisis and the creation of narrative, the role of testimony is to transfer to the witness a certain form of knowledge, 'knowledge of the way in which history is the body's business'.[37] If these starving bodies become the vehicle on which the violence of famine is inscribed, its recording by another human being, a witness, is inevitable—this is the very basis of a shared humanity. To not respond to such distress, as 'even soldiers of other nationalities' do, to not record such misery, would be unconscionable.

The doctor's wife focuses, instead, on what she has read rather than witnessed—the breakdown in traditional familial and social structures wrought by famine. She observes:

> The situation in the Punjab is not so miserable compared to Bombay and Bengal where people are starving due to lack of foodstuffs. The other day I read in a paper that many unclaimed children are wandering in the streets. Their parents are helpless to feed them, so they have turned them out of their homes upon God's mercy. Now foodstuffs are being sent there. Also, some co-operative societies have reached there. On reading of these events, one's hair stands on end. May God have mercy on all of us.[38]

A complex response of empathy and horror suffuses this letter-writer—relatively secure from food shortages herself—at how children too are victims of hunger. Writing in the context of modern-day Amnesty International's communications that make immediate the experiences of those who are suffering but physically distant, Elaine Scarry notes that the latter's 'ordinary life' may be unknown to the reader, 'except that it is known that that ordinary life has ceased to exist'.[39] The doctor's wife responds similarly: she may not have direct knowledge of the lives of the children thus turned out by their parents, but she recognises the extent to which this act subverts core social bonds as famine severs parental duties of care. Again, Yasmin Khan notes a different kind of famine observation, that by British soldiers themselves:

> [...] soldiers waiting for action in Burma now found themselves on the front line of a very different kind of calamity. They witnessed deaths more shocking than the violence of war itself [...] For the soldiers, the sights were distressing and disorienting. How could they justify their presence as colonial overlords if this was the result of British rule? How could they help alleviate such a tragedy? And what was the war all about if the empire was unable to protect its own inhabitants?[40]

Witnessing famine, then, starts exposing the brutality of empire, even for those fighting to protect it.

In Middle-Eastern and North African battlefronts—Egypt, Cyrenaica and Tripolitania in Libya, Palestine, Syria and the British Protectorate of Transjordan—rumours of a great and devastating famine sweeping parts of India, and particularly Bengal, in 1943 reached Indian soldiers, despite censorship of news and letters.[41] Contrasted against British soldiers' self-questioning of the enterprise of empire, Indian responses implicate themselves more directly in the material conditions of famine. A sepoy stationed at the Indian Division Headquarters in the Middle East writes home in a half-jocular vein: 'You have asked me to come back on leave as quickly as possible. But what is the use of coming home on leave to starve [...] Don't forget that here I eat 8 *chapaties* [sic] in one meal while you probably cook 8 *chapaties* [sic] for the whole family.'[42]

Other responses are considerably more empathic. A Havildar, part of the Sappers and Miners unit, writes:

> From my personal experience I can tell you that the food we get here is much better than that we soldiers get in India. But whenever I sit for my meals, a dreadful picture of the appalling Indian food problem passes through my mind leaving a cloudy sediment on the walls of my heart which makes me nauseous and often I leave my meals untouched.[43]

The soldier highlights his identification with this imagined community of sufferers through images of his own body, and his reactions are expressed in physiological terms—he visualises the walls of his heart being covered with 'cloudy sediment' at the thought of food shortage in India. The spectre of famine in India hovers, Banquo-like, before him every time he sits down to eat his rations carefully provided by the colonial British government, but while Banquo's ghost arouses guilt and fear in Macbeth, the Havildar feels only the pain of distant hunger in his nausea.

Indian emotional responses to famine move from nausea to madness, from being witness to victim, a co-sharer implicated in the same misfortune. How can the soldier's earnings help his family when the latter cannot afford to buy food because of soaring rates of wartime inflation?[44] A Havildar Clerk or junior officer writing to relatives in South India relates soldiers' helplessness caused by famine to the extraordinary conditions of the wartime marketplace:

> I am terribly sorry to learn about the food situation in India and it
> seems as if there is no salvation for me. From my earliest days to
> the present time, I have always been in this abyss of misery. It was
> with grim determination to see you all free from poverty that I
> allotted my whole pay of Rs. 85/- to you, but cruel Fate is deter
> mined to defeat me in all my purposes. What is the use of money
> when we are unable to obtain the necessities of life in exchange for
> it? The situation would drive even the most level-headed of us to
> madness and when we think of conditions in India we become crazy
> as lunatics.[45]

The letter highlights how the standard material benefits of serving
in the imperial army are no longer sustainable for the soldier and his
family because of the extraordinary economic conditions of war,
which have led to the famine and priced poorer sections of Indian
society out of food. Indivar Kamtekar notes how, despite all government efforts, taxes and loans could not raise enough money in wartime India, and more money was simply printed: 'There was an
outpouring of paper currency. The amount of currency in circulation in India multiplied about six and a half times during the war
years [...] Inflation was the inevitable result.'[46] This drastic reduction in purchasing power is an intensely traumatic experience for
the soldier even as he participates in, and witnesses, heavy fighting
on the battlefield—evident in his linguistic choices, filtered as they
are to us by the English translation: 'madness', 'crazy', 'lunatics'.
The Havildar Clerk's very identity as a soldier, then, is ruptured by
the recreation of hunger in the homeland within his mind.

The process by which empathy is generated with Indian soldiers
is re-enacted in another Havildar Clerk's letter, where he, writing
in Marathi, observes to his family:

> I am arranging that you may be provided with ration cards. And as
> you say, that it is difficult, dear, and grain is unobtainable. But look
> at these people in Bengal. Their attention is ten times worse than
> our home district. There are many Bengalies [sic] in the army here
> with me, and when they get their letters from home, they seem to
> be very worried and by their appearance, I guess that the public in

> Bengal is suffering badly. Many times they have shown me their
> letters and when I read their sufferings, it breaks my heart.[47]

Information about conditions at home was thus being shared
amongst Indian soldiers abroad through the circulation of letters,
bringing knowledge of the home-front to the warfront rather than
simply to an individual soldier. As this extract shows, soldiers were
also physically circulating their letters across regional differences.
The Havildar Clerk's letter is written in Marathi, widely spoken in
western India, and he expresses his solidarity for Bengali fellow
combatants as he reads their letters from home. Does 'reading'
itself, then, broaden to become understanding and commiserating?
The epistle reveals once again how writing and reading letters during the war blurs the borders of the private and the public, much as
the censorship reports themselves do. As communities of knowledge were created on international battlefronts, so too were these
deep bonds of feeling.[48]

Gajendra Singh has observed how images evoked in these letters
about the famine are seen as portentous for the rest of India, as a
soldier's letter, outlining his prediction for friends and family from
Sargodha district in Punjab in February 1944, demonstrates:
'Everyone in India knows well how people suffered in Bengal and
millions died of starvation and they want that you should die in the
same way.'[49] Writing to family in Bengal, another Havildar from a
Salvage Unit observes grimly: 'I am well acquainted with the distressing and famine-stricken conditions of the country, but it is not
the end of the sufferings now, everybody knows that we have to
undergo more trials than the present ones. The war has just begun
and before it comes to an end the people will be compelled to
devour the leaves of the trees to satisfy their hunger.'[50] This letter
presents a dark, proleptic vision of the terrible historical circumstances in which Indian people find themselves entrapped, within a
warring world, in an endless quest for food.

Civilian and military responses to the Bengal Famine were mediated through the panoptic gaze of the colonial censor in the Middle
East and North Africa, Lieutenant Colonel M.G.M. Mair,[51] who
decided on how much information to filter through to Indian troops,
and to the home-front. However, as Sanjoy Bhattacharya notes:

While the mention of certain issues of strategic import—like references to the location of troop encampments and details of the
movement of armed detachments—was deleted from the Indian
soldier's correspondence, he was allowed, and indeed, encouraged
to state his fears, or misgivings, about the contemporary political
situation, wartime problems that affected his family and particular
official policies.[52]

Bhattacharya believes that the knowledge thus gleaned was used as
the basis for British military propaganda. Thus, while censorship
practices played a significant role in communications between civilian and soldier, the censor's role was more about surveillance
rather than severely editing these exchanges. Yet, although the
censor's authoritarian voice may have shaped the content of these
military censorship reports, rarely do his own feelings find expression here. It is the acts of intercepting, reading and editing thousands of letters highlighting starvation and utter destitution, which
reveal changes in the censor's own perception of, and response to,
the Bengal Famine.

Towards the end of 1942, the censor's initial notes appear
begrudging and disbelieving: 'There are the usual grouses about
leave and moans from India concerning the cost of living and shortages but there is no evidence to show that this latter correspondence, much of which is highly coloured, is having any adverse
effect on the men.'[53] However, when such 'coloured' letters continue unabated, he makes a specific observation regarding Bengali
soldiers: 'A careful watch is being kept on the reactions of Bengali
troops to reports of the conditions in Bengal as reported in the
Incoming Mail portion of this report.'[54] He then observes how
important the soldier is as a financial provider to his family: 'There
is a feeling [in India] that the presence of the soldier from the Middle
East will help greatly towards the alleviation of the many wartime
hardships.'[55] Indian soldiers, however, did not cease fighting in protest against home-front conditions, and the censor highlights how
little incitement there is in the letters to antagonising colonial
authorities: 'It is somewhat refreshing, therefore, to note that
despite the terrible hardships which are being endured in India at
the present time, when the worst type of political crisis might well
be expected, letters couched in terms of political criticism are very

rare. The will to fight remains unaltered.'[56] Both soldiers and their family members, of course, knew that their letters were intercepted and read.[57]

The censor's focus then turns towards how Bengali soldiers in the Middle East represent their own emotions through letters: 'Letters from Bengalee [sic] personnel revealed that they were much upset by the distressing news from home though no tendency to panic was noted. All ranks however now feel acutely their inability to assist families with their pecuniary difficulties.'[58] At about the same time as this observation, in December 1943, he observes with some sympathy:

> The people of India have faced shortage of food and other essentials, famine, plague and pestilence and an all-round increase in the cost of living. The best of the young manhood, in many cases the breadwinners, have been enlisted into the armed forces. Yet no compensative increase of pay or family allowance has been granted to the Indian soldier. On the contrary, in hundreds of cases which come to light with monotonous frequency, conditions for his family grow progressively worse as the length of separation grows steadily longer. It is not surprising therefore, that much of the mail which reaches the troops consists of either complaints or pitiful stories of hardship.[59]

This is a clear indication to the War Office that the soldiers' salaries must increase if they are to keep fighting for the British through the famine years.

The censor's perspective on wartime hardship in India alters further as he continues to summarise the contents of letters from home: 'Letters vary from the angry and frustrated to the hopelessly heartsick. It is understandable that those who return to the Middle East do little to allay the anxieties of their comrades.'[60] From being responsible for the emotional monitoring of Indian troops and the removal of epistolary content considered inappropriate for the soldiers' 'morale', the censor himself becomes a witness to the lived realities of famine through life-writing. He comments on the nature of his work: 'Many alarming reports concerning conditions in Bengal and South India have to be suppressed here to prevent the spread of alarm and despondency. The number of letters containing such reports is however on the increase and some letters must inevitably get through.'[61] And he also reveals the psychological damage of continuing in his current role: 'deletion from such letters present problems which a humane censor finds very difficult'.[62]

The human thus disrupts, cutting across asymmetrical power structures that place the colonial censor in control of the Indian soldier and his family's words: the censor finds himself pausing before excising words further. Witnessing famine, then, makes letter writers record their empathy, highlight ruptures in social and economic bonds, and find themselves unable to eat meals placed before them. The censor too does not remain immune. If the pain of famine can 'unmake' the world, to use Scarry's word, perhaps it also suggests an 'unmaking' in the authoritative surveillance and deletion involved in the act of colonial censorship itself.

'Pyeter jwala': food, fire and feeling in Bibhutibhushan's Ashani Sanket

The exchange of Indian wartime letters on the famine provides us with glimpses into an almost unbearable proximity to the physical depletion generated by starvation on the individual body and the community. The Bengali novel I will now discuss investigates even further the intimate connection between the reader/witness and those who endure hunger. Bibhutibhushan Bandyapadhyay's Ashani Sanket is technically an incomplete novel. It was published serially in the Bengali magazine Matribhumi ('The Motherland') between January 1944 and 1946, but when the magazine folded, Bibhutibhushan never took up the novel again.[63] If the letter extracts can be seen as an example of serial writing that produces the censorship reports, the novel too here appears to take on a serial prose form. Again, while in their untimely termination both letters and novel draw attention to the unimaginable nature of hunger, they also underscore how hunger may be seen as a new form of connection between sufferer and reader/witness. As we shall see in Ashani Sanket, communities of knowledge and bonds of empathy are formed, both among the characters themselves, and in the readership of the serialised novel within the magazine Matribhumi. Matribhumi continued to be published throughout the war years on a monthly basis, and even increased its length and price in 1942.[64]

Ashani Sanket opens with the scene of two women bathing in the river in Notungan village. One of them is Ananga-bou, the Brahmin wife much loved in the *Kapali* or farming village community; the other is an elderly neighbour called Puntir Ma, who warns Ananga-bou of approaching danger—'Sister, you should get out of the water. A crocodile has come to the river' (59). The crocodile never makes its appearance, but Ananga-bou hears of its presence. A little later in the novel, rumours of a far-flung war reach her schoolteacher husband Gangacharan's ears, along with the news of a sudden spike in the price of rice (80). The proleptic image of the predatory crocodile thus establishes a key theme of the novel. *Ashani Sanket* is as much about the Notungan villagers themselves *becoming* food as it is about the encroaching lack of food they experience. How then—through surges in rice prices, or bodily sensations like the repeatedly endured '*pyeter jwala*' ('the burning of the stomach')—is famine registered in the lives of these villagers? The Bengal Famine is shown to dismantle the traditional structures of their world, but what effect has it on the characters' interiority, memory and desire?

Bibhutibhushan himself was not directly affected by the famine. His biographer Rushati Sen notes that, by 1943, he was a recognised author who spent the year travelling across Bengal, having finally achieved a degree of financial stability. However, from his very childhood Bibhutibhushan had been no stranger to poverty and hardship,[65] and had also cultivated a deep and intimate knowledge of the Bengali countryside and its village people, which the novel reflects. Two of his diary entries from 1943 specifically mention the famine. On 1 October 1943, Bibhutibhushan writes: 'A crowd of beggars up until such late hours of the night! All night they say—give us *phyan*! give us rice!'[66] And again, on 27 October 1943, he observes: 'On my way to Ghatshila, naked skeletal men and women were begging desperately—how much longer will we have to bear this sight? The world is filled with their despairing cries. The dead bodies form mountains.'[67] Yet *Ashani Sanket* does not focus on these mountains of dead bodies but is invested in the warmth, richness and inner life of its rural characters. As is the case with most of the villagers in Notungan, the geopolitical contours of a world at war on an industrial scale are beyond the imaginings of Ananga-bou and her husband Gangacharan, the protagonists in the novel, whose knowledge of place is formed only by journeying by foot or bullock cart across the villages of Bengal. The novel portrays their itinerant life through glimpses into the past, woven through with everyday realities of poverty and hardship. However, their life in Notungan, with which the novel begins, seems to bring about a reversal of fortune.

Bibhutibhushan reveals here how food becomes a structuring device for representing a harmonious relationship with the natural world as well as determining the nature of interpersonal connections on which Bengali village life operates. He tracks, for instance, Ananga-bou's journey from her bath in the river to her home in Notungan village at the start of the novel:

> Ananga's family's home was just beyond the cow-rearing locality, and consisted of two earthen rooms. The roof was thatched with hay, and there was a kitchen with two slanted thatched roofs. Papaya and arum plants lined the spick-and-span outer courtyard. Leaves from the native pumpkin plant curled around the bamboo branches placed on the roof, and next to the kitchen grew several aubergine and okra shoots. (59–60)

This is a cinematic portrayal of a village homestead, with the narrator's voice dwelling lovingly on the fruits of nature as he describes a home carefully nurtured by its inhabitants, where a symbiotic relationship has developed between human beings and the natural world. In addition to this yield of food from the earth, Gangacharan and Ananga-bou's access to food in Notungan village is assured since they are high caste Brahmins, Gangacharan shrewdly choosing to make his home in a place where no other Brahmins live. They are held in great respect here—Gangacharan has become the village schoolmaster and local physician, and is even believed to be the repository of mystical powers because of his Brahminical learning that can keep deadly diseases like cholera at bay. Performing such Brahminism reaps great benefits for Ananga-bou and himself, as the villagers gladly give them gifts of food in exchange for their presence in the village, and the couple finally starts believing that their time of want is over.

With such food negotiations interwoven into the first section of the novel, Gangacharan's increasing financial stability, the growth of his small school, and Ananga-bou's network of relationships in the village they had previously lived in—Bhatchala—are established. If, as Maud Ellmann argues, 'food is the prototype of all exchanges with the other, be they verbal, financial, or erotic',[68] *Ashani Sanket* highlights this in both social milieux and intimate spaces of encounter between husband and wife. When, for instance, the hungry Brahmin schoolmaster Durga Bhattacharya visits, Ananga-bou makes a special culinary effort—rice, *moong dal* or yellow lentils, papaya curry and fried lentil balls are presented to him as a marker of hospitality. Social bonds are sealed through this preparation and offering of food, locating maternal nurture within the gendered role of the housewife—the suffix '*bou*', meaning 'wife', hardly ever leaves Ananga-bou's name in the course of the novel. Again, erotic intimacy is suggested through the partaking of food from a single dish:

> [Ananga-bou] sat beside her husband and tossed a handful of *ghee*-covered puffed rice from Gangacharan's bowl into her mouth [...]
> Her laughter and the seduction in her eyes showed that she had not left her youth behind, she had not lost the power to steal away a man's heart.
>
> Gangacharan continued to stare at his wife, entranced. (85)

Different kinds of appetite, then—maternal, sexual and prandial—are enmeshed in these encounters with food.

Such interactions with food are sharply contrasted with the 'unnatural' conditions of being priced out of food in a fertile Bengal—the focus of the later section of the novel. As Amartya Sen argues in *Poverty and Famines*: 'Starvation is the characteristic of some people not *having* enough to eat. It is not the characteristic of there not being enough to eat. While the latter can be the cause of the former, it is but one of many possible causes.'[69] Bibhutibhushan's literary investment in the language of bounty and dearth in *Ashani Sanket* in the 1940s anticipates Sen's economic insight of 1981. The language of bounty is highlighted in early scenes where the author's cinematic eye affectionately lingers on a verdant rural Bengali landscape that becomes an intrinsic part of the characters themselves. This is seen, for instance, when Ananga-bou and her two boys take a trip to Bhatchala in their wealthy land-owning neighbour Mr Biswas's bullock cart, and stop by the riverside for a rest:

Ananga said to her sons: 'Come and sit in this shade and eat some puffed rice. We don't know when we will reach Bhatchala.'

Her eldest boy replied: 'Oh, just look at how many mangoes are budding on those trees! This season there will be plenty of mangoes, won't there, mother?'

'Just eat your puffed rice. We don't have time to look at all the budding mangoes.'

The two boys began running around by the riverside under the shade of the trees, chasing grasshoppers. Ananga managed to scold them back into the cart.

In the silent spring afternoon, swaying along the earthen road, the bullock cart passed under the shade of mango tree clusters, along with star-apple, banyan, bamboo and silk cotton trees. Sitting inside the cart, Ananga-bou started becoming drowsy. The elder boy said: 'Mother, you're dozing—do sit up!'

Embarrassed, Ananga replied: 'I should have splashed my eyes with some water. I'm feeling sleepy.' (72–73)

The puffed rice, budding mangoes and regional varieties of trees recreate the image of a gentle, beautiful Bengal, bearing the promise of food to come—a Bengali spring rather than an English autumn that anticipates mellow fruitfulness, with the possibility of filling 'all fruit with ripeness to the core'.[70] The trundling motion of the bullock cart that makes Ananga-bou drift off evokes the sleepy rhythm of such rural life, a slowness of time and pace out of joint with the military aeroplanes Gangacharan sometimes sees, both literally and metaphorically, 'flying over his head' (82).

Direct mentions of war in the novel, of which there are only a few, forge further links with food. An early verbal exchange between Gangacharan and Durga Pandit, another Brahmin teacher from the village of Kamdevpur, highlights that Allied defeats in Southeast Asia relate also to losses in food supplies:

'Have the Japanese taken over Singapore? What news of the war?'

'Why only Singapore, they've taken over Burma too. Didn't you know that piece of news?'

'No—um—hadn't really heard it. Burma? That's—'

'From where Rangoon rice comes from, brother...'

Now this was a new bit of news. A truly juicy piece of information to mull over and discuss tomorrow at Mr. Biswas's gathering. How was it that he didn't know this before? No one had said anything. And who would have known this in such a far-flung village, anyway? Although, to Gangacharan, all this was still rather hazy. He didn't really know exactly which direction Rangoon or Burma was in. East or south, and which region? Was it very far away? (87–88)

Ananga-bou's visit to the neighbouring village of Bhatchala takes place after such connections between food and war have been established, but before rising food prices directly affect the couple. It is this journey that becomes highly significant in the novel, indicating its turn to interiority, memory and desire.

As night falls, Ananga-bou sits on a mat on the threshold of her former home in Bhatchala, facing the moonlit lotus pond outside. Most of the village women who had come to welcome her have now gone home. Two of her dearest female companions—Moti-Muchini and the widow Kali—still remain. Memories of food weave themselves into Ananga-bou's happiness:

> Ananga-bou's heart was rejoicing today. After so many days she had come back to her old home and had met her old friends. So much time had gone by since she had seen such a moonlit night over the lotus pond! Although when she actually lived here, she was only able to eat sometimes and not at others. This same Moti-Muchini had plucked so many ripe mangoes for her, had even stolen ripe jackfruit from other people's trees to feed her. The female cowherd Kali had surreptitiously, under the noses of her brothers and their wives, brought Ananga-bou flattened rice or *chire*, made from new grain. (74)

The intimate space of female companionship created by the three women bears the history of food being given, gladly and generously, to Ananga-bou during times of duress, by those who do not enjoy her caste privileges but love her nonetheless. By recalling these moments of past nurture, Ananga-bou is then able to articulate her deepest desire for the future: 'What I really wanted was to build a little home right by the bank of the lotus pond [...] Wouldn't that be nice?' (75). And Kali responds: 'You can still build one. I'll bring you bamboo and hay and anything else that you might need from my father' (75).

The narrative moves on from this yearning for home in a gentle, nurturing Bengal to the month of *shravan* (the monsoon season), when even the ever hopeful and optimistic Ananga-bou starts fearing for the future in the seemingly endless struggle to obtain food. 'All the rice had suddenly disappeared from the land, just like camphor! Even the large market at Gobindapur did not have any rice' (108). The simile is telling—extraordinary forces at play in '*juddher bajar*' ('the war market') (105) make both the plentiful quantities of agricultural and natural produce, and their ready availability for Gangacharan and Ananga-bou as Brahmins, suddenly disappear. This strange vanishing reflects the lived realities of the 1940s—as Madhusree Mukerjee notes: 'Between January and July of 1943, even as famine set in, India exported 71,000 tons of rice, an unknown fraction of it through Calcutta's port.'[71] The situation was further aggravated by black-market profiteering and hoarding practices, most of which went unchecked, a rationing system introduced far too late, only when the famine was well underway, and permission to import food grains consistently being denied by the British government in London.[72]

War and famine, then, register in the novel not an as event but as everyday violence, through an extraordinary rise in food prices. Rural Bengal's natural abundance is not enough to support Notungan villagers as it had in the past; Bibhutibhushan's Gangacharan and Ananga-bou are depicted as priced out of rice in a market where uncontrolled hoarding and colonial wartime policies have simply made food disappear. Gangacharan and Ananga-bou's socio-economic identity can no longer simply be that of a poor Bengali Brahmin couple, living off school teaching and practising domestic frugality: they are inexorably connected to the devastating effects of a global war they know and care so little about. On first hearing of price surges in the marketplace, Gangacharan and Ananga-bou reflect on this very connection:

'You know, I heard that the price of rice will keep increasing, everyone is saying this.'
'It will go up more than six rupees? What on earth?'
'That's what everyone is saying. Apparently it's because of the war that this is happening—'
'Who is doing all this warring?!'
'That you won't understand. Our King has started fighting with Germany and Japan—apparently everything will now cost more.' (83)

Linguistic resonances further connect the characters' experiences of famine, with the novel being shot through with metaphors of fire. While the title of the novel itself, *Ashani Sanket* or *Intimations of Thunder*, evokes a distant, thunderous fire, we are also informed of a literal fire in Notungan's past that defaced a villager—his body was burnt when he was a boy and the scars have never faded (127). This character, nicknamed 'Jodu-pora' or 'burnt Jodu' by the villagers, is not a sympathetic portrayal of a disfigured man living in rural Bengal; rather, his burnt body becomes a physical realisation for the rapaciousness of war. A well-paid employee at the local brick-kiln, Jodu-pora gains access to hoarded rice, which he agrees to sell to a young woman in Notungan village, Kapali-bou—a close friend of Ananga-bou—in return for sexual favours when she is starving.[73] Here, a metaphoric use of Bengali language is shown to turn literal. Ananga-bou often affectionately uses the adjective *'porarmukhi'*, which she calls younger female companions like Moti-Muchini (74) when their last remark to her has been especially pert—*'porarmukhi'* means 'the girl with the burnt or accursed mouth'. But with the introduction of Jodu-pora in the novel, the word *'pora'* transforms instead into the horrifying predatory reality of his burnt body.

Transgressive sexual appetites are thus also associated with fire, as metaphors of rapacity continue throughout the novel. As the food scarcity worsens, Ananga-bou and her companions Moti-Muchini and Kapali-bou devise new strategies for feeding themselves. They make their way into the forest on the village outskirts, and are rooting amongst thorny bushes to dig out potatoes when a bearded man suddenly emerges from the roadside and makes straight for them. He marches silently and purposefully towards Ananga-bou as she watches in horror, while simultaneously trying to disentangle her hair from brambly bushes that prevent her from fleeing: 'Her dress was in disarray. In her exertions, her sweating face had become suffused with colour. The man was coming towards her like an insect inexorably drawn towards a burning flame' (123). Just as this ravisher is about to grab Ananga-bou's hand, Moti-Muchini intervenes, pushing the man with all her strength. He falls helplessly into the hole the women had dug to retrieve their precious potato.

In the novel, then, Bibhutibhushan views forced sexuality as part of the larger net of rapaciousness that he describes closing in on

Notungan village, with characters being marked as targets of consumption. As Maud Ellmann argues, representations of sexuality are often 'haunted by the imagery of ingestion',[74] and Ananga-bou's attacker desires to satiate yet another appetite. The imagery of a consuming fire continues to intensify—if Ananga-bou is 'a burning flame' (123) to her would-be ravisher, fire is also associated with the sparse, strange wartime market. Gangacharan goes to the 'bazaar of war' (105) to find that 'the price of items had soared like fire' (137), while a starving Moti-Muchini comes to Ananga-bou saying '*pyet jwalchhe*'—her stomach is 'on fire with hunger' (122). As the fires of thunder, sexual desire, war and hunger intersect with a literal disfiguring fire from the past and with each other, language is shown to register the sensation of burning. This, then, is how the characters experience famine in the novel—through an everyday burn.

As the famine progressively worsens, and hunger dominates the characters' relentless quest for food, we realise that Ananga-bou's home by the lotus pond in Bhatchala will never be built. This forms the novel's undertow of loss. Furthermore, Gangacharan's daydreams, built around his fervent longing to provide for his wife, are built into this narrative of unfulfilled desires too. While Ananga-bou scours the shrubbery near the village for food, Gangacharan walks miles nearly every day to see if there is anyone from whom he can buy rice, or who is willing to gift him rice, since donating food to a Brahmin is seen as a pious act in Hinduism. He hears of Nibaran Ghosh in the village of Shankarpur, who is rumoured to possess rice stores. When he reaches Nibaran Ghosh's house, however, the latter is unwilling to sell him any, but offers him a meal instead. The hungry Gangacharan, not having eaten properly in many days, is unable to resist. At the very thought of eating a full meal, images of delectable dishes swim before his eyes—fish stew cooked with small asafoetida balls, aubergine and potato curry, large prawns floating in a rich sauce, rice being mixed with the fish stew, eaten with chillies on the side (130–131). Yet, though Gangacharan eats on his own, his enjoyment of the food is haunted by memories of Ananga-bou rummaging through thorny brambly woods at home to gather edible leaves. He calculates how many rice balls she would be able to scoop up out of the unfinished rice on his plate and is determined to bring these remains back home for her: in the mathematics of food deprivation, even discarded, half-consumed rice finds a place as an index of love.

Ultimately, however, Gangacharan is far too embarrassed to request these leftovers from his host's daughter, Khyantamani. But later, in the soaringly expensive wartime marketplace in the nearest town, a luxurious and expensive pair of *sandesh* or sweetmeats transfixes him, and he imagines the joy of presenting these to his wife:

> Gangacharan began to gaze repeatedly at the pair of *sandesh*. How beautifully they had been made! The sweet makers were skilled.
>
> If only he could take them out of the packaging and place them straight into Ananga's hands!
>
> 'My love, see what I have brought you…'
>
> 'What is it, dear?'
>
> 'Such a lovely pair of *sandesh*, have you ever seen anything like it? I bought them just for you.'
>
> Never had he been able to put luxurious food into his wife's hands. Where would he get such food from, anyway? Had he ever seen days when money flowed plentifully into their household? And, on top of everything, there was this terrible famine. (138)

Through repeatedly evoking the image of Ananga-bou's hands, and evoking his own joy in placing the *sandesh* in them, Gangacharan's imagination transforms food from simply satiating appetite to becoming a symbol of enduring love.

However, Gangacharan's dreams of securing food remain unrealised. They jostle uncomfortably in the novel against the nightmarish spectres that human beings become. In the monsoon season, just as rice vanishes from the market, human wraiths drift into Notungan, begging endlessly for rice-starch. Nobody knows where they are from, or where they had been all this time. Half-naked, weary and gaunt, with nude children in tow, they visit Ananga-bou one day as she is busy in the kitchen. Standing at the threshold of the house, they clamour for rice-starch—'*phyan khaitam, phyan khaitam*'— which Ananga-bou rushes to provide them with. 'What kind of situation have such folk found themselves in, when they have to leave their native village and travel to unknown places with their children, only to beg for a mug of rice-starch?' she thinks (104–105). With tears in her eyes, Ananga-bou thinks of her own sons, busy studying at that moment in the village school. And yet, even then, the menace of war seems far from imminent: 'Everyone [in Notungan] still wondered, do people really die from not having enough to eat? Surely that danger could never befall them' (105).

Death by starvation comes to Notungan village in the form of Moti-Muchini. At the end of the novel, she is unexpectedly seen near Ananga-bou's house under a mango tree. Her body, with its swollen hands, feet and face, is almost unrecognisable. Gangacharan, on his way back home in the evening, has to ask her who she is:

> Moti spoke with great effort in a croaking voice: 'It's me, *dadathakur*.'[75]
>
> 'Who—Moti? Why are you here? What's happened to you?'
>
> 'I'm suffering from a terrible fever, *dadathakur*. Haven't eaten in three days. I want to eat a bit of rice.'
>
> 'Oh, I see! Can you get up and come with me?'
>
> Moti had no energy to rise to her feet. Gangacharan would not touch her. Therefore Moti remained lying where she was. (145)

Gangacharan, the educated Brahmin, adheres to the strictures of the Hindu caste system in not assisting Moti. As a '*muchini*' or female leather worker, a suffix that forms an inescapable part of her identity throughout the novel, she is considered an 'untouchable'. Later, when she is discovered to have died in the same location by Kapali-bou, her corpse becomes a village spectacle:

> Moti's dead body remained under the mango tree. So many people came to see it. They gazed on it from afar and left in fear. What had befallen Moti today could easily be their fate too. Her death seemed to open the villagers' eyes [...] The intimations of thunder brought about by the first death from starvation. (149)

Writing in the context of the 1981 Irish hunger strike in Long Kesh prison, Maud Ellmann notes that 'the starving body is itself a text, the living dossier of its discontents, for the injustices of power are encoded in the savage hieroglyphics of its sufferings'.[76] *Ashani Sanket* does not ascribe death to anyone else other than Moti-Muchini: Gangacharan and Ananga-bou, though undergoing severe hardships, remain alive when the novel ends. It is the most vulnerable character within the highly asymmetrical power structures of colonialism as well as the social and religious hierarchies of Bengali village life—a woman, an 'untouchable'—who diverts death from the main characters, much as, earlier in the novel, she had prevented Ananga-bou's rape by pushing the male assailant away. Moti-Muchini's body becomes the site in which the villagers read a portent of their own destiny. The subaltern speaks, but only through her own dead body. She becomes a symbolic warning for the future and a focus of attention only when she becomes a terrifying object consumed not only by the brutality of war but also indigenous caste and gender hierarchies.[77] Bibhutibhushan's penetrating gaze as a writer, then, reveals how all are equally implicated: caste hierarchies and gender asymmetries prove just as violent as colonialism, war and famine.

Ellmann's provocative and poignant conclusion to *The Hunger Artists* states: 'There are many nuances of nothingness: and every hunger artist eats a different absence, speaks a different silence, and leaves a different kind of desolation.'[78] How is this 'desolation' reflected in Bibhutibhushan's representation of Bengal famine sufferers? If anything, Bibhutibhushan's characters—not so much hunger artists, perhaps, as hunger victims, since they starve not by choice but as the uncontrolled outcome of an imperial war—resist 'desolation'. Food may be scarce and traditional Bengali village life largely destroyed, but parts of the village community are still shown to endure. After Moti-Muchini's death, people start escaping to the city, where they hear that the government is doling out food rations.[79] Kapali-bou, deciding to leave with Jodu-pora, comes to say goodbye to Ananga-bou, who, however, will have none of it: 'Stay with me. If I get to eat, so will you. You'll stay here with me like my younger sister. If we die from hunger, we'll both die together [...] Promise me, you won't go!' (151). Convinced, Kapali-bou goes to meet Jodu-pora to cancel her travel plans. A thwarted and enraged Jodu-pora tries to persuade her otherwise in the final lines of the novel:

Jodu-pora shouted after her: 'Listen to me, I want to say something to you!'
From afar, Kapali-bou looked back at him. She hesitated a little. Then she turned and walked away for good. (151)

If the Bengal hunger victims are to succumb to the inescapable lack of food in *Ashani Sanket*, they seek to exercise choice over how their lives end. The novel finishes with Kapali-bou's final severing of sexually exploitative ties with Jodu-pora. Preventing further capitulation to the economic forces brought into play by the Second World War, she refuses to remain an object of consumption, food for the predator. Her return to the female companionship and sisterly love of Ananga-bou in Notungan reaffirms the novel's emotional core by echoing Ananga-bou's evening of camaraderie with Moti-Muchini and the widow Kali in Bhatchala, where Ananga-bou had dreamt of her ideal home by the lotus pond. Kapali-bou's walking away from Jodu-pora, then, constitutes the novel's resistance by locating agency within a nurturing female community. We are not told what ultimately happens to her, or to any of the other characters, as Bibhutibhushan never took up the novel again after January 1946.[80] The novel is thus technically incomplete but leaves the reader with a final assertion of character agency. If Kapali-bou is to starve, she chooses how, and where.

'Jyano jhalsano ruti': *the poetry of hunger and war in Sukanta Bhattacharya and Samar Sen*

> O great life, no more of this poetry
> Now bring us to harsh, hard prose,
> Let pace, gentleness, rhythm be erased
> Strike today that pitiless hammer of prose!
> No longer is needed the grace of poetry –
> Poetry today I grant you leave,
> In the kingdom of hunger, the world is prose-filled,
> The full moon is like a burnt *ruti*.[81]

In this famous Bengali poem '*Hay Mahajeeban*' ('O Great Life', written between 1943 and 1947), the teenage poet Sukanta Bhattacharya announces the death of poetry. Through eight lines of terse, tight verse, he forges a direct correlation between the tumultuous political, economic and social changes in Bengal brought about by war and famine, particularly in the city of Calcutta, and poetic aesthetics. Poetry and prose are structured as oppositional modes of representation—the former associated with '*pada-lalitya-jhankar*' ('pace, gentleness, rhythm') and *'snigdhata'* ('grace'), and the latter characterised as *'kothin, kothor'* ('harsh, hard') and like a *'kora hathuri'* ('pitiless hammer'). Gentleness and grace are rapidly receding in this world; the hammer's beat is in the ascendant, drowning them out. Adorno famously said that there could be no poetry after Auschwitz;[82] Sukanta believes that poetry dies even earlier, with the Bengal Famine.

The poetry anthologised in Sukanta's first collection of poems, *Chharpatra* (*Passport*, posthumously published in 1948)—from where the poems discussed in this chapter have been chosen—was written between 1943 and 1947, the year of Sukanta's death.[83] These poems were precious to Sukanta: he kept publishers' proofs of them under his pillow in the Jadavpur tuberculosis hospital in Calcutta, showing them to his friend and fellow poet Arunachal Basu a few days before he died.[84] *Chharpatra* 'created a sensation when it first appeared' in 1948 as a publication targeted at Bengali audiences, enabling the creation of communities of knowledge and relationships of empathy among its readership.[85] Tanika Sarkar, among others, has noted the historical circumstances from where such poetry germinated—the Second World War came terribly close to Bengal with the Japanese advance westwards to India, and the city of Calcutta, for the first time, experienced modern warfare in the form of repeated Japanese bombing. War was accompanied by 'a killer famine, scattering rotting corpses all over city streets [...] Major debates about poetry accompanied new poetic forms in the post-Rabindranath era [...] Communist poets Subhas Mukhopadhyay and Sukanta Bhattacharya wrote with a simple and strong diction and critical energy.'[86]

The 1940s was a time of remarkable creative stimulus across India. Famine poetry in Bengal was born out of a thriving and youthful rupture with past literary traditions from the 1920s and 1930s onwards—a 'transition from an imperial to an internationalist scope for Bengali intellectual life'.[87] In her valuable overview of Bengali literature during the war years, Srimanjari further examines the nature of this debate: 'On the eve of World War II, there was a growing concern with literary realism. This triggered a debate on whether 'good' literature was based on *visuddha kalpana* [pure imagination] or the class struggle.'[88] She notes that Rabindranath Tagore himself participated in this discussion in 1939 'with the understanding that in literature, any overt concern with class struggle was bound to be a superficial exercise'.[89] Indeed, much of Sukanta's poetic rebellion—in diction, theme and composition—is a response to such Tagorean aesthetics, although he also acknowledges his great love for, and creative debt to, Tagore in poems such as 'Rabindranath-er Prati' ('To Rabindranath', written in 1943). This new group of poets, mostly young, male and from Calcutta, were often influenced by communist ideology, and opted for a more colloquial use of language in their poetry as they represented incisively the destitutions of the urban landscape.

Sukanta evokes a new urban soundscape in 'Hay Mahajeeban'. We hear echoes of large-scale wartime industrial production in India in the image of the 'kora hathuri' ('pitiless hammer') beating—the discordant sound of forging an unsettled world that leaves an older, quieter time behind. As war fronts in Egypt and the Middle East gained in strategic importance, India rapidly became an industrial powerhouse, required to supply ready-made products such as guns, uniforms, paper, steel and leather boots to a growing Indian Army.[90] The hammer's clangs thus erase the tripping grace and metre of poetic composition. Famine enters the poem in the seventh line as a macabre, despotic ruler over 'khudar rajya' ('the kingdom of hunger')—the reign of which has erased the desire for poetry, and, more importantly, eviscerated its necessity: 'Prayajan nei kabitar snigdhata' ('No longer is needed the grace of poetry'). Prose is warlike—symbolised by news bulletins and radio broadcasts, laden with the weight of disasters, as Sukanta describes in the first few lines of another poem, 'Khabar' ('News', written in 1945): 'Khabar ashe! / Dik diganta theke bidyutbahini khabar / Juddha, bidraha, banya, durbhikhhya, jhor' ('News arrives! / From all the corners of the world news at lightning speed; / War, revolution, flood, famine, storm').[91] How can we compose or enjoy poetry in such a world? It is an outmoded form, argues Sukanta, and needs to be set free—'Kobita tomay dilam aajke chhuti' ('Poetry, today I grant you leave').

Yet, unlike Adorno, Sukanta uses poetry itself to talk about its banishment; for all his trenchant declaration that poetry is dead, 'Hay Mahajeeban' itself draws heavily on poetic form, style and structure. The poem follows a strict rhyme scheme in the original Bengali (abcb), and uses alliterative devices such as 'kothin, kothor *godye ano'* ('bring us to harsh, hard prose'), where the repetitive Bengali consonants underpin the grimness of a world that cannot—must not—accommodate poetry. And the poem makes an aesthetic investment in dearth, reflected in its economy with words, compactness of structure and use of imagery. Beginning with a rhetorical address to life's greatness (*'hay mahajeeban'*), to the unexplored possibilities contained in the very acts of living and creating, it ends with the full moon as a piece of burnt flatbread (*'jhalsano ruti'*). By invoking *'godyer kora hathuri'*—the 'pitiless hammer of prose'—Sukanta thus forges instead a new kind of Bengali poem. Here the Keatsian—or even Tagorean—sense of abundant profusion in the world, inherent in the term *'mahajeeban'*, is whittled down by the strictness of the poetic form itself, until what we are left with is the orb of the *'jhalsano ruti'* hanging in the sky. Living, creating, writing, all have condensed into one image—food.

The poem alerts us to this reduced world by images of expulsion and erasure.[92] *'Pada-lalitya-jhonkar muchhe jak'* ('Let pace, gentleness, rhythm be erased') is connected to the image of the *'kora hathuri'* ('pitiless hammer'), which simultaneously makes a new world, and symbolises the authority behind a schoolmaster-like edict and judicial proclamation—*'Kobita tomay dilam aajke chhuti'* ('Poetry today I set you free.') Thus, the line *'Prayajan nei kobitar snigdhata'* ('No longer is needed the grace of poetry') ends with a dash, the diacritical mark a shorthand for our sharp intake of breath as we prepare for poetry's final sentencing—its banishment. The poem then reaches its climax in an image of both reduction and subversion. The full moon, that quintessential Romantic symbol, no longer possesses its old natural radiance conducive to creative inspiration. Instead, as Sukanta says in the poem *'Khabar'*: *'Purono bhanga chashmae jhapsa mone hoy prithibi'* ('Through these old broken glasses the world appears blurred').[93]

To Sukanta, the moon is still visible in the night sky, but to the starving people on earth its spherical shape becomes a visual reminder of subsistence food—the *'ruti'*—while its craters metamorphose into the *ruti*'s blackened, roasted parts. Bengali Romanticism's glasses have finally shattered with the force of a war-induced famine; Sukanta, in likening the moon to the poor man's food, highlights new ways of seeing and feeling. Instead of privileging an elite individual poetic consciousness, '*Hay Mahajeeban*' foregrounds a collective perspective shared by ordinary Bengali men and women that germinates from their suffering bodies. And as India increasingly becomes a crucible for industrialised war production, Sukanta takes the metaphor of re-form to the core of poetic craftsmanship itself. Following on from the interwar *Kallol* generation of youthful Bengali writers, he heralds, through this poem, the continued rise in the 1940s of a new Bengali literary modernism.[94]

Sukanta was a deeply empathic, troubled witness to the suffering engendered by the famine in Calcutta, although he himself came from a relatively well-to-do family that was spared its excesses. At the age of sixteen, while still in school, he signed up to the recently legalised Communist Party of India and remained a committed activist and anti-fascist until his death in 1947 at the age of twenty-one due to tuberculosis. Sukanta, in fact, is credited with founding the party's Youth Branch, officially launched on Bengali New Year's Day—14 April—in 1943, when the famine's worst effects were becoming manifest.[95] The Communist Youth Branch, under the supervision of Sukanta and other volunteers in the wartime People's Protection Committee, worked in ration shops to maintain queues of people, operated alms houses and partnered with the Red Cross to distribute milk in villages. After the famine, when epidemics of malaria, cholera and smallpox broke out due to malnutrition, the Youth Branch attempted to make the urban environment hygienic by clearing woody areas and lakes.[96] Hunger therefore becomes part of Sukanta's self-fashioning as a poet of his time, as he remained actively involved in relief and rescue work. He says in '*Rabindranath-er Prati*' ('To Rabindranath', written on the occasion of Rabindranath's death anniversary in 1943):

I am a famine's poet
Every day I see nightmares, the clear reflections of death.
My spring goes by waiting in food queues,
My sleepless nights are torn by the wail of vigilant sirens,
I feel horror at the unjust cruel spilling of blood,
I feel astonishment on seeing the cruel chains that bind both my
hands.[97]

War, famine and colonialism are fiercely interlocked in these six lines, as the emotions generated by the famine become symptomatic of a deeper malaise. The '*durbhikhher kobi*' ('famine's poet') begins with what he can see—his daily encounters with '*duhswapna*' ('nightmares') that become '*mrityur suspashta pratichhabi*' ('clear reflections of death'), evoking the strange feeling of being asleep during his waking hours, and linking the visions emanating from such seeming somnolence with death. Instead of holding the promise of new life, the poet's youth or springtime ('*amar basanta*')—and Sukanta was seventeen years old when he wrote these lines—is spent waiting in lines for food rations. His nights deny him sleep, with the siren's wail reminding him of war, and evoking in him a physical response to its violence—'*romancho*' ('horror') at '*ajatha nishthur raktapat*' ('unjust cruel bloodshed'). And the word '*nishthur*' ('cruel'), repeated in the final line, brings Sukanta back from imagining murder on distant battlefronts to the harshness inflicted on his own body, through the metaphor of chains. Through the charged polemical image of bound hands, he highlights how powerless he is as a colonial subject, how constrained by historical circumstance to being '*ek durbhikhher kobi*' ('a famine's poet'), and thereby powerfully links war and famine to India's experience of colonisation.

Shortly before his own death, in a letter to his friend and fellow poet Arunachal Basu, Sukanta writes: 'Nowadays I can only see the vultures of despair flying about. Hundreds upon hundreds of vultures have filled the skies of my future [...] I am weak in both body and spirit, I feel deeply helpless.'[98] Vultures in the sky were an ominous indication during 1943 of coming physically close to a famine-afflicted Bengal village.[99] This image is internalised by Sukanta here as symptomatic of his own fate, revealing the extent to which he is unable to separate himself from external circumstances, from his own time. His biographer Amiyo Bhattacharya notes that in 1942 Sukanta enjoyed good health but believes that overwork during the famine years led to him suffering from a range of serious illnesses, including malignant malaria and typhoid, which may have accelerated his eventual death from tuberculosis.[100] The image Sukanta uses of bound hands takes on a particular poignancy in this context.

While Sukanta's poetry re-politicises and reinvigorates Bengali poetic form, Marxist poet Samar Sen (1916–1987), also writing in the 1930s and 1940s, forges instead a transnational poetics, placing the emotions of hunger in Bengal within the parameters of larger literary imaginings. As Pritish Nandy notes, between 1936 and 1946, Samar Sen 'wrote five slim books of verse that created a sensation in the Bengali literary world and gave a new direction to modern Bengali poetry'.[101] The vigour and novelty of Sen's poems, when they were first published, made 'readers of Bengali poetry sit up',[102] and he became well known enough to be cited as a representative of new Indian poetry in a *Times Literary Supplement* piece in 1936.[103] This includes Sen's famine poetry and the attention he draws to poetic acts of witnessing for his Bengali readership.

Born in 1916 into an affluent, middle-class Bengali family, Sen came into regular contact with leading intellectuals—mostly male—in Bengali literature and politics: the revolutionary poet Kazi Nazrul Islam and modernist artist Jamini Roy, for example, were visitors to his childhood home. Sen read widely and voraciously, particularly enjoying British modernists such as T.S. Eliot. However, in 1946, he abruptly gave up on poetry altogether, becoming instead a journalist and editor of *Frontier*, a Calcutta-based news magazine.[104] Poetic composition, then, remained a mode of emotional, philosophical and critical reflection for Sen only during his youth, particularly during the Second World War. Tanika Sarkar, in fact, believes Sen to have produced 'a very different order of poetry: instead of strident hope, it was dark, angry, mocking, almost nihilistic, laced with a doom-laden beauty. It was poetry at the limit of itself and he stopped writing it after Independence.'[105]

Samar Sen did not directly experience or witness the Bengal Famine. He lived and worked in Delhi as a college lecturer from October 1940 to June 1944—most of the war years—and enjoyed a relatively financially stable married life at the time.[106] Although possessing strong communist sympathies and contributing funds to the Communist Party, Sen could not, like Sukanta Bhattacharya, bring himself formally to join the party. His poetic response to war, famine and Indian political upheavals during the 1940s remained ambivalent, offering strident political critique but steering away from polemic; his sympathies remained non-partisan. Sen's biographer Nityapriya Ghosh notes:

> He would write poems celebrating the virtues of a socialist life but thought it laughable when the Nazi Germans were still undefeated

in Russia. He would approvingly read the book 'Soviet Literature' but feel angry when critics found his poems Gandhiite and counter-revolutionary because of his sympathy for the sufferings of the free-dom fighters when the British government came down heavily on Congress workers during the Quit India movement.[107]

Writing to his friend Debiprasad Chattopadhyay on 5 September 1942, after the Quit India movement had been launched and was being violently suppressed, Sen acerbically expressed his own per-spective of communist collaboration with British colonial powers during this time: 'There are only one or two here who are intelli-gent communists. [...] These conceited animals are depressing me. The Party line towards the Japanese should be, of course, altered—that is unavoidable and natural but it is also true that our future, if we don't have a national government, will be like our toilets (not fitted with commodes but service latrines).'[108] Communist, anti-fascist and nationalist feeling are thus entangled in this response by Sen. While he remains alert to the destructive potential of colonial rule and his anti-fascist sympathies do not diminish his nationalist feeling, at the same time he is also sharply critical of the political direction provided by the contemporary communist leadership.

Sukanta's 'khudar rajya' ('kingdom of famine'), then, does not enter Sen's poetry with the same directness or experiential fervour. Rather, famine becomes an oblique suggestion, part of a war-rav-aged wasteland of decay and despair in India.[109] In the prose poem '9th August 1945' (written between 1945 and 1946), Sen probes the relationship of the historical moment to poetic emotion. Unlike Sukanta, who reduces poetic expansiveness to fixate upon a single image (the 'ruti' or flatbread) and probe its meanings, Sen's eye is sweeping and poetic technique cumulative:

> The blood-red evening of Nippon, deep rumblings reverberating through the clouds!
> In the rugged fields of north-east Asia
> Tawny herds of camel raise their necks and listen to this sound
> A red storm blusters its way through the clouds; there are sounds of a thunderous spring in Manchuria
> The deserts of Mongolia shake with the rolling of tanks,
> To the yellow body of the east rushes the violent flow of life-giving blood.[110]

The poem begins rather curiously. '*Nippon-er raktashondya*' ('the blood-red evening of Nippon') evokes mass death and defeat in the war for Japan. Blood-redness as a poetic colour scheme linked to war, in fact, had precedent in earlier Bengali poetry. On 31 December 1900, Tagore, recoiling from imperialist wars in South Africa and the suppression of the Boxer Uprising, where Indian soldiers had been put to service, wrote a poem called 'The Sunset of the Century', where he composed these lines: 'The last sun of the century sets amidst the blood-red clouds of the West and the whirlwind of hatred. / The naked passion of self-love of Nations, in its drunken delirium of greed, is dancing to the clash of steel and the howling verses of vengeance.'[111] Tagore sees crimson clouds as a symbol for organised violence that imperial countries employ to undergird their national interest, the clouds at sunset seeming to absorb their colour from the human bloodshed in wars born out of such competitive nationalism, a point I analyse more fully in Chapter 5. For Tagore, then, blood-redness becomes a trenchant critique of violence.

In the case of Sen's poem, however, this same colour has rather different connotations. The Soviet invasion of Japanese-occupied Manchuria began on 9 August 1945, ending six years of peace between Japan and Russia. It was to be the last campaign of the Second World War, where more than one million Russian soldiers faced 700,000 men of the Japanese army.[112] The 'red storm' or '*lal jhor*' thus indicates the success of revolutionary forces. Much more controversially, 9 August 1945 also marks the date the US dropped the second atomic bomb on Nagasaki; the first was detonated over the city of Hiroshima three days previously. Up to the end of 1945, approximately 100,000 people died in Hiroshima, and about 73,000 in Nagasaki;[113] on 15 August 1945, imperial Japan announced its surrender.[114] Yet, in the poem, there is a strange silence regarding the ethics of using the atomic bomb and the tremendous loss of Japanese civilian life. While the incarnadine Japanese evening, the approaching revolutionary spring storm over Manchuria and '*san-jibani rakta*' ('life-giving blood') are connected through different shades of crimson, blood-redness here remains at the level of meta-phor, evoking the richness of colour without representing horror. Indeed, the '*rakta*' or 'blood' in the sixth line quoted above is the very opposite of destruction—it is '*sanjibani*' or 'life-giving', a symbol for Sen of the end of fascism and the old conflicts brought about by the clash of imperial ambitions in the Second World War, a transfusion of youthful vigour and new life, animating '*prachyer pito deho*' ('the yellow body of the east').

The poem also creates sound—'*meghe meghe ghor shabdo*' ('deep rumblings reverberating through the clouds'), '*basanter bajradhwani*' ('the thunderous spring'), '*tank-er ghorghor*' ('the rolling of tanks'). With Russian tanks rumbling on the Mongolian border, and a revolutionary spring storm thundering as it gathers over Manchuria, Sen establishes a soundscape that becomes the harbinger of change in the east at the end of the war. The poem then moves on, as a contrast, to the decaying landscape of 'Hindustan', still under colonial rule. Here, Sen's humanity for the suffering of Indian people in a post-war, post-famine world is palpable:

> The flag of Empire flies high in Hindustan, dark sounds reverberate
> through the clouds;
> Here the cries of the malnourished child, the shame of the naked
> woman
> Fill village after village with subdued whisperings,
> Next to the grey fields the river smokily streaks. (30)

In this gloomy world, out of which colour seems to have leached, the soundscape too is muted. Sickly children crying signal widespread wartime malnutrition; the extreme shortage of cloth[115] is emblematised in the village women's humiliated nudity—yet these sounds are '*gumot kanakani*' ('subdued whisperings'), faint, dying out, the very opposite of the thunderous spring or rolling of tanks highlighted previously. This receding landscape and soundscape is contrasted against Sen's disaffection for organised Indian politics, its factions and opportunism in the next section of the poem:

> Here in the mountainous mists, at the end of the battles for the
> fortress of Bundi[116]
>
> The political leaders have returned to their individual camps;
> In all the confusion, the sworn enemy has today transformed into a
> friend,
>
> A friend into the enemy;

Here politics is simply to criticise and gossip, the quarrels of old
men;
Those who are enslaved by honour
Those who are self-destructive in obstinate, blind anger
In these terrible times it is they who hold court, it is they who
choose politics as their profession.

And dark sounds gather pace in the clouds
The saffron river's flow does not bring with it the flames of crops,
The violent flow of the water reveals a muddy delirium,
Only now and then is there a flash of fish.
But fishermen have forgotten the taste of *ilish*,
And a great death covers the shame of the naked women weav-
ers. (30)

The Bengal Famine, so far, had been suppressed in the poem; the
first mention of food occurs, in the twentieth line, with the river's
traditional associations of fertility transmuted in this enervated
'Hindustan' into impotence, an inability to create a harvest—'*nadir
geruya beg aane na phosoler agnishikha*' ('the saffron river's flow does
not bring with it the flame of crops'). The imagery of fire and famine that I analysed in relation to Bibhutibhushan's novel *Ashani Sanket*
is re-invoked in Sen's poem, but fire here is seen as a lack, a missing
vibrancy and force, rather than the experiential pain of famine.
Again, wartime death and madness seem to have been absorbed by
this river, in its '*uddam jowar*' ('violent flow') revealing a '*gholate
prolap*' ('muddy delirium').

   If '*meghe-meghe kalo shabdo bare*' ('dark sounds gather pace in the
clouds'), what does this thunder say at the end of Sen's poem? The
poem concentrates on the occasional '*machher jhalak*' ('a flash of
fish') in the churning river, like a glimpse into a vanished time, a
visual reminder of pre-war life in rural Bengal with its thriving rural
fish trade. The British colonial government's wartime 'denial' and
'scorched earth' policies, just before the onset of famine, however,
had led to the destruction of more than 20,000 boats plying on
rivers and their tributaries across the fertile Bengal delta, resulting
in Bengali fishermen's trade being entirely decimated.[117] Military
authorities did not want the Japanese to have easy access into India
from Bengal in case of an invasion, but 'took little note of the fragil-

ity of the Bengali economy and ecosystem'.[118] As Gandhi observed in 1942, 'to deprive the people in east Bengal of their boats [was] like cutting off a vital limb'.[119]

In Sen's poem, then, the metaphor of gustatory perception—*'ilisher swad'* ('the taste of *ilish*')—comes only at the end, as if held in check for so long.[120] The fishermen, previously connoisseurs in regional fish varieties, are represented here as victims of a terrible sensory forgetting, a cultural amputation, as it were, to continue Gandhi's simile. They cannot now even remember what the traditional Bengali culinary delight, the *ilish* fish, tastes like. And weaving, the well-known craft of Bengali villages, particularly that of east Bengal, is shown to die too along with its women—the Bengal Famine affected those who were financially precarious the most, resulting in an enormous decline in the numbers of village artisans.[121] The famine, then, registers in the poem not only as shortage of food in Bengal, but also as a vast and sweeping destruction of the primordial nubs of Bengali sensibility and cultural life. As a contrast to Sukanta's concept of 'great life' or *'mahajeeban'* with which we began our discussion of the hunger poetry of Bengal, this is a 'great death' or *'mahapran mrityu'*.

Conclusion

The 1943–1944 Bengal Famine provides us with a 'flare of light'[122] that brings into sharp focus features of turbulent life in 1940s India. Mass death on the streets of Calcutta and in Bengal's villages allows for a fresh critique of colonialism and global war itself. These socio-political and cultural currents of the time lead us towards a history of contested emotions. This chapter starts with photographs by communist journalist Sunil Janah, which urgently invite us to bear witness and make the catastrophic visible. It then uses different disciplinary perspectives drawn from literary scholar of European modernism Maud Ellmann and Indian economist Amartya Sen, among others, to shed light on the many-layered emotions of emptiness and dislocation that the letters, novel and poems raise. We also discover in the process how all three forms of writing enable the creation of communities of feeling among their readerships.

Let us consider the case of life-writing first. Letters sent to and by Indian soldiers foreground the various ways that the pain of famine is witnessed, imagined and represented. The letters also reveal the development of new and alternative associations and connections, where knowledge is shared and empathy built across differences, including disruptions in the role of colonial censorship itself. If the letter extracts demonstrate a wide-ranging survey of empathic responses, it is the literary texts that enable me to reveal how such an emotional history might be more evocatively or fully gleaned. Novelists like Bibhutibhushan, along with poets like Sukanta and Samar Sen, were giving form to public attitudes on war and famine, their insecurities and anxieties, and yearning and loss. Their literary re-imagining of famine reframes war writing itself, broadening the conception of war from simply battlefront violence to including colonised bodies on the Indian home-front.

Through its deft interweaving of images, Bibhutibhushan's novel *Ashani Sanket* highlights the rapacious and all-consuming nature of famine. The Bengali verb '*jwala*' ('to burn') returns with varied associations, finally devouring the body of the 'untouchable' leather worker Moti-Muchini. While schoolmaster Gangacharan dreams of placing luxurious food into the hands of his beloved wife Ananga-bou in *Ashani Sanket*, Sukanta sees his own hands chained by history—the '*durbhikhher kobi*' or 'famine poet' is a prisoner of his time. Samar Sen's modernist poetics, on the other hand, focuses on the psychological and cultural trauma inflicted by hunger. His famine poem culminates in a '*mahapran mrityu*' or a 'great death' of the traditional ways of Bengali life.

What specific role, then, do literary narratives occupy in unearthing such histories of trauma and suffering? And how might they change our understanding of the historiography of war and famine? The serialised publication of *Ashani Sanket* in the magazine *Matribhumi*, successfully targeting Bengali readership between 1944 and 1946, and the poetic innovations by Sukanta and Samar Sen that caused a sensation among their audiences in the 1940s, reveal to us how literary texts deepen their role as testaments to atrocity by generating an immediate empathy and fellow-feeling in their receiving publics. I argue in this chapter that creating a novel for Bibhutibhushan, and composing poetry for Sukanta and Samar Sen, become a means of alerting us to the emotional tow of a historical event, leaving enduring traces in writing. Even some eighty years later, history transforms into emotion in these literary texts, compelling us to participate in an empathic knowing.

3

'CLOSE TO ME AS MY VERY OWN BROTHER'

MALE FRIENDSHIPS IN INDIAN WAR WRITING

Fig. 3.1: 'West African and Indian troops bathing in a stream', c. 1944, Burma. Courtesy of the Council of the National Army Museum, London.[1]

Seven soldiers from across the British Empire enjoy a moment of merriment in a Burmese stream in 1944 in the photograph above. The image, taken by a British officer, draws our attention to men who are relaxed and at ease, apparently inattentive to the camera. It seems that military pursuits have been forgotten for a while—although the fully dressed West African infantryman towards the left of the photograph, carrying a Short Magazine Lee-Enfield Rifle over his shoulder, reminds us that war is never far away from their lives. Four Indian soldiers are washing themselves in a stream; the man on the right is giving his friend a scrubbing with soap and appears to be thoroughly enjoying himself. The two West African soldiers stand by, watching in amusement, as does the tall and well-built Indian soldier in the centre of the photograph. He, along with the West African soldier to his right, is stripped to the waist: the homoerotic gaze of the colonial lens lingers on their brown and black bodies.[2] Is the camera captivated by this moment of mirth? Is it poised to capture what might follow: when the men who stand by smiling and watching step into the stream, will they soap themselves, or be soaped? In reproducing this convivial moment, the colonial lens reveals its fascination with male intimacy and belonging. It visually recreates a reprieve of camaraderie and play between imperial soldiers, contrasted against the horror and trauma of jungle warfare with the Japanese in Burma. Such instances of interaction between soldiers from across the British Empire are rare in colonial photography of the Second World War. There is visually little that demonstrates sustained, or even brief, alliances between them. Against this context, the fact that this photograph highlights a seemingly spontaneous emotional connection forged between these men suggests to us its radical potential. This is a theme that I will explore more fully in this chapter.

This chapter begins by addressing how personal connections between men are mobilised during the Second World War, generating new understandings of intimacy and emotional worlds. It considers two memoirs and a novel, reflecting in each of the three texts how male bonding becomes intensified by wartime. It then turns to examine how these unpermitted male bonds transform into ways of 'unmaking' the rigid structures of wartime masculinity within which Indian soldiers are required to operate. The bonds represented in the memoirs and the novel, then, become 'the sites at which the most significant politics are being played out'.[3] Cross-cultural encounters between Indian men stationed in nearly every single international theatre of war during the Second World War— Greece, Italy, North Africa, the Middle East, Singapore, Burma, Malaya—and other soldiers and civilians formed an integral part of their experiences abroad. This was not a new occurrence: as Santanu Das and Anna Maguire, among others, have demonstrated, some thirty years earlier, the First World War fuelled an extraordinary range of colonial encounters amongst soldiers, doctors, writers, photographers and revolutionaries.[4] Such transnational 'contact zones' continued to be forged in the Second World War too.[5] However, male connections developed by Indian men were not simply the product of two global wars. Instead, they drew upon established Indian traditions of martial comradeship and fellow feeling, as well as long-standing anxieties regarding the nature of colonial masculinity,[6] which were interrogated and re-formulated during the war years. During the Second World War in particular, we see how the discourse of anticolonialist nationalism becomes central to the way male friendships are forged: at times, it fiercely underpins male solidarities, especially between Indian men; at others, it is questioned and resisted in favour of transnational bonding.

Whether anticolonialist, nationalist or transnational, the male connections examined in this chapter emerge as emotionally expansive and transgressive acts. To recognise how illicit and unpermitted they are, we need to understand them against the context of competing and conflicting constructs of Indian masculinity—the 'socially produced but embodied ways of being male'[7]—which were formed in pre-colonial and colonial India and inscribed into public discourse.[8] Pre-colonial Indian society has been viewed by historians such as Ashis Nandy as exhibiting a greater gender fluidity, a time where violence and the exercise of power were not necessarily associated with masculine tropes, and more nurturing forms of behaviour too were not always seen as feminine. It was Victorian colonial culture, Nandy argues, that transcribed the British middle-class qualities of perceived manliness, bravery and rationality as dominant values over what was considered to be degeneracy and feminine weakness in colonised subjects.[9]

Mrinalini Sinha, in her nearly thirty-year-old yet still influential study, which examines the constructs of the 'manly Englishman' and 'effeminate Bengali' in the late nineteenth century, extends into these ideological positions the influences of race and imperialism. It was politically self-conscious Indian intellectuals, according to Sinha, who were seen by colonial authorities as exhibiting 'a "perverted" form of masculinity'.[10] She traces the shifting contours of such effeminacy, evolving from an association with the entire population of Bengal to only Bengali Hindus, and then again broadening out to encompass the politically discontented middle-class 'natives' from across India.[11] Indian intellectuals, in turn, internalised and responded to what they perceived to be this crisis of masculinity and the decay of the male body. The rise of Bengal's physical culture movement between the mid-nineteenth century and the 1930s, for instance, was anticolonial in nature, linked to the growth of terrorist organisations against the British.[12]

If we consider 'war [to be] a domain in which meanings about gender are produced, negotiated and circulated',[13] what of its history before the dominance of British colonialism in India? Extending Mrinalini Sinha's argument of 'colonial masculinity' to older Indian practice, Rosalind O'Hanlon examines the construction of military identities during the eighteenth century among Rajputs, Marathas, Sikhs and Afghans, who formed part of the north Indian military labour contingent and provided service to Mughal armies. Juxtaposed against the indoor worlds of the court, household and harem, they formed 'peasant brotherhoods in arms'[14] which adhered to 'shared codes of martial masculinity' that promoted 'intercommunal fellow feeling'.[15] Male comradeship, then, stemmed from a well-established pre-colonial trajectory in Indian military history, but it was the two world wars that saw such feeling gain transnational scope.[16] The return of global war in 1939 and the widespread nature of colonial recruitment in India during the Second World War opened up these social formations to new groups of Indian men, pushing such emotional structures in fresh and unexpected directions.

On Christmas Eve 1945, the thirty-five-year-old John Baptist Crasta, serving in the Indian Army, returned home to India after four years away in Southeast Asia. He had spent three-and-a-half years of this time as a PoW under the Japanese. Although Crasta's 'happiness knew no bounds'[17] in being back home, his physical health had deteriorated terribly. 'Grievously weakened and ill' (90), he needed six months' sick leave to recuperate, with his mother nursing him. It was during this time that he scribbled in pencil on the yellowing stationery of his brother's shoe store in

Kinnigoli, south-western India, an account of his imprisonment. After India's independence, Crasta continued to work for the Indian Army as a Subedar Major or junior officer. His manuscript, which had no title or even chapter divisions, lay forgotten for fifty-one years—until it was recovered and published as a surprise for him by his son in 1997, only two years before his death. Crasta's son gave the memoir the title *Eaten by the Japanese*—an allusion to alleged cannibalistic practices by sections of the Japanese army during the war but here used metaphorically to signal his father's intense suffering as a PoW in Southeast Asia.

Yet, on reading the memoir, what is most striking is not the catalogue of physical privations which we might expect from this experience of captivity, but Crasta's generosity towards his captors. There are, of course, moments in the text when Crasta despairs of his own existence and highlights the sadism and cruelty of the prison guards. Remarkably, however, he also foregrounds moments of consideration and care, even affection, from Malayans, fellow Indian PoWs and, most significantly, his Japanese captors. This chapter examines these unexpected moments of male connection which illuminate Crasta's PoW years with the material and emotional sustenance he needs to keep living. In her book *The Consolations of Writing* (2014), Rivkah Zim analyses European prison literature, including writing from the Holocaust, and considers how prison writing reveals the importance of 'the life of the mind [...] produced from situations of captivity, confinement and persecution'.[18] In this chapter, I argue that Indian PoW accounts of the Second World War, instead, reveal the significance of the life of the emotions.

Apart from Crasta's *Eaten by the Japanese*, I study another PoW memoir, entitled *Whom Enemies Sheltered* (1983), by Indian officer R.G. Salvi, which explores Salvi's friendship with a lapsed enemy, the Italian soldier Romano. Here, I reveal how Salvi finds closer emotional affinities with a white soldier from a remote Italian village than he has with anyone else in wartime, and it is this homosocial bond that undoes the rationale of war for him. The imagined community formed by an insurgent Indian nationalism is destabilised in this memoir against the affirming, expansive nature of transnational male friendship, forged against the oppressive exercise of fascist power.

Finally, I move on from life-writing to consider a literary text—Baren Basu's Bengali novel *Rangrut* (*The Recruit*, 1950), which represents an alternative male fraternity. Studying how fiction can extend and enrich as well as contest historical sources, I argue that *Rangrut* is written as a polemical reaction to the idea of Indian—predominantly Bengali—men conforming to colonial ideals of order and obedience by becoming the British's '*bharate sainik*',[19] or the hired soldiers of imperial authority. It shows how Basu, responding to the charge of Bengali recruits serving the British being labelled '*desher shatru*' or 'national enemies' (311), portrays this group of colonial soldiers as a dissenting male community to justify their military service to a post-war Indian readership. Contrasted against life-writing, it is the form of the novel, I argue, which allows a more resistant imaginative mode of writing to be developed in its portrayal of transgressive male friendship.

The two memoirs have been selected from a small body of Indian PoW life-writing recovered from the Second World War, with care taken to highlight representations as diverse as possible. The first memoir discusses the emotions expressed by a rank-and-file Indian soldier held captive in a Japanese PoW camp, while the second considers the feelings of a high-ranking Indian officer as an escaped convict from an Italian PoW camp. The literary text, a rare and out-of-print Bengali novel published shortly after the war, is one of the very few Indian-language novels to have survived today and has been chosen for a comparative analysis of transgressive male friendship in a different, more imaginative mode of writing. Turning to the novel from the memoirs also takes us from the experiential aspects of incarceration to the psychological: the Bengali soldiers depicted here are not physically kept captive but *feel* confined by colonial authorities that govern every aspect of their lives. Colonised military life is itself a carceral emotion for them.

In the case of each work, I analyse how emotional relationships challenge the identities that the men initially embody. I start with Crasta's memoir, where these male connections comprise significant—if transient—moments of shared humanity, generosity and mutuality, even with Crasta's Japanese enemies. In Salvi's case, the comradeship he starts feeling for the Italian soldier Romano develops into a lasting bond with a former enemy. And it is Basu's novel

which charts the growth of a male 'affective community'[20] in opposition to imperial military authority, and ultimately to the war
itself. The perspective of the central character Amol evolves into
the philosophical and ethical core of the literary text. This chapter,
then, makes a case for why male bonding matters: such emotions
become ways of feeling that challenge established structures of
power through alternative anticolonial, nationalist and transnational imaginings.

'The kindest of all': Male intimacy across enemy lines in Crasta's Eaten
by the Japanese

The Indian PoW experience in the Second World War varied
sharply depending on where one was taken captive and who one's
captor was. John Baptist Crasta and R.G. Salvi's narratives are
inflected by differences in war fronts, military rank, social class and
individual agency. In May and June 1940, the Dunkirk evacuation
resulted in about 34,000 British and Empire servicemen becoming
PoWs of the Germans.[21] By the end of the war, approximately
200,000 British and Empire troops were imprisoned in PoW camps
in Germany out of a total of two million Allied PoWs.[22] Japan's
rapid occupation of British-controlled territory in Southeast Asia
between December 1941 and May 1942 saw more than 180,000
Allied troops, including colonial forces, taken captive.[23] Although
the precise numbers of Indian PoWs in Europe and East Asia are not
easy to determine, recent research suggests that about 15,000 Indian
PoWs were in German and Italian custody, and over 60,000 Indian
troops were captured in Singapore by the Japanese.[24]

The contrast was not simply one of numbers—the two fronts saw
differences in the treatment of prisoners too. It is important to note
at the outset that, in comparison with Germans in the Soviet Union,
Russians and Polish people in Germany, and Jewish people in Nazi
concentration camps, British and Empire PoWs were generally better off in Europe.[25] There are, of course, further layers of complexity to these statistics: Vandana Joshi in her illuminating work on
Indian *jangi qaidi*s (PoWs) in Stalag IVDZ at Annaburg in Germany,
highlights how the 4,323 Indian PoWs interned here were used as
slave labour in German industries, mines and farms.[26] At a time of

123

labour shortage, it was because of the work undertaken by these PoWs and other forced labourers that women in Nazi Germany were spared gruelling war work in factories and mines. In attempting to recover the experiential history of these men, Joshi terms them the 'twice colonised peasants and workers in uniform', who experienced life in 'a hostile and culturally alien land behind the barbed wire'.[27]

Indian officers in particular, however, were spared the rigours of labour in the camps, and led confined but fairly comfortable lives, a detail which Salvi's memoir corroborates. Captured by Rommel's *Panzerarmee Afrika* comprising German and Italian forces in June 1942 at the Battle of Gazala during the Western Desert Campaign, and then flown from Benghazi in Libya to Lecce in Italy, Salvi shows how Germany and Italy generally abided by the terms of the Geneva Convention in their treatment of Allied officers. Accommodation, food and medical provision were adequate, Red Cross parcels and mail received regularly, and the men granted time for sporting and cultural pursuits. In Lecce and Aversa in Italy, Salvi notes how Indian PoW officers were served coffee and bread twice a day and received a packet of cigarettes once a week, while Red Cross parcels ensured officers' access to tins of meat, fish, cheese and vitaminised chocolates. Salvi also observes how football and volleyball were popular in the camps, and that he had his first ever bridge lesson in the Aversa PoW camp.

In contrast, as Eleanor Bass comments on British PoW writing during the Second World War, Japanese PoW camps were administered in decentralised and disparate ways, with those imprisoned including Allied servicemen, non-combatant Europeans such as colonial officials, businessmen and their families, and thousands of Chinese and Southeast Asian civilians who were forced into slave work. Japan had not signed the 1929 Geneva Convention, but in 1942 agreed to abide by the spirit of the convention's terms. In practice, however, this was not followed. Camp locations ranged from Japan itself to Burmese jungle interiors; incarceration could mean solitary confinement in secret police gaols, hard manual labour in working groups, or accommodation in large, structured camp communities such as that of Changi in Singapore.[28]

If the Asia-Pacific war itself has been overshadowed in modern memory by the Normandy landings and Allied victory in Europe,

John Baptist Crasta's slim eighty-page memoir *Eaten by the Japanese* (written 1946, published 1997) stands at the crossroads of a double forgetting.[29] Memoirs such as *The Railway Man* (1995) by British writer Eric Lomax, representing Lomax's PoW experiences after the Japanese takeover of Singapore and documenting his forced labour on the infamous Burma-Siam railway, have had some purchase on public memory, mainly in Britain, but the non-INA Indian experiences under the Japanese have been almost entirely erased both in modern South Asia and the West.[30] It is no surprise then that one of the few scholarly articles on this topic, G.J. Doud's insightful piece on the Second World War and Indian PoWs, is entitled 'The Men who Never Were' (2010). Crasta's memoir is, significantly, one of the few first-hand Indian records of the Allied forces' overwhelming surrender to Japan in February 1942, the formation of the first INA under Indian commander Mohan Singh and its dissolution, and the resurrection of the INA under Subhas Chandra Bose.[31] In terms of political affiliation, Crasta utterly rejects the Japanese and along with them the INA, but his emotional responses towards certain Japanese captors highlight how unstable such political divisions are, and how unpredictable his own inner world.

Eaten by the Japanese starts with few illusions about colonial war or military glory. Crasta wryly begins: 'When Britain, fighting the Second World War, began to mobilise its Indian resources of whatever kind—vegetable, mineral or animal—my unit, 12 FB, was mobilised at Ambala early in 1941' (3). Human participation as raw material is here made indistinguishable from inanimate or other sentient life forms swept up by war. This lack of distinction anticipates Crasta's intense struggle as a PoW to preserve the integrity of being human. His memoir becomes a clear-eyed and unsentimental representation of slow bodily attrition due to tremendous hard labour and starvation: his greatest achievement, once Japan formally surrenders in August 1945, is to have remained alive when so many others did not. Born in Mangalore in South India into a Christian family, Crasta had joined the Indian Army during the interwar years at the age of twenty-three, presumably as a Havildar, although his exact rank remains unspecified. He becomes a PoW in Singapore in February 1942 during the Japanese takeover of Southeast Asia but categorically refuses to defect to the INA, a decision which has terrible consequences in acute deprivation. He observes:

> The only Red Cross amenity we received during our entire captivity
> was a peg of brandy and six ounces of milk on 1 January 1943 [...]
> It was rumoured that Red Cross comforts were received in suffi-
> cient quantity but were eaten up by the hungry Japanese—and what
> was left, by the INA men. (27–28)

The hierarchies of military power between the Japanese and their
PoWs, intersecting with and complicated by the formation of the
INA, manifest themselves through levels of access to PoW rations;
Crasta, as a PoW staunch in his rejection of the INA, receives the
smallest amount.

Shipped out in April 1943 with other Indian PoWs to an unknown
destination, Crasta ends his journey in the Japanese-occupied island
of New Britain in modern-day Papua New Guinea. His experiences
on board this 'torture ship' were made worse by being crammed in
with other PoWs. In the heat, suffocation and darkness, he asks
despairingly: 'Could Inferno be worse?' (31). Yet, even in the midst
of such suffering, Crasta feels a mixture of compassion and outrage
when he witnesses an outbreak of dysentery among Indian soldiers
on the ship. He writes:

> Brave, virile soldiers who would have defied anybody in battle were
> now helpless like babies and were groaning and rolling naked on the
> floor presenting a weird spectacle. I could not bear it and tears
> started trickling from my eyes as nothing in my life had moved me
> to that extent. Was this the penalty we were paying for being honest
> and principled? (37)

While Crasta's political and military allegiance, like that of the
dysentery-struck Indian men, remains with the Indian Army, this is
not necessarily because he sees himself as 'loyal' to the British, but
because to him joining the INA is analogous to defecting to the
Japanese—the antithesis of being 'honest' and 'principled'. He does
not consider the INA to possess separate political authority but as
instrumentalised by the Japanese for the latter's own ends. Crasta
wonders, in fact, whether Indian PoWs were being treated so
poorly because they had not co-operated with the INA, an opinion
corroborated in recent years by G.J. Douds, who observes that 'the
death rate for Indian PoWs who resisted Japanese overtures was

substantially higher than for their comrades who went over to the INA', and that 'Indians held captive in the Pacific region endured years of physical and mental persecution'.[32]

Crasta's empathy, however, is not restricted to fellow Indian PoWs. In its focus on sites of incarceration where there seem to be no traces of women at all, the memoir goes on to highlight male connections forged across ethnic and national differences, starting with East Asian communities more broadly and then with the Japanese themselves. Crasta speaks briefly but generously of Malay soldiers who join their ship at Sourabaya—'The Malays are a nice people, very polite and sociable. They pitied the Indians' (35). Later in the memoir, once they are in New Britain, he notes how a Japanese captor called Harai Joutouhei, in charge of their PoW group, was 'the kindest of all the Japanese I had met. He was a young fellow hardly thirty years old, good-natured and considerate' (55). This is because Harai consigns Crasta and other Indian PoWs to only several hours of light garden work near the Japanese head-quarters. Crasta also remembers other Japanese officers working in the same garden as having 'a kind word for us, which was very much appreciated' (55), and describes the emotional nourishment he believes the Indian PoWs needed from their captors: 'a few kind words and courteous treatment—and he [an Indian PoW] is quite satisfied. He is sentimental' (55).

Crasta's repetition of the word 'kind' in this context is signifi-cant, as is 'sentimental'. Although these are contingent moments of connection rather than a sustained development of homosocial bonds, they punctuate the ordeal of his PoW experience with inti-macy, warmth and humanity, attesting to the importance of the life of the emotions. Crasta, for instance, describes how he caught malaria in July 1943 due to a combination of torrential rain, wet clothes and bedding, and mosquitoes in New Britain:

> There on the ground I lay, shivering, helpless. The thin cotton blan-ket given to me being inadequate to protect me from the cold, I waited for the sun to warm me. I would shiver like a leaf. Then, seized by fever, my body would turn as hot as fire—I would become unconscious, then awake only to find myself perspiring. There was not a soul who could give [me] a sip of even cold water. (42)

127

This fundamental human need for water, both on sea and land, informs memory and metaphor in the memoir. Earlier, on board the 'torture ship', Crasta had asked some Malays for cups of water—an almost priceless commodity on board—and despite extreme rationing, was sometimes given one. These moments, then, when a sympathetic Malayan does give him water, transform into affect. It is against such contexts of acute physical deprivation and powerlessness that the word 'kind' has to be understood; when contrasted with Crasta's intense suffering, along with his feelings of loneliness, the word carries an enormous charge. In *The Consolations of Writing* (2014), Rivkah Zim focuses on the use of the same word while discussing Holocaust survivor Primo Levi's emphasis on kindness to strangers—'those different from ourselves'. Zim declares: 'Without that "kindness" we are not human beings.'[33] In Crasta's case, the word 'kind' transforms into an expansiveness of human feeling in response to another's distress—the very reversal of the totalising exercises of domination engineered by the Japanese that he had witnessed on board the 'torture ship'.

In its restrained, laconic style, the memoir continues to provide us with a catalogue of phantasmagoric experiences against which these moments of male connection are juxtaposed. When Crasta is sent to Rabaul, the capital of New Guinea, along with other physically capable PoWs to undertake heavy fatigue in unloading ammunition from cargo ships, he discovers that American planes had been bombing the city. In October 1943, he experiences one such raid himself, with about three or four hundred planes closing in on the harbour, supply centres and Japanese warships. After the planes depart, he witnesses utter chaos—'everybody in the heat of excitement [was] running here and there like madmen' (45). A bomb had exploded nearby, resulting in about thirty men taking refuge in a trench being buried alive in it. Crasta outlines the horror of the consequent destruction of the human form—'some corpses had already been dug out, their eyes glassy, mouths open with mud inside, presenting a ghastly sight. They had tried to scoop out the mud with their hands, feet and mouth in an attempt to free themselves, but had died in extreme agony' (45).

This gruesome incident occurs again only a month later, in November 1943, on a greater scale when American planes set alight huts and destroy the meagre belongings of Crasta and the other PoWs. The attack also results in further trenches collapsing and many more casualties, especially amongst the Taiwanese, who had by now joined Japanese forces at Rabaul. Crasta tells us:

> Everybody who was dug out had died. Several men standing outside the trench were mortally hit by splinters and dismembered, some losing arms, legs and having their stomachs ripped open. Some breathed their last after being dug out. The Taiwanese dug out hundreds of their comrades but finding it impossible to take out everyone, left the rest in the collapsed trench, Nature's own grave. (46)

In both instances, Crasta is disgusted by the violence of war but feels the need to describe it; he is simultaneously repelled and fascinated by the grotesque. Yet even such extreme violence eventually becomes normalised. Apparently bored by incessant American air raids, Crasta says a little later: 'Well! By now we had become accustomed to the bombers. They no longer scared us. Our only grievance against them was that they disturbed our sleep. Otherwise, they were welcome' (51). It is perhaps not boredom but rather a death-wish when in the constant presence of death: American planes become a combination of his 'only hope of deliverance or our end, either of which was desirable' (51). This yearning for self-annihilation is not felt by Crasta alone but shared by other Indian PoWs— Harbans Lal, Sen Gupta and Sardar Singh—who join him by 'never [taking] shelter during the air raids but gaz[ing] at the manoeuvres in the air' (51).

However, in July 1944, these three friends of Crasta meet a terrible end in a night-time air raid that catches them unawares. Crasta bears witness:

> Sen Gupta's head and thighs had been severed, Sardar Singh disembowelled, and poor Harbans Lal's skull had been cracked, his body thrown into the steel tub. These gentlemen died the most cruel death imaginable [...] I had had a narrow escape but my friends had not. (53)

This brief summary of bodily desecration cannot reveal the extent of Crasta's emotional anguish, which is transferred instead onto his memories of their past comradeship. He tells us: 'They had been quite hale and healthy the previous night: Harbans Lal, Sen Gupta and I had been talking till late that night, planning our post-war schemes, and now my only friends there were no more. I could not restrain myself, and tears rolled down my cheeks' (53). As Vanda Wilcox notes while analysing Italian recruits' mention of tears in First World War letters, witnessing violence and death was very difficult for soldiers to articulate, and that writing about crying becomes a metonym for expressing a complex and troubling range of emotions.[34] Crasta's small group had been a male community created as a product of war, dreaming together of freedom beyond their conditions of incarceration—a shared act that made such hopeful imaginings possible. In anger, despair and disbelief, Crasta views these deaths as a result of a political decision on the part of Indian PoWs, like his friends and himself, to not defect to the INA, and once again conflates the INA with Japanese forces: 'These men could very well have stayed back in Singapore and saved their own lives but came with the fatigue party to be away from the INA influence in vindication of certain principles' (53). In other words, the three PoWs had resisted the INA resistance, only to meet with disastrous consequences. But it was only in the company of such friends that Crasta could imagine a life after the war; when they die, his own death-wish continues unabated: 'They were dead, but their troubles were at an end [...] And we envied them!' (54).

Male communities continue to be remade as the memoir transforms at points into a ledger of gratitude to friendship. Crasta recalls his Christmas dinner of December 1944 by saying: 'I wish to record the names of the people who gave me considerable help as regards food, vegetables and so forth during these months' (59). PoWs Suraj Din, Franors, Giyat and Ramaswamy—whose only trace of existence in the memoir is in this brief note on the Christmas meal they once shared with Crasta—make it onto this list, highlighting how Crasta uses writing as a means of preserving the memory of their names. The meal itself is the very inverse of Christmas feasting and merriment, described in Crasta's usual dry style: 'A small anaemic fowl had been cooked in coconut milk with brinjals and tapioca. We got a bone each' (59). Yet, though the food is meagre, the formation of community and the enjoyment of companionship over this meal on Christmas Day for an Indian

Christian PoW becomes emotionally significant. It forges the way for Crasta to reveal the nature of his intimacy with other Indian PoWs, with whom he had little in common and yet who look after him with tenderness when he is most vulnerable. Crasta foregrounds the affection with which he is nursed in the summer of 1945 when once again he falls seriously ill:

> During these months, Rup Lal and Lance Naik Mohant Ram of 22 Battalion were of great help to me. Rup Lal and I ate together, and he shared with me whatever he could manage to get. Mohant Ram stitched our torn clothes and even washed them—something no one would have done in the circumstances. I did not belong to their unit, nor was of their place or caste.[35] Yet they, realising my helpless condition, did what they could to make me comfortable.
>
> During my illness and anxiety, Rup Lal comforted me and was my constant companion. I can never forget these two gentlemen as long as I live, and pray to God that He may amply reward them. (67–68)

It is by such acts of nurturing under conditions of extreme duress, simply to keep each other alive, that Crasta and his two fellow PoWs become allies in the fight against institutionalised suffering.

Even those men meant to serve as the instruments of inflicting suffering as prison guards are revealed to destabilise such categories. If, on one hand, Crasta draws our attention to sadistic Japanese commanders such as Koga Hugcho, nicknamed 'Koga the Devil' and described as 'a most unprincipled and inhumane brute' (61), he also remains alert to the presence of Japanese sergeant Meena Gunsou, 'an extremely considerate and amiable man' (64), like Harai Joutouhei mentioned earlier. Despite Crasta feeling at 'the limit of human endurance and degradation' (64) under Koga, remarkably, he never stereotypes or demonstrates antipathy towards all his Japanese captors. Crasta, in fact, represents Meena with considerable feeling: 'He knew how, when and to whom to be lenient. He had a fair education, knew a smattering of English, and had a liking for India' (64). It is this 'good Meena' (70), as Crasta fondly calls him, who tells the Indian PoWs on 16 August 1945 that peace had been declared and follows this up by saying that he wished to accompany the PoWs to India, where he would be happy to undertake any sort of work.

Is this a 'bottom-up' version of the pan-Asian solidarity envisaged by Japanese officer Captain Iwaichi Fujiwara when he brokered the establishment of the first INA under Indian commander Mohan Singh in Singapore? This was an emotional allegiance to the 'politics of anti-Westernism', as Cemil Aydin terms it. Despite the INA's contested history and Crasta's own antipathy towards this army, part of the reason behind its initial formation had been Japanese support for the Indian anticolonial independence movement, embodied in officers such as Fujiwara.[36] In the memoir, Crasta and Meena represent yet another version of such solidarity. Crasta's son Richard, who introduces, edits and annotates the memoir, notes at this point that his father later named his only daughter 'Meena', and that 'she turned out to be his most beloved child' (70). We are not told what ultimately became of 'the good Meena', except that he lingered on as this emotional trace in Crasta's post-war life.

When the end of the war is finally announced, it becomes, to Crasta, 'a second birth, resurrection from death'. Despite being a 'complete physical wreck', he 'thanked God that he gave me that day' (70). Yet even the final Allied rescue of these PoWs is fraught. Crasta notes the 'meanness or racial prejudice' (73) of British officer Major Rose, who, even as their liberator, denied the Indians small, precious comforts. Just as Crasta perceives the INA to be a front for the exercise of Japanese authority rather than its own force for securing Indian independence, ironically many British officers viewed all Indian PoWs under Japanese control as 'tainted' by the INA association and therefore as 'traitors'.[37] It is now the Australians who nurture the Indian PoWs until arrangements are made for the latter to leave the island in November 1945.

Crasta remembers this subversion of racial divides with gratitude: 'They gave us more than what we could eat, ungrudgingly, and better things than they gave their own soldiers—clothes, drinks, etc., etc. Australian soldiers would mingle freely and dine with us, disregarding all codes of etiquette. They hated the Americans and the British' (73). Is this evidence of a white Dominion state sympathising with Indian colonial subjects against a common imperial authority, or a reflection of a more democratic Australian society contrasted against the racial, hierarchical practices of British colonialism in India? Lapsing suddenly into the present tense, as though psychologically transported back to his PoW years, Crasta notes in an enigmatic emotional shorthand: 'We love the Australians. They are simple' (73). This word 'simple', like the previous use of the word 'kind', becomes Crasta's nomenclature for human fellow-feeling, developed in the absence of vertical relationships built on racial and colonial asymmetries. Both 'simple' and 'kind' represent a lateral movement that connects and unites by unmaking the structures that separate and stratify. It is this bond that I will examine further by studying a sustained homosocial relationship in the next PoW memoir, R.G. Salvi's *Whom Enemies Sheltered*.

'Our guardian angel': A transcendental homosocial relationship in Salvi's Whom Enemies Sheltered

> [...] if I had to choose between betraying my country and betraying my friend, I hope I should have the guts to betray my country.
>
> – E.M. Forster, *Two Cheers for Democracy* (1938)

Transnational male friendship, in R.G. Salvi's *Whom Enemies Sheltered*, locates itself within a wartime memoir-writing tradition of romance and unexpected relationships in the Italian countryside. Eleanor Bass highlights how, following Italy's Armistice with the Allies in September 1943, hundreds of British PoWs fled their camps, rescued by the goodwill of local Italians who 'welcomed prisoners into their communities and secreted them amongst their homes and haylofts'. This resulted in a romanticised literature of Allied evasion in the Italian mountain passes and farmlands, exemplified by Eric Newby's memoir *Love and War in the Apennines* (1971), which achieved notable prominence in Britain during the early 1970s.[38] In Salvi's memoir, anticolonial feeling is nowhere evident. Instead, his privileged Anglicised upbringing is emphasised, and his love for sport and adventure indicated in his preferences: 'Gunn and Moore's Autograph, or Slazenger's Queen, attracted me more than did Shakespeare's *Othello* or Shelley's "Skylark".'[39]

Born in Satara in west India, Salvi was studying for a bachelor's degree at Wadia College in Poona when war broke out. His grandfather had been Chief of the Baroda Army, and in tracing such a military lineage he romanticises his own participation in war: 'As a youngster, I had always imagined myself in the uniform of an army officer. Tales of adventure and acts of bravery had always attracted me' (1). Selected to enlist as a Second Lieutenant in the Maratha Light Infantry, it seems as though Salvi's route to elite military participation in the Indian Army is secured. Yet even in representations of Salvi's army life before his PoW years, the memoir anticipates a commonality of feeling in those moments where it pauses for reflection. En route from Bombay to an unknown wartime destination in 1942, Salvi recalls 'many a poignant scene' (11) at the train station, where people from different social classes enact a ritual of leave-taking. To Salvi, the platform itself seems to 'surge with emotion' (11), becoming the site where shared feelings arising from an impending separation from loved ones are expressed:

> With malice towards none and love to all they waved to us, cheering, shouting and praying for our safe return. Never before was I so moved. Never did I know that common grief brings us all so close, making us forget our worldly differences, and confirming that below our skins we are all the same. (11)

That differences can be but skin deep continues to form the thematic arc of the memoir. While stationed at Mina Camp in Egypt in April 1942, Salvi receives a letter from home informing him of his father's death. His initial response is to reach out to fellow officer Maharaja Vikram Sinh [sic] for emotional guidance. Vikram Sinh, or Vikramsinhrao Puar, king of the Maratha princely state of Dewas, had trained with Salvi at the same elite officers' camp in India, and Salvi feels his empathy keenly at this time of unexpected sorrow:

> The next moment Vikram Sinh was by my side. He consoled me as one would a younger brother. The tears, which I had controlled till now, flowed freely now. I sat down and wept. Never before had I known such sorrow. How I wished I had never left the shores of my country! For I felt that our separation was partly responsible for my father's fatal heart attack. (22)

These emotions of guilt and grief are partially mitigated by Vikram Sinh's solicitous fraternal nurturing, making him a 'true friend' (22). Sinh is willing to give up his own leave and accompany the battalion to the front, so that he, Salvi, could go home to India for a period of bereavement. Even though Salvi decides against this course of action, he feels 'a sense of gratitude towards this noble-hearted man. He was not merely a king but was endowed with kingly qualities too' (23). Throughout his interactions with Sinh, then, Salvi remains keenly aware of rank and royalty, providing us with an idealised portrait of a gracious Indian gentleman and ruler. Nonetheless, the textures of this relationship also reveal shared moments of fragility and tenderness between Sinh and Salvi, and it is such encounters that transform Mina Camp itself into an intimate male space across the divides of privilege.

When Salvi finally finds himself on the battlefront at Tobruk in modern-day Libya, he is stationed with Indian Sikh, Gurkha and Muslim soldiers as well as the Scottish Cameron Highlanders.[40] Rather than religious or racial difference, he emphasises the 'feel-ing of oneness' (26) of military life, along with the strong homo-social bonds he feels for British and Indian servicemen, drawing upon the 'shared codes of martial masculinity' analysed by Rosalind O'Hanlon in pre-colonial north India, discussed previously in this chapter. He writes:

> A Sikh would greet you with 'Sat, Siri, Akal,' while a Gurkha would salaam with a 'Jai Ramji Ki,' and the Marathas responded with a 'Ram Ram Saheb.' To the Camerons 'Oich Ayah.' Occasionally a Muslim would pass you with his 'Salaam-a-lekum.' Quite often the jawans would greet a comrade in the other's language. While we were there, the thought of language, religion, country or colour never entered our minds, nor did it affect in any way our admiration for one another. (26)

This may seem a romanticised depiction of colonial military life, a nostalgic evocation of the past in the forty-odd years that separated Salvi's lived experience of war from memoir writing, particularly since his memories are being filtered through a post-Partition, com-munal lens. Nonetheless, he creates a democratic space within the narrative through the use of words such as 'comrade'. The battle cry of the Maratha Light Infantry—'*Bolo Shri Chhatrapati Shivaji Maharaj Ki Jai*' ('All hail King Shivaji!')—also becomes a collective shout, and Salvi observes: 'Strange as it might seem today, even our British officers never hesitated to join in this battle-cry before launching an offensive' (33). It appears to be colonial military service itself, experienced as an Indian officer, that makes Salvi recognise the existence of a larger male fraternity, across racial, linguistic and religious separations.

At the Battle of Gazala during the Western Desert Campaign led by Rommel's *Panzerarmee Afrika* in June 1942, Tobruk transforms for Salvi into a desert battlefield where violence and intimacy rub uncomfortably, and sometimes exhilaratingly, against each other. Taken as a PoW by a German officer, Salvi finds a revolver on himself that he had forgotten to declare. In the midst of 'the dead and the dying' (36), he shoots his captor from behind with it: 'I pulled out the revolver, and mercilessly emptied the chamber into the back of that fine young officer' (36). Salvi's memory lingers admiringly on this German officer, on his youth and physical form even as he recalls this act of killing. Is there a trace of regret in the comment that follows soon after: 'How elusive was victory for him!' (36)? Or, instead, is this evidence of the 'thrill of destruction', as Joanna Bourke terms it?[41]

A little while later, Salvi is woken up from the trench in which he had taken shelter by the groans of a wounded British sergeant. He tells us: 'Unmindful of my own injury, I took him close to me and bandaged him. Then I took out his flask [of brandy] and helped him to have a swig' (38). Nursing the sergeant overnight in his arms, Salvi is recaptured by enemy forces in the morning, by which time the sergeant has died. While analysing the emotional lives of British soldiers on the Western Front during the First World War, Michael Roper has compellingly demonstrated the importance of soldiers' relationship with their mothers, and the emotional sustenance generated by those men who themselves took up a mothering role on the frontlines.[42] For Salvi too, the act of nurturing becomes a crucial aspect of forging relationships with other men. In the same 'unforgettable' (37) night, he crosses racial boundaries twice, first by becoming a killer but then also a carer, offering physical tenderness and drink to the dying British sergeant. These moments of heightened emotion and male intimacy culminate in an extraordinary interaction, this time across enemy lines, with a German officer and captor, who drives him in the morning to the aerodrome at Tobruk from where all PoWs were being transported to their camps. Depression engulfs Salvi on seeing so many PoWs under German control: 'A look of defeat and despair was seen stamped on every prisoner's face. It was indeed a dismal sight and made me feel sick and miserable' (39).

Perhaps this German officer, whom Salvi calls a 'kindly soul' (39), realises some of Salvi's unspoken emotions. He gifts Salvi a blanket from his own belongings, shakes his hand and wishes him well. Salvi notes with a mixture of surprise and pleasure: 'I was an Indian officer from the Allied army and as such his enemy. Despite this he had treated me with dignity [...] War is not a mere slaughterhouse after all—it has its soft and tender moments too!' (39–40). 'Soft' and 'tender', much like Crasta's 'simple' and 'kind', then become part of Salvi's vocabulary in representing male bonds on the battlefield in the memoir, despite their transient nature. This German officer's unexpected gesture of friendship forges a lasting moment of affinity between two men sharing military rank but separated by political and racial allegiances. There is even a forlornness in Salvi's tone, an undercurrent of the sorrow of separation, as he writes of being left at the aerodrome, blanket in hand, after the German officer's departure: 'His jeep drove off leaving clouds of dust and smoke behind. I stood there watching it silently till it disappeared into the distant desert land' (40).

In September 1943, after fourteen months in captivity, Salvi escapes into the Italian countryside with four Indian PoWs, where he first glimpses Romano, an Italian soldier returning home. Salvi recollects:

> He was a young man of about my age. He was fair and very attractive and out of clear, blue eyes, he gazed affectionately at us. He had the sort of face which immediately created confidence in us. He stopped as I wished him, 'Buon giorno', the only Italian phrase I knew then. Through our interpreter, he told us that his name was Romano. He had deserted[43] his Regiment immediately after the Armistice of the Italians with the Allied forces and was now returning home to his village. (66)

In representing the liminal space of the battlefront, the memoir had revealed unexpected affinities between Salvi and the second German officer he encounters; now in the Italian countryside, such affection is legitimised and deepened as Romano becomes the lapsed enemy. The memoir portrays Romano as Salvi's doppelgänger. When Salvi feels the oppressiveness of his escaped PoW condition—'in spite of being free we were hiding like owls, sitting in the hollow of a tree, frightened of the daylight' (67)—it is Romano who brings solace and succour in addition to nourishment. In assuring the escaped PoWs that the villagers would provide them with all assistance required, Romano becomes symbolic in the memoir of the village's collective efforts in resisting the fascist occupying powers. As German soldiers take over the village right after the Italian surrender, Romano, along with fellow Italians Sirio and Adelina, undergo considerable personal risk to keep Salvi alive and undetected as he continues to live in hiding in Adelina's cattle-shed, as well as in mountains, forests and shepherd's huts for eight months until May 1944, when Allied forces finally establish control of the village.

Romano becomes, for Salvi, a saviour figure amidst tribulations, the friend who undertakes arduous journeys in secret to keep him safe. When Salvi is heading for the mountains to hide, he recalls how Romano 'left us there, and embracing me warmly he wished us "Buona Notte—Arrivederci", as his eyes glistened with tears!' (78) His 'dear, heartening face' (81) rapidly transforms into possessing a more revelatory, even spiritual association. Waiting three days without food amidst an intense snowstorm in the mountains, Salvi sees 'a dark figure in the snow, at a distance. My heart throbbed a prayer, "Oh God! Let it be Romano!" And it was him, Romano! At that moment he appeared to me like God's own angel!' (81) Again, during Christmas Eve in 1943, when Salvi hides in Adelina's cattle-shed in the village, it is Romano who keeps him company late into the night:

> Romano disappeared into the darkness of that holy Christmas night, but he left a very warm glow within my heart! How deeply obliged I was to him. No words could suffice to express the nobility and sincerity that he showed at every step, in helping me and my companions. Even at the risk of his own life [...] I was touched to the very core of my heart, and my eyes grew moist.' (92)

Later, when he is back to hiding in the mountains, it is 'our guardian angel' (96) Romano who visits Salvi and the other escaped PoWs, bringing the news that German forces had searched Adelina's house thoroughly: if Salvi had not relocated, he would surely have been captured. This frisson of tension recurs in the memoir, following a common narrative pattern—Salvi remains alive and free, but only just, and each time reaffirms his reliance on Romano for food, information, safe journeys and male solidarity, thus starting to associate the former Italian soldier with spiritual succour.

In her book *Affective Communities*, which explores the 'messiness' of radical, socialist and anti-imperial politics at the turn of the nineteenth century, Leela Gandhi notes how the idea of the friend becomes 'a metaphor for dissident cross-cultural collaboration'.[44] In the figures of Romano and Salvi, this metaphor turns literal: Salvi in his escape and Romano in his protection are entwined in their combined resistance to German authorities. Is this because of the timing of their friendship, which is forged at an opportune political moment with the Italian fascist powers' formal surrender and the Allied progress into Italy? Yet their relationship appears to be much more than fortuitous politics. Perhaps it is also because Salvi finds closer emotional affinities with a white soldier from a remote Italian village than he has with anyone else in wartime. He becomes particularly aware of the contradictions inherent in this realisation when discovering that, among German spies who enter the village to track down the missing Indian PoWs, is an Indian man called Vasant. Salvi writes:

> Romano returned in the evening and stood, holding up his palm before my eyes. I simply stared at the letters written there—VASANT. Thousands of miles away from my motherland I was reading the name of an Indian on the hand of an Italian. How ironical! My own fellow countryman was being a traitor, wanting to catch me for the enemy, and here was an Italian, having no earthly connection with me, trying to shield me from the very bullet of the enemy! (98)

The imagined community formed by Indian nationalism is thus destabilised in the memoir against the affirming, expansive nature of transnational male friendship. Writing in 1938, E.M. Forster famously says, 'if I had to choose between betraying my country and betraying my friend, I hope I should have the guts to betray my country'[45]—a quote with which this section of the chapter began.

Salvi's and Romano's homosocial bond foregrounds this feeling: being chosen as a friend by an Italian rather than by one's countryman highlights the political value of the personal and intimate to Salvi as more enduring than that of any affiliation to the nation-state.

As Salvi and Romano's relationship intensifies, so too does the narrator's attention to landscape, demonstrated through a particularly revealing instance. In February 1944, the situation in the village becomes far too dangerous for Salvi to hide there any longer without being discovered by German soldiers. Salvi, Romano and several other Indian PoWs, who had also been seeking refuge in Villa San Sebastiano, walk for twenty miles until they reach forests near the hills of Casino. Arriving there, exhausted, they sleep; when Salvi wakes up, Romano is lying next to him, smoking. The two men start conversing, and Salvi tells us:

> Sitting there, gazing at the patches of sky visible through the tops of the teak trees, I was transported into an introspective mood. The atrocities of war had been something that I would probably never in my life forget. I had entered the battle, my young blood enthused by the romanticism of military life. But witnessing the sordid side of war had made me realise the worth of the divinely given human life [...] Here was Romano, lying down beside me, and in spite of a contrast in our skin colour, he had grown close to me as my very own brother.
>
> I felt the rough grains of the naked earth under my palms as I leaned back. It filled me with a sense of belonging. This bit of land was as rightfully mine as it was Romano's or anybody else's. I saw the pale blue sky above me—it was the same sky that I would have seen in my own country. Not only were the elements of Nature the same the world over, but human emotions too were universally alike. In adversity, strangers had extended a helping hand to me, regardless of petty prejudices. And war then seemed so futile! (103)

Salvi's vocabulary of touch here is fascinating: the earth is 'naked', its texture 'rough' as he cups the 'grains' in his 'palms'. The emphasis on land and soil echoes Shantilal Ray's memoir *Arakan Fronte* (1953) discussed in Chapter 1, where Ray notes: 'This is the first time I felt such a deep relationship with the earth' (42). Yet Salvi's experience of touching and feeling the earth is different to

Ray's. Ray embarks upon a complicated relationship with the earth as a nurturing marker of home as well as a symbol for the primeval terror of entombment and death. Salvi, on the other hand, transfers onto land the deep homosocial intimacy he feels for Romano. If the soil is where Salvi belongs and the sky that he sees remains unchanged no matter where he may be, he urges us to ask what these nationalist constructions of 'India' and 'Italy' are that affiliate him and Romano to certain territorial zones and enforce separations between them. When they feel an innate emotional bond, what do brownness and whiteness mean? This is also the point in the memoir where previous descriptions of Romano as a 'guardian angel' coalesce into Salvi's perception of life itself as 'divinely given': homosocial intimacy becomes a route into a form of spiritual insight. This remarkable feeling of transcendental expansiveness, where Salvi feels connected to a natural world without borders and consequently to 'my very own brother' Romano, unmakes the rationale of war for him. We are told in Salvi's wife Hansa's postscript to the memoir that after Indian independence he no longer worked in the army but for the Indian Civil Service.

The language of earth is used again to express love for Romano later in the memoir when Salvi and his fellow escapees make their way back towards the village in May and June 1944 and hide in the nearby mountains. Here, they hear from a shepherd boy grazing his flock about the suffering inflicted upon Romano by German forces. The shepherd boy tells them how the Germans stripped and whipped Romano: 'They were asking him all the time where you all were hiding. But Roma [sic] did not utter a word. He bore the agonising pain of the whip lash silently [...] Oh! It was a horrible sight!' (122). Hearing this, Salvi responds in anguished empathy: 'My heart twisted in pain. What made Romano bear such intense physical torture for our sake?' (122). He then says: 'I felt the earth begin to slip from under my feet and I was losing my balance. My courage was coming to an end, and I was confused and lost' (122). The ground slipping from under one's feet is, of course, an idiomatic phrase, but it is revealing that Salvi uses this phrase at the moment of narrating how he learnt about the physical suffering inflicted on Romano and chooses to replace 'ground' with 'earth'. The earth that he had physically felt with his palms, with all its attendant associations of male intimacy and transnational belonging, now becomes a metaphoric loss, rapidly vanishing in the wake of guilt at being the cause of Romano's pain.

When German forces finally retreat from the village in May 1944, Salvi no longer remains a PoW on the run. Instead, in a complete reversal of his fortunes, he becomes Allied commanding officer of Villa San Sebastiano and six neighbouring villages—an Indian soldier invested with supreme decision-making power over a region of the Italian countryside. However, parting with the Italian villagers, and Romano in particular, in September 1944 becomes a sorrowful ritual. At this moment, more than language, it is gestures of touch and the materiality of objects which communicate the intensity of emotion and become the repositories of memory. Salvi writes: 'I went to Romano and hugged him tightly. I took my wristwatch and put it around his wrist. He clasped my hands warmly, his clear blue eyes blurred with tears. Words were unnecessary' (133).

On board a ship for India, Salvi remembers staring at 'the faint coast of my country with mixed feelings [...] I was ecstatic at the thought of meeting my people soon. Every moment now took me closer to my dear ones. But I could not forget that far beyond this ocean, in a little village in Italy, I had left behind a loving people who were also my own' (135). This transnational notion of belonging, of forming an alternative male fellowship with Romano in resistance to the oppressive forces of fascism, beyond the affiliations and identities into which he had been born, becomes Salvi's enduring legacy from his Italian PoW years.

'Biplob roye gelo asamapto': a male community of resistance in Baren Basu's novel Rangrut

A young, nearly naked Indian man in the centre of a colonial photograph arches his neck as an imperious medical hand positions his head at the required angle. He closes his eyes too—is it in pleasure, pain or a recognition of subjugation? The hand belongs to a fully clothed and uniformed Indian medical officer, who listens to the sounds of the young man's heart and lungs through his stethoscope. This Indian medical officer leans over in concentration, in a position of command and ease; in contrast, the young man's arms hang

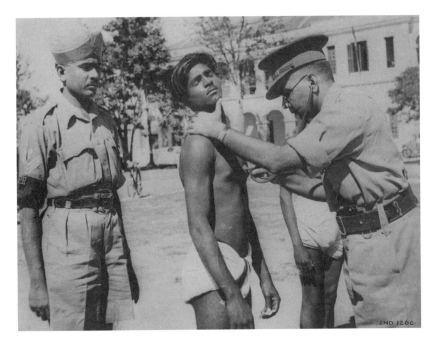

Fig. 3.2: 'Recruiting for the army in South India. The Recruiting Medical Officer in Bangalore examining a candidate's chest'. © Imperial War Museum.[46]

limply by his sides. To the left, the officer's uniformed aide, standing uncomfortably close to the examinee, looks on; from behind the officer, we catch a glimpse of the next barely clothed Indian recruit awaiting his turn for medical scrutiny. More Indian men like this one, the photograph suggests, are in the process of being transformed via military enlistment into Foucauldian 'docile bodies'.[47]

Shot through with homoerotic charge, this photograph dramatises how the colonised male body was fetishised during the war.[48] Colonial authorities generating propaganda material in India in the 1940s were aware that 'Indians needed to be portrayed in positions of authority ... working for the war effort spontaneously and on a self-organising basis.'[49] Thus, although the medical officer shown to be in charge here is Indian, the spectacle of colonial power acting upon the colonised remains unchanged. Moreover, it would have likely been a white British officer, professionally trained in photography, behind the camera.[50] And, rather than unequivocally evidencing 'indexical technology', in Christopher Pinney's use of the term, as its rather dry and bureaucratic caption might suggest, the photograph performs an imperial fantasy of domination and con-trol.[51] The young man being examined is from South India, typically classified as belonging to a 'non-martial' race.[52] Yet, as we know, British colonial powers from 1942 onwards were desperate to recruit men from across the subcontinent into the army, despite the threat that they considered this posed to their authority. It seems to have become all the more important here to stage a scene enacting this near-naked 'non-martial' young man's subservience to an impe-rial ethnographic and military gaze.

The photograph has close parallels with a representation of colo-nised male bodies performing military drill in Baren Basu's extraor-dinary Bengali novel *Rangrut*. Basu tells us that, when the Havildar-Major or junior officer in charge screams: 'Company, Atten-tion!', the men under his command respond, as though in slow motion:

> The silent feet of 500 men, making only a single sound, brought heel to heel [...] 500 men stood rigid like *kather putul*, puppets, clenching their butts, thrusting out their chests, keeping their eyes fixed ahead at 200 yards, holding both their arms clutched close together. From heel to head they stood sharp and upright! (99)

Of course, the male recruit in the colonial photograph is pliable and malleable in the doctor's hands rather than standing to attention. But Basu's point—about the physical obedience demanded by those higher up in the military colonial hierarchy—remains relevant to the visual dynamics of the photograph. For Basu, the recruits' syn-chronised obedience that must be on display draws attention to a collective '*jantrik prokriya*' (100) or mechanistic routine inherent in armies, especially colonial ones.

In the novel, Commanding Officer Major Ray lectures the men about how 'the enemy must be killed, and peace brought back to the country' (100) and how soldiers are never licensed to feel pain. After a hard day's work in heavy lifting and packing up their camp, however, the recruits feel exactly the opposite: they are bone-weary. One of them, a young man named Khogen, protests: 'We are men! We are not machines!' (100) and collapses with exhaus-tion. However, no one is permitted to assist Khogen: 'The men again stood rigid, chests thrust out. An unspoken curse raged within their hearts' (101). And then, on command, the company marches as one. A few of the recruits pause to look at Khogen's prostate body, but not for long:

> The beat of the mechanistic speed at which they moved was inter-
> rupted for a moment. It was on one of their own that this moment
> of delay was spent. *Danobiyo ek shaktir taronae*, chased by some
> demonic spirit, they moved forward, catching up with the missed
> beat of the march, moving their feet to the same rhythm—thump-
> thump-thump. (101)[53]

Maintaining this rhythm becomes, in Basu's *Rangrut*, an indicator of a lack of empathy, a failure of fellow-feeling—a reversal, in fact, of the expansiveness we saw in Crasta and Salvi's PoW memoirs— where the fatigued Khogen must be bypassed and forgotten instead of assisted. It is a type of military conformity that the male community of recruits ultimately resists in the novel not by simply challenging colonial authority but dismantling the structure of army discipline itself.

The final section of this chapter, then, takes a literary turn by focusing on Baren Basu's Bengali novel *Rangrut*, studying in particular the complex ways by which literature intersects with historical sources in foregrounding the creation of alternative male communities of belonging. Right from the beginning of this novel, Bengali men are represented as reluctant soldiers of empire. Left without much choice,[54] they work for the Indian Army during the 1940s, at a time when anticolonial movements were escalating, and feel despair at the nationalist political movements that surround them, which they yearn to be part of—but cannot. For many Indian intellectuals, including political leaders like Jawaharlal Nehru, the Indian military serving the British was dismissed as simply 'barbaric and mercenary', as Stephen Cohen notes.[55] Baren Basu uses the Bengali novel[56] to refute this allegation, making the case in *Rangrut* that the imperial soldiers of the Second World War harbour just as much nationalism as anyone else in undivided India—it is economic circumstances brought about by colonial rule that force them to sign up and serve the British. 'We joined the military to eat!'[57] exclaims a soldier in the military training camp early in the novel, and the novel is shot through with repeated references to hunger—'*pyeter dyay*' ('for my stomach', 14, 19), and its 'burning sensation' ('*pyeter jwala*', 14), resonating with images of fire and the suffering body explored in Chapter 2 on the Bengal Famine.

Basu is deeply invested in how his novel is received, crafting the ways by which this narrative of a dissenting male community formed out of colonial soldiers against oppressive imperial forces can be made to appeal to different types of readership. *Rangrut* is a rare and out-of-print novel in India, and it has proved very difficult to source information on Basu's life and war experiences. However, the Bengali edition which I use here reprints prefaces for various translations of the novel, including Hindustani, Telegu, Czech, Hungarian, Chinese and German versions, which provide illuminating glimpses into Basu's authorial perspectives and target readership. These prefaces endorse the 'authenticity' of the novel, emphasising that it is based on Basu's own experiences as a rank-and-file soldier in the Indian Army. They also focus on readership in communist countries during the 1950s and 1960s, attempting to draw an equivalence between experiences of fascism in these countries and service in the colonial military in India. 'Reading this novel,' declares Basu, 'the audience will inevitably think of fascist PoW camps.'[58] Freedom from fascism, then, and freedom from colonialism are positioned as contiguous.

But how 'authentic' a reflection of wartime experience is this? When we read historical material in the form of military censorship reports of letters exchanged by Indian soldiers stationed in the Middle Eastern and North African fronts, as we have done in Chapters 1 and 2, they suggest that the British looked after the interests of Indian soldiers carefully, as the latter were central to the war effort. The sappers or military engineers in the novel joke about the poor quality of rice and *dal* (lentils) slopped on their plates at the army canteen, and how they cannot afford to send money back home because they spend it on buying better food. But, in the extracts contained in the censorship reports, a Jemadar or junior officer writes from a Reinforcement Camp: 'I am having a good time here, good arrangements for "*khana*" [food], lot of things to eat free, you can have as many drinks as you like',[59] while an Indian engineer in the Ordnance Corps observes: 'Our British government made good arrangements for the soldiers. We get good food and fruit twice with tea. We are passing our days more comfortably here than in India.'[60] Srinath Raghavan corroborates the point by noting that obtaining high-quality food was a 'major incentive for joining the army'.[61] Furthermore, when the Burma front, on which this novel is focused, came under the Allied operating body known as the Southeast Asia Command in August 1943, the British remained careful about aligning their propaganda to the concerns of Indian soldiers.[62] If colonial authorities were alert enough to keep Indian soldiers' correspondence under surveillance and took care to assuage sepoys' worries about the Indian home-front, why would they undercut their efforts by recreating the conditions of a fascist camp in their own barracks?

I argue that in the novel Basu represents the barracks as a fictional oppressive space because of two main reasons: it allows him to develop the theme of growing political awareness amongst Bengali recruits that makes them ideologically align with the nationalist cause, and it enables him to build the anti-war thrust of the novel. Both these narratives become crucial to the formation of a transgressive male collective out of colonial soldiers, as opposed to being imperial loyalists. The soldiers respond to anxieties about a form of 'degenerate' Bengali masculinity under British rule going back to the nineteenth century, as discussed at the beginning of this chapter, which is reclaimed by their riotous uprising against colonial authority at the end of the novel. This literary strategy, then, enables Basu to show us how 'revolutionary' soldiers specifically from Bengal are, as a counterpoint to more traditional colonial military recruitment territories within India such as Punjab.

Despite Bengalis not being perceived as a traditional 'martial race', the region's contribution to the war effort, as we have seen, was significant. Recruitment from Bengal during the Second World War rose to 3.7 per cent of new recruits—it ranked as the fourth highest region in providing men, coming after Punjab, Madras and the United Provinces.[63] Out of approximately two-and-a-half million, about 100,000 men from Bengal served as recruits, although few participated directly in combat arms.[64] Indivar Kamtekar observes that most of the Bengali recruits were from towns, and about a third of them had technical training.[65] The novel bears this out. Amol—the principal character—is a young graduate from a middle-class, patriarchal Bengali family in Calcutta, who, along with fellow recruits, is assigned to a rail transport company and sent to the Burma front. Between 1942 and 1944, Allied rail transport facilities to the Indo-Burma front had become crucial in being able to send a steady flow of supplies to Dimapur in Nagaland, a strategic military post which the Japanese attempted—but failed—to take over in 1944.[66]

If Bengal's participation in the imperial war effort is considerable, how can Bengali soldiers also be portrayed as radical, anti-imperial and therefore not as '*desher shatru*' or 'national enemies' (311)? To address this question, Basu in *Rangrut* undertakes a self-fashioning of war experience meant for a post-independence readership in India—where the author fears that his protagonists will not be seen kindly—as well as for a post-war readership in communist countries. The novel directs its representation of dissent and political awakening inwards, within the colonial army and the processes of imperialism that generate the economic stresses under which colonised men sign up to war, rather than towards an external enemy such as the Japanese, who largely remain absent. And it is the novel form, in contrast to the memoir, that enables Basu to undertake this self-fashioning and develop a more resistant imaginative mode of writing.

Male community-building in *Rangrut* concentrates on the year 1942, corresponding to turbulent historical developments against the British Empire both within and outside India. By May 1942, as discussed previously, Japanese forces had gained rapid control over Burma and other British colonies in Southeast Asia, with catastrophic consequences for its inhabitants. In the novel, Amol and his fellow recruits become first-hand witnesses to the barely human conditions of British and Indian refugees fleeing from Burma into India. Internally too, the Quit India movement was launched in 1942. This anticolonial political event registers as trauma for the soldiers in the novel, particularly the sapper Panchkori, who is compelled to fire on Indian protesters, even though 'reverberating through the skies and the wind was that one cry: British—Quit India!' (185). Undergirding both occurrences, and woven through the entire novel, is the representation of war, particularly a colonial one, as automaton-like, mechanical and ultimately inhuman. It is this realisation that begins to build a community of resistance amongst the sappers.

The 1942 Burma evacuation in the wake of Japanese victories in Southeast Asia was the largest mass migration in history at the time.[67] It has been dwarfed in modern memory by subsequent cataclysmic events in South Asia—the 1943 Bengal Famine, the violence of Partition and the Burmese civil war. In their remarkable book *Forgotten Armies* (2004), Christopher Bayly and Tim Harper outline the scale of this evacuation, the desperation of refugees fleeing to India, and the inequalities of race and class that it glaringly exposed. Bayly and Harper recount: 'There were few parallels in history to this sudden and dramatic humiliation of an old and complacent supremacy—the British Empire in Asia—by an underrated and even despised enemy.' What survived was the Asian memory of 'abandonment and betrayal by their fleeing white masters in those terrible days of 1942'.[68] By autumn 1942, nearly 600,000 people had escaped from Burma into India via land and sea, of which 80,000 succumbed to disease, exhaustion and malnutrition.[69] With Japanese forces hard on their heels, British troops embarked on a hasty retreat over the high passes that connected north Burma with Assam in India. However, as Bayly and Harper note, 'Wealth and strength generally won out. [...] Little was done for the tens of thousands of civilian Indian refugees who were also attempting to struggle across into Assam without food or transport.'[70]

It is these horrific casualties of war that Amol and his fellow recruits Khogen, Ananta and others see on the Burma front, as their dissenting male fraternity gradually begins to form.[71] Khogen comments on the physical condition of the refugees, particularly the army officers who arrive on a steamer to the riverbank, resembling gaunt religious leaders: 'Look, look, the officers have all turned into padres! Long flowing beards, torn clothes and bare feet! The poor things have become like dried bats, like *chamchike!*' (123). The officers are followed by rank-and-file soldiers, walking like strange, unstable marionettes: 'They got off the boat with great enthusiasm but had no strength to move. The vitality of their bodies seemed to have been sucked dry' (124). The opposite of this desiccation, evoked through the similes of withered bats and dehydrated flesh, is highlighted in the body of a wounded refugee writhing in pain in front of Amol. His wound, covered in dust and sand, attracts flies; his foot is 'swollen like a banana tree', its colour 'red like the vermillion of *sindoor*' (141)—the signifier of a married woman, applied to the parting of her hair. Such common markers of Bengali cultural life become the only vocabulary by which the humanness of the body in pain can be recovered before it slips into the abject.

The Bengali sappers' encounter with the abject on the Burma border here serves two functions. On the one hand, it undercuts entrenched beliefs about the military, racial and political superiority of British imperialism and its 'civilising mission', with its promise of looking after colonial subjects. On the other, it exposes the night-marish dissolution of the human form resulting from war, affecting soldiers and civilian refugees alike. Both feed into the narrative's desire for an alternative male community that can overthrow colo-nialism and lay claim to nationalistic fervour, as well as challenge the fundamental premises of war that have such terrible conse-quences on the lives of 'ordinary' people. In direct contrast to colo-nial abandonment, Amol refuses to give up on a dying civilian refu-gee. He places the wounded man's head on his knee, sits on the bank of the river Brahmaputra and waits for fellow recruit Ananta to get help, telling Ananta: 'Today I understand that we face the same fate!' (125). As he waits, Amol wonders who the evacuee is—where is his home, his family? When Ananta finally returns with another soldier, there is nothing, in fact, that can be done: the wounded man has died, with his head still on Amol's lap—much as the British sergeant on the battlefield in Tobruk died in Salvi's arms in *Whom Enemies Sheltered*. The abject, splayed out in front of the living, is viscerally felt.

The soldier accompanying Ananta, who had been in Burma dur-ing the retreat, declares in despair: 'Did we enter the military sim-ply to die! As we advance forward, we die! As we retreat back-wards, we also die. We simply died, keep dying and in future will also probably die!' (126). Yet, in the case of 'total war', it is not simply soldiers who die—in Marina Mackay's words, the Second World War becomes a 'crushing totality [...] turn[ing] into a battle-ground everything it touched',[72] rendering civilians just as vulner-able as combatants. And here too in Amol's lap is a civilian refugee's body. Helpless, Amol and his two companions eventually cast the corpse into the river Brahmaputra, a no-man's land—or rather, water—between British-owned India and Japanese-occupied

Burma, but also the 'borderline'[73] in the novel of the human body's own frontiers, in which the wholeness of physical form disintegrates. The male community of resistance, created by Amol and the other sappers, then, is built in opposition to such abjection.

Along with their haplessness when faced with refugees from Burma, the Bengali sappers also feel anguish at being part of the machinery of colonial control in repressing the 1942 Quit India movement. They hear about the August *kranti* protestors targeting imperial military servicemen, with an army camp nearby being burnt down and soldiers injured on Guwahati's streets in the north-eastern province of Assam. Extracts from letters contained in military censorship reports discussed previously corroborate the fact that military symbols were often the focus of attacks by protestors during the Quit India movement. One such letter from an Indian woman in Hoshiarpur, Punjab, describes the mood in the country during the first week of September 1942: 'In Bombay, a huge crowd was returning from a lecture addressed by Sirdar Patel [*sic*]. On the way, it came across [a] military lorry and broke it into pieces.'[74]

Colonial authorities retaliated by opening fire on protesting crowds as well as public floggings and *lathi* or baton charges, with imperial soldiers participating in the quelling of these riots.[75] In *Rangrut*, it is the sapper Panchkori who perpetrates this violence on his Indian fellowmen in an incident that becomes deeply psychologically troubling for him. As he guards the military camp one night in August 1942, Panchkori sees the flames of lit torches held by Quit India protestors draw nearer and nearer. When Panchkori's scream of 'Halt!' has no effect on the torch bearers, he fires on them. The scene rapidly descends into a surreal phantasm: as the camp wakes up and firefighters rush to the scene, along with officers carrying revolvers, Panchkori collapses. We are told that 'in Panchkori's eyes the lights of the flares were still spinning! Spinning like nebula! Spinning and spinning!' (185). Later, we discover that the sappers must group together to nurse the troubled Panchkori back to health.

Panchkori is not the only one—the Quit India movement also emotionally affects other sappers through their family ties with Indian protestors on the home-front. One evening in the camp, when the men receive letters from home, they hear sobs coming from a sepoy named Shiben, who has received word that his brother in Calcutta has been shot dead by the imperial police. Amol's own letter from his younger sisters Rini and Mini also recounts the army firing on civilians. 'The whole country is calling people like you traitors,' (186) declares the letter, making Amol's eyes well up with tears. Later that night, new company orders are issued—all letters received and sent by the soldiers would be censored. These 'sharp scissors of censorship', says Basu, would 'snip away at all their emotional outpourings, slice away all their sadness'. It would only hold up their uniform 'for the world to behold' (311). Amol and his fellow recruits would be known as men obediently performing their imperial duties, while the Indian people would see them as 'barbaric', as 'animals', as 'having no such thing as humanity!' (311). It is against this political label of 'traitors' that Basu feels the need for an attempted literary redemption, to show how these men form an alternative emotional community which rejects compliance with colonial orders.

Towards the end of the novel, then, we discover how the sappers stop adhering to the demands of automaton-like behaviour and revolt to claim back their humanity. Basu tells us that it is 1945 and the war over, but the men from Bengal, not having been demobilised yet, are still on the Indo-Burma border. While on a route march, they are commanded by their tyrannical Havildar-Major not to sing in unison, a common practice during such marches. The men wordlessly challenge this order: without the song, their steps no longer mark time properly. In desperation, the Havildar retracts his command, allowing the men to sing as they march back to camp. It is the men's first significant victory against colonial military authority. The song they choose here is, importantly, the INA regimental song in Hindustani: '*Qadam qadam barhaye ja!*' ('Keep moving forwards, a step at a time!').[76] By co-opting the marching anthem of the INA, the men prepare the ground for the novel's frenzied conclusion, and legitimise their claims to an anticolonial, national male community. Keeping in mind the novel's communist sympathies and readership, Basu imagines this community as being one for 'ordinary' sappers: it excludes elite officers, British and Indian alike, and all those who benefit from the hierarchies and privileges of military life.

The sappers' transgressive emotions finally find their full release through the liberation of their imprisoned fellow soldier Rahman.

Commanded to dig a swimming pool for British officer Major Nelson and other high-ranking officers after the war, the Bengali men feel considerable resentment but nonetheless start working. Being unwell, Rahman takes a break from digging, only to be accused by a Subedar or junior officer of shirking his duties. Their confrontation escalates, and news later comes in that Rahman has been taken away and beaten badly. He is also sentenced to twenty-eight days' field punishment, which the sappers become determined to subvert. Basu's use of language here is evocative: 'They [the sappers] would prise him away! They would return him to their warm bosoms!' (318). In previously singing about their love for the motherland while they marched, it is as though the men themselves have imbibed maternal feeling; bringing Rahman back to them is like the return of a prodigal son, just like they themselves will one day return to their homeland, now that the war is over.

The following day, Rahman is brought forward to be tied to the crossbar of a goalpost in the parade ground by Major Nelson and an Indian Subedar—and the sappers are ready with their plan to thwart this punishment. When Rahman's body finally lifts upwards onto the crossbar and his cries of agony fill the camp, they take their cue. From the barracks comes the cry: 'British—Quit India!', immediately echoed by all the Bengali soldiers (319). Basu describes this moment of high drama through metaphors of fire: 'From every barrack there rose an incredible sound; the boys ran at the speed of comets towards the parade ground. From the middle of the field the entire Company announced thunderously: "British—Quit India!"'(319). Military discipline, in its demands for synchronicity and machine-like behaviour, breaks down entirely in the disobedient, revolutionary bodies of the men who 'laugh, dance, cry, scream, run across the field with Rahman's unconscious body' (319). The figures of military authority, both British and Indian, are now in trouble. The British officer Major Nelson pleads to the Subedar to save him, but the Subedar himself tries to run away. He is stopped in his tracks by the camp sentry, who cries: 'Halt!'—and this is where the novel ends.

In the Preface to the Bengali edition of *Rangrut*, echoing the title of Amalendu Sengupta's famous book *Uttal Challish: Asamapta Biplab* (1989), Baren Basu draws attention to the incomplete Indian revo-

lution—'*biplab roye gelo asamapto*'.[77] He considers how the anticolonial resistance fomented by the Quit India movement ended with
imprisonment, where the Indian National Congress leadership
found itself for most of the war years. He also foregrounds his disillusionment with elite Indian nationalism by declaring that, at the
end of the war, political leaders became far too engrossed in building the edifices of the nation—'*netara tokhon rashtrer prakar khara
korte byasto*'—resulting in the claim for freedom ('*muktir dabi*') from
everyday, despairing people ('*hotash manush*') remaining unfulfilled.[78] For Basu, a fraught justification and gesture towards
redemption for colonial soldiers such as Amol, Khogen and
Panchkori lies only in the possibilities of fictional form. Other than
Subhas Chandra Bose's Indian Legion in Germany, formed from
PoWs in Europe, and the INA, created from PoWs in Southeast
Asia, there had been very little organised military resistance by
Indian soldiers to the Indian Army during the Second World War.[79]
The feverish climax in which the sapper company unravels at the
end of *Rangrut* thus takes on a symbolic emotional significance.

By reclaiming Rahman's unconscious body and appropriating the
Quit India protestors' cry—'British—Quit India!'—the Bengali
sappers are shown to revolt against the immense power structures
of the Indian Army itself. They seek to subvert both colonial subjecthood and the obedient body desired by military authorities
through their collective action. Such re-imaginings of the transgressive male community also move beyond the national to take on a
transnational hue in moments when sappers like Panchkori express
solidarity with 'ordinary' soldiers across the world: 'Regardless of
which country soldiers are from, their situation is like ours. Within
the confines of such inhumane conditions, how much longer can
human beings survive? Now they are the ones who will stop the
war' (200). If such a 'people's resistance' remains unrealised for
Basu in his lived political experience during the war, it remains alive
in the imaginative scope and emotional possibilities of fiction.

Conclusion

In the two PoW memoirs and the Bengali novel, we journey from
life in extremis on the island of New Guinea off the coast of Australia,

to the transcendental possibilities of the Italian countryside, and finally to abjection and revolution on the banks of the river Brahmaputra on the Indo-Burma border. In each text, language registers emotion in distinct ways: we move from Crasta's sparse, economical words that leave much unsaid, to Salvi's romanticised flourishes, and finish with Basu's overwrought, hectic literary style.

Despite their locational and generic differences, in all three texts, unexpected male friendships challenge the foundations of power structures. In doing so, the memoirs and novel raise important questions regarding the possibilities of affective resistance and the potential for redemption inherent in the act of writing itself, which highlights the failure of power to be performed as it has been imagined. What, then, are these literary 'consolations of writing'? Why did Crasta compose his PoW account as soon as he returned to India in December 1945? As his severely malnutritioned and disease-ravaged body recovered, did writing itself become a form of therapy? If, as Rivkah Zim puts it, prison writing becomes 'one of the most important and durable'[80] methods we have of protecting ourselves against fear, uncertainty, persecution and the depletion of self, this chapter traces how Crasta's account transforms into an emotional testimony to survival. A crucial part of this is to record seeing humanity in his Japanese captors, to reimagine male communities beyond enemy lines.

Unlike Crasta, it took Salvi forty years before he could write *Whom Enemies Sheltered*, at first in Marathi and then to translate it into English. Does writing become remembrance for Salvi, a means of capturing the heightened wartime emotions of male bonding before they are lost forever? As we have seen, Salvi's contemplative moments lead to an undoing of the logic of war for him, when he questions the separations enforced by national and ethnic identities. Despite the vulnerability of being a PoW on the run from fascist powers, the homosocial relationship he shares with Romano, former foe and later friend, allows him to retain much of his own agency. The narrative therefore progresses in an arc of strengthening affection and affinity. Finally, Baren Basu's *Rangrut*, structured as an emotional and political bildungsroman, takes us through a series of episodes tracing Amol's journey from Calcutta to a military training camp, army barracks and the banks of the river

Brahmaputra, where the final fantasy of collective resistance against colonial power is enacted by its very own soldiers. Here, alternative male belonging is neither contingent nor singular but community-driven and overtly nationalist.

These three texts enable us to reassess historical scholarship on India and the Second World War by illuminating how male friendships forged by Indian men during this war have to reckon with both the discourse of anticolonial nationalism and transnational feeling. For Crasta, resolutely opposed to joining the INA, the possibilities of pan-Asian solidarities open up in his connections with Japanese captors. In Salvi's case, fellow Indians seek to turn him in to German forces, while his enemy-turned-saviour Romano leads him instead to safety and liberation. And even the novel *Rangrut*, with its highly politicised account of Bengali soldiers' war experiences, does not rein in its imaginative possibilities within the limits of nationalism. Characters like Panchkori in the novel feel a shared empathy for 'ordinary' soldiers across the world who fight in '*amanushik obyostha*'—'inhumane conditions' (200). The novel, then, also gestures towards a transnational anti-fascist alliance. It is only by placing the memoirs in dialogue with the novel that we realise the particular ways that each contributes to a new historical understanding: the reconfiguring of male friendship as an emotion of dissent.

4

'AN ANGUISHED HEART'

WITNESSING THE INDIAN HOME-FRONT

Fig. 4.1: 'New Indian Army recruits boarding the train to join their units'.
© Imperial War Museum.[1]

A recruitment photograph in north India from August 1942 archived at the Imperial War Museum highlights two young men standing in the light in front of a train, the shadow of both camera and camera-man falling upon them. The style of their clothing and headwear indicates that they are Muslim. Contrasted against these two men, several other nameless faces also look back at us from within the train's darkness: the photographer is just as observed here as he is himself the observer. Can we detect wariness in the eyes of the recruit seated on the left as he returns the camera's gaze? The photograph itself seems like a rushed job: the legs of the two men in the foreground have been cut off, as has one of their headcloths. Is time short, and the train about to leave?

And what can we make of the contrast between the men's traditional attire and the dominant backdrop of the train? Railways, as is well known, were seen by colonial authorities as a benevolent instrument of their presence, showcasing the British 'civilising mission' in India.[2] Such imperial modes of thinking, now sclerotic, have persisted into the twenty-first century. In this photograph, the train highlights the beginning of a transformative journey through which these newly recruited village boys would become imperial soldiers; the camera captures the moment when they are being taken to join their military units and made to serve in a highly industrialised global war. We do not, however, know what happened to these young men, or whether they ever returned home. The archives

Fig. 4.2: 'Parsi women taking a course of Air Raid Precaution (ARP) training at the Cusrow Baug Training School, Bombay. Stretcher bearers taking part in a demonstration'. © Imperial War Museum.[3]

remain silent. Their youthful fragility and the suppressed violence that undergirds colonial modernity are unsettlingly conjoined here.

Contrasted against this image of men from rural north India about to leave the home-front is another photograph from the Imperial War Museum archives, also from 1942. It focuses on four sari-clad young women from the Parsi community, wearing Air Raid Precaution (ARP) hats and bearing stretchers, their shadows sharp against the bright sunlight. The women are receiving ARP training in the city of Bombay, the major port for supplies during the Second World War and thus a potential target for Japanese bombing. The women's faces show concentration and focus, but they know they are being observed. Perhaps the smiles that we can also glimpse here indicate their awareness of the male photographer's gaze. This is a more purpose-filled photograph than the former: these urban women appear to be in command of their actions. The hesitancy and watchfulness that we discern among the rural men, about to travel to their military destinations by train and not knowing when they will return, is missing.

These gendered visual perspectives on war have striking textual corollaries if we turn our attention to literary texts written in English during the 1940s representing the Indian home-front. I start with a well-known Indian writer, Mulk Raj Anand, and assess his novel *The Sword and The Sickle* (1942), set in the 1920s and reflecting the political awakening of the returned soldier Lal Singh from Punjab. This book concludes Anand's 'Lalu' trilogy. Lalu's experiences in the First World War's Western Front comprise the famous second book of the trilogy, *Across the Black Waters* (1939), and his return home in the 1920s predates India's participation in the Second World War. By focusing on this novel, this chapter considers how, in Anand's view, the two world wars are intimately connected, and investigates in what ways Anand frames Lalu's return from the first global war through the lens of the second that he was living through while writing the novel.

From representations of the rural peasant-soldier turned political activist by an established Indian male author writing in England, the chapter turns to consider two poets—women from similar elite backgrounds in the 1940s—whose creative works have been excluded so far from the literary and historical canon. Educationist

Muriel Wasi and social welfare reformer Tara Ali Baig's 1940s English writing dramatises the conditions of a turbulent Indian home-front. In particular, my chapter reveals how both these women bear traumatic witness to the 1943–44 Bengal Famine through poetry, even if they do not directly experience starvation themselves. India might not have become a site for invasion and occupation by Axis forces, but to Wasi and Baig it is the slow violence of hunger and destitution through which war registers on the Indian home-front. Their poems, drawing upon formal Victorian lyric traditions or re-purposing modernist practices, are charged with a sense of citizen activism, and carefully represent the intense and visceral suffering they observed.

The participation of Indian women in the Second World War, and their responses to it, like Baig's and Wasi's, are varied and complex. Aside from women performing ARP duties, as the photograph above demonstrates, the Women's Auxiliary Corps (India), or WAC (I), was formed in 1942, arising from the crisis of losing Burma to the Japanese and the bombing of India's coastline. In February 1944, a women's naval section was formed to serve alongside the Royal Indian Navy.[4] The WAC (I) shared similarities with the creation of women's militias, guards and units across the world during the war—a global 'women's movement' into the public realm—and mirrored the fact that middle-class women were taking up political and social work in India. European and Indian women could join the WAC (I) as equals, a policy that caused disapproval in the British government, as this meant that Indian women officers could in theory command white men, disrupting both racial and gender hierarchies.

Women in WAC (I) were involved in a remarkably diverse range of jobs; they worked in anti-aircraft direction and plotting, parachute inspection and packing, as meteorologists and in radio-location teams, as cipher clerks, operators and in catering or housekeeping. Trained women also served as intelligence officers, translators and radio mechanics.[5] Yet recruitment into the WAC (I) was limited by caste and communal restrictions: Yasmin Khan notes that middle-class Indian women at the time did not mix socially or at work with men, and thus a substantial part of 11,500 women who made up this corps came from minority communities, being Anglo-Indian or Anglo-Burmese or belonging to the Indian Christian community.[6]

The WAC (I) constituted the work of only a particular privileged class of Indian women: there were also over 30,000 women serving as labourers on war contracts, undertaking intense physical activities in clearing scrubland for aerodromes, carrying bricks, constructing barracks and buildings, and bearing rubble and cement to and from building sites.[7] And new research into Indian wartime lives has revealed that over 70,000 'low-caste' and *adivasi* or indigenous women worked in coal mines, maintaining production levels in unsanitary conditions, enduring heat and hunger, and preventing the monthly loss of 385,000 tons of coal between August 1943 and February 1946.[8]

These participatory histories prove significant in understanding the wartime service of the two women writers, Muriel Wasi and Tara Ali Baig. Wasi had signed up to the WAC (I), while Baig volunteered with the Bombay Women's Service during the 1940s. It is important, I argue, in reading Anand, Wasi and Baig's gendered representations of the Indian home-front alongside one another to consider how each writer makes distinct choices of literary genre and form. Anand's use of the novel gives him scope to chart the rise of Lalu's disillusionment and politicisation, providing context and character in tracing this bildungsroman, and enabling Anand to stage his political belief in the urgent need for an anticolonial agrarian revolution in India. Lalu as witness to war serves a particular narrative function, by linking combat experience in the First World War to revolutionary politics in the home-front during the interwar years, shaped by the contested discourse of the Second World War. The colonial promise of land rights, among other reasons, lured Lalu to enlist; on his return home, he understands how evanescent these promises were. For Lalu, this is the beginning of the end of imperial benevolence. He realises that the only way to agitate for a fairer system for peasants and cultivators like himself is to join the insurgent political movements spearheaded by Gandhi and Nehru, on the one hand, and the Indian communists on the other.

Written in England between 1940 and 1941, and published in 1942—the year of the greatest Indian opposition to British rule since the 1857 Sepoy Rebellion—*The Sword and the Sickle* acts as a premonitory warning of the shape of things to come. Soldiers like Lalu, Anand suggests, have been disillusioned once; they are likely to be far more combative on their return from the second global war. Or perhaps Lalu's story is intended to serve as a cautionary tale against the act of signing up to imperial war service in the first place, when the rewards of such service—the right to a plot of land, or to the land of India itself—do not materialise. Why, though, does Anand write about an Indian soldier's return from the First World War in the early years of the Second? I argue that he forms part of a network of writers in English for whom the Second World War, or least its beginnings, is primarily felt as *recurrence* in literature—and we shall see how this theme becomes significant in Chapter 5, in our discussion of the writings of M.J. Tambimuttu and Rabindranath Tagore.

What traction is there, then, in reading Mulk Raj Anand, Muriel Wasi and Tara Ali Baig as witnesses to the Indian home-front in connection with one another? All three writers reveal themselves to be staunch anti-fascists—a political position strongly espoused by India's elite, such as communist revolutionary M.N. Roy and Congress leader Jawaharlal Nehru.[9] None of the three, however, unquestioningly support India's undemocratic inclusion in the Second World War. *The Sword and the Sickle* maps the structures of power in north India that oppress farmers, tracing these to their imperial source, and charts the rise of communism in the country as an expressedly *anticolonial* political movement, albeit with its own tensions and uncertainties. The novel, as we shall see, becomes a product of Second World War discourse in England, and the contested space that India occupied in determining its own independence while fighting fascist powers under the British.

Anand's retrospective consideration of the Indian home-front in the post-First World War years emerges almost exclusively as a masculine space; the imagined solidarity that the novel invokes at the end is male brotherhood. Wasi and Baig, on the other hand, take on representations of the Second World War in more direct but equally gendered ways. For Wasi, India after an imperial war can only be imagined through feminised suffering, in a recognition of lived bodily experience and emotion, of despair and pain felt across the country. Baig, perhaps, is the most overt of the three writers: for her, the violence of war in India explicitly registers through famine. Wasi and Baig's craft in writing poetry is far more restrained and fragmented than Anand's novel, providing us with only glimpses into their emotional lives as witnesses to war. Yet there is a particular textual charge that emanates from this poetry, from its very lack of exposition, which enables the partial nature of its images to dominate. As readers, we become immersed in both poems' subjectivity, immediacy and 'rawness' as testaments to war.

Indian home-front emotions as global history: Mulk Raj Anand's
The Sword and the Sickle

The photograph with which this chapter starts highlights a train as its dominant backdrop, carrying Indian village recruits to the heart of a second global war; *The Sword and the Sickle* begins some twenty years previously, with Lalu, the returned recruit, on a train being borne back home from the first. As he converses with fellow passengers, Lalu hears for the first time about the shooting at Jallianwallah Bagh in Amritsar; he displays his war wound on his thigh to his audience, only to have them compare it to the bullet-riddled body of their friend's son at this massacre. Anand provides us with the first of many glimpses into Lalu's febrile inner world in the novel:

> The war was over and though it did not happen in India, it seemed, from the talk of these people, to have happened to India. And what was more, from all this unrest and shooting and what not, it hadn't quite finished yet [...] Something in his soul cried out with the dead, for the dead, as if he were the ghost of himself, left behind, unhoused and quite detached from everyone, an utter stranger. He did not know what lay in store for him. And he felt afraid again and shrank back into himself.[10] (11)

The language used here to establish connections between battle-front and home-front violence is fascinating. The Anglo-Irish novelist Elizabeth Bowen observes in her Second World War novel *The Heat of the Day* (1948): 'War's being global meant that it ran off the edges of maps; it was uncontainable.'[11] It is this 'uncontainable' and unfinished nature of war that Anand highlights, not simply by the fact of its spreading across the world but in its deep penetration into colonised lands and their civilian populations. Right at the beginning of the novel, Lalu gains an insight into an Indian homeland that has dramatically changed during the war years, just as he himself has been radically altered by his experiences on the Western Front. On his return home, then, he can only be 'the ghost of himself', 'unhoused', 'an utter stranger'. Santanu Das has observed that Anand's Lalu trilogy explores what it is to become modern, the novels functioning as a site where different kinds of modernity—technological, cultural and political—intersect.[12] The unspoken question lingering in *The Sword and the Sickle* is—if the First World War has radicalised Lalu, what will the Second World War do to Indian soldiers? The ghost of the first global war, in the person of Lalu, returns to haunt the second.

It was Anand's friend and fellow BBC employee, George Orwell, who suggested the title *The Sword and the Sickle* while walking across Primrose Hill together in London during a blackout.[13] The title, taken from William Blake's short poem, functions as the novel's epigraph: 'The sword sang on the barren heath, / The sickle in the fruitful field; / The sword he sung a song of death, / But could not make the sickle yield.' The image of the sword recurs in *Letters on India*, a series of fictitious epistolary exchanges, also published in 1942, where Anand explains India's contemporary political conflicts to an imaginary socialist friend in England. In *Letters*, Anand assesses the attitudes of empire apologists—'We took it [India] by the sword and by the sword we shall keep it'[14] (17). The sword, of course, indicates violence in the novel too—the exploitation and thuggery of Indian landlords and British imperialists in the post-First World War years, while the sickle serves as the emblem of a rising political, and particularly communist, consciousness. Yet the sword can also be read as a symbol for war: it is precisely because Lalu has known what it is to live by the sword that he understands the potential and power of the sickle. The two images bleed into one another in the novel.

When the clash of European empires led to global crisis in 1939, such experiences of crisis reverberated across other political conditions and subjugations, principally that of empire and independence movements. The early years of the Second World War and crisis present, then, gave impetus to Indian writers to stage creatively crises past.[15] For Anand, this is the First World War and its aftermath; for fellow Indian writers abroad, like Ahmed Ali, it is the fall of Delhi in 1857 to the British. Ali's English-language novel *Twilight in Delhi*, published in 1940 with the Hogarth Press in London, becomes a melancholy ode to the city of Delhi and the vanishing of an Islamicate way of life under the Mughals. Ali too notes Indian home-front experiences of the First World War and the outbreak of Spanish flu in his novel, but he is predominantly interested in representing irrevocable decline and loss. Anand's making retrospective sense of the emotions of the First World War works rather differently—his principal character Lalu witnesses terrible hardship and poverty, but this is Lalu's political awakening and call to action, even if that action often has no direct or even necessarily positive outcome. The two world wars are intimately connected in Anand's writing, then, not only as event but also as narrative impetus—it is because he was living through the Second that he found potential in creatively representing the First. As Beryl Pong eloquently puts it in her analysis of temporalities in British literature during the Second World War, 'time here holds more than one war'.[16]

Perhaps Anand's greatest achievement as a novelist writing the Lalu trilogy in English is to decentre—or 'provincialise', to use Dipesh Chakrabarty's term—European perspectives of the world wars.[17] As Daniel Morse notes, the First World War represented in these novels is configured as 'part of Indian experiences and history rather than as a temporary crisis confined to a European stage'.[18] Building on a growing scholarly interest in Anand's broadcasting life in England, Morse analyses Anand's career at the BBC's Eastern Service during the Second World War years as well as his creative writing from the time.[19] Soon after being imprisoned in India for taking part in the 1921 non-co-operation movement, Anand had set off for England to study philosophy at the University of London, and became involved with the elite Bloomsbury circle, although never quite belonging to it.[20] Morse highlights how, from 1942 onwards, Anand worked closely with a select group of intellectuals from Britain and its empire—George Orwell, T.S. Eliot, Una Marson, Venu Chitale, M.J. Tambimuttu, William Empson and Narayana Menon—to create programme content for elite, English-speaking audiences in India. In particular, Anand's contributions to the BBC literary radio magazine *Voice*, first broadcast in 1942—the same year as *The Sword and the Sickle* was published—demonstrates how he was able to represent 'lines of continuity between the wars' and express 'a new perception of worldwide connectedness'.[21] Anand's broadcast themes spilled over into his novelistic creations. In *The Sword and the Sickle*, the representations of Lalu's private frustrations provide inroads into larger socio-political events in India, revealing the messy, complicated and unfinished nature of imperial war.

It is significant, then, that Anand foregrounds how returning home becomes a highly charged physical experience for Lalu, where the latter's body seems to tune in to a particular political frequency—'His head throbbed with the heat and he was on edge, as if he had suddenly become the vehicle for the most powerful impulses, as if the touch of the home air, the touch of the land, had electrified the lumbering, weary war-prisoner into a desperate seditionist' (59). This is not quite Salman Rushdie's Saleem Sinai in the fêted postcolonial Indian novel in English, *Midnight's Children* (1981), where Saleem acts as radio receiver for all children born on the stroke of Indian independence. Nonetheless, Anand's Lal Singh is 'handcuffed to history' too through his war service, and becomes an earlier prototype of Saleem—a character shot through with the conflicting political perspectives of anticolonial India.

Why did Anand think of reframing this Indian war history as universally important and relevant? In her insightful study of Anand's non-fiction writing, Sushiela Nasta argues that it was in the anti-imperial atmosphere of 1930s and 1940s London where Anand 'began to articulate an evolving but highly prescient global alternative to a predominant Euro-American vision of modernity, carving out a space to locate himself as well as his Indian subjects in history'.[22] During this time, Anand became a high-profile and influential advocate for this global view of history, one in which Britain's own past and that of its colonies could be understood and studied together. Elected President of the Progressive Writers' Association in 1935 at an inaugural meeting—attended by thirty-five Indians from Cambridge, Oxford and London universities in a back room of the Nanking Chinese Restaurant in Bloomsbury—Anand also co-wrote its manifesto.[23] This declared a new vision both for India and creative writing:

> We believe that the new literature of India must deal with the basic problems of our existence to-day—the problems of hunger and poverty, social backwardness, and political subjection. All that drags

us down to passivity, inaction and un-reason we reject as reaction-
ary. All that arouses in us the critical spirit, which examines institutions and customs in the light of reason, which helps us to act, to
organise ourselves, to transform, we accept as progressive.[24]

At the same time, underpinning this call to act, organise and
transform is Anand's clear-eyed understanding of India's critical
need to secure complete independence from British rule. This is a
theme he also took up in 1942 in *Letters on India*.[25] This collection of
letters makes a powerful case for India's freedom, pushing against
barriers in the minds of even anticolonial metropolitan British intellectuals who did not believe that the subcontinent was ready for
independence.[26] Continuing his polemic efforts in 1943, and making
an unusual choice of literary form, Anand wrote a play on the Bengal
Famine, which he rightly recognised as a manmade product of the
Second World War, and called it *India Speaks: Map of India*. This play
was first performed at the Unity Theatre in London in the same
year. Here too, metropole and colony are stylistically connected—
scenes set in India and England are enacted on stage at the same
time, the action crosscutting between them to convey a sense of
simultaneity.[27] It was this charged intellectual and activist milieu in
which *The Sword and the Sickle* was written and published.

Colonial authorities banned Anand's novels in India up until
1947, but *The Sword and the Sickle* was generally well received in
England when it was first published in 1942. I draw attention here
to the debates the novel generated in the 1940s because these firmly
situate the work within the tensions of Second World War discourse in England. Most of the reviews, though positive, omitted
discussing the role of imperialism in creating the Indian peasant
crisis that forms the novel's core. Perhaps this was a form of self-
censoring practice amongst reviewers, who remained conscious of
undermining the British war effort.[28] The only negative review came
in May 1942 from Ranjee Shahani in the *Times Literary Supplement*, in
which Shahani explicitly and disparagingly drew attention to the
anticolonial thrust of the book: 'What is really disagreeable, however, is the spirit of the novel; it tends to create bad blood between
Indians and British, which is a bad thing at any time and a dangerous
one at this hour.'[29] It was a question, then, of Anand's timing: dra-

matising the hardships of post-war Indian life in the 1920s is seen here as provocative and unnecessary during the international fight against fascism.

An affronted Orwell wrote a rejoinder to this review in *Horizon* in the same year: 'Mr Anand does not like us very much, and some of his colleagues hate us very bitterly; but so long as they voice their hatred in English they are in a species of alliance with us, and an ultimate decent settlement with the Indians whom we have wronged but also helped to awaken remains possible.'[30] Orwell's sentiments here are certainly paternalistic; nonetheless, he recognises the complexity of Anand's political position in England as both an antifascist and an anti-imperialist. As Anand himself would say, rather more directly, in *Letters*, 'Fascism is the twin brother of imperialism' (145), and it was not possible to oppose one without the other.

Significantly, Orwell's quote also highlights how novels such as *The Sword and the Sickle* were published, read and discussed within the imperial centre itself, lending writers like Anand a certain cosmopolitan status. This is viewed by Orwell as the product of linguistic choice—writing in English enables 'a species of alliance' with England and its readership, a perspective that synchronises with the BBC Eastern Service's own mission, in which both men were involved.[31] The novel, then, on its publication in England in the 1940s, led to discussion and debate but also contestation.

The Sword and the Sickle tells the story of a fraught, and ultimately doomed, peasant uprising in the state of Oudh in northern India, in which Lal Singh, the returned Indian soldier, plays a crucial role. It fictionalises an account found in Jawaharlal Nehru's *Autobiography* (1936) of a *kisan sabha* or farmers' union movement.[32] In his autobiography, Nehru highlights how the farmers and the Indian Congress Party started to work together, along with the ways by which the party influenced the farmers' union. Anand's own nonfictional account of this farmers' movement was published as *Letters on India* (1942), as mentioned previously, but it is the novel that intimately connects imperial war service to political agitation for land rights. The action of the book shifts from Punjab to Oudh in the United Provinces when Lalu is denied land by colonial authorities on account of his being exposed to seditious influences while taken PoW in Germany. Lalu joins the *kisan sabha* movement led by a renegade *zamindar* or landlord, Kanwar Rampal Singh, who has become a peasant leader, albeit a rather eccentric one.

The situation transforms into a crisis when the peasant Sukhua is evicted from his land while another peasant, Chandra, dies while undertaking *begar*, or forced unpaid labour. Lalu learns how to rouse his audience with speeches at political rallies and attempts to involve Gandhi and Nehru in championing peasant rights, with only partial success. He witnesses the founding of the *kisan sabha* and its victories—for instance, a court case levied against other peasants and himself is dismissed, to the accompaniment of a riotous demonstration. But this victory is transient: the leader Kanwar Rampal Singh and others are given orders to evict and then arrested for disobeying this injunction. The peasants, buoyed by their initial success, follow Rampal Singh to the northern city of Rae Bareili, where he is being held captive, as a sign of their support, but in a recreation of the horrors of Jallianwallah Bagh, are shot and killed by the colonial army. The novel ends, much like *Across the Black Waters* does, with Lalu taken to prison.

The Sword and the Sickle does not always make for easy reading. Scholars have thought the novel to be burdened by Anand's 'unflagging love of detail';[33] characters ventriloquise political positions in lengthy speeches; Maya, Lalu's love interest, makes brief appearances but mysteriously vanishes from the novel at other times, as though both protagonist and author have forgotten about her. The book has not received the attention of Anand's more famous works—*Untouchable* (1935), *Coolie* (1936) and, with the recent centenary of the First World War commemorated between 2014 to 2018, *Across the Black Waters* (1939). Yet I argue that the novel deserves our consideration in understanding how the politics of the Indian interwar years are retrospectively represented during the Second World War. In that sense, it is one of the most significant literary responses to Indian involvement in both world wars, locating the peasant-soldier from Punjab within the particularities of his social, political and cultural context, and linking the disillusionment with war service to a coalition of anticolonial and anti-class movements that hold promise for the future of an independent India.

Curiously enough, for a stridently anti-imperialist novel, the imperialists themselves are hardly to be seen. We encounter the 'old-school' officer Colonel Peacock interrogating Lalu on his return, offering him a pension but no land, and the hapless magistrate Mr Buckle, who is forced to withdraw the peasants' arrest warrant in court. Other than these, the novel does not concern itself with English characters. This is deliberate on Anand's part, of course, but to what end? In *Letters*, Anand tells us that the Sarkar or government serves as 'the ultimate landlord' (64), and in the novel he explicates further:

> And then had come the Angrezi Sarkar, like an invisible shadow, as one-eyed Sukhua had said, spreading over this anonymous countryside, where men and women and children and cattle had grown and died, nameless, like plants. And this Sarkar had built roads and begun to push the peasants out on them by rolling up their land, the land which had belonged to them for generations, and donating it to whoever the Ferungis liked. (188)

Anand's linguistic choices are pointed. If the countryside is 'anonymous', it resists private ownership and belongs to everyone; if the farming community and its animals are plant-like and 'nameless', they exist in a blend with the natural world, one indistinguishable from the other. In place of characters, imperial presence in the novel, instead, is apprehended as an 'invisible shadow', encroaching upon the peasants' lives and livelihoods until they have nothing left. We 'gaze at it,' Lalu introspects, 'as one gazes at a god' (188). Earlier in the novel, Lalu's uncle, the farmer-turned-revolutionary Harnam Singh bemoans in a similar vein, 'Oh, Hindustan! Hindustan! [...] This country is like a lean bullock that has been reduced to the bone by the Angrezi lion, son' (64). This comparison, highlighting the predator's appetitive urges, sharply evokes imperialism's rapacity, much like the metaphor of the crocodile in Bibhutibhushan's Bengali novel *Ashani Sanket*, discussed in Chapter 2. The image of the Angrezi or English lion is a nod, perhaps, to First World War recruitment posters depicting the colonial metropole as a lion, calling upon its imperial subjects to enlist. Again, warfront and home-front are revealed to be intimately connected, this time through both simile and iconography.

It is not, however, the interests of Indian nationalist leaders that the novel highlights either. *The Sword and the Sickle* forges new and radical ground in being able to create a separate space for grass-roots peasant concerns, distinct from national politics. As Angela Eyre notes, although the peasants are shown to need the intervention of political leaders to begin their rebellion, they also debate the ideas introduced by these leaders in a linguistically fluid and idiomatic medium facilitated by the novel.[34] Sometimes such discussions border on the humorous. When a political rally is organised in the village of Bansi to celebrate the anniversary of the Russian Revolution, Kanwar Rampal Singh is summoned to the train station to manage his men. The peasants have been protesting: they refuse to pay their train fare to travel from the town of Nanakpur to Bansi, much to the consternation of the station-master. 'Go, go, the old days of Sarkari Raj have gone, now it is peasant Raj, exactly as it is in Roos,' scoffs Mithu, a peasant ringleader (319). A little later, Madhu, another peasant, reflects thoughtfully, 'We must stone the eagles who sit on the lands' (324). These turns of phrase, like 'peasant Raj' and the upheavals in 'Roos', or the violent metaphor of stoning eagles, indicate how Anand brings revolution into the peasants' linguistic domain as this embryonic movement is shown to find its way.

Language, in fact, becomes an extraordinary tool in Anand's hands, evoking for us the tangible material and sensuous realities of the peasants' world. Anna Snaith has discussed how much Anand's novel *Untouchable*, highlighting a day in the life of Bakha, a young sweeper who cleans latrines, is bound up with faecal matter. Its purpose, she argues, is to 'inscribe and make visible the unknown, excremental abjection of the colonial margin in the aesthetic heart of the centre'.[35] The same desire permeates *The Sword and the Sickle*. Consider this section, in which Lalu discovers that a protest march he had organised on behalf of the peasants from Oudh to Allahabad is resulting in a gruesome and bloody end:

> Conscious of his responsibility for the misadventures into which he had led them, Lalu bent down and strained to lever the dead bodies with trembling hands. A sharp odour of decomposing flesh shot up to his nostrils from Chandra's body while his hands were smeared with blood from Nandu's neck. He sat up imagining the smell to be a whiff of the foul virulence of bacterial decay, ensuing from the

vegetation of the forest through which they had come. But, as he bent down again, there was no disguising the stink of the corpse. And, in a flash he realised that though Nandu's blood was hot now, it would soon be cold and the body would stink if it was carried all the way to Allahabad. (181–182)

The entire scene is an assault upon our senses. Dead peasant bodies decay; their acridity is speedy; Lalu's hands are 'smeared in blood' from Nandu, who has just been shot by Sheikh Hadayat Ullah, an agent of the scheming landlord, the Nawab of Nasirabad. The smell of death too is like gunfire, which assaults Lalu's nose with the same fatal certainty. Bacterial decay from the forest, like its human counterpart, also reeks, creating a pervasive odour of stagnation and rot. The planned protest march to Allahabad, where both bodies would have been borne aloft as symbols of injustice, cannot continue anymore. At every turn in the novel, the peasants come up against the brutality of landlords intertwined with the imperial state, and Anand's use of language foregrounds how visceral this experience is. And, as Eyre observes, the novel form itself enables discussions about the peasants deploying violence as a way of achieving their aims, modelling themselves on the Russian Revolution rather than Gandhian non-violence.[36] Indeed, Lalu's brief physical meeting with Gandhi in the novel is represented as far from fulfilling.

And yet, despite their partial success in political organisation, the novel ends in tragedy for the peasants. One of the final scenes depicts them running in hope across the river in Rae Bareili towards Lal Singh but being gunned down by soldiers of the Indian Army— the same army that Lalu was once part of. Lalu is both ashamed and troubled by this encounter, seeing the soldiers solely as powerful imperial agents: 'curiously, he who had once been a soldier and known how inept and awkward and human soldiers were, now felt dwarfed and frightened of this detachment' (373). In Letters, Anand highlights how the peasant movement had been successful, spreading across India from its origins in Oudh; the novel, however, showcases a far more conflicted and ambivalent picture, drawing attention to the movement's failure but also to a new resolution forming within Lalu.

Rather than a plan for a specific political programme, Lalu's vision of the future while he is in prison at the end of the novel is diffuse. 'Now is the time to change the world, to fight for Life and happiness,' he thinks (385). Kristin Bluemel believes that none of Anand's oppressed protagonists can 'envision a less oppressive, post-imperial future for himself or India', and to an extent that is a valid reading of The Sword and The Sickle.[37] It seems to me, however, that Lalu does not 'win' at the end because the novel resists coming to a neat conclusion about the various ideological strands it represents through different characters. Lalu remains confused about which path of action to pursue.[38] The idea of revolution, however, still remains significant. This is less a specific form of communist organisation, as advocated by the political leader Comrade Sarshar in the novel. Instead, to Lalu, revolution is shown to become a mode of feeling: 'a need of togetherness, Comrade, the need to curb malice among men, the need for men to stand together as brothers' (367). It is only by imagining this internationalist male solidarity and fraternal affection, cutting across class and caste divides, that Lalu can see from his prison 'the new dawn filtering through the doorways with that uncanny milk-white radiance which heralds the coming of a strong sun' (386). And this 'new dawn' brings to his mind thoughts of his wife Maya and their newborn son at home. Like the embryonic revolution, Lalu's son too is 'alive and kicking!' (386).

Before I conclude this section on how Anand represents Indian home-front emotions as interconnected global history, it is important to note that Lalu's political growth and radicalisation in The Sword and the Sickle takes place in an almost exclusively male world. Lalu's friends, fellow revolutionaries, political leaders and mentors, landlords and oppressors, and the peasants themselves are all men. The novel creates no space for charting a female political bildungsroman or even acknowledging women's involvement in the insurgent politics of the time. The only exception to the lack of women in the novel is Lalu's beloved Maya, the daughter of a landlord in Punjab, with whom he elopes to Oudh and later marries. But, after his elopement, Maya is often, guiltily, forgotten by both Lalu and Anand. While her sexuality is foregrounded, as is her promiscuity, Maya is represented as petulant and lacking interest in politics. Even when, later in the novel, she appears to support Lalu's cause, Lalu himself remains unconvinced by this. Lalu's affectionate nickname for Maya is 'childling', and she remains infantilised throughout the novel, a foil for the male protagonist's struggle and development.[39] There seems to be no critique here of north Indian patriarchal structures within which Lalu and Maya's relationship operates: this profoundly anticolonial novel, then, does not transform into a feminist one.

From the revolutionary masculine world of Punjab and Oudh in north India, I move on to a different emotional perspective—that of Indian women's responses to the Second World War. Here, I explore how women engage with the poetic and intellectual discourse on the war. Does war sharpen gendered experiences, establishing differences between home-front and battlefront, or does it blur such boundaries, providing women with greater opportunities in the public sphere and an enhanced sense of civilian responsibility? I also consider how writing by women reconfigures ideas of colonisation and nationhood as well as trauma and suffering endured in the home-front during the war.

'A woman plunged in misery': Acts of witnessing in Muriel Wasi and Tara Ali Baig's poetry

In the previous section, we read how Anand's novel *The Sword and the Sickle* traced the disillusioned imperial soldier Lalu's journey towards anger, radicalisation and the birth of an embryonic political movement in India. Although Anand is writing in the 1940s, the novel's context remains 1920s India. What historical, literary and emotional shifts occur when we consider, instead, writing from the 1940s about the Second World War, and by women? I will consider in this section two rare poems in English by Indian women writers, which were published just after the war in 1945, and form a small but significant body of work. The first is by educationist and teacher Muriel Wasi (1912–1995), who was Junior Commander at the Public Relations Directorate in the WAC (I) in the 1940s, and the second by reformist and child welfare expert Tara Ali Baig (1916–1989), who volunteered with the Bombay Women's Service during the war.[40] Wasi and Baig's poetry offer us a deeper, more pronounced inflection of the anger and injustice represented in Anand's text. The 1920s are seen in the novel as a time of oppression, violence and rebellion. By the 1940s, writing about the second global war has transformed into bearing witness not only to deprivation and misery but also atrocity in India. Unlike Anand, Wasi and Baig do not offer us specific ideological positions in their writing or trace the evolution of a particular type of politics. Nonetheless, their poems remain highly politically charged. In both cases, India is feminised, embodied as a starving and suffering woman—one with whom Wasi identifies and whose abjection Baig helplessly, and traumatically, records.

Indian women's emotional responses to the Second World War—an important and neglected field of scholarship—have proved, unsurprisingly, harder to recover than that of men.[41] This is because colonial war involvement studied from the Indian perspective has only recently been opened up to scholarly discussion, and within this the predominant focus continues to be on battlefront narratives, although shifts towards a more nuanced gendered analysis are forthcoming.[42] I have sought to remain alert to Indian women's responses in the Second World War throughout my book. In the Introduction, I highlighted female perspectives by examining the extraordinary all-women Rani of Jhansi regiment formed under the aegis of Subhas Chandra Bose's INA in Singapore and Burma. Sections of Chapters 1 and 2 have discussed extracts from letters—some by women—from Indian cities and villages as they wrote to men stationed at international battlefronts.

Several of these letters transform into complex repositories of feeling. Let us consider this extract by an Indian woman in Nabha, near Punjab, writing to her husband in Urdu in 1943:

> My dear husband, you should do your work sincerely and faithfully. Try to defeat the enemy and show your bravery in the battlefield. Do not blame me and your mother. Come soon with the crown of success. My husband, I request you to serve the Government with your whole heart and never be disappointed.[43]

As noted in Chapter 1, this exhortation to a soldier by his wife to continue carrying out his duties abroad intersects with the objectives of colonial structures of power, which lay claim to his war service for as long as required. In that sense, this is a conservative epistle, seeking to keep the imperial soldier in his place. But other emotions jostle against one other here. Why does the soldier's wife anticipate that her husband might be 'disappointed' with the 'Government'? Did his previous letter express some disquiet, even though it passed under the censor's gaze? Many letters in the archive, as I have observed before, highlight how much Indian soldiers desired leave and how little this was allotted to them. Was this soldier longing for leave too and desiring to come home, and is this his wife telling him not to return just yet? Perhaps even more fascinating, then, is the soldier's wife's instruction—'Do not blame me and your mother.' The letter, of course, was translated from the original Urdu into English, so that the colonial censor could assess its contents, and the language that reaches us, therefore, is mediated. Nonetheless, the evocation of 'blame' on the part of the womenfolk of the family is curious. Is the soldier's wife suggesting that men serve on the battlefront simply for the benefit of women on the home-front, and that this makes the former resentful? Or is she instead hinting that the soldier might think he needs to return home for the sake of his wife and mother, and that he should not disgrace himself by taking such a course of action? The only way the soldier can come home, it seems, is 'with the crown of success': imperial military service is conflated here with notions of upholding masculine valour and familial honour.

If this Indian wife from Nabha reveals to us the key role played by women in generating intricate emotional networks between battlefront and home-front through life-writing, how can we assess Indian women's creative responses to conflict by studying the poetry of Wasi and Baig? The exceptional nature of Wasi and Baig's English poems is acknowledged in the Preface to the anthology in which the poems appear, *Poems from India by Members of the Forces* (1945), selected and edited by former British soldiers in India R.N. Currey and R.V. Gibson, and published in December 1945. Its Preface states:

> In a book which aims at increasing understanding between British and Indian, we are glad to be able to include examples of work by Indian writers, two of whom are women. These writers can speak from 'inside' where we can only record visitors' impressions [...] We should have liked more poems from Indians and more from women.[44]

OPPORTUNITIES FOR

YOU

**EXCELLENT OPPORTUNITIES
EXIST FOR YOUNG MEN TO
SECURE EMPLOYMENT**

IN

THE ROYAL INDIAN NAVY
THE INDIAN ARMY
AND
THE INDIAN AIR FORCE

VACANCIES

PILOTS	STOKERS
WIRELESS OPERATORS	AIRFORCE MECHANICS
SIGNALLERS	MOTOR MECHANICS
MOTOR DRIVERS	MACHINEMEN
ENGINE DRIVERS	FITTERS
ENGINE DRIVERS (MARINE)	MOULDERS
MOTOR BOAT DRIVERS	TURNERS
MOTOR DRIVER INSTRUCTORS	ELECTRICIANS
SEAMEN	CLERKS (COMBATANTS) MATRICULATES
SEPOYS	CLERKS (NON-COMBATANTS) MATRICULATES
FIREMEN	BAKERS

AND OTHER TRADESMEN

FOR PARTICULARS APPLY TO THE NEAREST RECRUITING OFFICE

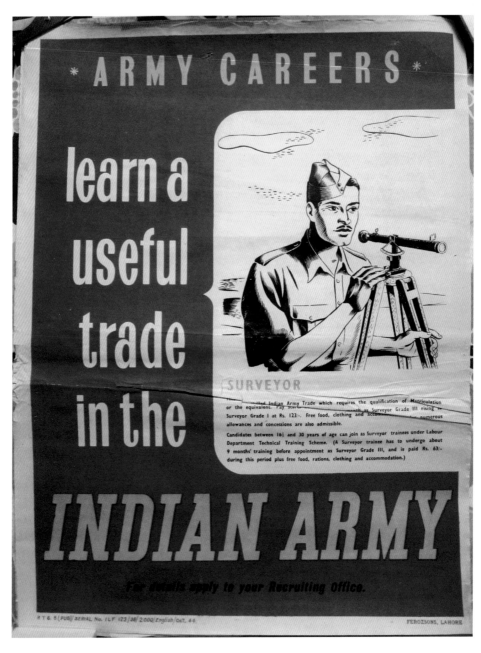

Figs 1a and 1b: Colonial propaganda advertised the war as a training opportunity to learn crucial skills and become employable in a post-war, newly industrialised India, c 1940s. See Introduction, p. 16. (Images courtesy of Jyotirmoy Bareria)

Figs 2a, b and c: Three Japanese propaganda pamphlets targeted at Indian people, with English translations by the author. These were likely air-dropped on the Indo-Burma border between 1943 and 1944.

a: 'O sleeping elephant! Arise! Take this opportunity to break the chains that the English have imposed upon you, and become free!' (© IWM, LBY K. Aerial 3 / 3896)

b: 'A group of defeated nations whose destruction is inevitable is eyeing India's natural wealth and riches. Do not be taken in by their beguiling and sweet words!' Words written on the flag: 'We accept your self-rule'. (© IWM, LBY K. 82/1516-2)

c: 'This is not the time to fight amongst yourselves. Become united and fight together for your freedom! Creating division is the hallmark of English rule.' Script on the men's back and thigh: 'Muslim League' and 'Indian National Congress'. (© IWM, LBY K. 82/1516-2)

ON WAR WORK IN BRITAIN: No. 3

**INDIANS
IN CIVIL
DEFENCE**

FOR VICTORY

Mr. Dorai Ross, one-time merchant and rubber-planter in the Straits Settlements, was in London when war broke out. Immediately he set about forming an Ambulance Service composed of Indians living in London. One hundred Indians of various religions and castes, and of different callings, including doctors and barristers, joined the unit. During the London Blitz, Auxiliary Ambulance Station 50, Indian Section, proved itself to be one of the most efficient units in Great Britain. Above are two Indian ladies of this unit, dressed for immediate action.

G.P.D. 365/13/21/1

Fig. 3: Two Indian women from the Auxiliary Ambulance Station 50, Indian Section, during the London Blitz, 1940s. (© IWM, Art.IWM PST 16288)

Fig. 4: 'A Hindoo Kitchen': Edward Bawden's painting of the Royal Indian Army Service Corps in Zghorta, in modern-day Lebanon, 1940s. (© IWM, Art.IWM ART LD 2220)

Fig. 5: Anthony Gross's painting of Indian casualties at a field hospital in Egypt in 1942. (© IWM, Art.IWM ART LD 2722)

Baig and Wasi's poems are thus selected for the anthology at the end of the war as part of an inclusive idea of representing male and female responses to war, shifting focus from combat to conflict, and incorporating both battlefront and home-front perspectives as well as Indian and English voices. Currey and Gibson acknowledge in the Preface that the days of empire are numbered in India by the end of the war: British soldiers are simply 'visitors', passing through. This context lends the two Indian women's poems urgency and greater meaning. Contrasted, then, against British soldier-poets' responses to India as international frontline and site of foreignness, the women are seen as conceiving of India as home, and there is a desire for further such insight from the editors: 'We should have liked more poems from Indians and more from women.' The Preface alerts us to the workings of war memory at the immediate end of the war by highlighting how such comparative and diverse perspectives in terms of race and gender were considered significant in 1945.[45]

In the poem 'To India' (56), Muriel Wasi provides us with a non-combatant and civilian war volunteer's response to violence, physical hardship and famine in undivided India. Muriel Wasi—formerly de Costa—joined the WAC (I) as a privileged Indian woman from a Roman Catholic background in Goa. Her parents were both doctors, but from an early age she demonstrated an interest in literature, which they fostered. Wasi recalls the cosmopolitanism of dining-table conversations at home, which centred on Gandhi and the 1919 Jallianwallah Bagh massacre, but also on Darwin, Pasteur and Italian music.[46] After studying at Madras University, Wasi read philosophy at the University of Oxford from 1937 to 1940.[47] She provides an idealised recollection of these early years in her memoir *The Narrow Corridor* (published posthumously in 2005), written in her seventies, and credits the Oxford experience with forging the foundations of her career as a journalist, educationist and university teacher. Back in India, from the 1940s onwards she worked at the Ministry of Education and as a teacher at St. Stephen's College, followed by Jesus and Mary College, both leading Delhi educational institutions.[48] Unsurprisingly, then, the corpus of her own writing mostly comprises prose works focusing on the educational and the instructive.[49]

The poem 'To India' is, unusually, a creative response to war from Wasi, which employs fascinating emotional structures. Composed on the cusp of historical change, it foregrounds complex interplays between ideas of orientalism, nationalism and the end of empire without directly referencing the war. Wasi writes:

> I do not claim thee as mine own
> When loud the stranger world applauds thy mystery;
> The lure intangible, the hidden power
> That draw men to thee in the frighted hour
> Of fading life. For these I love thee not.
> Alas! I know thee not.
>
> But when the stranger looks aghast at thee,
> At filth and hunger, crying poverty,
> When stunned with sight of endless sluggishness
> He turns away in civilised dismay –
> Ah then! I know thee as thou art –
> A woman plunged in misery: an anguished heart,
> An aching body rent today with cry
> Of starving hollowness.
> Then to retreating worlds let me proclaim
> That I am thine and that I bear thy name. (56)

A plangent lyric, the poem is steeped in late Victorian language, the archaic use of 'thee' forming one such instance. Wasi here rejects essentialised ideas of a 'spiritual', mystical India that the 'stranger world' conceives of. Perhaps she is thinking here of the context of her poem's publication in a volume dominated by British male writers and read by a mainly British audience. She, however, self-consciously takes on the task of representing the 'real' India—'I know thee as thou art'—and draws upon a familiar literary trope of imagining the Indian nation as mother, spearheaded as early as the nineteenth century by Bengali writer Bankimchandra Chattopadhyay in the song 'Vande Mataram' in his 1881 novel *Anandamath*.[50] Wasi's nationalist image represents this 'Mother India' as abject, 'plunged in misery' with 'an anguished heart'. She also locates embodied suffering within this gendered maternal figure, whose 'aching body [is] rent today with cry / Of starving hollowness'.

Reading the poem alongside Wasi's memoir, which is a highly reflective and introspective piece of writing, is illuminating because it reveals how Wasi negotiates her own relationship to the Second World War as a non-combatant Indian woman. Bearing witness is part of this negotiation. The memoir's title—*The Narrow Corridor*— is striking. Wasi explains in fuller detail the significance of this title towards the end of the memoir:

> For years now I have seen my life less in time or achievement than in special moments of being within a narrow corridor of a crowded moving train. The populated space contains people of all kinds, who frequently interrupt the growth of what I conceive to be the essential spiritual identity of a private man or woman [...] For it seems to me that it is only by a constant retreat into one's narrow corridor that one achieves an understanding of what life is about.[51]

The language used here—from the phrase 'moments of being' to the image of being held within the corridor of a moving train— bears a remarkable resemblance to that of Virginia Woolf's autobiographical writing and the influence of British modernist thought on Wasi.[52] The metaphor of the narrow corridor carves out Wasi's need for the philosophical and ethical responses to the vicissitudes of life in times of war. In particular, the years when Hitler came to power—the 'Hitler years', as she terms it in the memoir—become of crucial importance here. Wasi was at Oxford then and remembers clearly how 'the persecuted intellectual fled from Nazi-occupied Europe [and] tended to come Oxford-wards'. To her, Oxford becomes the symbol of 'courage' and 'an independence of mind' in 'those deeply troubled times'.[53] This youthful witnessing of acts of political and academic sanctuary changes the nature of the war for Wasi. She becomes staunchly anti-fascist, believing that 'Indian independence was imperative, but Hitler was clearly the worse of two enemies.' On her return to India after 1940, however, 'Hitler's war' is no longer enacted for her on a global political scale but becomes a moment of individual transformation. This is because the war gives her the 'opportunity to see and know India'. Her extensive travels across India up until 1947 result in her 'claim[ing] to have seen most of the subcontinent and to have a pretty clear picture of India's countryside, her cities and people, their historied [*sic*] past and their problematic future [...] This made the political life of the forties intelligible to me.'[54]

Although Wasi does not mention being part of the WAC (I) and her role as a non-combatant at the Indian home-front in the memoir, the psychological effects of war service are discernible in the poem. Like Mulk Raj Anand, although she abhorred fascism and ideologically supported the Allied cause during the war, Wasi's travels across India also revealed to her the deep-rooted violence of colonialism. She describes how she joined the Military Public Liaison Unit in Assam in north-east India during the war, journeying her way through Calcutta, where she witnessed utter abjection in 'the grotesque horrors of a famine'.[55] To me, this is why the real 'Mother India' in the poem is a woman to Wasi, one who feels empty and agonised—'an aching body rent today with cry / Of starving hollowness'. Her witnessing of others' pain merges with ideas of imminent independence and nationhood to inform Wasi's personal identity at the end of the poem: 'I am thine and [...] I bear thy name,' she says of India. This 'Indianness' is affirmed and enacted within the poem before an external, presumably Western audience, an identity that she uses as a counterpoint to 'the stranger [who] looks aghast at thee'.

Ideas of belonging and separation, underpinned by contrasting representations of India as homeland and site of foreignness become gendered in Wasi's poem. The 'stranger' who 'turns away in civilised dismay' at the end of empire from India is male; the 'remainer' poet who identifies herself with 'Mother India' is female. At one level, this gendered binary plays into stereotypes of East and West, action and inaction, civilisation and destitution. But here the familiar literary trope of the Indian nation conceptualised as the suffering body of a woman, I argue, powerfully brings together the experiences of colonialism, war and famine in ways more immediate and visceral. After all, the vast majority of famine victims in Bengal were rural women, some of the most vulnerable members of a highly stratified colonised society.[56] The poem also interrogates the purpose of Western male 'civilised' action when its only response to intense suffering is to turn away. The British wartime writer Wrenne Jarman establishes a similar, if reductive, distinction between male action and thought versus female felt experience and loss in her poem 'Letter to Claudia' (1948) when she says: 'Of what use glory, since it cannot heal? / Men are but dreamers: only we are real.'[57] Wasi might have said the same.

There are fascinating points of emotional intersection and difference between Wasi's poem 'To India' and activist, feminist and politician Sarojini Naidu's poem 'The Gift of India' (1915), composed during the First World War. The two poems share the mannered vocabulary and imagery of the late Victorian lyric, but channel their use for very different purposes during distinct historical moments. Naidu, speaking of Indian soldiers dying in the First World War, imagines herself fused into the gendered image of the anguished mother, and theatrically declares:

> Lo! I have flung to the East and the West
> Priceless treasures torn from my breast,
> And yielded the sons of my stricken womb
> To the drum-beats of the duty, the sabres of doom.[58]

The poem, while inhabiting the perspective of yet another representation of the 'Mother India' literary trope, sees war only in terms of battlefront experience, as does the Indian soldier's wife writing to her husband from Nabha—to use James Campbell's words, as 'combat gnosticism'.[59] It is male bodies that are mutilated here, the horror of which is defused through romantic simile and symbolism:

> Scattered like shells on Egyptian sands,
> They lie with pale brows and brave, broken hands,
> They are strewn like blossoms mown down by chance
> On the blood-brown meadows of Flanders and France.[60]

This is a decimation that Naidu strategically connects to the Indian nationalist project: India's 'gift' of death to empire that must be recompensed.[61] Like the ghost of Hamlet's father, in the last line of her poem, she provides an exhortation to colonial powers that borders on the threatening: 'And you honour the deeds of the deathless ones / Remember the blood of thy martyred sons!!'[62] Indian men dying in the First World War function as political leverage here: through her linguistic identification with the mother figure whose sons go to battle, Naidu implicates herself in war ideology, even though this is ultimately to serve nationalist ends.

To Wasi, on the other hand, empathic observation remains paramount: she sees the figure of Mother India reflected in the wreckage of the feminised body on the home-front. In fact, the only way she chooses to highlight her identification with this 'Mother India' figure is by evoking a powerful sense of belonging: 'I am thine and [...] I bear thy name.' These two distinct poetic representations of female mourning foreground dramatic changes between the two world wars and Indian political developments towards independence. Early into the First World War, Naidu both implores and seeks to coerce the British Empire to recognise the war contribution of the 'sons' of her 'stricken womb'; writing thirty years later, Wasi's poem is much less strategic and instrumental. At the end of the Second World War, it was evident that Indian independence was imminent. Wasi is therefore critical, but stoical, about the 'civilised' male gaze from 'retreating worlds' who can only 'look aghast' at India. It is enough that she herself understands, identifies and remains.

Tara Ali Baig's poem 'Bengal Famine, 1943', as its title foregrounds, engages with the emotional realities of famine in the Indian home-front in more direct ways than Wasi's. Again, as in Wasi's case, the poem is an unusual creative endeavour from Baig: her writing consists mainly of non-fictional prose works, the most well-known of which are a biography of Sarojini Naidu, whose First World War poetry we have just discussed, and tales for children.[63] Baig's poem is divided into two sections—the first focusing on famine as witnessed by passers-by and illicit grain hoarders, and the second composed from the perspective of the famine sufferers themselves. Contrasted to Wasi's Victorianism, Baig is much more of a modernist, using fragments of language that draw our attention to images evoking suffering and death, the directness of her voice reminiscent of Kamala Das's English poetry. The first section begins:

> Cities paved with bones
> And dying hands...
> Pass them by.
> Leave them in their rags.
>
> Who is the microscopic I
> Who can defy such death
> Such desolation?

See her with cracking breasts,
Ancient face mirrored in ancient eyes beneath:
Mouthing at the air;
The empty air.
See death with her tired stare...
Death everywhere.

Who am I?
The microscopic I,
In all this desolation and despair? (48)

We find here an Indian urban landscape transforming itself into a graveyard, where gestures of supplication ('dying hands') are only met with indifference ('Pass them by. Leave them in their rags.'). The short, sharp line breaks reflect the fragmentation of the body into bones, hands, 'cracking breasts', 'ancient eyes'. Like the letters written during the Bengal Famine discussed in Chapter 2 reveal, the body is no longer an individual human form here, but an amalgamation of disjointed parts. Even the spectator in the poem can only view the body in pain in its broken pieces. There is, unusually, a repeated questioning of the spectator's selfhood in the poem ('Who am I?') and an emphasis on its terrible diminution ('the microscopic I'). In Baig's poem, it is subjectivity itself that seems to have shrunk, throttled under the pressures of bearing witness to famine. This intense circumscribing of individual emotion in a lyric, which conventionally enables the expression of personal, meditative and reflective feeling, highlights Baig's modernist experimentation with literary form.

The use of the present tense in these stanzas gestures to a classic representation of war trauma, which we find most famously depicted in a male First World War poet's battlefront experience—Owen's 'Dulce Et Decorum Est' with its lines: 'In all my dreams before my helpless sight, / He plunges at me, guttering, choking, drowning'.[64] Baig brings this representation of war trauma to the Indian home-front, to the violence of famine. The present tense in both Owen and Baig signifies a continuous replay of the same action: both poets are locked in a moment of horror in time from which there is no release. Baig's injunction to the reader to look upon the famine victim—'See her with cracking breasts'[65]—is both a re-enactment of trauma and an admonition: the very worst thing we could do is not even to look, not even bear witness. As we observe the suffering, there is a sense of time and motion slowing down. Death as embodied in this desiccated woman has 'her tired stare', while the action of 'mouthing at the air' reflects a slowness of movement, suggesting also that sound has somehow been shut out, so that, despite trying to speak, the woman cannot be heard. The witness, the 'microscopic I', is hapless against such a torrent of suffering.

Yet, as Shoshana Felman observes while analysing Camus' *The Plague* (1947) and its relationship to bearing testimony, 'the historical crisis of the witness brings about a certain form of cognition [...] seeing leads to knowing, a knowing that, in some ill-understood way, might be ground breaking'.[66] It is by radically changing the witness—in this case, Baig herself—that the literary narrative can impart its knowledge to history. And what is the nature of this knowledge? Baig here bears witness to the suffering of the famine-inflicted body, crucially transforming this event, which may be otherwise understood in terms of the statistics of the dead, into an intimate 'carnal knowledge of victimisation'.[67]

The Bengal Famine left a profoundly traumatic impression on Tara Ali Baig, although she was based in Bombay at the time and, coming from a wealthy background, suffered no food shortages herself. Born in 1914 as Tara Gupta in East Bengal, she was able to attend university in Dhaka. Like Muriel Wasi, Baig married into a Muslim family, attributing her ability to do so without opposition to her family's close association with the monotheistic reformist sect within Hinduism, the Brahmo Samaj, which encouraged such progressive thinking.[68] In 1944, her husband, Mirza Rashid Ali Baig, was appointed the Director of National War Front in India and served as a high-ranking diplomat in India and abroad after independence,[69] while Baig herself went on to become the first Asian woman President of the International Union for Child Welfare in Geneva.[70] In a revealing interview conducted by British businessman and broadcaster Charles Allen in 1975 and 1976, Baig highlights the impact left on her by war and famine, seen through the prism of her class privilege. In this interview, she proclaims her perspective of the Indian role in the war as pawns for the British: 'We were just cats' paws, we were just tools of the whole power game and we had nothing to say in the matter and our men were being killed and our people were being involved without it being our war.'[71]

The interview highlights how Baig participated in civilian war work without necessarily supporting the way in which India had been co-opted into becoming a belligerent by the British Raj. Like Mulk Raj Anand and Muriel Wasi, she too became staunchly anti-fascist but remained deeply critical of colonialism. Baig was highly active as a wartime civilian in India: she established a hospital committee to look after Indian officers who were being sent overseas to Libya, and also during the 1940s worked with the Bombay Women's Volunteer Service, a civil organisation established to support the war effort. In the face of imperial indifference, she also made efforts to support areas in South India, such as Bijapur, which were undergoing gruelling wartime food shortages—'this whole area had been starved literally to be able to keep the war effort going'. She recounts how 'at that time there were just four of us and we collected enough money to feed 60,000 people for one solid year in order to keep them alive during that period' and that 'there was nobody else to take this load'.[72]

The famine in Bengal evokes an even more emotionally raw reaction from Baig during her interview, when she states that 'millions of people [...] died through no fault of theirs. It was part of another power game altogether.'[73] Here, Baig appears to view the famine as Amartya Sen does, although in humanitarian rather than economic terms. Sen's famous thesis on the Bengal Famine, discussed in more detail in Chapter 2, views it as the outcome of a process by which certain groups of people were priced out of food because of fluctuations in their purchasing abilities, brought about through an exercise of imperial power in a war economy. Baig's poem, in highlighting the complicity of Indian hoarders in this manufacturing of hunger, also reveals further levels of political awareness that Sen touches on.[74]

The poem continues:

'Rice water' he asked,
'Only water from the rice, no more.
Keep the light white grains to feed your wife,
Plump, golden wife,

Shuddering behind her sacks of hoarded grain.
Keep it.
Give me the water to revive

The vision through the pain:
The clean hearth and copper vessels,
And paddy lush with rain
Growing like sons. (49)

Attempts by the government to introduce price controls on rice created a 'black market' in Bengal, encouraging sellers to withhold stocks.[75] It is one such 'hoarder' who is represented in Baig's poem, seen through the eyes of a male famine victim. The poem, then, reveals through its literary frame what Indivar Kamtekar observes about unequal class relationships during wartime India: 'War discloses those who call the shots. Some people starved; other people ate more than they had ever done.'[76] Baig offers us this same juxtaposition through a terrible contrast of femininity, starting with the figure of the 'ancient' starving woman and then depicting the hoarder's 'plump, golden wife' shielded behind the illicit stockpile of food. Even the meagre sustenance of *phyan* or 'rice water' is denied to the former farmer and now famine victim. His homestead, copper cooking pots, the ripening paddy in the field—all contain within them intimations of the future, of nourishment by food, of renewal, all of which have now been obliterated.

The ability to procure rice becomes symbolic here of securing one's family line through supplies of adequate food. In her poem, Baig writes of the starving farmer's desire to envision 'paddy lush with rain / Growing like sons'—a potent simile that provides insights into the legacy of the famine instead of confining the event simply to 1943. It is the potential of familial continuity, of a culture and way of life, that the famine has extinguished. The poem later goes on to talk of 'the sons turned bone and ash upon the wind, / The empty farmstead / And the scattered kin' (49). As we saw in Chapter 2 in the analysis of Bibhutibhushan's novel *Ashani Sanket*, hunger, once again, is connected here with fire—the sons of the famine sufferer seem to have burnt away in the scorching heat of starvation. The poem continues inexorably:

Remember you are nothing brother…
Not even clay.
So fill the river and despoil the earth. (50)

It is the disappearance of this entire generation of rural lives that the
poem mourns, those who are denied even the capacity of nourishing
the soil through their bodily decay after death. Baig's grim use of
the word 'despoil' shows how far removed from empathy we have
to be to view the victims of this terrible famine as ruining the earth.

From bearing witness, Baig shifts in the second part of the poem
to write from the collective perspective of famine sufferers in the
first person:

The road to the city is hard.
The city is hard with shut doors.
The stone walks of the city burn our feet.
We do not understand.

We do not understand shut doors
And people passing heedless in the street.
Above all we do not understand
Why we hunger,
Why our homesteads lie deserted,
Our fields fallow.

[…]

We do not understand,
Why only death has pity.
Death is all that remains,
The only harvest for what we sowed.
We do not understand
Why only death should be our harvest. (50–51)

Baig imagines the famine victims as rural cultivators habituated to
the rhythms of agricultural life, the destruction of which makes
them unwanted foreigners in a city that they have been forced to
journey to out of necessity. The victims cannot comprehend the
indifference of the city-dwellers, but most importantly, do not
understand how it is that they have no home to return to and no
crops to reap. All that the famine victims are now left with is the
inexorable presence of death, 'the only harvest'.

I want to pause here and consider whether Baig's appropriation of voice in this way is problematic. The use of the first person by Baig, a highly privileged Indian intellectual and writer, essentialises the three million victims of the Bengal Famine, speaking for them as one homogenised body. Recent historical interpretations have in fact questioned the 'passivity' of the famine sufferers as represented by Baig, recording how hunger marches and looting of grocery shops and grain traders' warehouses took place alongside mass deaths.[77] The poem in this final section re-enacts the conundrum of Spivak's famous essay 'Can the Subaltern Speak?' (1988), where Spivak questions: 'How can we touch the consciousness of the people, even as we investigate their politics? With what voice-consciousness can the subaltern speak?'[78]

In examining the influence of Spivak's essay, Rajeswari Sunder Rajan has highlighted Spivak's choice of an 'imperfect' subaltern example in ending 'Can the Subaltern Speak?' with the story of Bhubaneswari Bhaduri, a middle-class woman from 1920s Calcutta who committed suicide because she was unable to carry out the assassination required of her by the nationalist terrorist group she had joined. Spivak's 'resistance to literalism' here, Sunder Rajan argues, is 'an invitation to rethink the relation between the figural and the literal'.[79] Perhaps we too need to undertake a similar rethinking in considering Baig's use of the first-person voice to represent famine victims, and question here how literary narrative may depart from historical writing. After all, literature is interested in forms of representation that foreground in complex ways how others' experience is imagined, and empathy registered. Although the use of a first-person voice to represent all famine sufferers is undoubtedly fraught, composing the poem becomes for Baig a way of alerting us to the emotional legacy of a historical event which does not end with the removal of corpses from the streets of Calcutta in 1943 but leaves enduring traces in art and literature.

In her interview with Charles Allen some thirty-five years later, Baig describes the extremity of her own response to the famine: 'As a person I reacted very violently to all this, but violently only to the extent that one was hapless and all that one could do was to try to help the people.'[80] The refrain in this final section of her poem, 'We do not understand', emphasises the violence enacted on the bodies of these famine victims in the city with its 'shut doors' and people 'passing heedless', concluding with 'We do not understand / Why only death should be our harvest.' By channelling both her 'violent' reaction and 'hapless' feeling as witness into literary response, Baig is able to record this pain, and pass on to readers an empathic, imaginative form of knowledge rooted in the body. The importance of this act of writing and representing is recognised by the editors Currey and Gibson, who say of Baig in the Preface: 'She speaks with sensitive understanding of a disaster which impressed every British soldier who witnessed anything of it, but appears among British writers to have numbed rather than inspired expression.'[81] The subaltern's voice—or rather, their voices—becomes figurative, a symbol in Baig's literary imagination, through which, in Sunder Rajan's words, Baig reveals her 'labour of affect'.[82] The composition of the poem, then, is both an emotional and an ethical response.

While in Wasi's poem India during the Second World War is imagined as gendered, Baig's response is more complicated. Baig moves from observing a woman famine victim to a starving male farmer, culminating in a communal dirge mourning the untimely death of an entire generation of rural lives from a first-person perspective. Yet both poems retain a shared thematic focus by addressing war trauma in India—through hunger, suffering and hardship. There is much, in fact, to connect Wasi and Baig as individuals too—they were of similar age, and had remarkably similar lived experiences, receiving university education (rare for Indian women in the 1940s) and marrying outside their own religious backgrounds into Muslim families. Perhaps most significantly, they were both present in India during the 1940s, seeing first-hand the turbulence of anticolonialism, nationalism, war and famine on the home-front.

Wasi seems more committed to anti-fascism and support for the war than Baig, which might explain the former's non-combatant role in the WAC (I). Baig, on the other hand, views India as a battleground for rival imperialisms during the war—'we were just cats' paws'—but nonetheless feels a nationalistic urge to help 'our people'. Both women were invested in their communities as wartime citizens. This engagement continues even beyond the war years, transforming into a reformist zeal—for Wasi in the field of Indian education and Baig with her international interest in child welfare—

when in different ways they align themselves to larger post-war humanitarian concerns. But it is their literary responses to conflict, I argue, written as young women, which highlight how important they were as witnesses to war trauma at home.

Conclusion

We began this chapter by considering two photographs—one showing the fragility and hesitancy of male rural recruits from north India, about to be taken away by train to their military units, and the other highlighting the more poised assurance of urban women of Bombay bearing stretchers and practising their ARP training. Where do such gendered experiences of the Second World War intersect, and what of the emotions they generate? After all, Anand was composing *The Sword and the Sickle* in England in the early 1940s, while Wasi and Baig were based in India, their poetry published in 1945, just after the end of the war. Although geographically separate, as elite intellectuals writing in English during the war years, Anand, Wasi and Baig's politics and modes of creative expression are interconnected. Their use of the English language enabled them to access a more international readership. Anand's novels, banned in India during the war years, were being read and reviewed in England, while Wasi and Baig's poems were published in an anthology of verse specifically targeted at a British readership. All three writers also engage in a conscious and often combative self-fashioning of Eastern experience for this audience. Furthermore, they position themselves both as anti-fascist, establishing links with a transnational political movement, as well as anticolonialist, by locating their writing within the particularities of the Indian home-front.

Finally, how can we assess Anand, Wasi and Baig's political activism, which influences how they witness the Second World War, through their creative writing? 'Literature bears testimony,' writes Shoshana Felman, 'not just to duplicate or to record events, but to make history available to the imaginative act whose historical unavailability has prompted, and made possible, a holocaust.'[83] The nature of literary testimony, then, responds to a moment of historical crisis, to a failure of imagination that results in acts of violence, suffering and horror. For Anand, this crisis is represented by imperial demands repeatedly made upon India during two global conflicts, and the disillusionment and radicalisation experienced by the character of Lalu in a turbulent Indian home-front that is growing more politically conscious. To Anand, this is how the two world wars are interconnected.

Wasi and Baig, on the other hand, by bearing witness, become custodians of a fragile yet terrible historical experience that needs literary preservation. Wasi represents the Bengal Famine through the image of the suffering woman who starves; Baig sees her own individuality and subjectivity become suffocated by the sheer extent of the calamity of hunger she can see—'Who am I? / The microscopic I, / In all this desolation and despair?'. From Anand's novelistic world of violent political turmoil, I have traced in this chapter how India's home-front transforms into the site of atrocity through poetry. Both creative forms make the role of Indian writer as witness become all the more significant during the Second World War. Chapter 5 will explore in more detail the nature of this historical crisis and the role of poetry as testimony.

5

'CRISIS IN CIVILISATION'

HOW POETRY BECOMES TESTIMONY

Under the lee of the great European rock,
We rape and are not satisfied
But the Other One lurking behind—the wicked voyeur,
Rattles his glad sabres and grows bloody-eyed.

– M.J. Tambimuttu, *Out of This War* (1941)

I had at one time believed that the springs of civilisation would issue out
of the heart of Europe. But today when I am about to quit the world that
faith has gone bankrupt altogether.

– Rabindranath Tagore, *Crisis in Civilisation* (1941)

What is the nature of historical crisis, and how does it shape our understanding of the Second World War and India? As Richard Overy notes, the term 'crisis' is often employed in hindsight, but those who lived through the world wars were conscious of confronting 'an age of chaotic, dangerous transition'.[1] This acute sense of crisis became closely linked to the nature and purpose of European civilisation and the violent forces it unleashed, both within Europe and without. Even during the late nineteenth century, there was a sharply felt sense of doom encroaching upon European civilisation, which was further cemented by the advent of war. Overy observes of the First World War, 'The very fact that the war had even happened, that the populations which regarded themselves as the bearers of modern civilisation had indulged in such an orgy of

193

blood-letting and destruction, called in question the ability of those same states to rebuild the world they had destroyed.'[2] The Second World War with its sixty million dead, the Holocaust and the atomic bombing of Hiroshima and Nagasaki, revealed how devastating the return of global war had been across the world. Once again, it urgently called into question—even as the war itself was progressing, and not simply as retrospective assessment—the geography of ruination and the sense of civilisational catastrophe.

If the centrality of civilisation to nineteenth-century European self-consciousness transformed into an 'ideological plank for overseas power and expansion before the outbreak of the First World War',[3] twentieth-century ideas of civilisation were more deeply interwoven with the concept of a cultural crisis and its relationship to emotional worlds.[4] The genocide brought about by the Second World War rendered European civilisation 'the grandest of illusions': a continent that had considered itself the touchstone of civilisation across the world had revealed the barbarism at its heart.[5] As Walter Benjamin put it in his 'Theses on the Philosophy of History' (1940), early into the Second World War, there is 'no document of civilisation that is not at the same time a document of barbarism'.[6]

This chapter looks closely at the wartime writings of two male South Asian writers—the relatively little-known Tamil poet M.J. Tambimuttu (1915–1983) and the much older and renowned Indian poet-philosopher Rabindranath Tagore (1861–1941), who died while the war was ongoing—to assess how each represented the Second World War as civilisational crisis in their poetic and philosophical work of the 1930s and 1940s. In doing so, I not only recover and analyse the work of a marginalised wartime writer from South Asia based in London but also move away from more traditional Tagorean scholarly approaches,[7] recontextualising Tagore himself as a witness to war as he neared the end of his life. Reading Tambimuttu and Tagore—writers whose works were written and circulated in different contexts—in conjunction with one another proves to be highly productive. Tambimuttu charts a series of diasporic responses as he lives through the London Blitz in his little-studied long poem *Out of This War* (1941), which meditates on the nature of time, and the fraught relationship between civilisation, modernity and barbarity. Tagore, on the other hand, views the Second World War as the culmination of his long-held beliefs on the nation-state and its rapacity, which undergirds the very basis of European civilisation and colonial power, and also causes its destruction. Here, I draw upon Tagore's prose and poetic works in Bengali from the early twentieth century, as well as his 1938 letters in English to Japanese poet Yone Noguchi and last published essay in English, *Crisis in Civilisation* (1941).

In this chapter, by considering Tambimuttu and Tagore's creative responses alongside one another, I advocate for the testimonial function of poetry from South Asian writers in bearing witness to global war. If poetry highlights a form of aesthetics that 'defends the autonomy of the lyrical voice', it also focuses our attention on intense moments of subjective experience and the meanings we can ascribe to them.[8] The late modernist poetry of Tambimuttu, inspired by T.S. Eliot, deliberately highlights the emotional discontinuities and ruptures caused by the London Blitz, engaging with the confusion and dislocation arising from continuous aerial bombardment. It begins with, and returns to, the English home-front, but encompasses a sense of historical time and a global fraternity of suffering. Tagore's corpus of poetic vocabulary, on the other hand, which suffuses not only his poetry but also philosophical writing, establishes emotional structures that are prophetic and doomladen—and rapidly transforming into lived reality with the recurrence of global war. He does not focus on a particular home-front but instead investigates what the underlying causes of repeated world wars are.

Both Tambimuttu and Tagore foreground the importance of the fragmentary nature of poetic writing, rich in metaphor and imagery, as well as its multifaceted and ambiguous nature. For these two writers, as we shall discover, it is poetry that opens up the creative possibilities of emotion and upholds the value of subjective experience. Poetry for them operates as testimony because it is able to highlight the effects of suffering that are not yet fully assimilated or understood but only glimpsed at. Yet there is value in this partial, and deeply felt, emotional knowledge.

'How soon / Will the thunder drop?' The London Blitz and
M.J. Tambimuttu's poetic testimony

Fig. 5.1: Still from the silent film 'Air Raid Damage, London, Indian AMPC',
November 1940. © Imperial War Museum.[9]

A short film archived at the Imperial War Museum focuses on
Indian 'lascars' or seamen in the Auxiliary Military Pioneering
Corps clearing up Sloane Square Tube station in London after a
bombing attack during the Blitz in November 1940. I have chosen
to highlight two distinct moments from this film here. The first
image shows us the men assessing the scale of the damage and clearing the rubble; the second homes in on a uniformed Indian 'lascar'
wearing a hard hat and holding a shovel, squarely facing the camera,
about to move more debris. He is being observed by a passer-by on
the left and supervised by a uniformed British soldier on the right,
most likely a corporal, according to the stripes displayed on the left
arm. This rare footage uses panning shots that survey the destruction caused by bombing but is distinctive in its use of close-ups of
the Indian men. The 'lascars' are a novelty to the camera: it repeat-

Fig. 5.2: Still from the silent film 'Air Raid Damage, London, Indian AMPC', November 1940. © Imperial War Museum.

edly zooms in on their faces and bodies, trying to capture changing flickers of expression as they dig, drill, hammer, shift rubble and hoist buckets. The men, aware they are being filmed, occasionally return the camera's gaze.

The physical presence of Indians during air raids in London was considerable. As recent scholarship has revealed, Indians served as volunteers in civil defence, working as both ARP wardens and ambulance workers. Florian Stadtler names Bengali novelist and BBC broadcaster Sudhindranath Ghose in Ealing, activist and editor Krishna Menon in Camden, and doctor and politician C.L. Katial in Finsbury as prominent ARP wardens.[10] Again, the Auxiliary Ambulance Station 50 (Indian Section), set up in St Pancras by the merchant Dorai Ross, comprised about a hundred Indian men and women from a range of professions, including doctors and barristers, and became well known for the quality of medical services provided.[11] Indian 'lascars', recruited from docks and ports, also became members of the Auxiliary Military Pioneer Corps, formed in 1939 to assist in clearing obstacles, fixing roads and undertaking repair-work, as we have seen above.[12]

London did not only witness a strong Indian presence during the Second World War: the city also became a site of 'transnational mixing'.[13] Wendy Webster notes how Canadians, Africans, Australians, Indians, Newfoundlanders, New Zealanders, Maltese and West Indians journeyed to Britain during the Second World War. In addition, over a quarter of a million Irish men and women undertook war work in Britain or volunteered for the British armed forces, along with over half a million German and Italian PoWs being held captive in Britain.[14] In London, and across the rest of the country, then, there were complex interactions between different national, ethnic and racial groups during the war.[15] Furthermore, we have seen in our discussion of Anand's *The Sword and the Sickle* in Chapter 4 how London, as the imperial centre, also functioned as an anticolonial site in the 1930s and 1940s, being the place where literary manifestos aimed at addressing the problems of contemporary India were formulated, and where anti-imperialist Indian novels and plays in English were published and performed, debated and contested.

It was in this intellectual milieu that poet, editor, critic and broadcaster M.J. Tambimuttu (1915–1983) published his response to the London Blitz in a long poem entitled *Out of This War* in 1941.[16] This comprises one of his few creative works from the war period—his time in London from 1938 to 1949 was spent more on commissioning and publishing poems in the magazine that he founded, *Poetry London* (1939–1951), than in writing them. Again, as we have seen in Chapter 4, Tambimuttu has been recognised as a regular participant in BBC radio programmes on the Eastern Service during the Second World War, particularly *Talking to India* and *Voice*.[17] The long poem *Out of this War* might have been obscured by Tambimuttu's editorial and broadcasting roles, but it nonetheless provides us with his complex testimonial response to global war. The poem covers a remarkable philosophical narrative arc, tracing the poet's arrival in London from Ceylon (modern-day Sri Lanka), experiencing aerial bombing and the trauma of the Blitz, and then turning to the crisis in civilisation prompted by the Second World War. The poem is divided into six sections, entitled

'Preface', 'The Hero', 'Air Raid', 'The Spreading Cross', 'Statements (with Connections) and Postscript', and concluding with 'The Elegy for the Dead'.

While Indian intellectuals such as Rabindranath Tagore foreground the predatory rapaciousness of both First and Second World Wars in their writing, as I shall explore later in this chapter, they seldom had direct experience of bombing or invasion.[18] Tambimuttu, instead, bears poetic witness to the everyday trauma of air raids and the consequent devastation of London. He also adopts a highly self-conscious perspective in the poem through which a profound critique of the political structures that undergird global war is foregrounded. The poem establishes causal links between the two world wars and interrogates the purpose of Western violent action. It culminates in an examination of savagery and barbarism, and laments for a global brotherhood of suffering created by war.

Right from the length of the poem and its use of sections to establish thematic separations, we recognise the obvious influence of T.S. Eliot's *The Waste Land* (1922).[19] There are also similarities with other modernist poems, such as Ezra Pound's *Hugh Selwyn Mauberley* (1920).[20] Tambimuttu here attempts to create a deliberate diffuseness and ambiguity of expression in line with British modernist aesthetics and aimed at a British readership—but only with partial success. The *Times Literary Supplement* in 1941, for instance, reviewed *Out of This War* as 'powerful, penetrating' but also 'too rhetorical'.[21] Nonetheless, Tambimuttu does manage to establish connections here with the aesthetics of other Blitz poetry. 'Where shall the innocent, curly head shelter from the blast' evokes images of vulnerable childhood, such as in Dylan Thomas's 'A Refusal to Mourn the Death, by Fire, of a Child' (1946). The lines: 'The bombs and tombs are falling on Leicester Square. / Hour-glass sand aflame on the roof-tops; the mouth / Of fear eating air we breathe', engenders an atmosphere of tangible urban terror, witnessed first-hand.

The Second World War generated a spectrum of responses from South Asian writers, both in Britain and South Asia, during the 1940s. As Ruvani Ranasinha observes, many such writers viewed the war as a civilisational crisis—a theme that will recur later in this chapter in my discussion of Tagore and his intellectual responses to war. Iqbal Singh (1912–2001) and Ahmed Ali (1910–1994),[22] contributing editors to the radical London literary magazine *Indian Writing* (1940–1945), for instance, considered the British to be using Indian soldiers in the war as 'cannon fodder', and commented on 'the spectacle of innocent nations and peoples being dragged into the homicidal delirium of rival imperialist powers'.[23] This shares similarities with the female activist and poet Tara Ali Baig's response to India's involvement in the war, discussed in Chapter 4—'We were just cats' paws.'[24]

Tambimuttu, coming from an Anglicised upbringing in Ceylon, where his family, being landowners and colonial bourgeoisie, held privileged class and caste positions, displayed no such obvious anti-colonial leanings during the war. His background was literary: Tambimuttu's grandfather owned and edited one of the first newspapers published in Tamil and English in Ceylon, while his father was also an editor and set up his own press.[25] Receiving a colonial education, he had English as his first language and Latin as his second but achieved little fluency in his native Tamil.[26] During the war years, Tambimuttu gained acceptance into an elite intellectual world in London, aided, as Ruvani Ranasinha argues, by his class background, English education and love of Western literature. He also invented a royal ancestry to be accepted into his new cultural milieu: the BBC addressed its correspondence to 'Prince Tambimuttu'[27]—an act that highlights his attempts to subvert racial hierarchies by invoking an exoticised class privilege and prestige.[28]

Tambimuttu's main literary and cultural circle centred on the intellectuals of Soho and Fitzroy Square—which he is credited with nicknaming 'Fitzrovia'[29]—while his magazine *Poetry London* gained a reputation for promoting modern poetry, particularly encouraging the talent of younger, mainly European poets.[30] It published, among others, Dylan Thomas, Kathleen Raine, George Barker and David Gascoyne, by all of whom he was held in much affection.[31] Indeed, George Orwell's letter to Alex Comfort, editor of the poetry magazine *Lyra* (1942), tells us that Tambimuttu had secured for himself a place in London's 1940s literary scene that was often denied to other South Asian writers:

> I saw you had a poem by Tambimuttu. If you are bringing out other numbers you ought to get some of the other Indians[32] to

write for you. There are several quite talented ones and they are very embittered because they think people snub them and won't print their stuff. It is tremendously important from several points of view to try and promote decent cultural relations between Europe and Asia.[33]

Tambimuttu, then, was accepted into this elite British cultural milieu but did not espouse any overtly anticolonial political positions in the 1940s. He was later sharply criticised by Anand—who held much more radical political views—for being a 'brown Englishman'.[34] There is also no evidence of him participating in ARP or other civilian wartime duties in London. A revealing extract from British Army officer Russell McKinnon-Croft's memories of wartime London with Tambimuttu highlights, in fact, how *little* the war signified to the latter, except in altering the physical environment in which he socialised and discussed poetry:

In the unreal claustrophobia of the 'phoney war' we lived out our counterpoint to the humbug and sterility of leaflet raids, Ministry announcements, empty war news bulletins [...] played music, read and talked poetry, ate in odd little restaurants and cafés where the rationed food grew steadily more wan [...]
Then I went off to war in greater earnest in the Mediterranean. So that it was the beginning of 1945 before I saw Tambi again. No real change, thank God [...] He gurgled at my multicoloured medal ribbons: an aesthetic gesture, merely. Otherwise, the war—happily—might never have been.[35]

Yet, despite all Tambimuttu's apparent nonchalance in front of his friends, the war *had* been, and it had left its mark on him. His complex background placed him at the cross-section of various threads of influence—colonial elitism, British modernism and the lived experiences of the Blitz—which are reconfigured in the long poem.[36] His response to war, then, is a complicated and ambivalent one, registered through a highly stylised, mannered and often laboured poetic vocabulary. The poem's orientalism is itself filtered through British modernist influences, such as those of Eliot, Spender and Auden, while its borrowing of Christian symbolism draws upon Tambimuttu's Roman Catholic familial heritage.[37]

201

While writing about British life-writing and literary responses to the Blitz, Beryl Pong notes that, during the Second World War, there was a shift in attitudes to death from the First. This was not simply due to mass killings in Europe and elsewhere, but because civilian aerial bombardment, for both the Allies and Axis forces, resulted in European home-fronts and battlefronts becoming indistinguishable. 'The need to find a new attitude towards death,' she observes, 'creates a new paralysis of capacity that requires its own grammar of anxiety, its own style and aesthetics. [...] Even if one does not die in an air raid, one accepts this as a future possibility, again and again.' While confronting this repetitious nature of one's own mortality, death becomes palpable in the 'anticipation of retrospection', which becomes a way of surviving the present but also preserving it for analysis and examination at a later date.[38] From the very title of Tambimuttu's work—*Out of This War*—we understand how crucial this 'anticipation of retrospection' is to the functioning of the poem. *Out of This War* does not simply serve as an emotional and philosophical testament to wartime suffering; it also charts an imaginary roadmap through the war. The return of global war provides Tambimuttu with the poetic opportunity for interrogating the structures of civilisation in the West. But it is romanticised memories of Eastern life, as we shall see, depicted through images of ripeness and fertility, which symbolise the poet's desire for a lost past, taking him beyond the horrors of war.

The poem begins with a section entitled 'Preface':

I roll the suns of twenty-five summers in my fist,
Their bellies filled with fruits and corn and thunder.
The many-flavoured waters of the East slide in my veins,
And I am ripe for plunder. (9)

Here, Tambimuttu is engaged in self-orientalism, playing up Eastern qualities that readers from the West project onto him. This is evident in the stereotypes of Ceylon that he draws upon, with its 'many-flavoured waters', a tropical climate of thunderstorms, and the abundance of agricultural produce in fruit and corn—a sensuous rather than spiritual essentialism. Yet the fourth line jostles uncomfortably against such images. If Tambimuttu is establishing a correlation here between territorial Ceylon and himself, a process by which he seems to become the physical embodiment of a lush and verdant East, is he also not criticising the political consequences of the country's fertility and profuseness—an invitation for colonial forces to 'plunder'? Yet this is both critique and coquetry: in seeing himself as the embodiment of Ceylon in the West, Tambimuttu also flaunts his exoticism and erotic appeal—being 'ripe for plunder' here operates at the level of both colonial politics and individual sexuality.

Writing a little later in the 'Preface', Tambimuttu continues:

> Here, Death is measured with Big Ben or theodolite;
> The cerements of mansions, neat on the washing line.
> Neatly brewed and bottled, the heady liquor,
> Lies different on the tongue, to our simple wines.
>
> Tapes and set-squares, cones, tangents,
> The formal property of the cupboard brain;
> Are projected into further lines, cones and tangents,
> A nut too well precisioned for my head. (10)

As Sukhdev Sandhu notes, the poem projects a stereotypical binary between a 'sophisticated' London and the 'simple' East.[39] But Tambimuttu also questions the foundations of such sophistication and rationality when it results in mass death. Here, he focuses on the organisation that structures life in the imperial metropolis, where alcohol is industrially produced and generates greater intoxication, seeming 'different on the tongue', and where urban architectural neatness also creates a feeling of excess within the poet's mind. Tambimuttu witnesses the measure of mortality in the strikes made by Big Ben during the Blitz; the theodolite, or instrument used for calculating angles in horizontal and vertical planes, here reveals only the precise mathematics of death.

Stephen Spender, whose work Tambimuttu published, makes a similar point about the geometry of killing in his poem 'Air Raid Across the Bay at Plymouth' (1942) when he highlights how 'triangles, parallels, parallelograms, / Experiment with hypotheses / On the blackboard sky, / Seeking that X / Where the enemy is met'.[40] In Tambimuttu's poem, London's luxury homes are imagined as shrouded corpses wrapped in cerement or waxed cloth, strangely conflated with the image of clothes neatly displayed on the washing line. Is this a production line of death, hung out to dry, transforming city into cemetery? Again, while London may become in the poem the site of 'tabulation and notation'[41] with its 'tapes and set-squares, cones, tangents', it is also foregrounded as a place aflame and destroyed. The last few lines of the 'Preface' highlight the image of firefighters struggling to subdue the effects of incendiary bombs in the 'boiling, gutted air'—where 'the bloody heaps of her harvests ris[e] / And the hairy long-armed men juggl[e] with fire' (10).

Tambimuttu's more pointed wartime interrogation centres on the very concept of opposing sides, and the hostile political discourse this generates, in the poem's next section, 'The Hero':

> The Teutonic Rilke will cover the Hero with laurel;
> Genghiz Khan allow him a hundred oyster brides.
> But remember, the hero is a fool with a theory
> That wouldn't work—the fire in his head was sand.
>
> [...]
>
> No better than vegetable, we have need of root and plot;
> Denied, a crimson crime will branch from the crime.
> Who fights, not the hero, but the oppressor,
> Denied the love of reason, to make him different.
>
> The Hero will sit him down with Bible and book
> Learn the stories of Indian, German and Pole.
> War as the evil branching on the outraged body
> Will steal from the stalking grave and wash it whole. (11)

Here, the German-language poet, denoted by the 'Teutonic Rilke', praises the nationalist 'Hero', while aggressors, symbolised by Genghiz Khan, reward the 'Hero' by fulfilling all his desires, indicated by the 'hundred oyster brides'. The 'oppressor', in contrast, is defined as such, Tambimuttu believes, because he is 'denied the love of reason, to make him different'. The poem, then, by investigating the causes of global war, is sensitive to acts that stoke conflict amongst nations, including that of the propaganda-spreading 'Hero'.

Tambimuttu does not distinguish between the 'stories' of 'Indian, German and Pole' here, although he is writing in a political context where in 1939 Hitler had invaded Poland and India been declared a belligerent in the war without consultation by British political powers. These 'stories' become representative of various narratives of nationhood, which the poet links to war: when the 'Hero' teaches those fighting the 'oppressor' these 'stories', war—imagined as a corrupt plant 'branching' on the 'outraged body'—threatens to engulf the latter. This is clunky poetry, with uneasy transitions between images, and there is some justification for literary critics who in the 1980s thought that *Out of This War* was 'clumsy, prosaic and portentous'.[42] Nonetheless, these three concepts are made to align in the final line, functioning as Tambimuttu's conscious philosophical critique: death, imagined as a 'stalking grave', is in constant secret surveillance of humanity; war enables death to spread across the human body; nationalism feeds such cancerous growth.

In his book *Tense Future* (2015), Paul Saint-Amour reads the interwar years themselves as an anticipation of violence. He highlights how the traumatic and discursive effects of the First World War could not be contained within a particular timeframe—'the memory of one world war was already joined to the spectre of a second future one'. For Saint-Amour, the term 'interwar' resonates with proleptic charge, 'making the future seem a predetermined site of catastrophic violence and therefore capable of inflicting damage in the present'.[43] Tambimuttu proposes just such a relationship between the First and Second World Wars in 'The Hero':

A Primary Evil to rim the earth with war.
The evil resides not in itself but causes
– The mutilated page in the book, the suffered slight,
The gnawing hunger and our accusing losses.

To rise up on the martyred blood and shriek vengeance,
And plunge the angry bayonet in the scabbard of blood,
Is the Secondary Evil, without recompense
That times the bomb of another war. (12)

Belligerence thus cannot be contained within the war years themselves but spreads itself across time. The First World War, seen in the poem as a 'Primary Evil', circumscribes the world in conflict, arising only from perceived losses—'the mutilated page', 'the suffered slight'—while the Second World War, the 'Secondary Evil', is imagined as vengeful, vindictive and blood-thirsty. The grammatic construction of the second stanza blurs agency; we are not sure who 'rise[s] up on the martyred blood' and 'plunge[s] the angry bayonet'. Is this an allusion to the rise of Hitler, or to the devastating economic effects of the 1919 Treaty of Versailles? Or is it simply a reference to the warmongering of nations the second time round? In any case, Tambimuttu further affirms the interconnectivity between the wars, saying a little later: 'The one [is] unformulated without the other. / The resentful hand not met with force / Use violence again will not bother' (12). And such a war-generated 'Evil', the poet believes:

> [...] probes into the infinite reaches of space
> And graded life below, the Buddha said.
> Evil is the all-flavouring element
> Blowing equally on the new-born and the dead. (12)

Tambimuttu responds here to the global 'idealist' moment, highlighted in Stephen Spender and John Lehmann's anthology *Poems for Spain* (1940), where they publish, among others, Auden's poem 'Spain', and in whose introduction Spender stresses the crucial role of poets in the international anti-fascist struggle.[44] We see again how Tambimuttu frames his critique of the world wars as products of Western civilisation by referencing the Buddha— another Eastern source of spirituality. But if 'Evil' seems like pervasive dust here, invading both those alive and dead, can a way 'out of this war' even be imagined? Tambimuttu provides us with a flicker of redemptive hope when he writes: 'Half this battle and the murder over'; / The hero stirring in the common weed and seed' (12). As a counterpoint to the fatal growth of conflict fuelled by the war 'hero', this is an alternative, albeit tentative, portrayal of heroism, located in images of regeneration, in plant life sustained within the ordinary and the everyday.

From a philosophical and political detour of the historical causes of the two world wars, *Out of This War* returns to London, transforming nightmarish landscapes into poetic testimony in 'Air Raid', its third section. Living through air raids left a significant psychological impact on Tambimuttu. In a wartime broadcast made in 1941, entitled 'The Man on the Street' for the BBC radio series targeted at India's English speakers, *Talking to India*, he describes London's streets as 'unreal and intangible' by the 'dim blue lighting' during blackouts and air raids.[45] But if on the radio he discusses the city's *The*

Waste Land-like wartime appearance, Tambimuttu in the poem deepens his focus on the meaning of time itself during air raids:

> This iron moment stretches over Europe
> Like the clang of a deep bell.
> The vacant squares, staring stony-eyed to the moon
> Will never stir or tell
> How soon, ah how soon
> Will the thunder drop
>
> On our sad head...
>
> Our hungry star is dying over Europe
> A silent mouth in the burning cell;
> And as the dead eye slants from the ruins to the sky –
> Quick danger of eyes and hell –
> Will it cry, will it cry
> When will the murder stop
> On the blameless head. (13)

For Auden in 'Spain', time is marked by the relevance of political action—'yesterday' is 'all the past' and 'today the struggle';[46] for Tambimuttu, waiting for the bomb is a form of timelessness, resonating with Saint-Amour's insight into the experience of air raids being moments when 'the familiar coordinates against which time's measure could be taken were gone'.[47] The city here has turned into battlefield, as violence overflows and spills beyond frontlines into the very heart of civilian spaces, as Beryl Pong notes. There is a deeply felt tragedy evoked at the extent of civilian deaths, with Tambimuttu's repeated use of adjectives such as 'innocent' and 'blameless'. He castigates such deaths as 'murder', and this word acts as a refrain throughout the long poem: in the Prufrockian invocation to time quoted below, he likens war in the month of September to 'murder' and 'thrust'. Again, if the West is seen as an arena for action in contrast to a spiritualised, contemplative East, this 'time of action' is ethically challenged by Tambimuttu for being 'plunder, rape, devilry':

> Time was and time will be
> For building and erection
> Time for work and time for rest.

This, this is September time: time of action
Time for murder and time for thrust,
For plunder, rape, devilry.

The word 'plunder' echoes its earlier use in the poem, when Tambimuttu, seeing himself as the embodiment of a fertile Ceylon, declared that he is 'ripe for plunder'. Poetic language points us to connections that are not explicitly made: the violence of war and the violence of colonialism seen as manifestations of the same desire to possess and control. Bringing back to mind the enemy that must be fought, Tambimuttu continues:

This is no summer to weigh the merits of war
While the iron Junker loads the sky
Against us. In our jackets of nightmare
We shall stoke the ship, until the boilers crack
Like our hollow bones. But where, where
Will we find us after wreck? (14)

The recurrent imagery of fire in the poem—from the firemen working hard to quench flames and the 'hungry star dying over Europe'—finds another expression in the poet's images of endlessly stoking the fires of British ships as suitable retaliation against the bombs dropped by German aircraft. But, instead of ship against aircraft, nation against nation being locked into conflict with one another, the question that preoccupies Tambimuttu the most is where ordinary people will find themselves 'after wreck'—another refrain in the poem. How do we make our way out of the violence engendered by our experience of historical time? What lies on the other side of war?

This civilian realisation of Wilfred Owen's 'pity of war' finds expression through a complex philosophical world view in which Tambimuttu's Christian heritage brushes against a more Eastern sense of deep time, both of which are filtered through an Eliotic sense of the interconnectedness of all time.[48] The title of the fourth section, 'The Spreading Cross', along with the vocabulary of 'mercy' and 'the day of reckoning', foregrounds a Christian sense of how war could have been averted and the possibility of atonement for terrible violence:

A simple book of his, the awful other's want,
A little mercy on the clean surgeon's knife
Would have avoided all this. Who can say?
Today the cars of war run only when life
Is stranded for reason. And when the day
Of reckoning descends and someone, perhaps he, the other has to pay –
Where will we find us after wreck? (15)

In the metaphor 'the cars of war', Tambimuttu links conflict to processes of mechanisation separated from the natural rhythms of life, which are 'stranded', in an odd turn of phrase, 'for reason'. The preposition 'for' makes the meaning of the line ambiguous—is it *because* of excessive reason that life is stranded? Or is it because life during war is *bereft* of reason? The exact relationship between life and war, although predicated as oppositional, is left ambivalent.

In continuing his investigation into historical time, Tambimuttu reveals his trenchant critique of European imperialism through his use of the binary between 'man' who falls 'on the lap of Europe from the south' and the 'savage' who is 'slaughtered' (18). This rational-savage paradigm is rapidly internalised as a psychological divide, where savagery is imagined as the dark underbelly of everyday life:

Thus, we are double-faced. Behind the easy façade
Of custom, acquired grace or intelligence,
Lurks the Neanderthaler with a savage grin. (19)

He then writes:

Under the lee of the great European rock,
We rape and are not satisfied
But the Other One lurking behind—the wicked *voyeur*,
Rattles his glad sabres and grows bloody-eyed. (19)

In his tracing of a history of humanity making its way into Europe, with its 'slaughtering' of the 'savage', Tambimuttu highlights that barbarism itself was not dominated and eradicated. Rather, sheltered by the powerful edifice of European civilisation, it was replaced by a continuing 'rape'—and the word here resonates with the vocabulary of 'plunder' used previously in the poem.[49] Witnessing such action, the 'wicked voyeur'—the internalised savage the poet believes to be within all of us—is spurred on in his need for blood-thirstiness. For Tambimuttu, the idea of savagery is not restricted to an imperial trope but inherent in human nature itself. It is wartime that exposes such 'savagery', resulting in the normalisation of such behaviour in the heart of European metropolitan life:

> In the corner of the street, in the traffic,
> Watch him grin his sadist syllables. Now
> He is exploding the guns and battleships.
> What next? Shall we throw him out? (19)

The Second World War is, in other words, 'savagery' itself coming home to Europe, another form of the 'rape' and 'plunder' it had previously inflicted on colonised countries. This point is also made by Tagore, which I shall discuss in the next section, as well as noted by scholars analysing perspectives of the First World War beyond Europe. Santanu Das, in discussing the responses of the intellectuals Aurobindo Ghose, Muhammed Iqbal and Tagore to the First World War, observes: 'The massacre on the Western Front made a mockery of the narrative of progress woven around Western technological modernity. How could Europe continue with its claim of "civilising mission" when it could not even contain its own barbaric violence?'[50] In *Out of This War*, Tambimuttu reveals his interest in precisely such themes—industrial progress and the natural rhythms of life, 'savagery' and reason, mass death and 'civilisation'. The difference lies in that, for the Second World War, barbarism is no longer confined to any frontline: home-front and battlefront are more blurred than they have ever been. And the 'Postscript' with which this fifth section concludes shows us yet a different kind of 'murder':

> Honour us, please, we are fighting for man and civilisation
> But we are murdering the wit to become civilised. (19)

Here, Tambimuttu sees the Second World War (like the anti-nationalist Tagore, and radicals Iqbal Singh and Ahmed Ali of the London-based periodical *Indian Writing*) as a civilisational crisis. In post-war years, this viewpoint would increasingly be held by a cross-section of intellectuals such as Frantz Fanon and Jean-Paul Sartre, which I shall briefly discuss in the final section on Tagore.

In the final section of the poem, 'Elegy for the Dead', Tambimuttu returns to the idea of the 'uncontainable' in Elizabeth Bowen's sense of the multiplying theatres of war. This section does not aim to bury the dead like Eliot's *The Waste Land*, but to mourn them in great transnational sweeps, in which soldiers and civilians alike are included. 'Elegy for the Dead' comprises dense verses with vivid but often obscure imagery. Tambimuttu's empathy finds keenest expression in recording the Chinese victims of Japanese aggression, but he also simultaneously realises that these millions of deaths will be rendered 'unimportant':

> [...] look, on the sharp coast of China;
> Whirled the lantern of Death. Humbly they lie
> Gunned on the evil that laid them low—What evil
> Hand did they deal in this game of Greed!
>
> Die
> Progeny of the Sun, yellow brother, unimportant;
> But the exultant Sin has fallen on our courtyards,
> And after the worlds are hung in the Nothingness, together
> We'll heave a different world of sandalwood and myrrh. (20)

It is a strange combination of compassion and orientalism by someone who is himself 'oriental'. The problematic phrase 'yellow brother' views the Chinese in highly racialised terms but also establishes a fraternity of suffering. The 'different world' that will be built after the war is left as ethereal rather than practical, the combination of sandalwood and myrrh suggesting a fusion of Eastern faiths with Christian belief in a shared spirituality.

Continuing his emphasis on the 'uncontainable' nature of the war, Tambimuttu evokes a range of suffering, experienced at the same moment in time across the world, in the conclusion of the poem:

> Propose a meaning for the thousand dead,
> Our children fallen on the careless shame.
> The mouths of ash are sighing in France
> And the hoarded woe blowing from China.
> Blood runs dry, this bread is cracked,
> Our limbs are freezing and our trousers patched. (23)

Give back the robe of splendid sap,
Lap us in the gold, the power and ooze
Of rounded hours in the melon's belly
Singing: throats of the sun-filled juice.
Diffuse the laws and purple thrones
Over the plains and weaving Life
Knifed to a cross of blood we'll break
A white Freedom from such harsh roots. (24)

Spiritual regeneration through the Eucharistic ritual of transubstan-
tiation, where the offering of bread and wine becomes the body and
blood of Christ, is no longer possible in wartime—the 'blood runs
dry', the 'bread is cracked'. Instead, the suffering human body is
numb with cold, but also burnt out and reduced to ash. In this
context, Tambimuttu's return to the exoticised, sensuous East—
although he does not explicitly name it as such—is charged with
yearning. It is not simply a re-invention of himself for a Western
readership but his own journey through memory into a highly
romanticised past—a world of 'splendid sap' and 'the sun-filled
juice'—inflected with a Chaucerian sense of verdant nature with its
'ooze'.[51] Only in such nostalgic memories can life find its regenera-
tive impulse again, where there is the possibility of redemption after
humanity's Christ-like suffering during war.

Tambimuttu's *Out of This War*, then, reveals to us how poetry
operates as testimony by using literary form to reinscribe trauma
whose effects are only partially assimilated. After all, Tambimuttu
composed this poem as he was living through the Blitz and not when
the war was over. The circular narrative of the poem, beginning and
ending with visions of a lush and verdant East, establishes a poetic
continuity between images that are often fragmentary and diffuse—
firefighters in London, the causes of recurring global war, the dark
underbelly of savagery permeating Western 'civilised' life, the
death of civilians in Europe and China, and the seemingly eternal
suspension in waiting for the bomb to fall. It is the form of poetry
that enables this multidirectional and often ambiguous approach—
cutting across chronologies of time and place, drawing upon
Christian and Eastern symbolism—to make sense of the act of witnessing. In the next section, on Rabindranath Tagore, we shall dis-

cover how such poetic testimony deepens into becoming an intense, almost visceral response to civilisational crisis.

Time of monsters: Rabindranath Tagore and the culmination of a civilisational crisis

Two years before the start of the Second World War, on 10 September 1937, the seventy-seven-year-old Rabindranath Tagore fainted due to an attack of erysipelas, a form of cellulitis, at his home in Shantiniketan, and remained in a coma for sixty hours, hovering between life and death. After recovering, between 25 September and 25 December, he composed a cycle of eighteen poems published under the title *'Prantik'* ('The Borderland', 1938).[52] Written for a Bengali audience in Tagore's own homeland, India, these are, as Sudhir Kakar has observed, 'some of the finest meditations on death and afterdeath in world literature'.[53] However, the final poem in the cycle, *'Naginira charidike'* ('Everywhere the serpents'), reveals that Tagore was not simply focusing on individual philosophical reflections on the nature of dying but remained highly politically engaged. From the turn of the nineteenth century into the twentieth, Tagore had become increasingly despairing of the aggressive militarism of the world. The violence of the 1899–1902 Boer War was followed by the First World War, where Tagore's critique of nationalism and celebration of the relationship between East and West 'found some of their most powerful and compelling shapes as well as a global audience'.[54] And then came the 1930s, with Japanese belligerence in the East, and the rise of Franco, Hitler and Mussolini in the West.

This chapter, as we have discussed, considers what the affective possibilities are in bearing poetic witness to global war and intensely felt historical crisis. It is in Tagore's writing during the 1930s and 1940s, in response to global events that culminated in the Second World War, that we find some of his most profound creative, metaphoric and symbolic outpourings. Born in May 1861, Tagore formed a critical part of Bengali intellectual life, later becoming an acclaimed figure in world literature and receiving the Nobel Prize for Literature in 1913. In bearing witness to the Second World War, Tagore borrows extensively from his own corpus of poetic vocabulary used in previous writing. The evocations of this vocabulary morph across some thirty years, accruing greater emotional potency towards the end of his life because we recognise them as established leitmotifs in his worldview. One such recurrent theme is Tagore's interrogation of the nation and its manifestations in the forms of colonialism, imperialism and global conflict, which attain a climax with the Second World War. The imagery he uses for his poetic—and prophetic—questioning is weighted with the sense of the bestial and depraved, where serpents and demons, along with predatory, appetitive urges, abound. As Gramsci would say, 'The old world is dying, and the new world struggles to be born: now is the time of monsters.'[55]

In 1937, on the brink of the recurrence of a world war, and having himself returned from the borderland between life and death, Tagore wrote these lines in Bengali:

Nagini-ra charidike phelitechhe bishakto nishwas,
Shantir lalita bani shonaibe byartha parihas –
Bidae nebar age tai
Dak diye jai
Danober shathe jara songramer tore
Prostut hotechhe ghore ghore.

Everywhere the serpents hiss their poisonous breath,
The gentle message of peace will play on in futile mockery –
Before I take my leave then
Let me call out
To those who are arming themselves,
For battle with the demon, in home after home.[56]

Before analysing this further, I want to draw our attention to an earlier, deeply disturbing poem that Tagore composed, also in Bengali, connecting the natural world with the horror and scale of human violence.[57] On 31 December 1900, the last day of the nineteenth century, Tagore wrote:

Shatabdir surja aji rakta-megh majhe
Asta gelo, hingshar utshobe aaji baje
Astre astre moroner unmad ragini
Bhayankari.[58]

From May 1916 to February 1917, Tagore gave a series of high-profile lectures in English in Japan and the United States, which formed the core of his book *Nationalism* (1918) and opened up his ideas to a global audience. He selected this poem as one of five pieces originally written in Bengali to form a poetic conclusion to this book. Tagore himself translated the above lines into English, which I have referred to in Chapter 2 while analysing Samar Sen's famine poetry:

> The last sun of the century sets amidst the blood-red clouds of the West and the whirlwind of hatred.
>   The naked passion of self-love of Nations, in its drunken delirium of greed, is dancing to the clash of steel and the howling verses of vengeance.[59]

The Bengali poem was written in the context of the Boer War, and it was translated into the English version in *Nationalism* during the First World War, yet the two contexts are connected as philosophical and ethical structures in Tagore's thinking.[60] The Bengali poem does not explicitly mention nationalism—indeed, Tagore famously said that there was no linguistic equivalent for the word 'nation' in Bengali.[61] Instead, it powerfully suggests in subsequent lines that the '*hingshar utshob*' ('display of hate') is rooted in '*svartha*' ('selfishness') and '*jatiprem*' ('love of one's clan'). This latter meaning suffuses Tagore's English translation of the first two lines, leading us to the evocative phrase 'self-love of Nations', personified as dancing in its mad celebration of violence. To Tagore, then, both the Boer War and the First World War have the same provenance—they are rooted in the idea of the nation-state, towards which he maintained trenchant opposition throughout his life.

The two Bengali poems discussed above, '*Shatabdir surja*' (1900) and '*Naginira charidike*' (1937) are interlinked both philosophically and semantically. The connections continue to deepen as we read them in conjunction with each other. In the former, Tagore introduces the symbol of the serpent, connected by a strategically placed hyphen to the notion of civilisation itself:

Dayaheen sabhyata-nagini
Tulecche kutil phona chokkher nimeshe
Gupto bishodonto tar bhori teebro bishe.

The merciless civilisation-serpent
Has raised her deceitful hood in the blink of an eye
Filling her hidden fangs with pungent poison.

In the latter poem, the serpent is re-invoked, this time as an opening dramatic centrepiece:

Naginira charidike phelitechhe bishakto nishwas,
Shantir lalita bani shonaibe byartho porihas

Everywhere the serpents hiss and spit their poisonous breath,
The gentle message of peace will play in futile mockery.

If in Tagore's imagination the Boer War becomes the single serpent which guilefully raises its head to attack in 1900, the image of many serpents hissing and spitting refer to the political antagonisms of 1937. The duplicitous snake has multiplied: in the same year as the latter poem's composition the second Sino-Japanese war began, while only two years afterwards, in 1939, India was compelled by the British to enter the Second World War as a belligerent after Hitler's invasion of Poland. If we consider Rustom Bharucha's argument that Tagore 'consolidated his universal humanist position not with the acumen of a political theorist, but with all the ambivalence and metaphoric richness of a poet',[62] we recognise in the composition of '*Naginira charidike*' Tagore's keenly felt creative response to the increasing hostility of the world on the brink, once again, of a global war, and the continuing symbolic importance of the poisonous snake.

From his travels across East Asia, particularly China and Japan in the 1920s and 1930s, Tagore remained, as Pankaj Mishra says, 'preternaturally alert to, and fearful of, the violent hatreds still to be unleashed across Asia, beginning with the Japanese invasion of the Asian mainland'.[63] Mishra notes that, in their last years, Tagore's like-minded contemporaries across Asia—Liang Qichao and Kang Youwei from China and Phan Boi Chau from Vietnam—had found themselves increasingly opposed to mainstream hardline political thinking and therefore in a political minority, like Tagore himself.[64] '*Shantir lalita bani*' ('the gentle message of peace') seemed to be out of joint with time, mocking the state of the world in the late 1930s.

Tagore undoubtedly remained attuned to political developments in Asia during the interwar years, but his public comments on immediate events leading up to the Second World War, and on Nazi rule in particular, are few.[65] He was, in private, deeply critical of both Britain and France's political positioning in enabling the rise of fascism in Europe—with Franco's takeover of Spain, Italy's invasion of Ethiopia, the German occupation of Czechoslovakia and Hitler's domination of the 1938 Munich Agreement.[66] In 1933, however, he writes how the 'very Europe which had once reviled Turkey now flaunts Fascism' and thinks of Germany, 'in which the light of Europe's culture was at its brightest', as having 'torn up all civilised values—with what ease has an unspeakable devilry overtaken the entire country!'[67] In 1937, Tagore also contributed a piece against fascism to a public appeal promoting the Republican side of the Spanish Civil War, published in a pamphlet called 'To the conscience of humanity', which contained statements from French intellectual Romain Rolland and novelist and First World War survivor Henri Barbusse. Here, he writes in an unusually activist tone: 'This devastating tide of International Fascism must be checked [...] come in your millions to the aid of democracy, to the succour of civilisation and culture.'[68] The pamphlet did not go unnoticed—it resulted in a public rebuke from Joseph Goebbels at the Nazi Party's largest rally in Nuremberg in September 1937, where Goebbels mentioned Tagore by name as one of those belonging to a 'world liberalism' offering support to Republican Spain.[69]

As such a 'world liberal', Tagore directly critiqued the rise of Hitler only once in a public statement in June 1934 for N.E.B. Ezra, the editor of a Zionist newspaper in Shanghai, in language that is surprisingly measured. Tagore writes:

> As regards the Hitler regime in Germany, we read different versions of it. And certainly it cannot be denied that the German people were goaded to many acts of desperate folly by the humiliations imposed on them by the victorious nations of the War. Nevertheless, if the brutalities we read of are authentic, then no civilised conscience can allow compromise with them. The insults offered to my friend Einstein have shocked me to the point of torturing my faith in modern civilisation.[70]

Tagore's restraint may stem from the fact that the ideology of German fascism sharply contradicted his own experiences in

Germany as recently as 1930, when he had first met Einstein.[71] I would also argue that Tagore's perspective is highly attentive here to historical developments: rather than viewing Hitler's rise to power as single-minded megalomaniacal control over Germany, he sees it instead as a product of social, political and economic factors stemming from the hinterland of the First World War. It is, however, the personal that becomes Tagore's route to the most pointed political critique in the passage. His friendship with Einstein—who had had to leave Berlin in December 1932, never to return to Germany because of Nazi persecution[72]—brings Tagore to the vexed topic of 'modern civilisation', which 'tortur[es] his faith'. Empathy for the suffering of a friend, then, draws out his strongest condemnation, which is linked to the failure of modern civilisation itself.

It is also important to note here that there do not seem to be any references to the Holocaust anywhere in Tagore's writing, but this is possibly because he did not live to learn of such atrocity. During the final years of his life, Tagore was nearly eighty years old, suffering from ill health and unable to travel until his death in August 1941. It is likely that he did not know of the systematic extermination of Jewish people and other ethnicities and communities in concentration camps, which emerged as German state policy between summer 1941 and 1942.[73] And once Hitler invaded the Soviet Union on 22 June 1941, Tagore, even from his deathbed, continued to ask for news of Russia, believing that they alone could stop the 'monsters'.[74]

Returning to Tagore's thinking on civilisation, we discover that its relationship to barbarity has long roots. Tagore's Bengali essays, written during the early years of the twentieth century and aimed at a Bengali readership in India, highlight the germination of his philosophy on civilisation and its connection with barbarity, which his 1934 public statement for N.E.B. Ezra also foregrounds. I will consider two such essays briefly, one written before the First World War and the other in its midst, as valuable context to Tagore's last piece of writing during the Second World War and his most considered exegesis on modern civilisation and its discontents. This is *Sabhyatar Sankat*, a speech given on his eightieth birthday three months before his death, and later translated into English and published as *Crisis in Civilisation* (1941).[75] In the first of these two early Bengali essays under consideration, '*Birodhmulak Adarsha*' ('The Conflict-Rooted Ideology', 1901), Tagore analyses what he considers to be Europe's return to barbarism.[76] During the years preceding the First World War, he alerts us to the '*laraier nesha*' (592) or intoxication for conflict, where increasing tensions were being fomented between England and other nation-states in cultural discourse. He observes, for example, how newspapers, with their representations of '*shatrujati*' (593) or enemy nations, feed their readers '*pratyohik bish*' (593)—everyday poison. This emphasis on the politics of difference creates an '*ondhota*' (594) or blind separation between people, believes Tagore, subjecting them to the disease of what he terms '*nationtantra*' (594) or the ideology of nationalism. War and nationalism are thus established as intimately connected: the 'ideology of nationhood is rooted in the ideology of conflict' (595), he states uncompromisingly. This relationship is then triangulated with the introduction of '*prabhutva*' (271) or desire for dominance, in the essay '*Laraier Mul*' ('The Cause of War', 1914).[77]

In '*Laraier Mul*', Tagore describes the First World War as '*bonike sainike larai*' (270) or the battle between the business class and the soldiering class. Here, he again shifts away from direct political analysis to focus on revealing the structures underpinning the first industrial-scale war spreading itself across the globe. Business, says Tagore in the essay, has had a '*gandharva vivaha*' ('secret wedding', 271) with imperialism, which he describes as a wholly new form of dominance—the ability of one country to rule over another even though both may be separated by oceans. '*Eto boro bipul prabhutva*' (271)—such vast dominance—as Europe over Asia and Africa had never been seen before in the world. He then highlights how Germany, being a latecomer to this metaphorical feast of empire, hurries in towards the end, deciding to claim what it can with '*gayer jor*' ('physical might', 292). He concludes, importantly, by arguing that the seizing of power by force outside Europe has now been internalised on Europe's own body—'*aaj taha nijer gaye bajitechhe*' (272). Germany's desire for power, Tagore believes, is but a product of modern European civilisation; the barbarity with which such notions of civilisation were shot through has now returned home.

As Santanu Das notes in relation to the First World War, 'the violence on the Western Front was nothing wholly new but an extension into Europe of the barbarity that imperial Europe had inflicted in other parts of the world'.[78] And with the advent of the Second World War, this barbarity, in Tagore's eyes, leads to an implosion of Europe itself.

Tagore is almost uncannily prescient in highlighting such connections during the early years of the twentieth century, before the transformations wrought by two global wars. In the previous section of this chapter, I focused on how Tamil poet Tambimuttu came to a similar conclusion about European barbarity, but this was in relation to the Second World War and articulated much later, in 1941. It is this crucial link between European imperialism in Asia and Africa and barbarity in the form of totalitarianism and violence within Europe itself that is taken up in the post-Second World War years by Hannah Arendt in *The Origins of Totalitarianism* (1951) and acknowledged by Jean-Paul Sartre in his famous Preface to Frantz Fanon's *The Wretched of the Earth* (1961). Sartre writes in the context of Algeria's war of independence against French rule—'Now, which side are the savages on? Where is barbarism? Nothing is missing, not even the tom-toms; the motor-horns beat out '*Al-gér-ie fran-çaise*' while the Europeans burn Moslems alive.'[79] Tagore had come to the same realisation, that savagery and barbarism lay at the heart of civilisation, nearly sixty years before.

In Tagore's *Crisis in Civilisation* (1941), these interconnected thoughts find their final expression two years into the Second World War. Unlike '*Laraier Mul*', which diagnoses the causes of the First World War, this essay never mentions war directly. Instead, it reflects upon how Tagore falls out of love with European, and in particular English, civilisation. Tagore begins by recalling the liberal and humanistic potential of English influence for his generation of intellectuals, 'a prominent beneficiary of the British economic and cultural reshaping of India'.[80] Edmund Burke and Thomas Macaulay's speeches, Shakespeare's plays and Byron's poetry dominated Indian thinkers' minds, and they believed that their independence would inevitably result from the generosity inherent in the ruling race.

Tagore here struggles to find an apposite Bengali translation of the word 'civilisation', just as he had with the term 'nation', because

Indian society, to him, is historically founded on '*sodachar*' (723), the proper ways of conducting oneself, which then transformed into the 'rigid regulations of society' (723), the injustices of which were quelled through the liberating influence of English education. He remembers visiting England as a child and hearing British reform politician and orator John Bright speak in parliament—this, to him, is 'large-hearted, radical liberalism [...] overflowing all national narrow bounds' (722), which he believes India was able to welcome and imbibe, even if such liberalism was manifested in people of a foreign race. In an insightful essay on Tagore and nationalism, Sukanta Chaudhuri comments on this syncreticism in Tagore's long view of Indian history, with 'each encounter creat[ing] a new civili-sational synthesis', and India's 'impulse to such a synthesis' during Tagore's own lifetime too.[81]

However, negotiating such a synthesis becomes problematic when under British imperial rule. Tagore also realises in *Crisis in Civilisation* that those who claim 'civilisation' in its highest forms for themselves can, under the influence of 'national self-interest' (723), just as quickly disown them. Although India's resources continue to underpin the wealth of England, the 'so-called civilised race' (723) becomes entirely indifferent and hostile to the suffering of many hundreds of thousands of Indian people. This crucial point is further emphasised when Tagore contrasts subjugated India with other regions that have either never experienced imperial rule or have successfully shaken it off. He speaks of a 'mighty and prosperous' Japan (723); idealistically—and naively—of Soviet policies in com-bating disease and illiteracy and bringing together nomadic desert communities; Persia being freed of European interference and thus being able to develop; and future possibilities for Afghanistan. In contrast, India, 'smothered under the dead weight of British admin-istration' (724), cannot change or renew itself.

This disillusionment with the deceitful nature of civilisation is represented by a literary trope repeatedly used by Tagore in his writing—that of predatory hunger in relation to the nation. We find this metaphor powerfully employed in the poem 'The Sunset of the Century' (1918), discussed earlier, where he declares:

The hungry self of the Nation shall burst in a violence of fury from its own shameless feeding.

For it has made the world its food,
And licking it, crunching it, and swallowing it in big morsels,
It swells and swells.[82]

Again, two years previously, while still in the midst of the First World War, Tagore, in a famous passage in his lecture 'Nationalism in Japan' (1916), sees the progress undergirding Western dominance as opposed to belief in humanity, and significantly, as parasitic:

> The political civilisation which has sprung up from the soil of Europe [...] is carnivorous and cannibalistic in its tendencies, it feeds upon the resources of other peoples and tries to swallow their whole future [...] Before this political civilisation came to its power and opened its hungry jaws wide enough to gulp down great continents of the earth, we had [...] never such a sight of fearful and hopeless voracity, such wholesale feeding of nation upon nation [...] never such terrible jealousies with all their ugly teeth and claws ready for tearing open each other's vitals.[83]

As Rustom Bharucha has pointed out, Tagore's opposition to the nation is 'almost pathological [...] bordering at times on hysteria: a hysteria that is embodied in the *excess* of language that spills into shifting registers of revulsion and fear directed at the monstrous, almost vampire-like mechanisms of the nation'.[84] We witness here such linguistic excess at play, with the ruthless evolutionary logic of a Tennysonian 'nature red in tooth and claw'[85] being transposed onto an imperial climax, and conceptualised through metaphors of the animal body, with open jaws, grotesque teeth and claws ready for attack. Aggressive nationalism, European civilisation and war are thus inseparable in Tagore: they produce the same predators. Towards the end of *Crisis in Civilisation* (1941), he returns to this image in 'the demon of barbarity' which has 'given up all pretence and has emerged with unconcealed fangs, ready to tear up humanity in an orgy of devastation' (726). Tagore here plays upon the theme of recurrence discussed in Chapter 4 while analysing Anand's novel *The Sword and the Sickle* but gives it a more profound philosophical inflection. The Second World War is perceived in the essay as a cyclical pattern of predatory destruction born out of European civilisation—and now ready to self-annihilate.

Tagore's disenchantment with European civilisation and intense anticolonial feeling in *Crisis in Civilisation* does not, however, seek to glorify a militant Asian nationalism in its place. In the famous exchange of letters published in English-language newspapers in 1938, a year after the start of the second Sino-Japanese war, Japanese poet Yone Noguchi sought his friend Tagore's approval for Japan's aggressive attack on China in what the former terms as 'the war of "Asia for Asia"'.[86] Noguchi, although educated in America and forming friendships on the international literary scene with W.B. Yeats, Ezra Pound and Tagore, became a hardened Japanese nationalist in the 1930s and 1940s.[87] He published a poem in 1944 with the openly murderous title 'Slaughter Them! The Americans and British are our enemies', where his former love for America and Britain cultivated through literary reading transforms into disillusionment with and antipathy towards the West:

> The ties of the past are a dream
> America and England in the old days were for me countries of
> justice:
> America was the country of Whitman,
> England the country of Browning;
> But now they are dissolute countries fallen into the pit of wealth,
> Immoral countries, craving after unpardonable dreams.[88]

In Tagore, however, Noguchi meets with intransigent opposition. Tagore emphatically declares in his response, evoking the language of rapacity yet again, that 'no amount of special pleading can change the fact that in launching a ravening war on Chinese humanity, with all the deadly methods learnt from the West, Japan is infringing every moral principle of which civilisation is based' (6). This is a sharp reversal of his previous Japanophilia. Earlier in October 1937, when Indian revolutionary and exile in Japan Rashbehari Bose had cabled Tagore, requesting the latter to 'prevent Congress and Nehru's anti-Japanese activities' for the sake of 'Indo-Japanese friendship', Tagore's refusal is similarly categorical:

> I, along with the rest of Asia, did once admire and look up to Japan
> [...] But Japan has not taken long to betray that rising hope and
> repudiate all that seemed significant in her wonderful, and, to us

223

symbolic awakening, and has now become itself a worse menace to the defenceless people of the East.[89]

Out of four letters that were publicly exchanged, Tagore's first letter to Noguchi considers Japan to be guilty of the seemingly oxymoronic term 'scientific savagery' (7). As Pankaj Mishra notes, he repeatedly considers in his writings the metaphor of modern civilisation as a machine.[90] In *Crisis in Civilisation*, Tagore argues that 'mastery over the machine' (723) on whose back England conquered the world was denied as a means of progress to India but became hugely beneficial to Japan as a rising Asiatic power. To Noguchi, however, he highlights how the Japanese adoption of science should be contrasted against a 'larger humanity' (7) that the country, to Tagore, had entirely rejected. There are fascinating connections here between Tagorean thought and Baren Basu's novel *Rangrut*, discussed in Chapter 3, where Basu sees the synchronised military display of men in the Indian Army as '*jantrik prakriya*' or 'mechanistic routine' (100). The competitive and inhuman drive for technological superiority that brings nations to war for Tagore is internalised in Basu's novel by male bodies as they collectively perform military drill—it is the men themselves who become the machine. Basu ends the scene with an evocation of the Tagorean demon of war as the men press onwards, marching in time and unable to express fundamental fellow-feeling and empathy by helping their fallen comrade Khogen: 'Chased by some demonic spirit (*danobiyo ek shaktir taronae*), they moved forward' (101).

The parochial perspective of 'the doctrine of "Asia for Asia"' (7), then, that Tagore accuses Noguchi of espousing, returns us to a repugnant 'moral cannibalism' (7), where even the last vestiges of ethical belief are devoured. For Tagore, Noguchi's request becomes an 'instrument of political blackmail', possessing 'all the virtues of the lesser Europe which I repudiate and nothing of the larger humanity that makes us one across the barriers of political labels and divisions' (7). As Sukanta Chaudhuri has astutely pointed out, 'for Tagore, at base, the political *is* the ethical'.[91] Aggressive territorial acquisition, whether initiated by Europe or Japan, remains unconscionable to him because it kills our obligations towards other human beings, and in doing so, leads us down the road to ultimate self-destruction: we are implicated in our own moral death. This was a perspective Tagore shared with M.K. Gandhi, in spite of their many differences.[92]

Ethical considerations, then, become crucial in shaping Tagore's poetic and intellectual testimony to war. The body politic as ethical domain is interrogated by him through the metaphor of disease.[93] In his final letter to Noguchi, Tagore thinks of Japan's hostility towards China by imagining Asia as a 'riddled body', from whose 'bleeding heart' the 'bullets of hatred' need extracting (20). The silence of its people 'bodes disaster, like unconsciousness of disease in its painless progress of ravage' (9). Santanu Das raises the important question as to whether Tagore truly believed imperialism to be a Western disease that infected Japan, and whether such a belief was underpinned by an essentialist assumption of a spiritual East and a power-hungry West. Das notes how, in an earlier piece of writing, Letter No. 15 in 'Japanjatri' ('Travelling in Japan', 1919), Tagore considers Japan's hardened militarism arising as a consequence of European ambitions of world domination:

> In the whole of Asia only Japan realised one day that Europe could be countered only through that force through which she had become triumphant in the whole world. Otherwise, she must have to fall under her wheels, and once she has fallen, there would be no way of rising ever again.[94]

But, by the Second World War, witnessing Japan's depredations in China, Tagore's thinking has significantly reversed. In his final letter to Noguchi, he suggests that silent, and therefore complicit, Japanese citizens have internalised war as a disease, enabling it to tear the Asiatic body apart from within. Whether instigated by the East or the West, then, the demon of war manifests itself in similar ways and becomes just as culpable. Tagore tells Noguchi ominously: 'You are building your conception of an Asia which would be raised on a tower of skulls' (7), another prophetic image that brings to our minds some of the most horrific excesses of the Second World War.

Tagore's first letter to Noguchi expresses some hope for the future. He affirms that 'true Asian humanity will be reborn. Poets will raise their song and be unashamed, one believes, to declare their faith again in a human destiny which cannot admit of a scientific mass production of fratricide' (10). Bharucha has argued how,

225

just as Asia was orientalised by the West within the framework of European world history, Tagore too indulges in 'Orientalist utopianism' by seeing the Asia of his past as essentialised into 'a primordial fellowship and genealogy'.[95] Tagore is, then, inventing an Asia as well, although one that differed from Western conceptions of the continent. This 'oneness' amongst the countries of Asia, for instance between India and China, was conceptualised by Chinese scholars such as Liang Qichao in terms of fraternity, as a relationship between brothers.[96] In Tagore's letter to Noguchi, the idealistic harmony of an Asian brotherhood between China and Japan is ruptured by 'fratricide', against which poets must protest.

Even as he hopes for a future Asian reunification in his first letter to Noguchi, Tagore knows by the time he writes the second that this is a lost cause. Once more, he evokes the imagery of a broken human body, saying that he cannot ask the 'cripple'—referring to China after the fall of Canton and Hankow to the Japanese—to 'forget the memory of this mutilation as easily as you want me to' (21). He again ends on a note of dark prophecy: 'Wishing your people whom I love, not success, but remorse' (21). Yone Noguchi never responded again to Tagore; in 1945, Japan was 'fire- and nuclear-bombed into submission'.[97] Tagore and Noguchi's own fragile brotherhood ended across ideological divides.

What, then, is the role of the poet and intellectual as witness at a time of increasing world hostility? The question seems all the more relevant in the twenty-first century, just as it was in the 1930s. Tagore declares to Noguchi that the discerning mind must critique aggressive nationalism and militarism, and respond to state-sponsored propaganda, or 'hourly doses of poison' (8), recalling the 'pratyohik bish' of 'Birodhmulak Adarsha'. He cannot accept 'separation between an artist's function and his moral conscience', believing that abdicating from 'direct responsibility' is a 'philosophy of escapism' and a 'symptom of the modern intellectual's betrayal of humanity' (9). The 'rest of the world' (9) too needs to express judgement—as Tagore himself once wrote of the West: 'You may force your things into our homes, you may obstruct our prospects of life—but we *judge* you!'[98] It is a sombre Tagore, however, who says in *Crisis in Civilisation*: 'I had at one time believed that the springs of civilisation would issue out of the heart of Europe. But today when I am about to quit the world that faith has gone bank-rupt altogether' (726). At the age of eighty, he was a deeply dis-heartened man.

For Tagore as poetic witness, the resurgent violence of the Second World War manifests itself in his writing as a profound civilisational crisis. There is a remarkable affinity between Bibhutibhushan Bandyopadhyay's novelistic response to the famine, discussed in Chapter 2, and Tagore's poetic response to war: the predatory crocodile with which the novel *Ashani Sanket* begins is but a form of Tagore's all-consuming demon. Unlike the political theo-rist Clausewitz, who famously sees war philosophically and strategi-cally as the 'continuation of politics by any means',[99] Tagore's poetic imagination views war as disastrous in outcome for humanity, lead-ing to 'the crumbling ruins of a proud civilisation strewn like a vast heap of futility' (726) in *Crisis in Civilisation*—in other words, the remains of the world after the demon has feasted.

'I tremble to think of the future,' Tagore had once said to a Jewish friend living in Palestine, 'if the year 1940 ends as it has begun, with slaughter on every side, with history being made only in terms of outrage and violence'.[100] Written three years before this remark, the poem '*Nagini-ra charidike*', with which this section began, shows Tagore, as he bids farewell to the world, addressing those who cannot escape the devastation that such a future will inevitably bring:

Bidae nebar age tai
Dak diye jai.
Danober shathe jara sangramer tore
Prostut hotechhe ghore ghore.

Before I take my leave then
Let me call out
To those who are arming themselves,
For battle with the demon, in home after home.

The demon of violence and barbarity is evoked once again, but this time Tagore's tone is unusually militant,[101] spurring on those ready to fight this demon. His call is answered, two years after his death, by the young self-proclaimed '*durbhikhher kabi*' or famine poet Sukanta Bhattacharya in the poem '*Rabindranath-er Prati*' ('To

227

Rabindranath', written in 1943). Although Tagore did not live to see it, the Bengal Famine devoured the countryside that he had loved dearly, that had 'unleashed [in him] a love of natural land-scapes, a regard for the everyday, the domestic and the fragmentary, as well as an insight into the plight of the rural poor'.[102]

At a time when the streets of Calcutta were witnessing the terrible casualties of the famine in mass migrations from villages to the city, Sukanta the activist-poet and famine-relief worker writes his response to Tagore, playing on the latter's words in 'Naginira charidike':

> Tai aj amaro visvas
> 'Shantir lalita bani shonaibe byartha parihas.'
> Tai ami cheye dekhi protigya prostut ghore ghore,
> Danober shathe aaj sangramer tore.

> That is why today I too believe
> 'The gentle message of peace will play in futile mockery.'
> That is why I see the resolve and readiness in home after home,
> For battle with the demon today.[103]

The demon of war has, in 1943, transformed into the demon of hunger, which must be combated—but Tagore's extraordinary metaphoric foresight, dominated by images of predatory and rapa-cious appetitive urges, had long since anticipated the connection.

Conclusion

In her analysis of Albert Camus's novel *The Plague* (1947) as a monu-ment to witnessing, Shoshana Felman asks the searching question, 'What does it mean to be subject to history?'[104] She is interested neither in perpetrators nor in immediate victims but in history's onlookers and witnesses. This chapter too has addressed the same question, by considering how poetry as testimony responds to a moment of historical crisis, to the absolute failure of imagination that results in acts of violence, pain and trauma in the first place. It has also examined how two South Asian writers and intellectuals interrogate the concept of civilisation itself, framed by the return of global war. I have read M.J. Tambimuttu's early work and Rabindranath Tagore's late writing together here to examine the scope, range and complexity of poetic and literary testimony from

South Asian perspectives as a reaction to the Second World War. While Tagore's responses to the war continue right up until his death in August 1941, Tambimuttu has a more prolific record of participating in wartime broadcasts and editing poetry in post-war years than of composing poetry. Yet living through the Second World War makes him write creatively.

How does such testimonial writing shape our understanding of the Second World War in South Asia? And how does it work as an interpretive tool? These questions bring us back to the philosophical perception of the second global war as civilisational crisis. Ideas of decay and degeneration about Europe had persisted from the late nineteenth century onwards into the twentieth century and been accelerated by the First World War. It is, however, in Tagore's thinking that we find a profound critique of the structures of European civilisation itself—right from his poem composed on the last day of the nineteenth century to his final published work in the midst of the Second World War, self-consciously titled *Crisis in Civilisation*. Tagore had realised that colonialism itself was a form of barbarianism, and that global war meant that the violence Europe had inflicted on other parts of the world was now coming home. He sees the Second World War as a profoundly destructive, self-anni-hilating force, capable of reducing the world to rubble.

For Tambimuttu, barbarity lurks at the heart of civilisation itself, spurred on by colonial conquest and plunder. The savage that he considers to be living within us all is unleashed by global war and not simply restricted to an imperial trope. Bearing witness to the crisis of the London Blitz as he lives through it, then, becomes a means of establishing deep historical connections—between the First and Second World Wars, for instance, in their competing and terribly destructive nationalisms, one preparing the way for the next. If wait-ing for the violence of the next bomb takes one out of time, as it were, what connects the victims of war across the world is the simul-taneity of their present suffering, from China to Dunkirk and London. It is only by evoking nostalgic dreams of a verdant, lush East, rich in sunshine and fruit, where ripeness is all, that Tambimuttu can find imaginative release from privation and escape the civilisa-tional crisis brought about by Western violence.

Tagore had long since anticipated this civilisational crisis. His poetic testimony highlights the dangers of aggressive militarism and hardened nationalism through the prophetic and metaphorically resonant imagery of cannibalism and the ever-hungry demon of conflict. But his is also a deeply personal crisis. If political philosophy for Tagore merges into ethics—if the political is the ethical— the poetic and philosophical writings of his final years underscore how deeply disillusioned he is with humanity. Intensely critical of European civilisation for instigating violence and barbarity through colonialism and global war but faced with the realities of Japanese aggression in China towards the end of his life, Tagore realises that the East too holds few redemptive political possibilities.

Yet the imaginative potential inherent in hope never entirely fades away. After the imminent 'cataclysm' referred to in *Crisis in Civilisation* (726), Tagore is still somehow able to envision a world after war with a new historical dawn, born from the eastern horizon where the sun rises. Perhaps the 'daunting task of starting over', as Paul Betts terms it, then, begins for Tagore in the east.[105] If human beings in his time have failed to prevent 'the scattered rubble of history' (726), there is still hope in the 'unvanquished Man' (726) of the future, embarking on a fresh path to reclaim his 'lost human heritage' (726). Even as he takes leave of this world, then, Tagore poetically anticipates in his very last essay a new age for humankind beyond the rubble of the 1940s.

AFTERWORD

Indian involvement in the Second World War found significant literary representation in 1992, with Sri Lankan-Canadian author Michael Ondaatje's Booker Prize-winning novel *The English Patient*. The book portrays the character of Lieutenant Kirpal Singh, or Kip as he is known, the Indian sapper and bomb defusal expert, making his way to Italy during the war. Towards the end of the novel, appalled by the atomic bombs that devastate Hiroshima and Nagasaki, Kip discovers in himself an intense anger against Western nations, accompanied by a pan-Asian solidarity. As Caravaggio, another character in the novel, thinks, 'the young soldier is right. They [the Allies] would never have dropped such a bomb on a white nation.'[1] But feelings of pan-Asian comradeship in Indian soldiers, or amongst Indian civilians on the home-front, were diffuse by the end of the war. Samar Sen's poem '9th August 1945', for instance, discussed in Chapter 2, taking its title from the date of the Nagasaki bombing, talks of '*Nipponer raktashandya*' or 'the blood-red evening of Nippon'[2] as poetic symbolism alone. This incarnadine twilight becomes the harbinger of change in the poem, bringing in its wake the end of the war and the collapse of fascism. On the other hand, Gandhi, when asked in 1946 for his response to the atomic bomb, unequivocally stated: 'Unless now the world adopts non-violence, it will spell certain suicide for mankind.'[3] Contemporary Indian reactions to this moment of horrific violence at the end of the war, then, remained varied, contested, divided.[4]

India's records of the Second World War have largely remained dormant for over eighty years, as public memory has narrowed into a Eurocentric and US-focused remembrance. Recollections of imperial military service rubbed uncomfortably against post-war processes of decolonisation, which privileged narratives of resistance to the British Empire in South Asia. Rather than shaping Indian national identity, as it did in the UK, the Second World War was hijacked by momentous events in the post-war years—independence from the Raj, the trauma of Partition and communal violence—along with postcolonial amnesia. Ironically, these memories are missing in history because the war itself accelerated the processes of decolonisation, and in doing so wrote colonial involvement out of public consciousness in both the UK and India. The marginalisation of Indian war experiences was the result of the birth of modern South Asia: its time was out of joint. As Joanna Bourke observes, 'memory itself is a battlefield, in which there are high stakes involved'.[5] For both Britain and South Asia, remembering the Raj became—and remains—problematic and contentious. This was because, as Raghu Karnad puts it, 'The years 1939–1945 were not a break from a colonial world order that came before and resumed after. Rather, it was the climax of colonialism: when imperial mania finally came back home and Europe began to consume itself.'[6]

In August 1944, an Indian Viceroy's Commissioned Officer (VCO) based in Italy—like Kip in Ondaatje's novel—wrote to his family in Urdu: 'I heard on the BBC that the Government of India has restarted discussion of India's independence with Mr Gandhi. I hope that whatever results from these talks, our rights will be safeguarded.'[7] Here, the VCO is anxious about his status as an imperial soldier when colonialism has ended: he realises how problematic his situation might be in a post-war India that has successfully negotiated independence from the British. An entire year before the end of the war, while still stationed abroad, Indian soldiers in their letters home foreground their emotional investment in a world beyond the war. A sepoy writes in Bengali: 'I am in a fix to know what to do after my demobilisation, which is not far off. So for God's sake kindly deposit my allotted amount in the Savings Bank from now onwards, for my rainy days.'[8]

If growing his family allowance in the bank becomes this Bengali sepoy's strategy for confronting an unknown future on his return home, a Non-Commissioned Officer (NCO) finds himself entirely at a loss as he contemplates a saturated job market in the aftermath of war. He writes in Hindustani: 'The war may be over any day now and it is my constant anxiety to find what I shall do after the war. I cannot depend on getting one of the civilian jobs reserved for demobilised men; there will be many claimants [...] The problem defies solution, and the more I think of it the more depressed I feel.'[9] Economic concerns continue to dominate the soldiers' emotional worlds as they anticipate a world beyond war; such imperatives remain just as important as they had been during the recruitment years.

For many Indian soldiers who remained stationed abroad even after 1945, this post-war world took considerably longer to arrive. While the Indian home-front became the site of rebellion against the British Empire, selected Indian troops continued to serve in colonial struggles that played out in the immediate years after the war. The 5th Indian Infantry Division fought for the Dutch empire in Surabaya to suppress the Indonesian demand for independence in September and October 1945, while the 20th Indian Division battled guerrillas near Saigon to consolidate once again the French empire in 1945 and 1946.[10] But if Indian troops returned to their imperial roles in the immediate aftermath of war, there were other narratives of resistance being created. Writing about the working people of Australia, Indonesia and India who boycotted Dutch shipping in Australian waters in support of Indonesian independence at the end of the Second World War, Heather Goodall draws our attention to cross-border working-class solidarities. In particular, she highlights new meanings of internationalism that were being forged in 'that brief period of hope after the end of World War II, when colonialism seemed to be in its death throes but when the horrors of Partition and the bitter polarisations of the Cold War were still barely imagined'.[11]

If the violence of the Second World War bled into militant efforts to re-establish European colonial dominance in Southeast Asia after 1945, it was also directed inwards, to the Indian home-front, with catastrophic consequences. The sale of arms and ammunitions on the black market soared in post-war years, with military police in Calcutta, for instance, trying to locate US army men and Indian civilians illegally selling off unused American military equipment.[12] In addition to this destabilising phenomenon, political scientists Saumitra Jha and Steven Wilkinson have highlighted how, during Partition, districts in Punjab which contained significant numbers of men with combat experience saw much higher levels of ethnic cleansing, leading them to conclude that 'exposure to combat in external wars helps veterans, often from minority or non-elite groups, to develop skills at private organisation and violence'.[13] Indian soldiers who had been trained to kill for the Allies turned the tactics they had learnt onto other Indian men and women, as the scramble for communal homelands began in the subcontinent.

The end of the war, then, was not the end of conflict for India— rather, a continuum of violence was established beyond 1945, to which imperial military service contributed. The prolonged absence of Indian war narratives from public consciousness can perhaps be partially explained by the trauma of Partition, as the 'home' that soldiers had imaginatively invested with such longing and desire while stationed abroad became a ruptured and bloodied country soon after their return. As Yasmin Khan notes, even for the twentieth century, Partition is remembered for the scale of its violence—resulting in the deaths of half-a-million to one million women, men and children—and for its indiscriminate brutality.[14] Modern South Asia still lives in the long shadow of the national and communal animosities born out of the immediate post-war years.

What are we to make of the silence that surrounds Indian war narratives and their emotional undertow, which has only recently begun to be interrogated? A revealing insight into the immediate post-war attitude to this history is seen with British author Compton Mackenzie. Commissioned to write on India and the Second World War, Mackenzie was told by an Indian National Congress minister in 1946 that there was no interest in this book as 'he and his party had not considered it their war'.[15] Meanwhile, in the UK, the Indian Army's Commander-in-Chief Auchinleck campaigned for a monument in central London in memory of this army during the Second World War; without formal backing, his plan died out by 1949.[16] Both nationalist narratives and post-imperial inertia left Indian soldiers out in the cold, as unaccommodated men. Indian civilian responses to war remained even more buried, or were interpreted through other historical lenses, such as famine, communism, antifascism and the independence struggle.

Perhaps it is unsurprising that the life-writing and literary materials used throughout this book end before the return of Indian soldiers to their homeland: they are in danger of being subsumed by more dominant historical events. Salvi's memoir only touches upon his emotional response on seeing the shores of India from his ship, which recalls to him the Italian 'home' he has left behind; Shantilal Ray in *Arakan Fronte* concludes with a surge of nationalist feeling on the Indo-Burma border, knowing that he is about to journey home, yet not representing the actual return. Abid Hasan's memoir, *The Men from Imphal*, invested in the symbolic significance of the INA's political resistance to the British Empire, does not discuss the lived experiences of these men after 1945. Crasta does mention his return to India from Southeast Asia, but this is summarised rather perfunctorily in a few sentences before the memoir ends. Anand's novel *The Sword and the Sickle*, although born out of Second World War tensions and cultural discourse, depicts the return of Lal Singh after the First World War.

Military censorship reports on soldiers' letters too are only available up until March 1945, while none of the poets, philosophers and novelists analysed here seek to represent an emotional history of India in the post-war years. It is outside the scope of this book to consider the complex range of psychological and social realities which demobilised Indian soldiers in their millions came home to, along with the trauma of families whose men never returned.[17] This post-war perspective is an important area for future research, as is a detailed examination of the changing politics of war remembrance itself.

Alongside an analysis of the visual, my book has opened up the life-writing narratives of those women and men whose wartime emotions, even today, 'rest in caches private and unvisited',[18] and whose literary responses to this war have been overlooked. I have also attempted in the process to expand the broader cultural and literary focus of Second World War research itself, not only by including Indian emotions in response to this war, but also considering what such war service signified outside Europe and the USA. Furthermore, I have argued for the testimonial, ethical and representational value of literature in our engagement with this marginalised history, paying attention to how Indian literary texts complicate the emotional histories arising from the fraught socio-political contexts of this war. Future research on the Second World War will, I hope, continue to reveal further emotional nuances of colonial participation, including African and West Indian involvement.

My own engagements with twenty-first-century South Asian memories of the war have revealed how vibrant, intimate and enduring they are, drawing attention to the disjunction between private remembrance and public recognition. A feature piece I wrote for *The Telegraph* (India) in 2015, entitled 'Bengal boys of the "good war"', brought rich stores of war memorabilia in the form of photographs, uniforms, newspaper cuttings, private papers and family wartime memories to my attention. In several cases, this led to interviews with surviving veterans, including an eighty-nine-year-old woman, who had, as a teenager, worked in the Women's Auxiliary Territorial Service in India within the Signals section. Today, she is no more. South Asian war memories, I learnt, include not only the personal but also the cultural. I was alerted to the existence of both the memoir *Arakan Fronte* and the novel *Rangrut* by a Bangladeshi reader of my *Telegraph* article, who generously sent me copies of both these out-of-print works. It is, then, as much for those alive today who have quietly continued to remember the war, as for those who experienced its lived realities in the 'stormy decade'[19] of the 1940s, that I have attempted in this book to recover and re-animate Indian emotions of the Second World War within history.

NOTES

INTRODUCTION: 'V' FOR VICTORY?

1. Ministry of Information's Second World War Official Collection of Photographs, c. 1 December 1941, Imperial War Museum (hereafter abbreviated as IWM), K 1254.
2. For a brief history of the 'V' for Victory symbol, see <https://www.iwm.org.uk/history/where-does-v-for-victory-come-from> [Accessed 30 July 2022]. British soldiers in the Second World War were sometimes photographed flipping the 'V' as an insult. See <https://www.warhistoryonline.com/war-articles/wwii-3.html?safari=1&Exc_D_LessThanPoint002_p1=1> [Accessed 30 July 2022]. I thank Daniel Todman for alerting me to the many layers of meaning in this gesture.
3. I use the word 'India' throughout the book to refer to undivided India as it existed during the Second World War, comprising the modern South Asian countries of India, Pakistan and Bangladesh. Burma had already been separated from British India in 1937. Other place names in the book follow the same naming convention—thus, I use 'Calcutta' and not 'Kolkata'; 'Ceylon' and not 'Sri Lanka'; the princely state of 'Travancore', now part of the southern Indian state of Kerala; the British protectorate of 'Trans-Jordan' and not the country of Jordan, and so on.
4. There is general academic consensus on the figure of two-and-a-half million recruits from India serving in the Indian Army in the Second World War. See, for example, Srinath Raghavan, *India's War: The Making of Modern South Asia, 1939–1945* (London, Penguin: 2016), p. 1, and Florian Stadtler, 'Britain's Forgotten Volunteers: South Asian Contributions to the Two World Wars', in *South Asians and the Shaping of Britain, 1870–1950: A Sourcebook*, ed. by Ruvani Ranasinha, Rehana Ahmed, Sumita Mukherjee and Florian Stadtler (Manchester: Manchester University Press, 2013), pp. 80–135 (p. 91). Yasmin Khan notes that there were over two million Indian men being demobilised at the end of the war. See Yasmin Khan, *The Raj at War: A People's History of India's Second World War* (London: Bodley Head, 2015), p. xi.
5. Ashley Jackson, *The British Empire and the Second World War* (London: Hambledon Continuum, 2006), p. 353.

6. Recruitment figures for African soldiers from the British Empire are difficult to determine with precision. They include Nigerians, Gold Coasters, Sierra Leoneans and Gambians who formed the Royal West Africa Frontier Force (RWAFF)—Britain's West African colonial army—numbering about 155,000 men. The African Auxiliary Pioneer Corps served in the Middle East. Its recruitment records contain little information, but approximately 250,000 East and Central Africans served in British colonial military units during the war, while in southern Africa, about 36,000 pioneers signed up to this Corps. In addition, the Northern Rhodesia Regiment and the Somaliland Camel Corps, along with the King's African Rifles, confronted Italian forces when Italy officially entered the war in 1940. The Native Military Labour Corps, formed out of unarmed African men and resulting from racial segregation policies in South Africa where black soldiers were not permitted to join South Africa's Union Defence Force, comprised about 76,000 men. These figures do not include the Tirailleurs Sénégalais, who served under the French Empire during the war and numbered between 200,000 and 350,000 African men. See Timothy Parsons, 'The Military Experiences of Ordinary Africans in World War II', in *Africa and World War II*, ed. by Judith Byfield, Carolyn Brown, Timothy Parsons and Ahmad Sikainga (Cambridge: Cambridge University Press, 2015), pp. 3–23 (pp. 5, 6, 20).

   In addition, nearly 6,000 West Indian men were recruited into the Royal Air Force. A Caribbean Regiment comprising 1,000 soldiers was raised in 1944 and sent abroad, but never saw active service. See 'Together: Background Information, Some Facts and Figures', in *Together: The Contribution Made in the Second World War by African, Asian and Caribbean Men and Women* (London: Imperial War Museum, 1995).

7. As Indian soldiers led itinerant lives during the war, such 'V's continued to resurface across the world in various forms, finding representation in the narratives the soldiers wrote. The memoir *Whom Enemies Sheltered* (1983) by Indian officer R.G. Salvi, discussed in Chapter 3, highlights how, as an Allied prisoner under the Germans and Italians in North Africa, Salvi was taken from one city to another in Cyrenaica (modern-day Libya), where civilians, 'in retaliation to Churchill's famed victory sign [...] would gesture with an upside down "V". Here, the gesture was stripped of its unifying force into one of mockery, humiliation and defeat. See R.G. Salvi, *Whom Enemies Sheltered: A Saga of Human Love in the Midst of World War II* (Mumbai: Bharatiya Vidya Bhavan, 1983), p. 45. All further references are to this edition, and page numbers are provided in parentheses within the body of the text. 'V's also made their way onto commemorative Indian stamps in 1945, where India was represented as

the centre of the world, pierced through its middle by a sword and the two arms of the 'V' protruding on either side.

8. Roland Barthes, 'Myth Today', in *Mythologies*, trans. by Annette Lavers (London: Vintage, 2009; first pub. 1957), pp. 131–187 (p. 139).
9. Photo by Izis /Paris Match via Getty Images.
10. Roland Barthes, 'Myth Today', p. 149.
11. Ibid., p. 169.
12. Ibid., p. 142.
13. Srinath Raghavan, *India's War*, p. 64.
14. Gajendra Singh, *The Testimonies of Indian Soldiers and the Two World Wars: Between Self and Sepoy* (London: Bloomsbury, 2014), Appendix II, p. 256.
15. Srinath Raghavan, *India's War*, p. 64.
16. Appendix 13, in Nandan Prasad, *Expansion of the Armed Forces and Defence Organisation 1939–1945*, in *Official History of the Indian Armed Forces in the Second World War, 1939–1945*, ed. by Bisheshwar Prasad (Combined Inter-Services Historical Section, India and Pakistan, 1956).
17. *India and the War, 1939–1945, The Facts* (London: Information Department, India Office, 1946), p. 12. The numbers of those killed are from the online records of the Commonwealth War Graves Commission (CWGC) for the Indian Armed Forces, reconfirmed via an email exchange dated 5 February 2021 between the author and Roy Hemington, Records Data Manager, CWGC. These figures remain disputed.
18. Yasmin Khan, *The Raj at War*, p. 90.
19. Taj ul-Islam Hashmi, *Pakistan as a Peasant Utopia: The Communalisation of Class Politics in East Bengal, 1920–1947* (Delhi: Routledge, 1992), p. 223. The translation from the Bengali is mine.
20. Ibid., p. 224. The translation from the Bengali is mine.
21. A *takhallus* is the poetic name of a writer in Urdu. Here, Nawazish signs his full name as 'Nawazish Ali Mushtaq'.
22. Nawazish Ali Mushtaq, *Jangi Safarnama* (*Journey Through War*) (Lahore: Qureshi Book Agency, c. 1944). I am very grateful to Ghee Bowman for generously sending me Nawazish Ali's poem. This is a rare find from modern-day Pakistan. More on Nawazish Ali's life and poetry can be found in Ghee Bowman's own book *The Indian Contingent: The Forgotten Muslim Soldiers of Dunkirk* (Cheltenham: History Press, 2020). I am also indebted to Priyanka Basu and Farha Noor for their interest in this poem, and in helping me find a suitable English-language translator. And finally, my thanks to Ajmal Kamal for his wonderful translation of this challenging work.
    Ajmal notes that *qissas* or stories like Nawazish Ali's would be composed in verse using rhyming couplets, to be recited orally to a mostly

non-literate and usually male live audience in a *chaupal*-like gathering or community setting in a village or a *mohalla*. When printing became common, by the turn of the twentieth century, such long or short *qissas* began to be published as booklets. The purpose, however, remained the same: they were to be read by a literate person to a live audience. In many cases, the person reciting the *qissa* memorised it after a few readings and no longer needed the booklet itself, which would be kept safe inside the house for future reciters and gatherings.

The poem is not dated; however, it ends with the defeat of the Japanese in Burma, which presumably means it was composed after 1944.

23. Yasmin Khan, *The Raj at War*, p 16.
24. *Crises and Creativities: Middle-Class Bhadralok in Bengal, c.1939–52* (Hyderabad: Orient Black Swan, 2009), p. 54.
25. Ibid., pp. 54–55.
26. Priyamvada Gopal, *Insurgent Empire: Anticolonial Resistance and British Dissent* (London: Verso, 2020).
27. Robert Gerwarth and Erez Manela, 'The Great War as a Global War: Imperial Conflict and the Reconfiguration of World Order, 1911–1923', *Diplomatic History*, 38. 4 (September 2014), 786–800 (p. 791).
28. Santanu Das, *India, Empire and First World War Culture: Literature, Images, Songs* (Cambridge: Cambridge University Press, 2018), pp. 59–60.
29. For recent scholarship on the Amritsar Massacre, see Kim Wagner, *Amritsar 1919: An Empire of Fear and the Making of a Massacre* (New Haven, CT: Yale University Press, 2019), where Wagner assesses the relationship between state violence and colonial fear.
30. Letter from Rabindranath Tagore to Lord Chelmsford, Viceroy of India, dated 31 May 1919, in *Selected Letters of Rabindranath Tagore*, ed. by Krishna Dutta and Andrew Robinson (Cambridge: Cambridge University Press, 1997), p. 223.
31. Robert Gerwarth and Erez Manela, 'The Great War as a Global War', p. 791.
32. Ibid. Also see Erez Manela, 'Imagining Woodrow Wilson in Asia: Dreams of East-West Harmony and the Revolt against Empire in 1919', *The American Historical Review*, 111.5 (December 2006), 1327–1351, for an analysis of how intellectual elites in China and India began to see Woodrow Wilson as a political leader who could transform international relations founded on imperialism and domination into more equitable exchanges, mainly based on the League of Nations.
33. The start of the Second World War is contested. Hitler's invasion of Poland marks the beginning of hostilities in Europe; in Asia, however, the war dates back to 1931–1932 with the Japanese invasion of

Manchuria, and then China proper in 1937. India's participation in the war as a belligerent, however, was linked to Britain's own involvement, which began from September 1939 with the German attack on Poland. See Richard Bessell, 'Death and Survival in the Second World War', in *The Cambridge History of the Second World War, Part II, The Social Practice of People's War, 1939–1945*, ed. by Michael Geyer and Adam Tooze (Cambridge: Cambridge University Press, 2015), pp. 252–276 (p. 253).

34. Srinath Raghavan, *India's War*, p. 9.

35. Extract from H.N. Brailsford, 'India—the Path to Victory', 22 October 1939, in The Public and Judicial Department, India Office Records at the British Library, hereafter abbreviated as IOR/L/PJ. File reference 5706 (1939).

36. Alan Jeffreys, *The British Army in the Far East 1941–1945* (Oxford: Osprey Publishing, 2005), p. 15.

37. Tanika Sarkar, 'Time in Place: Urban Culture in Decades of Crisis', in *Calcutta: The Stormy Decades*, ed. by Tanika Sarkar and Sekhar Bandyopadhyay (New Delhi: Social Science Press, 2015), pp. 461–474 (p. 464).

38. Kris Manjapra, *M.N. Roy: Marxism and Colonial Cosmopolitanism* (New Delhi: Routledge, 2010), p. xiv. Manabendra Nath Roy initially favoured the Indian National Congress's position of offering conditional support for the war until the summer of 1940. But from July 1940 onwards, he fully supported the 'anti-fascist' war and separated himself entirely from the Congress position. See Amit Kumar Gupta, *Crises and Creativities: Middle-Class Bhadralok in Bengal, c.1939–52* (Hyderabad: Orient Black Swan, 2009), p. 44.

39. Raghu Karnad, *Farthest Field: An Indian Story of the Second World War* (London: William Collins, 2015), p. 49.

40. Sugata Bose, *His Majesty's Opponent: Subhas Chandra Bose and India's Struggle Against Empire* (Cambridge, MA: Harvard University Press, 2011), particularly the chapters entitled 'The Terrible Price of Freedom' (pp. 201–237) and 'Roads to Delhi' (pp. 238–303).

41. Sugata Bose, *His Majesty's Opponent*, p. 275.

42. Ibid., p. 279.

43. Many of the women were teenagers from the rubber plantations of Malaya, who had never seen India, but nonetheless enlisted in the INA, funding its activities by donating their gold jewellery and other valuables. The Ranis, in the end, were never sent to the frontline. For an important study of this women's regiment, see Joyce Lebra, *Women Against the Raj: The Rani of Jhansi Regiment* (Singapore: Institute of Southeast Asian Studies, 2008).

44. For a detailed account of Noor Inayat Khan's life and war service, see

Shrabani Basu, *Spy Princess: The Life of Noor Inayat Khan* (Cheltenham: History Press, 2008).

45. Letter by The Marquess of Zetland, Secretary of State for India, to the Home Department of the Government of India on 12 November 1939, L/PJ/5706 (1939), IOR/BL.

46. Yasmin Khan and Gajendra Singh, 'Introduction', in *An Imperial World at War: The British Empire, 1939–45*, ed. by Ashley Jackson, Yasmin Khan and Gajendra Singh (London: Routledge, 2016), pp. 1–9 (p. 5).

47. Raghu Karnad, *Farthest Field*, p. 23.

48. Michele Louro notes how India's struggle for independence was entwined in wider debates against imperialism, capitalism and fascism across the world. She also observes how Nehru's concerns about fascism led him to draft foreign policy initiatives that were approved by the Indian National Congress between 1937 and 1939. The Congress, for instance, sympathised with the Republican cause in Spain, denounced fascism, and raised funds for food and medical supplies for the Republicans. Nehru also organised public demonstrations in support of the Chinese cause and arranged for Japanese goods to be boycotted. He also persuaded the Congress to send its own medical unit to China in 1938. See Michele Louro, *Comrades against Imperialism: Nehru, India, and Interwar Internationalism* (Cambridge: Cambridge University Press, 2018), p. 214.

    Florian Stadtler notes how the India League, a political group based in London with strong ties to the Congress, did, however, support the war effort in Britain, but foregrounded India's crucial role in Allied victory as the lynchpin for Indian independence after the war. See Florian Stadtler, 'Britain's Forgotten Volunteers', p. 91.

49. Extract from *Harijan*, 25 November 1939, L/PJ/5706 (1939), IOR/BL.

50. Extract from statement issued by Clement Attlee, Leader of the Labour Party called 'India and the War', published in *The Times*, 21 October 1939. L/PJ/5706 (1939), IOR/BL.

51. Quoted in the newspaper *The Indian*, 19 October 1939, published in Kuala Lumpur, Microfilm No: 2075, National Archives of India, hereafter referred to as NAI.

52. Quoted in Manu Bhagavan, *India and the Quest for One World: The Peacemakers* (London: Palgrave Macmillan, 2013), p. 12.

53. Manu Bhagavan, *India and the Quest for One World*, p. xiv.

54. Ibid., p. 13.

55. Amit Kumar Gupta, *Crises and Creativities*, pp. 57–58.

56. Devika Shetti, *War over Words: Censorship in India, 1930–1960*, (Cambridge: Cambridge University Press, 2019), p. 162. Yasmin Khan, *The Raj at War*, p. 37.

57. Not all of India suffered during the war. Indivar Kamtekar notes how 'contemporary assessments of Punjab portray the war almost as a fairy-tale time, when more gold and silver were worn and dollops of ghee were gulped down with tea: prosperity in Punjab took the completely convincing form of eating more'. See Indivar Kamtekar, 'A Different War Dance: State and Class in India 1939–1945', *Past and Present* 176.1 (2002), 187–221 (p. 176).

58. Jonathan Friedman, 'Law and Politics in the Subsequent Nuremberg Trials, 1946–1949', in *Atrocities on Trial: Historical Perspectives on the Politics of Prosecuting War Crimes*, ed. by Patricia Heberer and Jürgen Matthäus (Lincoln, Nebraska: University of Nebraska Press, 2008), pp. 75–101 (p. 75).

59. L.C. Green, 'The Indian National Army Trials', *The Modern Law Review*, 11.1 (1948), 47–69 (p. 49).

60. A remarkable letter now housed at the National Archives of India (NAI), Delhi, attests to the tremendous emotional force of this trial. The letter is filed amongst the private papers of General Cariappa, who served as a senior officer in the Indian Army and was appointed president of the INA Red Fort court-martial. On 28 November 1945, a certain Jemadar B.I. Ganapathy, stationed in Burma with the South East Asia Command, made an impassioned plea to Cariappa on behalf of the arrested INA men.

    Ganapathy notes how the expatriate Indian community in Burma 'owe their existence to the Indian National Army' after the region was taken over by Japan, because Subhas Chandra Bose had left behind thousands of men to protect them. He highlights how forsaken imperial responsibilities were appropriated by this nascent national force, that 'during the time of trouble it is the Indian National Army that were [sic] discharging the actual duty of the British administration in safeguarding the lives of millions of British Indian subjects all over the Eastern islands here' and that the Indian expatriate community 'worship Subhas Chandra Bose as a second god who has given them a second life'. See 'Letter to General Cariappa from Jemadar Ganapathy', dated 28 November 1945, Cariappa Private Papers, (1912–1972), NAI.

61. See Peter Ward Fay's chapters 'Trial at the Red Fort' (pp. 464–492) and 'The Triumph of the INA' (pp. 493–524), in *The Forgotten Army: India's Armed Struggle for Independence, 1942–1945* (Delhi: Rupa, 1994).

62. Yasmin Khan, *The Raj at War*, p. ix.

63. Quoted in Srinath Raghavan, *India's War*, pp. 77–78.

64. MSS EUR T3, 'Field Marshall Sir Claude Auchinleck', interviewed by Charles Allen (1972–1974), Oral Archives, British Library.

65. Florian Stadtler, 'Britain's Forgotten Volunteers', p. 97.

66. For a detailed account of the Indian Army's campaigns in the Middle East and North Africa, see Srinath Raghavan, *India's War*, particularly the chapters 'Into Africa' (pp. 95–121), 'The Oil Campaigns' (pp. 122–149), 'Fox Hunting' (pp. 150–175) and 'Around the Mediterranean' (pp. 356–375).

67. Yasmin Khan, *The Raj at War*, pp. 36–37.

68. Srinath Raghavan, *India's War*, p. 99.

69. See Srinath Raghavan, *India's War*, particularly the chapter 'Around the Mediterranean' (pp. 356–375).

70. *India and the War, 1939–1945, The Facts* (London: Information Department, India Office, 1946), p. 14.

71. Indivar Kamtekar, 'A Different War Dance', p. 190.

72. A.G. Fernandes and K. Someswara Rao, 'Nutrition Work in the Indian Army', *Special Report Series—Indian Council of Medical Research*, 36.36 (1961), 73–96 (p. 77).

73. Yasmin Khan, *The Raj at War*, p. 38.

74. Ibid.

75. Santanu Das, *India, Empire and First World War Culture* (Cambridge: Cambridge University Press, 2018). See, in particular, the chapter 'The Imperial-Nationalist Self', pp. 39–74.

76. Anirudh Deshpande, *Hope and Despair: Mutiny, Rebellion and Death in India* (Delhi: Primus, 2016), pp. 19–20.

77. Johannes Voigt, *India in the Second World War*, pp. 163–164.

78. Benjamin Zachariah, 'The Creativity of Destruction: Wartime Imaginings of Development and Social Policy, *c.* 1942–1946', in *The World in World Wars: Experiences, Perceptions and Perspectives from Africa and Asia*, ed. by Heike Liebau, Katrin Bromber, Katharina Lange, Dyala Hamzah and Ravi Ahuja (Leiden: Brill, 2010), pp. 547–579 (pp. 554–555).

79. Srinath Raghavan, *India's War*, p. 78.

80. Benjamin Zachariah, 'The Creativity of Destruction', p. 554.

81. Srinath Raghavan, *India's War*, p. 74; Gajendra Singh, *The Testimonies of Indian Soldiers and the Two World Wars*, Appendix II, p. 256.

82. See Gajendra Singh, *The Testimonies of Indian Soldiers and the Two World Wars*, pp. 11–34, for a detailed analysis of the colonial 'martial races' theory. Also see Heather Streets, *Martial Races: The Military, Race and Masculinity in British Imperial Culture, 1857–1914* (Manchester: Manchester University Press, 2004).

83. Firozkhan Noon, 'Resettlement of Soldiers', *The Asiatic Review* (July 1944), 287–295 (p. 288).

84. Srinath Raghavan, *India's War*, p. 74.

85. Anirudh Deshpande, *Hope and Despair*, pp. 22–23.

86. Srinath Raghavan, *India's War*, p. 74. There are older assessments of Indian

Army recruitment numbers in military histories. See, for example, Frederick Perry, *The Commonwealth Armies: Manpower and Organisation in Two World Wars* (Manchester: Manchester University Press, 1988), p. 117, and Johannes H. Voigt, *India in the Second World War*, pp. 163–164.

87. Firozkhan Noon, 'Resettlement of Soldiers', p. 288.
88. Anirudh Deshpande, *Hope and Despair*, p. 23.
89. Srinath Raghavan notes, though, that Indian recruits from the old 'martial races' were still prioritised for the majority of front-line, combatant roles. See Srinath Raghavan, *India's War*, p. 76.
90. Gajendra Singh, *The Testimonies of Indian Soldiers and the Two World Wars*, p. 14. Singh quotes Frederick Sleigh Roberts, Commander of the Madras Army between 1880 and 1885, and then Commander-in-Chief of the Indian Army, writing in 1897 about Madrassi and Bengali men: 'Each cold season I made long tours in order to acquaint myself with the needs and capabilities of the men in the Madras Army [...] But long years of peace, and the security and prosperity attending it, had evidently had upon them, as they always seem to have on Asiatics, a softening and deteriorating effect; and I was forced to the conclusion that the ancient military spirit had died in them, as it died in the ordinary Hindustanis of Bengal and the Mahratta of Bombay, and that they could no longer be safely pitted against warlike races.'
91. Quoted in Indivar Kamtekar, 'A Different War Dance', p. 192.
92. Srinath Raghavan, *India's War*, p. 69.
93. This connection between Indian soldiers and their homes is noted by the director of military intelligence on 20 March 1943. Quoted by Indivar Kamtekar, 'A Different War Dance', p. 192.
94. Srinath Raghavan, *India's War*, p. 83.
95. Ibid., p. 85.
96. Ibid., p. 86.
97. Quoted by Tarak Barkawi, 'Culture and Combat in the Colonies: The Indian Army in the Second World War', in *Journal of Contemporary History*, 41.2 (2006), 325–355 (p. 331).
98. Anirudh Deshpande, *Hope and Despair*, p. x.
99. A.G. Fernandes and K. Someswara Rao, 'Nutrition Work in the Indian Army', p. 78.
100. Other publications, such as Lara Feigel's *The Love-charm of Bombs: Restless Lives in the Second World War* (2013), Gill Plain's *Literature of the 1940s: War, Postwar and 'Peace'* (2013) and Leo Mellor's *Reading the Ruins: Modernism, Bombsites and British Culture* (2011), remain contained within European parameters. Beryl Pong's *British Literature and Culture in Second World Wartime: For the Duration* (2020) offers powerful interpre-

tations on the relationship between late modernism, war and a fear of both past and future, but its focus is British and Irish writing. *The Cambridge Companion to the Literature of World War II* (2009) does not include perspectives from non-white colonies.

101. In addition, Gajendra Singh has interrogated sepoy perspectives in *The Testimonies of Indian Soldiers and the Two World Wars: Between Self and Sepoy* (2014); Tarak Barkawi has examined how imperial forces such as the Indian Army functioned in cosmopolitan terms in *Soldiers of Empire: Indian and British Armies in World War II* (2017); and Ghee Bowman has explored Muslim soldiers' lives in Europe in *The Indian Contingent: The Forgotten Muslim Soldiers of Dunkirk* (2020).

102. Amalendu Sengupta, *Uttal Challish: Asamapta Biplab* [*The Turbulent Forties: An Incomplete Revolution*] (Calcutta: Pearl Publishers, 1989).

103. Elizabeth Edwards, *Raw Histories: Photographs, Anthropology and Museums* (Abingdon: Routledge, 2001), p. 237.

104. James Campbell, 'Combat Gnosticism: The Ideology of First World War Poetry Criticism', *New Literary History*, 30.1 (1999), pp. 203–15.

105. For a comprehensive history of colonial state censorship in India, see N. Gerald Barrier, *Banned: Controversial Literature and Political Control in British India, 1907–1947* (Columbia, MO: University of Missouri Press, 1974). Barrier views the period between 1930 and 1947 as one of confrontation between the state and Indian publishing outfits.

106. Sara Ahmed, *The Cultural Politics of Emotion* (Edinburgh: Edinburgh University Press, 2004), p. 4.

107. See Santanu Das, *India, Empire and First World War Culture*, p. 25.

108. Vasudha Dalmia, *Fiction as History: The Novel and the City in Modern North India* (Albany, NY: State University of New York Press, 2019), p. 406.

109. Shabana Mahmud, '*Angare* and the Founding of the Progressive Writers' Association', *Modern Asian Studies*, 30.2 (May 1996), 447–467.

110. Bhisham Sahni, 'The Progressive Writers' Movement', *Indian Literature*, 29.6 (116) (November–December 1986), 178–183. Also see Progressive Writers' Association, The Open University's 'Making Britain' project, <https://www.open.ac.uk/researchprojects/makingbritain/content/progressive-writers-association> [Accessed 31 May 2022].

111. Amit Kumar Gupta, *Crises and Creativities*, p. 68.

112. Ibid., pp. 79–80.

113. For a history of the Left's involvement in the Indian national movement, including the Second World War years, see Irfan Habib, 'The Left and the National Movement', *Social Scientist*, 26, 5/6 (May–June 1998), 3–33.

114. Amit Kumar Gupta, *Crises and Creativities*, p. 98.

115. Ibid., p. 122 and p. 120.
116. Ibid., p. 120. He also notes that the youth in Bengal were far more captivated by the Quit India movement than the 'people's war' philosophy (p. 116).
117. Sanjukta Sunderason, *Partisan Aesthetics: Modern Art and India's Long Decolonisation* (Stanford, CA: Stanford University Press, 2020), p. 7.
118. Ibid., p. 8.
119. In my translations of Bengali texts into English, I have in general privileged the transfer of sense from Bengali to English, rather than the transfer of the linguistic meaning of each word. This process of translation, of course, has itself become an interpretative act.

1. 'THE THING THAT WAS LOST': RE-CONCEPTUALISATIONS OF HOME IN INDIAN LIFE-WRITING FROM THE WAR

1. October 1943, IWM, IND 2431. This is unlikely to have been taken by the No. 9 Army and Film Photographic Unit, as mentioned on the Imperial War Museum's website, as this unit was not officially established until 1945. See Fred McGlade, *The History of the British Army Film & Photographic Unit in the Second World War* (Solihull: Helion, 2010), p. 162.
2. Email conversation between the author and Helen Mavin, Head of Photographs, Imperial War Museum, London, dated 13 July 2021.
3. Srinath Raghavan, *India's War*, pp. 78–79.
4. IWM, IND 1300. It is not known who the photographer was in this case, but many of the photographs in this series state on the back 'With the compliments of the Principal Information Officer, Government of India'. In 1941, a year before this photograph was taken, the first Indian, J. Natarajan, was appointed to the post of Principal Information Officer in India. Natarajan later authored the book *History of Indian Journalism* (Delhi: Publications Division, Ministry of Information and Broadcasting, Government of India, 1955). The British Ministry of Information and the Government of India were working closely together in producing wartime publicity material. See Philip Woods, 'From Shaw to Shantaram: The Film Advisory Board and the Making of British Propaganda Films in India, 1940–1943', *Historical Journal of Film, Radio and Television*, 21.3 (2001), 293–308.
5. Salman Rushdie, 'Imaginary Homelands', in *Imaginary Homelands: Essays and Criticism 1981–1991* (London: Vintage, 2010), pp. 9–10.
6. Claudia Siebrecht, 'The Tears of 1939: German Women and the Emotional Archive of the First World War', in Lucy Noakes, Claire Langhamer and Claudia Siebrecht, eds, *Total War: An Emotional History* (Oxford: Oxford University Press, 2020), pp. 78–97 (p. 81).

7. Devleena Ghosh, 'Burma–Bengal Crossings: Intercolonial Connections in Pre-Independence India', *Asian Studies Review*, 40:2 (2016), 156–172. See also Amitav Ghosh's multi-generational historical novel *The Glass Palace* (London: Harper Collins, 2000), which begins in Mandalay at the end of the nineteenth century and concludes in the post-Second World War years.

8. Srinath Raghavan, *India's War*, p. 95.

9. Ibid., p. 170 and p. 374.

10. Frederick Perry, *The Commonwealth Armies*, p. 118. There is also a selection of letters from the CMF, dated between January and August 1944, housed at the National Archives at Kew, but these are far fewer in number. See WO 204–10381 CMF Censorships Reports.

11. In the 1941 census undertaken by the colonial government, only 13 per cent of the population in the Punjab were literate. This lowered to 8 per cent overall in the United Provinces, out of which a meagre 2 per cent of women were literate. Bombay had a 30 per cent literacy rate for men and 9 per cent for women, and Bengal 25 per cent for men and 7 per cent for women. Southern India, represented by Travancore and Cochin, had much better rates of literacy—56 per cent for men and 34 per cent for women. See M.W.M. Yeatts, *Census of India 1941, Volume 1, Part 1—Tables* (Simla: Government of India Press, 1943), pp. 31–32.

12. See, for example, Gajendra Singh's chapter '"The Perils of 'Oriental' Correspondence": Living the Space of Conditioned Testimony' (pp. 65–98) for an account of how these censorship reports were created in both wars. Gajendra Singh, *The Testimonies of Indian Soldiers*.

13. For a comprehensive history of censorship reports and those monitoring soldiers' morale, along with official statistics relating to rates of sickness, battle exhaustion, desertion, absence without leave and self-inflicted wounds in colonial armies, see Jonathan Fennell, *Fighting the People's War: The British Commonwealth Armies and the Second World War* (Cambridge: Cambridge University Press, 2019).

14. Devika Sethi, *War over Words*, p. 123.

15. Ibid., p. 133. See 'Part III Political or Military?: Censorship in India during the Second World War', pp. 123–172, for a full analysis.

16. Gajendra Singh, *The Testimonies of Indian Soldiers and the Two World Wars*, p. 92.

17. The First World War letters have been recovered through the efforts of historians such as David Omissi and Rozina Visram. See David Omissi, *Indian Voices of the Great War: Soldiers' Letters, 1914–18* (London: Palgrave Macmillan, 1999) and Rozina Visram, *Asians in Britain: 400 Years of History* (London: Pluto Press, 2002).

18. James Hinton, *Nine Wartime Lives: Mass-Observation and the Making of the Modern Self* (Oxford: Oxford University Press, 2010), p. 6.
19. Hermione Lee, *Body Parts: Essays in Life-Writing* (London: Chatto & Windus, 2005), p. 2.
20. Santanu Das, 'Reframing life/war "writing": objects, letters and songs of Indian soldiers, 1914–1918', *Textual Practice*, 29.7 (2015), 1–23 (p. 12).
21. Srinath Raghavan, *India's War*, p. 371.
22. Elleke Boehmer, *Indian Arrivals, 1870–1915: Networks of British Empire* (Oxford: Oxford University Press, 2015), p. 21.
23. Srinath Raghavan, *India's War*, p. 74.
24. Ibid.
25. Ibid., p. 79.
26. Indivar Kamtekar, 'A Different War Dance', p. 191.
27. *Middle East Military Censorship Reports: Fortnightly Summaries Covering Indian Troops, August 1942–April 1943*, L/PJ/12/654, British Library India Office Records, 21 October to 4 November 1942 and 30 September to 6 October 1942. All future references to these reports are abbreviated to *MEMCR 654*.
28. *Middle East Military Censorship Reports: Fortnightly Summaries Covering Indian Troops, April 1943–October 1943*, L/PJ/12/655, British Library India Office Records, 21 April to 5 May 1943. All future references to these reports are abbreviated to *MEMCR 655*.
29. Indrani Chatterjee, 'Introduction', in *Unfamiliar Relations Family and History in South Asia*, ed. by Indrani Chatterjee (New Brunswick, NJ: Rutgers University Press, 2004), pp. 3–45.
30. *MEMCR 655*, 21 April to 5 May 1943.
31. Heather Streets, *Martial Races*, p. 26.
32. *MEMCR 655*, 21 April to 5 May 1943.
33. For an analysis of colonial paternalism in the Indian Army, see Gajendra Singh, *The Testimonies of Indian Soldiers*, p. 62: '[…] discourses of colonial paternalism, of the officer as *ma-bap*, and the soldier as child, intruded into the language of legal procedure and then came to be enshrined in Indian military law'.
34. Rajit Mazumdar, *The Indian Army and the Making of Punjab* (Hyderabad: Orient Blackswan, 2003), p. 177.
35. Srinath Raghavan, *India's War*, p. 74.
36. *MEMCR 655*, 14 July to 27 July 1943.
37. Ibid.
38. Report from 19 May to 1 June 1943, *MEMCR 655*.
39. The colonial censor notes, for example, that stamps were being stolen

and sold by postmen in Karachi, who were subsequently arrested. *MEMCR 655*, 16 June to 29 June 1943.

40. Yasmin Khan, *The Raj at War*, p. 37. Also see pp. 38–39: 'At least one postman was accused of charging for handing over a letter and routine complaints about the post office flooded in [...].'

41. *MEMCR 655*, 11 August to 24 August 1943.

42. *MEMCR 655*, 19 May to 1 June 1943.

43. *MEMCR 655*, 14 July to 27 July 1943.

44. *MEMCR 654*, 26 August to 1 September 1942.

45. *Middle East Military Censorship Reports: Fortnightly Summaries Covering Indian Troops, November 1943–March 1944*, L/PJ/12/578, British Library India Office Records, 12 January 1944 to 25 January 1944. All future references are abbreviated to *MEMCR 578*.

46. Vanda Wilcox, '"Weeping tears of blood": Exploring Italian soldiers' emotions in the First World War', *Modern Italy*, 17:2 (May 2012), 171–184.

47. We are told very little about this sepoy's background in the military censorship reports, so it is difficult to be specific about the form of lamentation he might be influenced by. Considering, though, that a significantly large ethnic group in the Indian Army comprised Muslim men, we can read this letter through the prism of the Islamic traditions of mourning in the *marsiya*, which itself drew upon Iranian literary traditions. *Marsiyas* were poems expressing ritualised grief for the death of a person, or commemorating a sorrowful event. See, for example, Madhu Trivedi, 'Appropriating an Iranian Literary Tradition: Marsiya in the Indian Context', *Journal of the Indian Musicological Society*, 36–37 (2005/2006), 149–172.

48. *MEMCR 655*, 19 May to 1 June 1943.

49. The colonial censor quotes a British Captain who highlights the central role played by Indian troops in this victory: 'It was most fitting that the 4th Ind. Div. should capture Von Arnim. Believe me I've yet to meet the match of either Gurkha's or Punjabi's [*sic*]—they're bloody fine infantry and stop at nothing. Boy am I glad though I'm in artillery—I'd not be infantryman for love nor money!! It's far too dangerous.' *MEMCR 655*, 30 June to 13 July 1943.

50. *MEMCR 655*, 19 May to 1 June 1943.

51. See, for example, Walter Robson, *Letters from a Soldier* (London: Faber and Faber, 1960) and Tamasin Day-Lewis, ed., *Last Letters Home* (London: Macmillan, 1995).

52. Lucy Noakes, 'Communities of Feeling', in *Total War: An Emotional History*, pp. 116–136 (pp. 129–130).

53. *MEMCR 655*, 16 June to 29 June 1943.
54. *MEMCR 655*, 14 July to 27 July 1943.
55. Susheila Nasta, *Home Truths: Fictions of the South Asian Diaspora in Britain* (London: Palgrave, 2001), p. 1.
56. *MEMCR 655*, 19 May to 1 June 1943.
57. Indivar Kamtekar, 'A Different War Dance', pp. 200–201.
58. There were certain exceptions—the top military recruiting region of Punjab during the time of the Bengal Famine was flourishing in agricultural production. See Indivar Kamtekar, 'A Different War Dance', pp. 216–217.
59. There are numerous imperial and military histories on this topic. See, for example, Christopher Bayly and Tim Harper, *Forgotten Armies: Britain's Asian Empire and the War with Japan* (London: Penguin, 2004); Peter Ward Fay, *The Forgotten Army*; Bisheshwar Prasad, *The Arakan Operations 1942–45, The Reconquest of Burma June 1942–June 1944: Vol 1* and *The Reconquest of Burma June 1944–June 1945: Vol 2*, in Bisheshwar Prasad ed., *Official History of the Indian Armed Forces in the Second World War* (Delhi: Pentagon Press, 2012).
60. *India and the War, 1939–1945, The Facts* (London: Information Department, India Office, 1946), p. 14.
61. Douglas Ford, '"A Conquerable Yet Resilient Foe": British Perceptions of the Imperial Japanese Army's Tactics on the India-Burma Front, September 1942 to Summer 1944', *Intelligence and National Security*, 18.1 (2003), 65–90 (p. 66).
62. Avijit Gupta, 'Landforms of Southeast Asia', in *The Physical Geography of Southeast Asia*, ed. by Avijit Gupta (Oxford: Oxford University Press, 2005), pp. 38–64 (pp. 42–45).
63. Christopher Bayly and Tim Harper, *Forgotten Armies*, p. 369. Bayly and Harper observe how, 'to the people of Asia the world had been turned upside down' with the suddenness of Japanese victories (p. xxix). They refer to an English doctor, Oscar Fisher, who noted in his diary that the Japanese bombing on Penang was like H.G. Wells's *War of the Worlds* being lived out. Bodies covered the streets days after the city had been taken over. Over 3,000 were injured and killed in Penang alone (p. 119).
64. Bayly and Harper, *Forgotten Armies*, p. xxxi.
65. Elleke Boehmer, *Indian Arrivals, 1870–1915*, p. 63.
66. James Campbell, 'Combat Gnosticism: The Ideology of First World War Poetry Criticism', *New Literary History*, 30.1 (1999), pp. 203–15.
67. For a rich discussion on Bengali writing on Burma during the Second World War, including poetry and women's memoirs, see Chapter 5, 'World War II and Burma: Heroism, Violence and Exodus (1938–48)'

(pp. 129–162) in Parthasarathi Bhaumik, *Bengalis in Burma: A Colonial Encounter (1886–1948)* (New Delhi: Routledge India, 2022).

68. Shantilal Ray, *Arakan Fronte (On the Frontlines at Arakan)* (Calcutta: Bengal Publishers, 1946), p. 42. All further references are to this edition, and page numbers are provided in parentheses after quotations within the text. The translation from the Bengali is mine.

69. Roland Barthes, 'Death of the Author', in *Image Music Text*, trans. by Stephen Heath (London: Fontana Press, 1977), pp. 142–148 (p. 146). An unusual aspect of Shantilal Ray's use of literary references is that he often slightly misquotes them. Perhaps the quotes are not intended to serve as a display of erudition but demonstrate instead how interwoven literary references are in Ray's modes of thinking, feeling and writing. The memoir includes lines from lyricist and composer Atul Prasad Sen, devotional poet and composer Rajanikanta Sen, poet Rangalal Bandyopadhyay, poet and dramatist Michael Madhusudan Dutta, medieval devotional songs or *kirtans* from the book *Chandidaser Padabali*, and Hindustani songs.

70. Rabindranath Tagore, *'Sonar Tari'* <http://bichitra.jdvu.ac.in> [Accessed 23 July 2022]. The translation from the Bengali is mine.

71. Gaston Bachelard, *The Poetics of Space* (Boston, MA: Beacon Press, 1958), p. 20.

72. Sigmund Freud, *'Das Unheimliche'* or 'The Uncanny' (1919), in *The Standard Edition of the Complete Psychological Works*, ed. and trans. by James Strachey (London: Hogarth Press, 1953–74), XVII, pp. 219–252 (p. 219).

73. Alan Jeffreys, *The British Army in the Far East 1941–45*, pp. 32–33. The 'Admin Box' was the administrative area of the 7th Indian Division at Sinzweya in the Arakan province.

74. Bayly and Harper, among other scholars, note the cosmopolitan make-up of this army, with 70 per cent of soldiers being Indians, Gurkhas, Burmese and East and West Africans. See Bayly and Harper, *Forgotten Armies*, p. 294.

75. Rupert Brooke, 'The Soldier', in *Poetry of the First World War: An Anthology*, ed. by Tim Kendall (Oxford: Oxford University Press, 2013), p. 106.

76. Elaborate Japanese bunkers in Burma, in fact, were constructed to be impervious to bombardment and resilient to the use of heavy weaponry and became a significant threat to Allied forces advancing. Douglas Ford, 'A Conquerable Yet Resilient Foe', p. 81.

77. Nihar Ranjan Gupta was well known in the 1930s for his Bengali detective stories featuring the sleuth Kiriti Ray. See Sisir Kumar Das, *A History*

of Indian Literature, 1911–1956, Struggle for Freedom: Triumph and Tragedy (Calcutta: Sahitya Akademi, 2005), p. 259.

78. Mrinalini Sinha, *Colonial Masculinity: The 'Manly Englishman' and the 'Effeminate Bengali' in the Late Nineteenth Century* (Manchester, Manchester University Press, 1995).

79. Imagining the nation as mother was an Indian literary commonplace, spearheaded as early as the nineteenth century by Bengali writer Bankimchandra Chattopadhyay with the song '*Bande Mataram*' in his 1882 novel *Anandamath* (*The Abbey of Bliss*).

80. Frantz Fanon memorably investigated the psychology of colonialism through works such as *Black Skin, White Masks* (1952), followed by post-colonial scholars such as Ngũgĩ wa Thiong'o in *Decolonising the Mind* (1986) and Ashis Nandy in *The Intimate Enemy: Loss and Recovery of Self under Colonialism* (2009).

81. Tobias Rettig, 'Recruiting the All-female Rani of Jhansi Regiment: Subhas Chandra Bose and Dr Lakshmi Swaminadhan [*sic*]', *South East Asia Research*, 21.4 (2013), 627–638.

82. Shantilal Ray, part of the Indian Army, would not have met the INA men at Kohima and Imphal since he was stationed a few hundred miles away in the coastal Arakan province. Instead, his encounter with the INA would have been a little earlier, in February 1944, at the Battle of the 'Admin Box' discussed in the previous section of this chapter, when INA men led by Major L.S. Misra enabled the 7th Indian Division to be trapped on the eastern side of the Mayu range in the Arakan frontline. This offensive established the 'reputation of the INA as a fighting unit'. See Sugata Bose, *His Majesty's Opponent*, p. 270.

83. Tarak Barkawi, 'Culture and Combat in the Colonies', p. 329.

84. See Tarak Barkawi, 'Culture and Combat in the Colonies', p. 341; Sugata Bose, *His Majesty's Opponent*, p. 275, for numbers of INA soldiers in Imphal and Kohima.

85. Sugata Bose, *His Majesty's Opponent*, p. 277.

86. Hugh Toye, *The Springing Tiger: A Study of the Indian National Army and of Netaji Subhas Chandra Bose* (Delhi: Allied Publishers, 2009), p. 187.

87. Arjun Appadurai, 'Patriotism and Its Futures', *Public Culture*, 5.3 (September 1993), 411–429 (p. 413).

88. En route to Russia via Saigon and Taipei in August 1945, Subhas Chandra Bose died from his injuries in an aeroplane accident, which brought the hopes of India's armed struggle for independence to an end. Rumours of Bose being alive have repeatedly resurfaced in India. See Sugata Bose's final chapter 'A Life Immortal' (pp. 304–327) in *His Majesty's Opponent*.

89. See, for example, Shah Nawaz Khan, *My Memories of the INA and Its Netaji* (Delhi: Rajkamal Publications, 1946) and C.J. Strachey, 'How I came

to join the Indian National Army', *The Oracle* (Calcutta: Netaji Research Bureau, January 1982), pp. 53–56.

90. The 'Indian Legion' was formed by moving PoWs from the Indian Army from Italy to Germany in December 1941. Sugata Bose notes that, between December 1941 and December 1942, the Indian Legion grew to comprise four battalions. See Sugata Bose, *His Majesty's Opponent*, p. 212 and p. 225.

91. Sugata Bose, *His Majesty's Opponent*, pp. 232–237.

92. General Slim's words, quoted in Sugata Bose, *His Majesty's Opponent*, p. 280.

93. Tapan Raychaudhuri, 'Indian Nationalism as Animal Politics', *The Historical Journal*, 22.3 (September 1979), 747–763 (p. 763).

94. Tapan Raychaudhuri, 'Indian Nationalism as Animal Politics', p. 763.

95. Abid Hasan Safrani, *The Men from Imphal* (Calcutta: Netaji Research Bureau, 1971), p. 1. All further references are to this edition, and page numbers are provided in parentheses after quotations within the text.

96. Sugata Bose, *His Majesty's Opponent*, p. 277.

97. Santanu Das, *Touch and Intimacy in First World War Literature* (Cambridge: Cambridge University Press, 2008), p. 35.

98. Sugata Bose, *His Majesty's Opponent*, p. 280.

99. Peter Ward Fay, *The Forgotten Army*, pp. 300–301.

100. Quoted in Fay, *The Forgotten Army*, p. 302.

101. Sugata Bose, *His Majesty's Opponent*, p. 252; Fay, *The Forgotten Army*, pp. 223–238.

102. Ibid., p. 252.

103. Ibid.

104. The quote is from Kwame Anthony Appiah's essay 'Cosmopolitan Patriots', although Appiah uses the phrase in a somewhat different context, arguing for how people from different cultures and traditions can come together. See Kwame Anthony Appiah, 'Cosmopolitan Patriots', *Critical Inquiry* 23:3 (1997), 617–639 (p. 638).

105. Fay quotes an apposite Indian proverb in this context: 'On the way to Delhi I met many men, and they were all my brothers.' See *The Forgotten Army*, p. 235.

106. Amartya Sen, 'Is Nationalism a Boon or a Curse?', *Economic and Political Weekly*, 43.7 (February 2008), 39–44 (p. 44).

107. Ibid., p. 43.

108. Cemil Aydin, *The Politics of Anti-Westernism in Asia: Visions of World Order in Pan-Islamic and Pan-Asian Thought* (New York, NY: Columbia University Press, 2007), p. 186.

109. Amartya Sen, 'Is Nationalism a Boon or a Curse?', p. 40.

110. Ibid., p. 44.

111. Rajat Kanta Ray, *The Felt Community: Commonalty and Mentality Before the Emergence of Indian Nationalism* (New Delhi: Oxford University Press, 2003), p. 26.
112. In 1943, Malaya had nearly one million expatriate Indians, Thailand about 60,000 and Burma 800,000. See Sugata Bose, *His Majesty's Opponent*, pp. 247–248.
113. Sugata Bose, *His Majesty's Opponent*, p. 246.
114. Janaki Thevar describes going to hear Bose speak at a rally in Kuala Lumpur. At the end of the speech, she gave him her earrings and gold chain. See Sugata Bose, *His Majesty's Opponent*, p. 247.
115. Sugata Bose, *His Majesty's Opponent*, p. 247.
116. Ibid., p. 266.
117. See Endnote 88.
118. Yasmin Khan, *The Raj at War*, p. xi.
119. Sugata Bose, *His Majesty's Opponent*, p. 324.
120. Jayita Sarkar, 'How WWII shaped the crisis in Myanmar', <https://www.washingtonpost.com/outlook/2019/03/10/how-wwii-shaped-crisis-myanmar/> [Accessed 26 January 2022].

2. 'EVERY DAY I WITNESS NIGHTMARES': HUNGER AND THE HOME-LAND

1. Susan Sontag, *Regarding the Pain of Others* (London: Penguin, 2003), pp. 70–71.
2. Emilia Terracciano, *Art and Emergency: Modernism in Twentieth Century India* (London: I.B. Tauris, 2018), pp. 75–76.
3. See Emilia Terracciano, *Art and Emergency* (2018).
4. See Judith Butler, *Precarious Life: The Powers of Mourning and Violence* (New York, NY: Verso, 2006).
5. Ariella Azoulay, *The Civil Contract of Photography* (New York, NY: Zone Books, 2008), p. 17.
6. Joshi also commissioned other artists, such as Chittoprosad Bhattacharya, Zainul Abedin and Somnath Hore, to document the famine visually. See Emilia Terracciano, *Art and Emergency*, p. 100.
7. Emilia Terracciano, *Art and Emergency*, p. 105.
8. Ibid., p. 75.
9. Ibid., p. 97.
10. Ibid., p. 71.
11. James Vernon, *Hunger: A Modern History* (Cambridge, MA: Harvard University Press, 2007), p. 35.
12. Ibid., p. 35.

13. This is author and activist William Digby's estimate, cited by James Vernon in *Hunger*, p. 51.

14. The exact number of the famine dead is debatable, but over three million seems to be the recent scholarly consensus. See, for example, Srimanjari, *Through War and Famine* (Hyderabad: Orient Blackswan, 2009), p. 2; Madhusree Mukerjee, *Churchill's Secret War: The British Empire and the Ravaging of India during World War II* (New York, NY: Basic Books, 2011), p. i; Janam Mukherjee, *Hungry Bengal: War, Famine and the End of Empire* (London: Hurst & Company, 2015), p. 3.

15. Srimanjari, 'Map of Bengal Famine Intensity, 1933–1944', *Through War and Famine*, pp. 188–189.

16. Srimanjari, *Through War and Famine*, p. 209; Srimanjari, 'War, Famine and Popular Perceptions in Bengali Literature, 1939–1945', in *Issues in Modern Indian History: For Sumit Sarkar*, ed. by Biswamoy Pati (Mumbai: Popular Prakashan: 2000), pp. 258–290 (p. 261).

17. Ibid., p. 212.

18. Indivar Kamtekar, 'A Different War Dance', p. 212.

19. Srimanjari, *Through War and Famine*, p. 126.

20. Quoted in Benjamin Robert Siegel, *Hungry Nation: Food, Famine, and the Making of Modern India* (Cambridge: Cambridge University Press, 2018), p. 23.

21. Lizzie Collingham, *The Taste of War: World War Two and the Battle for Food* (London: Allen Lane, 2011), pp. 125–126.

22. Ibid., p. 124.

23. Collingham notes that an exception to this was the creation of the Middle East Supply Centre, which managed to control hoarding and high inflation rates. See *The Taste of War*, pp. 126–132.

24. Indivar Kamtekar, 'A Different War Dance', p. 218.

25. See Amartya Sen, *Poverty and Famines: An Essay on Entitlement and Deprivation* (Oxford: Clarendon Press, 1981). Two selections from further economic analyses of the famine include Omkar Goswami, 'The Bengal Famine of 1943: Re-examining the Data', *Indian Economic and Social History Review*, 27.4 (December 1990), 445–463, and Mark B. Tauger, 'The Indian Famine Crises of World War II', *British Scholar* 1.2 (2009), 166–196.

26. Iftekar Iqbal, *The Bengal Delta: Ecology, State and Social Change, 1840–1943* (London: Palgrave Macmillan, 2010), p. 160.

27. Sugata Bose and Ayesha Jalal describe the Bengal Famine as 'one of the more catastrophic, though least publicised, holocausts of the Second World War' in Sugata Bose and Ayesha Jalal, *Modern South Asia: History, Culture, Political Economy* (Delhi, Routledge: 2011; first pub. 1997), pp. 158–159. Indivar Kamtekar, in a perceptive comparative article on

government policies and class relations in India and the UK during the Second World War, analyses how interrelated famine was to Indian policies of wartime resource extraction, 'A Different War Dance', p. 212. See also a rigorous study of famine and war in 1940s Bengal in Srimanjari, *Through War and Famine* (2010); an examination of British colonial policy, particularly Winston Churchill's role, resulting in the Bengal Famine in Madhusree Mukerjee, *Churchill's Secret War* (2011); the interconnectivity between war, famine and the 1946 Noakhali communal riots in Bengal in Janam Mukherjee, *Hungry Bengal* (2015); and the relationship between famine and nation-building in Benjamin Siegel, *Hungry Nation* (2018). Emilia Terracciano in *Art and Emergency* (2018) sees the famine as political catastrophe through the artwork it inspired; Sourit Bhattacharya in his article 'Writing famine, writing empire: food crisis and anticolonial aesthetics' in Liam O'Flaherty's *Famine* and Bhabani Bhattacharya's 'So Many Hungers!', *Irish University Review*, 49.1 (2019), 54–73, focuses on the relationship between literary content and historical conditions relating to famine; in *Partisan Aesthetics* (2020), Sanjukta Sunderason looks at how the political was produced through the visual art of the famine.

28. Dan Hicks, *The Brutish Museums: The Benin Bronzes, Colonial Violence and Cultural Restitution* (London: Pluto Press, 2020), p. 153.

29. Achille Mbembe, 'The Power of the Archive and its Limits', in *Refiguring the Archive*, ed. by Caroline Hamilton, Michele Pickover and Verne Harris (Cape Town: New Africa Books, 2002), pp. 19–27 (pp. 21–22).

30. *MEMCR*, IOR/L/PJ/12/655, 11 August to 24 August 1943, A *maund* was an Indian unit of weight equivalent to approximately 37 kg.

31. *MEMCR*, IOR/L/PJ/12/655, 8 September to 21 September 1943, and 8 September to 21 September 1943.

32. *MEMCR*, IOR/L/PJ/12/655, 2 June to 15 June 1943, Indian troops in Cyprus.

33. *MEMCR*, IOR/L/PJ/12/655, 25 August to 7 September 1943.

34. *MEMCR*, IOR/L/PJ/12/655, 2 June to 15 June 1943, Indian troops in Palestine, Syria and Transjordan.

35. P. Priya, 'Malabar Famine of 1943: A Critique of War Situation in Malabar (1939–45)', *Proceedings of the Indian History Congress*, 75, Platinum Jubilee (2014), 628–638. Benjamin Siegal notes that relief workers were worried that scarce resources from south India would be transferred to help Bengal. See Benjamin Siegel, *Hungry Nation*, p. 28.

36. *MEMCR*, IOR/L/PJ/12/655, 21 April to 5 May 1943.

37. Shoshana Felman and Dori Laub, *Testimony: Crises of Witnessing in Literature, Psychoanalysis and History* (New York, NY: Routledge: 1992), p. 111.

38. *MEMCR*, IOR/L/PJ/12/655, 25 August to 7 September 1943. Experiences of famine across India varied enormously, and the Punjab region, during the famine years, experienced considerable comforts. See Indivar Kamtekar, 'A Different War Dance' (p. 176). Yet Punjab also responded emotionally to Bengal's famine—as Benjamin Siegel notes, the president of Ludhiana's Sikh Missionary College published poetry in the daily newspaper *Akali*, requesting the people of Punjab to reduce their consumption and send food to Bengal. See *Hungry Nation*, p. 34.

39. Elaine Scarry, *The Body in Pain: The Making and Unmaking of the World* (Oxford: Oxford University Press, 1985), p. 9.

40. Yasmin Khan, *The Raj at War*, pp. 213–214.

41. See Sanjoy Bhattacharya, 'British Military Information Management Techniques and the South Asian Soldier: Eastern India during the Second World War', *Modern Asian Studies* 34.2 (April 2000), pp. 483–510. Bhattacharya notes how 'a characteristic structure of censorship was developed in this period, wherein ostensible official intervention was reduced to the bare minimum, even though the examination of troops' mail continued unabated' (p. 487). Although famine-related news was heavily censored, as we shall see in the following discussion on the colonial censor's responses, the sheer scale of the crisis in food could not be entirely suppressed from Indian soldiers.

42. *MEMCR*, IOR/L/PJ/12/655, 11 August to 24 August 1943.

43. *MEMCR*, IOR/L/PJ/12/655, 2 June to 15 June 1943.

44. See, for example, Janam Mukherjee's explanation of price rises and shortage of goods in *Hungry Bengal*: 'By December 1941, the price of rice had risen by nearly 75 per cent since the declaration of war. Rice was in high demand as part of the war effort, particularly to feed industrial labour. Wheat prices had risen still more sharply, and so rice was also in high demand in western India and the Middle East as a hedge on wheat. This precipitated a drain of rice from eastern India, exasperating other difficulties in the food supply that war entailed [...] Refugees from Burma also continued to pour in, and local shortages of sugar, coal, matches, raw cotton, cotton yarn, piece goods, paper and cooking fuel, were making life increasingly difficult for many millions' (p. 55).

45. *MEMCR*, IOR/L/PJ/12/655, 22 September to 5 October 1943.

46. Indivar Kamtekar, 'A Different War Dance', p. 200.

47. *MEMCR*, IOR/L/PJ/12/655, Indian Troops with Central Mediterranean Forces, 8 September to 21 September 1943.

48. Benjamin Siegel notes the formation of corresponding communities within undivided India itself: 'Photographs and journalism and the affec-

tive bonds of charity tied Indians inextricably to Bengal and made its suffering their own'. See Benjamin Siegel, *Hungry Nation*, p. 48.

49. Quoted in Gajendra Singh, *The Testimonies of Indian Soldiers and the Two World Wars*, p. 95.

50. *MEMCR*, IOR/L/PJ/12/654, 27 January to 9 February 1943.

51. Gajendra Singh, *The Testimonies of Indian Soldiers and the Two World Wars*, p. 92.

52. Sanjoy Bhattacharya, 'British Military Information Management Techniques and the South Asian Soldier', p. 488. Also see Sanjoy Bhattacharya, *Propaganda and Information in Eastern India, 1939–45: A Necessary Weapon of War* (London: Curzon, 2001) for a discussion of colonial eastern India, treated as a single administrative unit during the course of the conflict for strategic purposes.

53. *MEMCR*, IOR/L/PJ/12/654, 5 November to 19 November 1942.

54. *MEMCR*, IOR/L/PJ/12/655, Indian troops in Egypt, Cyraenica and Tripolitania, 25 August to 7 September 1943.

55. *MEMCR*, IOR/L/PJ/12/655, 8 September to 21 September 1943.

56. Ibid.

57. Gajendra Singh, *The Testimonies of Indian Soldiers and the Two World Wars*, pp. 67–69.

58. *MEMCR*, IOR/L/PJ/12/578, Indian Troops with Central Mediterranean Forces, 1 December to 14 December 1943.

59. *MEMCR*, IOR/L/PJ/12/578, 15 December to 28 December 1943.

60. *MEMCR*, IOR/L/PJ/12/655, Indian Troops with Central Mediterranean Forces, 8 September to 21 September 1943.

61. *MEMCR*, IOR/L/PJ/12/655, 22 September to 5 October 1943.

62. *MEMCR*, IOR/L/PJ/12/655, 8 September to 21 September 1943.

63. Bibhutibhushan Bandyopadhyay, *Ashani Sanket* (*Intimations of Thunder*) (Calcutta: Mitra and Ghosh, 2015; first published serially between 1944 and 1946 and in novel form in 1959). All references are to this edition of the novel, and page numbers provided in parentheses within the text. The translation from the Bengali is mine.

64. It has proved difficult to trace readership figures of the Bengali magazine *Matribhumi*, which first started publication in 1938. The editors celebrated the magazine entering its fifth year in 1942, despite wartime hardships, in a short piece that reconfirmed its commitment to 'serving the country and its people' ('*desher or dosher sheba kora*'). They also noted the price of the magazine was increasing, as sixteen extra pages had been added to the publication since the beginning of 1942. This increase in length suggests that the magazine's circulation was improving, and that a slightly more costly magazine would not deter its readership. *Matribhumi* (*Motherland*, vol. 5, Magh—Chaitra, 1349; 1943 in the

English calendar), <https://archive.org/details/dli.bengal.10689.3186/ page/n51/mode/2up> [Accessed 23 July 2022]. I am very grateful to Supriya Chaudhuri and Purbasha Auddy for all their efforts in assisting me with this reference.

65. Rushati Sen, *Bibhutibhushan Bandyopadhyay* (Calcutta: Paschimbanga Bangla Academy, 1995), p. 33. All translations from the Bengali are mine.
66. Ibid., p. 25.
67. Ibid., p. 26.
68. Maud Ellmann, *The Hunger Artists: Starvation, Writing and Imprisonment* (London: Virago, 1993), p. 112.
69. Amartya Sen, *Poverty and Famines*, p. 1.
70. John Keats, 'To Autumn' (1819), in John Barnard, ed., *John Keats: The Complete Poems* (London: Penguin Classics, 2nd edition, 1977), p. 434.
71. Madhusree Mukerjee, *Churchill's Secret War*, p. 130. Mukerjee also believes that Ceylon, the Middle East and South Africa, where rice exports were principally directed, were better supplied with grain than India.
72. See, for example, Srimanjari, *Through War and Famine*, p. 147; Amartya Sen, *Poverty and Famines*, pp. 75–83; Janam Mukherjee, *Hungry Bengal*, pp. 141–142.
73. Sexual intercourse in exchange for food rations became increasingly common in Bengal during the famine. See Srimanjari, *Through War and Famine*, pp. 201–206. See also Urvi Khaitan's work on women as sex workers during war and famine. '"The Women had saved the Situation": Indian Women's Work in War and Famine', <https://blog.royalhist-soc.org/2021/05/04/the-women-had-saved-the-situation-indian-wom-ens-work-in-war-and-famine/> [Accessed 16 March 2022].
74. Maud Ellmann, *The Hunger Artists*, p. 39.
75. '*Dadathakur*' is a Bengali word for respectfully addressing a man, which acknowledges both Gangacharan's seniority to Moti-Muchini in terms of age, and his status as a learned man and priest in the village.
76. Maud Ellmann, *The Hunger Artists*, p. 16.
77. Ananga-bou later manages to convince her husband to perform funeral rites for Moti-Muchini's body, assisted by Durga Bhattacharya and Kapali-bou. She herself remains far too weak after childbirth (p. 150).
78. Ellmann, *The Hunger Artists*, p. 113.
79. Food rationing, in fact, only began towards the end of 1943, when the full scale of the famine was evident. There are many harrowing accounts of Bengal Famine victims on the streets of Calcutta. See, for example, first-person perspectives in the chapter 'On the Street' by Madhusree Mukerjee in *Churchill's Secret War* (pp. 169–190).

80. In the preface to the first edition of the novel, published posthumously in August 1959, Bibhutibhushan's wife Roma Bandhyopadhyay describes its publication history. Roma Bandhyopadhyay also notes how, after Bibhutibhushan's unexpected death, many of his papers were lost, and it was with difficulty that she pieced the manuscript together from the *Matribhumi*'s old files, with help from two editors. See 'Preface to the First Edition' by Roma Bandhyopadhyay, p. 4.

81. Sukanta Bhattacharya, '*Hay Mahajeeban*' ('O Great Life') in *Chharpatra* (*Passport*) (Calcutta: Kamini Prakashalaya, 2008; first pub. 1948), p. 64. The poems in this collection were written between 1943 and 1947. All references to Sukanta's poetry are to this edition and page numbers provided in parentheses within the text. The translation from the Bengali is mine. '*Ruti*' is a Bengali variant of the more commonly known Indian '*roti*'.

82. Theodore W. Adorno, 'Cultural Criticism and Society' in *Prisms*, trans. by Samuel and Shierry Weber (Cambridge, MA: MIT Press, 1983), p. 34.

83. Dipesh Chakrabarty, *Provincializing Europe: Postcolonial Thought and Historical Difference* (Princeton, NJ: Princeton University Press, 2000), p. 282.

84. Amiyo Bhattacharya, *Kabi Sukanta Bhattacharya O Shei Samay (The Poet Sukanta Bhattacharya and Those Days)*, (Calcutta: Charu Press, 2008), pp. 306–307. The translation from the Bengali is mine.

85. Pritish Nandy, 'The Poets', *Journal of South Asian Literature: Bengali Poetry Issue*, 9.4 (1974), 177–181 (p. 177).

86. Tanika Sarkar, 'Time in Place: Urban Culture in Decades of Crisis', pp. 461–474, p. 462.

87. Kris Manjapra, 'From Imperial to International Horizons: a Hermeneutic Study of Bengali Modernism', *Modern Intellectual History*, 8.2 (2011), 327–359, p. 340.

88. Srimanjari, 'War, Famine and Popular Perceptions in Bengali Literature', p. 259.

89. Ibid.

90. In *The Raj at War*, Yasmin Khan reflects on India's position as a huge industrial powerhouse for the British Empire. See, for example, p. 84.

91. Sukanta Bhattacharya, '*Khabar*', p. 10.

92. Such images of expulsion may have been informed by Sukanta's own boyhood experiences of being dismissed from Deshbandhu High School in Calcutta for organising a student strike, which his biographer and brother notes affected him deeply. See Amiyo Bhattacharya, *Kabi Sukanta Bhattacharya*, pp. 138–139.

93. Sukanta Bhattacharya, '*Khabar*', p. 11.

94. See Kris Manjapra, 'From Imperial to International Horizons'.

Manjapra's definition of modernism is particularly relevant to my chapter. He uses modernism 'to refer to artistic experimentation in colonial Bengal that sought to represent the abject aspects, injustices and irrationality of life, but also sought to stimulate political resistance and spiritual renewal' (p. 329).

95. Amiyo Bhattacharya, *Kabi Sukanta Bhattacharya*, pp. 193–194 and pp. 225–231.
96. Ibid., pp. 242–243.
97. Sukanta Bhattacharya, *'Rabindranath-er Prati'*, p. 7.
98. Amiyo Bhattacharya, *Kabi Sukanta Bhattacharya*, p. 296.
99. The image of vultures is also used by Tara Ali Baig in her poem 'Bengal Famine, 1943', which I analyse in Chapter 4, where she says: 'The vulture hovers mighty on the wing, / Searching the waving rice for the corpse of Spring.' See R.N. Currey and R.V. Gibson, eds, *Poems from India by Members of the Forces* (Oxford: Oxford University Press, 1945), p. 50.
100. Amiyo Bhattacharya, *Kabi Sukanta Bhattacharya*, pp. 279 and 291.
101. Pritish Nandy, 'The Poets', *Journal of South Asian Literature: Bengali Poetry Issue*, 9.4 (1974), 177–181 (p. 180).
102. Amalendu Bose, 'Introduction', in *The Complete Poems of Samar Sen*, trans. by Pritish Nandy (Calcutta: A Writer's Workshop Publication, 1970), pp. ix–xxxiii (p. xix).
103. Nityapriya Ghosh, *Makers of Indian Literature: Samar Sen* (Calcutta: Sahitya Academy, 2001), p. 4.
104. Ibid., p. 67.
105. Tanika Sarkar, 'Time in Place: Urban Culture in Decades of Crisis', p. 462.
106. Nityapriya Ghosh, *Samar Sen*, pp. 37–53.
107. Ibid., p. 19.
108. Ibid., p. 21.
109. Samar Sen thought that, in English poetry after the First World War, T.S. Eliot was the best poet, because 'Eliot expressed despair, as nobody else could do'. See Nityapriya Ghosh, *Samar Sen*, p. 47.
110. Samar Sen, '9th August 1945', in *Sankalita Samar Sen (The Selected Writings of Samar Sen)*, compiled by Sabyasachi Deb and Somesh Chattopadhyay (Calcutta: Calcutta Publishers, 1950), p. 9. All references to this poem are from this edition, and page numbers are provided in parentheses within the text. The translation from the Bengali is mine.
111. 'The Sunset of the Century', in Sisir Kumar Das, ed., *The English Writings of Rabindranath Tagore, Vol. II: Essays* (Calcutta: Sahitya Akademi, 1996), p. 466.

112. Martin Gilbert, *The Second World War: A Complete History* (London: Phoenix, 2009; first pub. 1989), p. 715. The Soviet declaration of war against Japan was made late at night on 8 August, coming into effect from 9 August.

113. Death rates from the atomic bombs dropped over Hiroshima and Nagasaki are disputed and controversial, with significant variation over numbers. The estimates cited here are from the Committee for the Compilation of Materials on Damage caused by the Atomic Bombs in Hiroshima and Nagasaki's *Hiroshima and Nagasaki: The Physical, Medical and Social Effects of the Atomic Bombings*, trans. by Eisei Ishikawa and David Swain (London: Hutchinson, 1981), pp. 113–114.

114. Martin Gilbert, *The Second World War: A Complete History*, p. 717.

115. Srimanjari in *Through War and Famine* draws attention to cloth being a key wartime shortage in Bengal. See pp. 199–202.

116. 'The fortress of *Bundi*' is a reference to a famous poem by Tagore, commonly anthologised in school textbooks, satirising the militaristic ambitions of two Rajput kings.

117. Yasmin Khan, *The Raj at War*, p. 95.

118. Ibid., p. 95.

119. Quoted in Yasmin Khan, *The Raj at War*, p. 95.

120. Yasmin Khan, *The Raj at War*, p. 95.

121. Srimanjari notes how a shortage of yarn and looms affected the craft of weaving during the war years, and placed artisan weavers at the mercy of moneylenders. Srimanjari, *Through War and Famine*, p. 173.

122. Indivar Kamtekar, 'A Different War Dance', p. 189.

3. 'CLOSE TO ME AS MY VERY OWN BROTHER': MALE FRIENDSHIPS IN INDIAN WAR WRITING

1. This photograph is from an album of 36 photographs compiled by Captain E.B. Mee (later Major), Royal Signals, 81st West African Division, Burma, 1944–1945. National Army Museum, image 1996–08–382–4. I thank Peter Johnston for drawing my attention to this photograph.

2. Colonial homoerotic desire for men of colour was conceptualised in a complex variety of ways. See, for example, Deanna Heath, 'Torture, the State, and Sexual Violence against Men in Colonial India', *Radical History Review*, 126 (2016), 122–133 (p. 130).

3. Brinda Bose and Subhabrata Bhattacharya, 'Introduction', in *The Phobic and the Erotic: The Politics of Sexualities In Contemporary India*, ed. by Brinda Bose and Subhabrata Bhattacharya (Calcutta: Seagull Books, 2007), pp. ix–xxxii (p. xiii).

4. See Santanu Das, Anna Maguire and Daniel Steinbach, eds, *Colonial*

Encounters in a Time of Global Conflict, 1914–1918 (Abington: Routledge, 2021).

5. See Anna Maguire, *Contact Zones of the First World War: Cultural Encounters across the British Empire* (Cambridge: Cambridge University Press, 2021).

6. The most significant scholarly analysis of colonial masculinity in India and its accompanying anxieties is Mrinalini Sinha's *Colonial Masculinity: The 'Manly Englishman' and the 'Effeminate Bengali' in the Late Nineteenth Century* (1995).

7. Sanjay Srivastava, '"Sane Sex": The Five-Year Plan Hero and Men on Footpaths and in Gated Communities: On the Cultures of Twentieth-Century Masculinity', in *Masculinity and Its Challenges in India: Essays on Changing Perceptions*, ed. by Rohit K. Dasgupta and K. Moti Gokulsing (Jefferson, NC: McFarland & Company, 2014), pp. 27–53 (p. 28).

8. Studying men through the lens of gender has, on the whole, received relatively little consideration in the history of South Asia. Rosalind O'Hanlon calls this the 'peculiar social invisibility of masculinity' in her 1997 essay on north Indian male cultures, while Rohit Dasgupta and K. Moti Gokulsing remark upon the same unseen or unnoticed aspect of masculinity arising from its very normativity in their 2014 edited anthology of essays on the challenges faced by the study of male gender and sexuality in India. Even today, Indian masculinity—or masculinities in its variant forms—is an emergent field of academic study.

9. Ashis Nandy, *The Intimate Enemy: Loss and Recovery of Self Under Colonialism* (Oxford: Oxford University Press, 1989).

10. Mrinalini Sinha, *Colonial Masculinity*, p. 2.

11. Ibid., p. 16.

12. Ibid., p. 21.

13. Linsey Robb and Juliette Pattinson, 'Becoming Visible: Gendering the Study of Men at War', in *Men, Masculinities and Male Culture in the Second World War*, ed. by Linsey Robb and Juliette Pattinson (London: Palgrave Macmillan, 2017), pp. 1–24 (p. 8).

14. Rosalind O'Hanlon, 'Issues of Masculinity in North Indian History: The Bangash Nawabs of Farrukhabad', *Bulletin (Centre for Women's Development Studies)*, 4.1 (March 1997), 1–19 (p. 7).

15. Rosalind O'Hanlon, 'Issues of Masculinity in North Indian History', p. 16.

16. Santanu Das observes how Indian PoW memoirs from the First World War, such as Mokkhada Devi's *Kalyan-Pradip* (1928) and Sisir Prasad Sarbadhikari's *Abhi Le Baghdad* (1957), can be read as a form of cosmopolitanism in extreme situations, revealing both male vulnerability and capacity for empathy. See '"Their Lives have become Ours": Occupation,

Captivity and Lateral Contact in Mesopotamia, 1914–1918' (pp. 239–273), in Santanu Das, *India, Empire and First World War Culture*.

17. John Baptist Crasta, *Eaten by the Japanese: The Memoir of an Unknown Indian Prisoner of War* (New York, NY: Invisible Man Press, 2012; first pub. 1997), p. 78. All further references are to this edition, and page numbers provided in parentheses within the text.

18. Rivkah Zim, *The Consolations of Writing: Literary Strategies of Resistance from Boethius to Primo Levi* (Princeton, NJ: Princeton University Press, 2014), p. 7.

19. Preface to the Russian edition of Baren Basu's *Rangrut* (1956), from Baren Basu, *Rangrut* (Calcutta: Sandharan Publishers, 1950). All references, unless specified, are to this Bengali edition of the novel. The translations from the Bengali are mine, and page numbers are provided in parentheses within the text.

20. See Leela Gandhi, *Affective Communities: Anticolonial Thought, Fin-de-Siecle Radicalism and the Politics of Friendship* (London: Duke University Press, 2006).

21. Arieh J. Kochavi, *Confronting Captivity: Britain and the United States and their Prisoners of War in Nazi Germany* (Chapel Hill, NC: University of North Carolina Press, 2005), p. 9.

22. Kochavi, *Confronting Captivity*, p. 1.

23. Gavan Daws, *Prisoners of the Japanese* (London: Simon and Schuster, 2006), p. 18.

24. G.J. Douds, 'The Men Who Never Were: Indian PoWs in the Second World War,' *South Asia: Journal of South Asian Studies*, 27.2 (2010), 183–216 (p. 185).

25. Niall Ferguson, *The War of the World: History's Age of Hatred* (London: Allen Lane, 2006), pp. 442–44; 496–99; 530–31.

26. Vandana Joshi, 'Between Erasure and Remembrance: Shreds from the Lives of South Asian Prisoners of War in Stammlagers, Arbeitskommandos, Lazaretts and Graves during World War II (1939–45)', *Südasien-Chronik—South Asia Chronicle*, 5 (2015), 144–168, (p. 150).

27. Vandana Joshi, 'Between Erasure and Remembrance', p. 151 and p. 160.

28. Eleanor Bass, '"A Threat to One's Skin": Representing the Human Body in Second World War Writing' (unpublished doctoral thesis, King's College London, 2015), p. 226. Bass also observes, however, that there were exceptions to this pattern—a few camps in Asia had favourable living conditions, while European camps like Salonika in Greece became notorious for starvation, disease and violence.

29. For a history of letters sent by PoWs and civilian internees in East Asia during the Second World War, see David Tett, *A Postal History of the*

Prisoners of War and Civilian Internees in East Asia during World War Two, Volumes 1, 2 and 3 (Saint Paul, MN: BFA Publishing, 2002, 2003, 2004). I am grateful to Ghee Bowman for providing me with this reference.

30. Eric Lomax, *The Railway Man* (London: Vintage, 2013; first pub. 1995).
31. For a detailed history of the evolution of the INA, see Peter Ward Fay, *The Forgotten Army*.
32. G.J. Douds, 'The Men Who Never Were', p. 185 and p. 214.
33. Rivkah Zim, *The Consolations of Writing*.
34. Vanda Wilcox, '"Weeping tears of blood": Exploring Italian soldiers' emotions in the First World War', *Modern Italy*, 17:2 (May 2012), 171–184.
35. I read Crasta's use of 'caste' here more of an indicator of religious difference—his own Christianity contrasted against the Hindu beliefs of Rup Lal and Mohant Ram. Furthermore, Indian Christians are often known to come from Dalit or *adivasi* (indigenous) backgrounds. I am inferring that Rup Lal and Mohant Lal were Hindus based on their names. There is no direct mention of their religious faith in the memoir.
36. See, for example, Cemil Aydin, *The Politics of Anti-Westernism in Asia*, p. 184. Aydin says: 'The creation of the Indian National Army (INA) in 1942, with its ranks composed of Indian soldiers from the surrendered British troops in Singapore, became the most memorable project to embody pan-Asianist slogans [...] Major Fujiwara Iwaichi (1908–1986) gained the trust of Indian officers mainly through his own sincere commitment to the project.' Aydin also calls Iwaichi an 'idealistic Japanese figure on the ground' (p. 184).
37. G.J. Douds, 'The Men Who Never Were', p. 211.
38. Eleanor Bass, '"A Threat to One's Skin"', p. 259.
39. R.G. Salvi, *Whom Enemies Sheltered: A Saga of Human Love in the Midst of World War II* (Mumbai: Bharatiya Vidya Bhavan, 1983), p. 1. All further references are to this edition, and page numbers provided in parentheses within the text. The reference to Gunn and Moore's Autograph is to a type of cricket bat, while Slazenger Queen is a tennis racquet.
40. This is a reference to the 2nd Battalion of the Queen's Own Cameron Highlanders, which was stationed in Egypt and Libya in 1942. See the Regimental Association of the Queen's Own Highlanders (Seaforth and Cameron): <http://www.qohldrs.co.uk/html/camerons_history.htm> [Accessed 28 July 2022].
41. Joanna Bourke, *An Intimate History of Killing: Face-to-Face Killing in Twentieth-Century Warfare* (New York, NY: Basic Books, 2000), p. 2.
42. Michael Roper, *The Secret Battle: Emotional Survival in the Great War*

(Manchester: Manchester University Press, 2009). See, in particular, 'Part II Mothering Men', pp. 119–201. See also Santanu Das, *Touch and Intimacy in First World War Literature* (Cambridge: Cambridge University Press, 2005).

43. Although Salvi uses the term 'deserted' here, Romano in fact left the Italian Army and returned home to the village of Villa San Sebastiano only after the Italian Armistice with the Allies had been signed in September 1943.

44. Leela Gandhi, *Affective Communities*, p. 10.

45. E.M. Forster, *Two Cheers for Democracy* (San Diego, CA: Harcourt, 1951), p. 68.

46. This photograph is part of a collection on recruitment for the Indian Army in South India in August 1942, held by the Imperial War Museum, IWM, IND 1260. I am grateful to the Imperial War Museum's 2021 'Provisional Semantics' project, where I was academic adviser, for drawing my attention to this photograph, and to Aashique Ahmed Iqbal for his thoughts on the homoerotic nature of wartime colonial photography in India.

47. 'A body is docile that may be subjected, used, transformed, and improved [...] Discipline is a political anatomy of detail.' See Michel Foucault, 'Docile Bodies', in *The Foucault Reader*, ed. by Paul Rabinow (London: Penguin, 1991, first pub. 1984), pp. 179–187 (p. 183).

48. Philippa Levine draws attention to the near-ubiquitous nakedness of the bodies of people of colour in colonial photography, where 'nakedness, as distinct from the nudity inherited from the [Western] classical tradition, increasingly became emblematic of colonial primitiveness, savagery, and inferiority.' Philippa Levine, 'Naked Truths: Bodies, Knowledge, and the Erotics of Colonial Power', *Journal of British Studies* (January 2013) 52.1, 5–25 (p. 9).

49. Philip Woods, 'From Shaw to Shantaram: The Film Advisory Board and the Making of British Propaganda Films in India, 1940–1943', *Historical Journal of Film, Radio and Television*, 21.3 (2001), 293–308 (p. 300).

50. Fred McGlade notes that training for Indian cameramen was established in India in 1943–1944. See Chapter 7, 'The South-East Asia Campaign', in Fred McGlade, *The History of the British Army Film & Photographic Unit in the Second World War* (Solihull: Helion, 2010), pp. 155–183 (p. 157).

51. Christopher Pinney, *Camera Indica: The Social Life of Indian Photographs* (London: Reaktion Books, 1997). See especially Chapter 1, '"Stern Fidelity" and "Penetrating Certainty"', pp. 16–71.

52. See the Introduction to this book for more details.

53. This critique of the automaton-like behaviour mandated from soldiers has long-established literary roots. First World War poet Isaac

Rosenberg's 'Marching' (1916), for instance, composed from the perspective of a marching soldier, talks of how:

> My eyes catch ruddy necks
> Sturdily pressed back.
> All a red-brick moving glint.
> Like flaming pendulums, hands
> Swing across the khaki—
> Mustard coloured khaki—
> To the automatic feet.

See *Collected Poems: Isaac Rosenberg* with an introduction by Will Jonson (CreateSpace Independent Publishing, 2013), p. 17.

54. Amit Kumar Gupta notes that the numbers of people who were educated and unemployed in Bengal were rising during the war years, and that home-front paid opportunities in the ARP and civic guard units, along with medical and engineering departments, were not significant. The rising rates of inflation also sharply affected the value of salaries. In fact, the middle class campaigned for a separate Bengali regiment in the Indian Army to facilitate further recruitment, although this did not yield any results. See Amit Kumar Gupta, *Crises and Creativities*, p. 60.

55. Stephen Cohen, *The Indian Army: Its Contribution to the Development of a Nation*, pp. 106–107.

56. For an insightful history into the development of the Bengali novel, see Supriya Chaudhuri, 'The Bengali Novel', in *The Cambridge Companion to Modern Indian Culture*, edited by Vasudha Dalmia and Rashmi Sadana (Cambridge: Cambridge University Press, 2012), pp. 99–123.

57. Baren Basu, *Rangrut* (Calcutta: Sandharan Publishers, 1950), p. 37. All references, unless specified, are to this Bengali edition of the novel. The translations from the Bengali are mine.

58. From the Preface to the Czech edition (1953).

59. *MEMCR*, IOR/L/PJ/12/578, Indian Troops in Egypt, Cyrenaica and Tripolitania, 15 December to 28 December 1943. A Reinforcement Camp is where troops are held until their units are ready to receive them.

60. *MEMCR*, IOR/L/PJ/12/655, 2 June to 15 June 1943.

61. Srinath Raghavan, *India's War*, p. 385.

62. Sanjoy Bhattacharya, 'British Military Information Management Techniques and the South Asian Soldier', p. 497. Indian letters from the Burma front have not yet been recovered.

63. Srinath Raghavan, *India's War*, p. 74.

64. The numbers of recruits from Bengal in the Second World War tend to vary. I have calculated the figure of about 100,000 men from the per-

centages provided in Srinath Raghavan's *India's War*, p. 74. Brian Cloughley, the former deputy head of the UN military mission in Kashmir, makes it a higher figure of 170,000 men in *A History of the Pakistan Army: Wars and Insurrections*, fifth ed. (Oxford: Oxford University Press, 2016), p. 150.

65. Indivar Kamtekar, 'A Different War Dance', p. 192.
66. Srinath Raghavan, *India's War*, p. 406.
67. Christopher Bayly and Timothy Harper, *Forgotten Armies*, p. 167.
68. Bayly and Harper, *Forgotten Armies*, p. xxix.
69. Ibid., p. 167. These figures are contested.
70. Ibid., p. 169, pp. 177–178.
71. For a fascinating analysis of Bengali evacuee writing on Burma in 1942, see Chapter 5 'World War II and Burma: Heroism, Violence and Exodus (1938–48)' (pp. 129–162) in Parthasarathi Bhaumik, *Bengalis in Burma: A Colonial Encounter (1886–1948)* (Delhi: Routledge India, 2022).
72. Marina Mackay, 'Introduction', in *The Cambridge Companion to the Literature of the Second World War*, ed. by Marina Mackay (Cambridge: Cambridge University Press, 2009), pp. 1–12 (p. 1).
73. Julia Kristeva and Leon S. Roudiez, *Powers of Horror: An Essay on Abjection* (New York, NY: Columbia University Press, 1982), p. 7.
74. *MEMCR*, IOR/L/PJ/12/654, 2 September to 8 September 1942. Sardar Vallabhbhai Patel was a senior member of the Indian National Congress and the first Deputy Prime Minister of independent India.
75. There is a rich body of academic literature on the Quit India movement. For a recent account, See, for example, Sachi Chakravarty, *Quit India Movement: A Study* (Delhi: New Century Publications, 2002).
76. Sugata Bose, *His Majesty's Opponent*, p. 271. The Bengali men in the novel sing: '*Zindagi hyan pyar se, pyar se bitae jao / Zindagi hain kaumki, kaum se bitaye jao.*' (This life is made by love, live it with love / This life belongs to the motherland, spend it for the motherland') (p. 273). The second line is misquoted from the INA song: '*Ye zindagi hain qaum ki / Tu qaum pe lutaye ja!*' ('This life belongs to the motherland / Give it up for the motherland!'). See Satis Chandra Maikap, *Netaji Subhas Chandra Bose and Indian War of Independence* (Calcutta: Punaschya, 1998), p. 352.
77. Amalendu Sengupta, *Uttal Challish: Asamapta Biplab* [*The Turbulent Forties: An Incomplete Revolution*] (Calcutta: Pearl Publishers, 1989).
78. Preface to the Bengali edition (1950).
79. Sikh soldiers in the Hong Kong and Singapore Royal Artillery refused to wear steel helmets, as this would require them to cut their hair. Eighty-five Sikh soldiers were detained and court-martialled in January 1941. See Srinath Raghavan, *India's War*, p. 183. Indian sepoys' individual agency in negotiating 'loyalty' towards and 'dissent' against impe-

rial employers is also increasingly being argued for. See, for example, Gajendra Singh, 'The Anatomy of Dissent in the Military of Colonial India during the First and Second World Wars', *Edinburgh Papers in South Asian Studies*, 20 (2006), 1–45. Also see Singh's book *The Testimonies of Indian Soldiers in the Two World Wars* (2014).

80. Rivkah Zim, *The Consolations of Writing*, p. 2.

4. 'AN ANGUISHED HEART': WITNESSING THE INDIAN HOME-FRONT

1. August 1942; Imperial War Museum, IND 1304.
2. Ian J. Kerr, 'Representation and Representations of the Railways of Colonial and Post-Colonial South Asia', *Modern Asian Studies*, 37 (May 2003), 287–326.
3. 1942; Imperial War Museum, IND 1492.
4. Alan Harfield, 'The Women's Auxiliary Corps (India)', *Journal of the Society for Army Historical Research*, 83. 335 (Autumn 2005), 243–254.
5. Yasmin Khan, *The Raj at War*, p. 171 and Frederick Perry, *The Commonwealth Armies*, p. 114. Also see Yasmin Khan, *The Raj at War*, pp. 154–155, and Urvi Khaitan, '"The Women had saved the Situation": Indian Women's Work in War and Famine' <https://blog.royalhistsoc.org/2021/05/04/the-women-had-saved-the-situation-indian-womens-work-in-war-and-famine/> [Accessed 9 March 2022].
6. Yasmin Khan, *The Raj at War*, pp. 273–274.
7. Ibid.
8. Urvi Khaitan, 'Women beneath the Surface: Coal and the Colonial State in India during the Second World War', *War and Society*, 39.3 (August 2020), 171–188.
9. See Michael P. Ortiz, 'Spain! Why? Jawaharlal Nehru, Non-Intervention, and the Spanish Civil War', *European History Quarterly*, 2019, 49(3), 445–466, for a fascinating analysis of how Indian internationalism and anti-colonialism in the 1930s, manifested in Nehru's support for the Republican cause, furthers our understanding of the Spanish Civil War.
10. Mulk Raj Anand, *The Sword and the Sickle* (Liverpool: Lucas Publications, 1986; first pub. 1942). All further references to this novel are provided within the text, with page numbers in parentheses.
11. Elizabeth Bowen, *The Heat of the Day* (New York, NY: Anchor Press, 2002), p. 347.
12. Santanu Das, 'Entangled Emotions: Race, Encounters and Anticolonial Cosmopolitanism', in Santanu Das and Kate McLoughlin, eds, *The First World War: Literature, Culture, Modernity* (Oxford: Oxford University Press, 2018), pp. 240–261 (p. 248).

13. George Orwell, *All Propaganda is Lies, 1941–1942*, vol. 13 of *The Complete Works of George Orwell*, ed. by Peter Davison (London: Secker and Warburg, 1998), p. 337.

14. Mulk Raj Anand, *Letters on India* (London: Routledge, 1942). All further references to this work are provided within the text, with page numbers in parentheses.

15. Ahmed Ali outlines how stocks of *Twilight in Delhi* were destroyed in the Blitz, resulting in the novel being forgotten for the next twenty-five years. Ahmed Ali, Introduction to *Twilight in Delhi* (New York, NY: New Directions, 1994; first pub. 1940), p. xvii.

16. Beryl Pong, *British Literature and Culture in Second World Wartime* (Oxford: Oxford University Press, 2020), p. 42. Pong also notes the interconnectedness of the two world wars in Elizabeth Bowen's short stories. See the chapter 'Stopped Clocks' in her book, pp. 79–103.

17. Dipesh Chakrabarty, *Provincializing Europe: Postcolonial Thought and Historical Difference* (Princeton, NJ: Princeton University Press, 2000).

18. Daniel Morse, *Radio Empire: The BBC's Eastern Service and the Emergence of the Global Anglophone Novel* (New York, NY: Columbia University Press, 2020), p. 125.

19. See the chapter 'The End of Empire: Mulk Raj Anand's Comparative Modernisms' in Daniel Morse's *Radio Empire* (pp. 114–150).

20. Leela Gandhi, 'Novelists of the 1930s and 1940s' in *A History of Indian Literature in English*, ed. by Arvind Mehrotra (London: Hurst, 2003), pp. 168–92 (p. 175).

21. Daniel Morse, *Radio Empire*, p. 115 and p. 125.

22. Susheila Nasta, 'Negotiating a "New World Order": Mulk Raj Anand as Public Intellectual at the Heart of Empire (1924–1945)' in *South Asian Resistances in Britain 1858–1947*, ed. by Rehana Ahmed and Sumita Mukherjee (London: Bloomsbury, 2012), pp. 140–60 (p. 140).

23. Progressive Writers' Association, The Open University's 'Making Britain' project, <https://www.open.ac.uk/researchprojects/making-britain/content/progressive-writers-association> [Accessed 7 February 2022].

24. <https://www.open.ac.uk/researchprojects/makingbritain/content/progressive-writers-association> [Accessed 7 February 2022]. The Progressive Writers' Association in England in 1935 led to the formation of the All-India Progressive Writers' Association in India in 1936, with the Indian writer Premchand as chair. See also Ahmed Ali, Introduction to *Twilight in Delhi*, p. xvi.

25. Anand was commissioned to write *Letters on India* in the early 1940s based on an invitation from Herbert Read at Routledge. Anand worked with Herbert Read, George Orwell and other intellectuals at the BBC

Eastern Service. See Susheila Nasta, 'Negotiating a 'New World Order', p. 149.

26. Bluemel notes how *Letters on India* met with opposition even from life-long socialists. Leonard Woolf, who wrote an introduction to the book, was disapproving of the text, considering it to be 'extreme', 'one-sided' and 'filled with a lot of nonsense'. Anand, who must have been shocked by such a response, wrote a rejoinder—'I am convinced that in your zeal to warn Tom Brown [the fictitious English socialist friend in the book] against my one-sidedness you have almost gone to the Amery extreme.' Quoted in Kristin Bluemel, *George Orwell and the Radical Eccentrics: Intermodernism in Literary London* (New York, NY: Palgrave Macmillan, 2004), p. 82 and p. 92. Also see Anna Snaith, 'Introducing Mulk Raj Anand: the Colonial Politics of Collaboration', *Literature & History*, 28.1 (May 2019), 10–26 (pp. 21–23).

27. Daniel Morse, *Radio Empire*, pp. 129–136.

28. Angela Eyre, 'Organised Peasant Resistance in Fiction: *The Sword and The Sickle* and *The Lives of Others*', *South Asia Multidisciplinary Academic Journal*, 21 (2019), 1–18 (p. 3).

29. George Orwell, *All Propaganda is Lies*, p. 337.

30. Ibid., p. 381.

31. Daniel Morse notes that, 'to counter German propaganda, which stressed that the war had little to do with India, the Ministry of Information conceded that it was more important to project Britain as a source of freedom and inspire Indian listeners to counter the fascist powers than it was to further the narratives pushed by the Colonial Office during the interwar years' (*Radio Empire*, p. 114).

32. Saros Cowasjee, *So Many Freedoms: A Study of the Major Fiction of Mulk Raj Anand* (Delhi: Oxford University Press, 1977), p. 116.

33. Leela Gandhi, 'Novelists of the 1930s and 1940s', p. 178.

34. Angela Eyre, 'Organised Peasant Resistance in Fiction', pp. 6–7.

35. Anna Snaith, 'Introducing Mulk Raj Anand: the Colonial Politics of Collaboration', p. 19.

36. Angela Eyre, 'Organised Peasant Resistance in Fiction', p. 7.

37. Kristin Bluemel, *George Orwell and the Radical Eccentrics*, p. 71.

38. Saros Cowasjee, *So Many Freedoms*, p. 121.

39. Kristin Bluemel draws our attention to the symbolic function of Maya in the very fact of her pregnancy and motherhood. In the novel, we learn that Lalu and Maya's baby is born two months premature (p. 377). This, in real terms, would have made the baby's life precarious, belying the novel's hopeful ending. Instead, the baby, described as 'alive and kicking', is seen as a sign of revolution continuing to be relevant and important. Kristin Bluemel, *George Orwell and the Radical Eccentrics*, p. 193.

40. See R.N. Currey and R.V. Gibson, eds, *Poems from India by Members of the Forces* (Oxford: Oxford University Press, 1945). Both Wasi and Baig's poems are from this anthology—see p. 56 and pp. 48–51. All further references to these poems are provided in parentheses within the text. Also see the contributors' pages for Baig (p. 159) and Wasi (p. 165).

41. The exceptions tend to be books focused on 'celebrity' women of war, such as Noor Inayat Khan, a resistance agent who was part of the Special Operations Executive. She was executed at Dachau in 1944. See Shrabani Basu's *Spy Princess: The Life of Noor Inayat Khan* (Cheltenham: The History Press, 2008).

42. The recent surge of academic interest in India and the Second World War has seen, for example, Gajendra Singh and Srinath Raghavan focus on sepoy experience in *The Testimonies of Indian Soldiers and the Two World Wars* (2014) and *India's War: The Making of Modern South Asia, 1939–1945* (2016), respectively. Yasmin Khan's *The Raj at War* (2015) does consider the role of women in the war, but as part of a broader social analysis. Urvi Khaitan's research on Indian women labourers and miners during the Second World War is breaking new ground in this field.

43. MEMCR 654, 24 March to 6 April 1943.

44. Currey and Gibson, eds, *Poems from India*, pp. vii–viii.

45. It was only in later years that Second World War remembrance was to become far more reductive, Eurocentric and US-focused.

46. Muriel Wasi, *The Narrow Corridor: Moments in A Woman's Life* (New Delhi: Promilla and Co., 2005), p. 18.

47. See contributor's page for Wasi (p. 165) in *Poems from India* and Muriel Wasi, *The Narrow Corridor*, p. 25.

48. Partha Chatterjee, 'Book Review: Bricks and Mortar for Educational Reform', *India International Centre Quarterly*, 48.1 (Summer 2021), 132–135.

49. Muriel Wasi, *The Narrow Corridor*, p. 64.

50. See, for example, a discussion of Bankimchandra's novel and the nation as mother in Tanika Sarkar, 'Birth of a Goddess: "Vande Mataram", "Anandamath", and Hindu Nationhood', *Economic and Political Weekly*, 41.37 (September 16–22, 2006), 3959–3969.

51. Muriel Wasi, *The Narrow Corridor*, p. 58.

52. Although I have not been able to find any evidence that Muriel Wasi read Virginia Woolf, there are clear parallels between Woolf and Wasi's language here. The phrase used by Wasi, 'moments of being', is the title of a collection of autobiographical essays by Woolf, published posthumously in 1972. Again, Woolf says of herself: 'I see myself as a fish in a stream; deflected; held in place; but cannot describe the stream.' See Virginia Woolf, 'A Sketch of the Past', in *Moments of Being*, ed. by Jeanne

Schulkind and intro. by Hermione Lee (London: Pimlico, 2002), p. 92.
In the image of the narrow corridor within 'a crowded, moving train',
we find a similar sense of Wasi being pressed in on all sides and yet moving along with the flow. I am very grateful to Bárbara Gallego Larrarte
for alerting me to these connections.

53. Muriel Wasi, *The Narrow Corridor*, pp. 29–30.

54. Ibid., pp. 31–33.

55. Ibid., p. 31.

56. Srimanjari notes how adult males abandoned women and children in
large numbers during the Bengal Famine. Her analysis highlights how
the famine exacerbated the already vulnerable socio-economic position
of rural women who had no land-ownership rights and only a small
amount of control in domestic and economic affairs. She cites a private
statistical survey carried out in Contai in the district of Midnapur in late
September 1943, where, out of approximately 500 people begging for
food, 2 per cent were men, 53 per cent were women and 45 per cent
children. Desperate women often turned to prostitution, mostly near
military cantonments, or committed suicide. See Srimanjari, 'Women
in War and Famine', in *Through War and Famine* (pp. 195–211).

57. Wrenne Jarman, 'Letter to Claudia', in *The Distaff Muse: An Anthology of
Poetry written by Women*, ed. by Clifford Bax and Meum Stewart (London:
Hollis and Carter, 1949), p. 135.

58. Sarojini Naidu, 'The Gift of India', in *The Broken Wing: Songs of Love,
Death and Destiny 1915–1916* (London: William Heinemann, 1917),
p. 5.

59. James Campbell, 'Combat Gnosticism', pp. 203–15.

60. Sarojini Naidu, 'The Gift of India', p. 5.

61. See Santanu Das's perceptive analysis of this poem in *India, Empire, and
First World War Culture* (pp. 315–317).

62. Sarojini Naidu, 'The Gift of India', p. 6.

63. See a list of Tara Ali Baig's prose works on WorldCat <http://www.
worldcat.org/wcidentities/lccn-n50017949> [Accessed 15 February
2022].

64. Wilfred Owen, 'Dulce Et Decorum Est' (1920), in *The Oxford Book of
War Poetry* (Oxford: Oxford University Press, 2015), ed. by Jon
Stallworthy, p. 189. We can trace the history of such analysis of trauma
to Freud, who, in *Beyond the Pleasure Principle* (1920) describes how the
traumatised subject of war neurosis '*repeat[s]* the repressed material as
contemporary experience instead of, as the physician would prefer to
see, *remembering* it as something belonging to the past'. See Sigmund
Freud, 'Beyond the Pleasure Principle', in *The Standard Edition of the

Complete Psychological Works, ed. and trans. James Strachey (London: Hogarth Press, 1953–74), XVIII, pp. 7–64 (p. 18).

65. There are echoes from British modernist poetry here too, for example, Eliot's evocation of aridity and infertility in the lines: 'Here is no water but only rock / Rock and no water and the sandy road'. T.S. Eliot, 'What The Thunder Said', in *The Waste Land* (London: Faber & Faber, 2002; first pub. 1922), p. 47.

66. Shoshana Felman and Dori Laub, *Testimony: Crises of Witnessing*, p. 110.

67. Ibid., p. 111.

68. Women in higher education were rare in the 1930s. Baig was one of only twenty-five girls—compared to 500 boys—at Dhaka University. For this, and more biographical details of her life, see 'Transcript, Tara Ali Baig interviewed by Charles Allen between 1975 and 1976', British Library MSS EUR/T77–78, pp. 1–62 (pp. 1–17).

69. Transcript, 'Tara Ali Baig interviewed by Charles Allen', p. 1.

70. 'Members of the Symposium', in *The Family and Its Future*, ed. by Katherine Elliott (London: Wiley, 1970), pp. 217–224 (p. 217).

71. Transcript, 'Tara Ali Baig interviewed by Charles Allen', pp. 17–18.

72. Ibid., pp. 17–18.

73. Ibid., pp. 18–19.

74. Sen also notes other related factors that led to the terrible famine conditions: price speculation, panic hoarding, administrative chaos, the inability to export cereals from other Indian provinces into Bengal. The 'manufacturing' of this famine is further highlighted when Sen observes that crop production in Bengal in 1943 was in fact 13 per cent higher than in 1941, when there was no famine. See Amartya Sen, 'The Great Bengal Famine', in *Poverty and Famines*, pp. 52–83.

75. See, for example, Madhusree Mukerjee's analysis, where she argues that the Bengal administration had issued 5,000 licences for grain procurement, enabling licence-holders to store rice to enhance their own profit margins. She continues: 'whereas natives "hoarded", which was at least in principle a penal offence, white men "stockpiled"—which was not only legal but recommended.' See *Churchill's Secret War*, p. 188.

76. Indivar Kamtekar, 'A Different War Dance', p. 216.

77. See, for example, Janam Mukherjee's *Hungry Bengal* (2015), where Mukherjee argues that the 'notion that famine victims died passively, without resistance and without a fight, however, is a claim that cannot live up to historical scrutiny', p. 12.

78. This was first published as Gayatri Chakravorty Spivak, 'Can the Subaltern Speak?', in *Marxism and the Interpretation of Culture*, ed. by Cary Nelson and Lawrence Grossberg (London: Macmillan, 1988), pp. 271–313 (p. 285).

79. Rajeswari Sunder Rajan, 'Death and the Subaltern', in *Can the Subaltern Speak? Reflections on the History of an Idea*, ed. by Rosalind Morris (New York, NY: Columbia University Press, 2010), pp. 117–138 (p. 122).
80. 'Transcript, Tara Ali Baig interviewed by Charles Allen', pp. 18–19.
81. Currey and Gibson, eds, *Poems from India*, p. viii.
82. Rajeswari Sunder Rajan, 'Death and the Subaltern', p. 128.
83. Shoshana Felman and Dori Laub, *Testimony: Crises of Witnessing*, p. 108.

5. 'CRISIS IN CIVILISATION': HOW POETRY BECOMES TESTIMONY

1. Richard Overy, *The Inter-War Crisis, 1919–1939* (London: Longman, 1994), p. 91.
2. Ibid., p. 10.
3. Paul Betts, *Ruin and Renewal: Civilising Europe after the Second World War* (London: Profile Books, 2020), p. 2.
4. Ibid., p. 15.
5. Ibid., p. 3.
6. Walter Benjamin, 'Theses on the Philosophy of History', in Hannah Arendt ed., *Illuminations* (New York, NY: Schoken Books, 1968), pp. 253–264 (p. 256).
7. As Ramachandra Guha notes, Tagore's enormous output of creative works—poems, plays, novels and songs—remain his best-known works, particularly within Bengal. See Ramachandra Guha, 'Introduction: Travelling with Tagore', in Rabindranath Tagore, *Nationalism* (London: Penguin, 2009), pp. vii–lxviii (p. xlix). Again, Tagore's less-studied lectures and essays are now increasingly attracting scholarly attention, but from the perspective of the history of ideas and political philosophy. See, for example, recent publications such as K.L. Tuteja and Kaustav Chakraborty, eds, *Tagore and Nationalism* (Delhi: Springer India, 2017). Expanding on Santanu Das's work on Tagore and the First World War in *India, Empire and First World War Culture* (2018), I look at Tagore here as a war writer in relation to the Second World War.
8. Antony Rowland, *Poetry as Testimony: Witnessing and Memory in Twentieth-Century Poems* (Abingdon: Routledge, 2014), p. 4.
9. IWM, AYY 57. I am very grateful to Suzanne Bardgett at the IWM and Ansar Ahmed Ullah at the Swadhinata Trust for their help in locating this film. The digitised version of this film can be found here <https://www.iwm.org.uk/collections/item/object/1060033045> [Accessed 24 July 2022]. Its caption reads: 'Company of Indian members of the AMPC (Auxiliary Military Pioneer Corps), recruited mainly from Lascars at docks and ports, clearing up Sloane Street underground station, London,

after air raid. Indian troops under the command of Lieutenant-Colonel N S Taylor.'

10. Florian Stadtler, '"Home" front: Indian soldiers and civilians in Britain, 1939–45', in *Culture, Conflict and the Military in Colonial South Asia*, ed. by Kaushik Roy and Gavin Rand (Abington: Routledge, 2018), pp. 258–76 (p. 264).

11. Florian Stadtler, '"Home" front: Indian soldiers and civilians in Britain', p. 264. Also see <https://www.iwm.org.uk/collections/item/object/33292> [Accessed 6 April 2022].

12. See Ansar Ahmed Ullah, 'The South Asian seaman's role during the wars', 2012 at the Imperial War Museum: <https://www.iwm.org.uk/sites/default/files/transcripts/2018–04/The%20South%20Asian%20seaman's%20role%20during%20the%20wars%2C%20Ansar%20Ahmed%20Ullah%20.pdf> [Accessed 25 March 2022].

13. Wendy Webster, *Mixing It: Diversity in World War Two Britain* (Oxford: Oxford University Press, 2018), p. 12.

14. Ibid., pp. 9 and 6.

15. Ghee Bowman notes how Indian soldiers in Force K6, comprising animal transport companies, were received in England, Scotland and Wales during the Second World War years. These men were often posted to remote rural locations. See Ghee Bowman, *The Indian Contingent: The Forgotten Muslim Soldiers of Dunkirk* (Cheltenham: The History Press, 2020).

16. M.J. Tambimuttu, *Out of This War* (London: Fortune Press, 1941), pp. 1–24. All further references are to this edition, with page numbers given in parentheses next to quotations from the text. As the title page of the poem notes, the sections 'Air Raid' and 'The Spreading Cross' were previously published in the little magazine *Kingdom Come* and 'Elegy for the Dead' in *Poetry London*.

17. Daniel Ryan Morse, *Radio Empire*, p. 115.

18. Anticipating enemy air raids, 300,000 Bengalis were recruited into the Air Raid Protection (ARP) service, the Civic Guards and the Home Guards in Calcutta during the war. Japan did bomb Calcutta several times between December 1941 and 1944. In particular, the attack on Kidderpore Docks in December 1943 caused extensive damage and claimed the lives of at least 335 dockworkers, although this was nowhere near the scale of the German Blitz on London, Coventry and other major British cities, which continued from September 1940 until May 1941. London itself was bombed by the Luftwaffe for fifty-seven consecutive nights. See Janam Mukherjee, 'Japan Attacks', in *Calcutta: The Stormy Decades*, pp. 93–120 (p. 112).

There is a wealth of academic literature on the Blitz, out of which the following are a few highlights from a literary and cultural perspective: Beryl Pong, *British Literature and Culture in Second World Wartime: For the Duration* (Oxford: Oxford University Press, 2020); Susan R. Grazel, *At Home and under Fire: Air Raids and Culture in Britain from the Great War to the Blitz* (Cambridge: Cambridge University Press, 2012); Marina MacKay, *Modernism and World War II* (Cambridge, Cambridge University Press, 2007); Mark Rawlinson, *British Writing of the Second World War* (Oxford: Oxford University Press, 2000). The Japanese invasion of India in 1942 via the cities of Calcutta by land and air and Madras by sea was also fearfully anticipated, but never eventually took place. See Indivar Kamtekar, 'The Shiver of 1942', *Studies in History*, 18.1 (2002), 81–102.

19. T.S. Eliot and Tambimuttu shared a fruitful professional relationship, with Tambimuttu viewing 'Uncle Tom' as his mentor, and Eliot holding *Poetry London* in high regard. In fact, Eliot said: 'It is only in *Poetry London* that I can consistently expect to find new poets who matter.' See Poologasingham, *Poet Tambimuttu: A Profile* (Colombo: Associated Newspapers of Ceylon Ltd, 1993), p. 22 and p. 17.

20. I am grateful to Supriya Chaudhuri for alerting me to this connection.

21. Quoted in Ruvani Ranasinha, *South Asian Writers in Twentieth-Century Britain*, p. 118.

22. We encountered Ahmed Ali's English-language novel *Twilight in Delhi* (1940) in Chapter 4, while discussing Anand.

23. Ruvani Ranasinha, 'South Asian broadcasters in Britain and the BBC: Talking to India (1941–1943)', *South Asian Diaspora*, 2.1 (2010), 57–71 (p. 60).

24. Transcript, 'Tara Ali Baig interviewed by Charles Allen', pp. 17–18.

25. Ruvani Ranasinha, *South Asian Writers in Twentieth-Century Britain*, pp. 105–106.

26. Ibid., p. 104.

27. Ibid., p. 110.

28. Ranasinha also notes that Tambimuttu did not necessarily isolate himself from other South Asians, remaining close to friend and fellow writer Alagu Subramaniam. See Ruvani Ranasinha, *South Asian Writers in Twentieth-Century Britain*, p. 109.

29. M.J. Tambimuttu, 'Fitzrovia', in *Tambimuttu: Bridge Between Two Worlds*, ed. by Jane Williams (London: Peter Owen, 1989), pp. 223–235 (p. 233).

30. Ruvani Ranasinha, 'South Asian broadcasters in Britain and the BBC', p. 60.

31. Ruvani Ranasinha, 'Textual Culture and Reception (1870–1950)', in *South Asians and the Shaping of Britain, 1870–1950*, ed. by Ruvani

Ranasinha, Rehana Ahmed and Sumita Mukherjee (Manchester: Manchester University Press, 2013), pp. 147–206 (p. 149).

32. Tambimuttu, of course, was from Ceylon and not undivided India.

33. Quoted in Ruvani Ranasinha, *South Asian Writers in Twentieth-Century Britain*, p. 117.

34. Anand says, 'One important lapse on Tambi's part was not to remember that he came from the disinherited society [...] He took no part, for instance, in the freedom struggle of Sri Lanka that was going on [...] These poets were mainly concerned to become brown Englishmen. Tambi was already one.' See Mulk Raj Anand and Jane Williams, 'Talking of Tambi: The Dilemma of the Asian Intellectual', in *Tambimuttu: Bridge Between Two Worlds*, pp. 191–201 (p. 195–196).

35. Russell McKinnon-Croft, '*Der Erl-König*: A Personal Memory of Meary James Tambimuttu', in *Tambimuttu: Bridge Between Two Worlds*, pp. 52–55 (p. 53–54).

36. Life-writing sources show little evidence to suggest that Tambimuttu expressed strong anticolonial feelings during the war years. Tambimuttu does overtly criticise the imposition of English culture and history at the expense of indigenous ones in an autobiographical essay entitled 'Swami Rock, Raga Rock', but this is written towards the end of his life. See M.J. Tambimuttu, 'Swami Rock, Raga Rock', in *Tambimuttu: Bridge Between Two Worlds*, pp. 28–45 (p. 28).

37. Ruvani Ranasinha, *South Asian Writers in Twentieth-Century Britain*, p. 103.

38. Beryl Pong, *British Literature and Culture in Second World Wartime*, p. 31.

39. Sukhdev Sandhu, *London Calling: How Black and Asian Writers Imagined a City* (London: Harper Collins, 2003), p. 193.

40. Stephen Spender, 'Raid Across the Bay at Plymouth', in *The Terrible Rain: The War Poets 1939–45*, ed. by Brian Gardner (London, Methuen and Co. 1966), p. 60.

41. Sukhdev Sandhu, *London Calling*, p. 193.

42. See, for example, A. Trevor Tolley, *The Poetry of the Forties* (Manchester: Manchester University Press, 1985), p. 122.

43. Paul Saint-Amour, *Tense Future: Modernism, Total War, Encyclopaedic Form* (Oxford: Oxford University Press, 2015), p. 8.

44. Stephen Spender and John Lehmann, eds, *Poems for Spain* (London: Hogarth Press, 1939).

45. Quoted in Ruvani Ranasinha, *South Asian Writers in Twentieth-Century Britain*, p. 122.

46. W.H. Auden, 'Spain' (1937), in *Poems for Spain*, p. 55.

47. Paul Saint-Amour, *Tense Future*, p. 4.

48. See, for example, the lines: 'Time present and time past / Are both perhaps present in time future, / And time future contained in time past. /

If all time is eternally present / All time is unredeemable', in T.S. Eliot, 'Burnt Norton', in *Four Quartets* (London: Faber & Faber, 2011; first pub. 1943), p. 1.

49. There are again clear parallels with *The Waste Land* in the evocation to the 'Other One lurking behind'. See, for example: 'Who is the third who walks always beside you? / When I count, there are only you and I together / But when I look ahead up the white road / There is always another one walking beside you'. T.S. Eliot, 'What The Thunder Said', in *The Waste Land*, p. 48.

50. Santanu Das, *India, Empire and First World War Culture*, p. 401.

51. See, for example: 'Whan that Aprill, with his shoures soote / The droghte of March hath perced to the roote / And bathed every veyne in swich licour, / Of which vertu engendred is the flour', in Geoffrey Chaucer, 'Prologue', in Geoffrey Chaucer and Jill Mann, *The Canterbury Tales* (London: Penguin, 2005), p. 3.

52. Sudhir Kakar, ed., *Death and Dying* (Delhi: Penguin, 2014), p. 93.

53. Ibid., p. 94.

54. Santanu Das, *India, Empire and First World War Culture*, p. 387.

55. Slavoj Žižek paraphrases Antonio Gramsci in this English translation. Slavoj Žižek, 'A Permanent Economic Emergency', *New Left Review*, 64 (August 2010), 85–95 (p. 95).

56. Poem 18, *'Prantik'* ('The Borderland'), in *Bichitra: Online Tagore Variorum*, <http://bichitra.jdvu.ac.in> [Accessed 7 April 2022]. All translations from Bengali in this chapter, unless otherwise specified, are mine.

57. See, for example, Sukanta Chaudhuri, 'Tagore, Nationalism and Imperialism', in *Tagore and Nationalism*, pp. 67–75; and Santanu Das, 'Post-war World and the 'Future of all Humanity': Aurobindo, Iqbal and Tagore', in *India, Empire and First World War Culture* (pp. 367–405).

58. Poem 64, *'Naibedya'*, in *Bichitra: Online Tagore Variorum* <http://bichitra.jdvu.ac.in/> [Accessed 7 April 2022].

59. 'The Sunset of the Century', in *The English Writings of Rabindranath Tagore, Vol. II: Essays*, p. 466. These quoted lines are Tagore's English translation of Poem No. 64 in *'Naibedya'*.

60. For an analysis of linguistic differences between Tagore's Bengali and English writing, see Santanu Das, 'Post-war World and the "Future of all Humanity"' (pp. 367–405).

61. *'Nation ki?'* ('What is the Nation?'), in *Atmashakti*, Shravan 1308 (1901) in *Rabindra Rachanabali*, Vol. 3, pp. 513–519 (p. 518). This volume is one of twenty-six volumes of *Rabindra Rachanabali* (Calcutta: Viswa Bharati, Ashwin 1346–Baishakh 1372 [September 1939–May 1965]). All further references are to this edition.

62. Rustom Bharucha, *Another Asia: Rabindranath Tagore and Okakura Tenshin* (Delhi: Oxford University Press, 2009), p. 67.

63. Pankaj Mishra, *From the Ruins of Empire: The Revolt against The West and the Remaking of Asia* (London: Allen Lane, 2012), p. 241.

64. Ibid., p. 240.

65. Krishna Dutta and Andrew Robinson, eds, *Selected Letters of Rabindranath Tagore* (Cambridge: Cambridge University Press, 1997), p. 437. Tagore's nephew Soumyendranath Tagore was arrested in Germany by the Nazis in 1933 on the charge of seeking to assassinate Hitler. He denied this charge and was expelled from Germany. We do not know his uncle's response to this incident. See '"Ruled by Criminals": Germany's Regime of Inhuman Brutality—Soumyen Tagore's Bitter Experience', *Amrita Bazar Patrika*, 2 June 1933. I am very grateful to Ole Birk Laursen for this reference.

66. Amit Kumar Gupta, *Crises and Creativities*, p. 43.

67. Quoted in Ramachandra Guha, 'Introduction: Travelling with Tagore', p. xlvii.

68. Krishna Dutta and Andrew Robinson, eds, *Selected Letters of Rabindranath Tagore*, pp. 492–493.

69. Krishna Dutta and Andrew Robinson, *Rabindranath Tagore: The Myriad-Minded Man* (London: Bloomsbury, 1995), pp. 351.

70. Krishna Dutta and Andrew Robinson, eds, *Selected Letters of Rabindranath Tagore*, p. 437.

71. Krishna Dutta and Andrew Robinson, *Rabindranath Tagore: The Myriad-Minded Man*, p. 344.

72. Brownshirt thugs raided Einstein's villa at Caputh, Germany, where Tagore and Einstein had spoken. They were supposedly searching for arms. See Krishna Dutta and Andrew Robinson, *Rabindranath Tagore: The Myriad-Minded Man*, p. 344.

73. Nikolaus Wachsmann, for example, notes how gas chambers inside new death camps in occupied Poland were set up between December 1941 and July 1942. See Nikolaus Wachsmann, 'The Dynamics of Destruction: The Development of the Concentration Camps, 1933–1945', in *Concentration Camps in Nazi Germany: The New Histories*, ed. by Nikolaus Wachsmann and Jane Caplan (New York, NY: Routledge, 2009), pp. 17–43 (p. 30).

74. Quoted in Amit Kumar Gupta, *Crises and Creativities*, p. 56.

75. Rabindranath Tagore, *Sabhyatar Sankat* (Calcutta: Viswabharati, 1941). Tagore also translated the speech into English, calling it *Crisis in Civilisation*—see *The English Writings of Rabindranath Tagore, Vol. III: A Miscellany*, ed. by Sisir Kumar Das (Calcutta: Sahitya Akademi, 1996), pp. 723–726. All further references are to this English edition.

76. '*Birodhmulak Adarsha*' ('The Conflict-Rooted Ideology'), Ashwin 1308 (1901), in *Rabindra Rachanabali*, Vol. 10, Chaitra 1348 (March 1942), pp. 592–596.

77. '*Laraier Mul*' ('The Cause of War'), Agrahayan 1321 (1914), in *Rabindra Rachanabali*, Vol. 24, Poush 1354 (December 1947), pp. 269–272.

78. Santanu Das, *India, Empire and First World War Culture*, p. 369.

79. Jean-Paul Sartre, Preface to Frantz Fanon's *The Wretched of the Earth*, <https://www.marxists.org/reference/archive/sartre/1961/preface.htm> [Accessed 25 April 2022].

80. Pankaj Mishra, *From the Ruins of Empire*, p. 220.

81. Sukanta Chaudhuri, 'Tagore, Nationalism and Imperialism', p. 73.

82. 'The Sunset of the Century', in *The English Writings of Rabindranath Tagore, Vol. II: Essays*, p. 466. These quoted lines are Tagore's English translation of '*Naibedya*', Poem No. 65.

83. 'Nationalism in Japan' (1916), in *The English Writings of Rabindranath Tagore, Vol. II: Essays*, pp. 436–452 (p. 440).

84. Rustom Bharucha, *Another Asia*, pp. 67–68.

85. Alfred Tennyson, Canto LVI, *In Memoriam A.H.H.* (Charleston, SC: BiblioLife, 2009; first pub. 1850), p. 80.

86. *Poet to Poet: Full Text of Correspondence between Yone Noguchi and Rabindranath Tagore on the Sino-Japanese Conflict* (Calcutta: Reprinted from the Viswa-Bharati Quarterly, Volume IV, Part 3, January 1939), p. 1. All further references are to this edition, and page numbers are provided in parentheses within the text.

87. See, for example, Masayo Duus, *The Life of Isamu Noguchi: Journey Without Borders*, trans. by Peter Duus (Princeton, NJ: Princeton University Press, 2004), which has valuable information on Isamu's father, Yone Noguchi, as well.

88. Donald Keene, ed., *So Lovely a Country Will Never Perish: Wartime Diaries of Japanese Writers* (New York, NY: Columbia University Press, 2010), p. 14.

89. Krishna Dutta and Andrew Robinson, eds, *Selected Letters of Rabindranath Tagore*, pp. 485–486.

90. Pankaj Mishra, *From the Ruins of Empire*, p. 231 and p. 224.

91. Sukanta Chaudhuri, 'Tagore, Nationalism and Imperialism', p. 69.

92. Consider Gandhi's words in *Hind Swaraj*: '[…] if we become free, India is free. And in this thought you have a definition of Swaraj. It is Swaraj when we learn to rule ourselves.' Mohandas Gandhi, *Hind Swaraj: or, Indian Home Rule* (Ahmedabad: Navajivan Pub. House, 1989; first pub. 1909), p. 84. Sukanta Chaudhuri notes that Tagore and Gandhi had separate means of arriving at such a conclusion. See Sukanta Chaudhuri, 'Tagore, Nationalism and Imperialism', p. 69.

93. Rustom Bharucha, *Another Asia*, p. 69.

94. Quoted in Santanu Das, *India, Empire and First World War Culture*, p. 394.

95. Rustom Bharucha, *Another Asia*, p. 73.

96. Ibid., p. 74.

97. Pankaj Mishra, *From the Ruins of Empire*, p. 250.

98. Rabindranath Tagore, 'Judgment' (1925), in *The English Writings of Tagore, Vol. III: A Miscellany*, pp. 549–558 (p. 556).

99. Claude von Clausewitz, *On War* (Princeton, NJ: Princeton University Press, 1993; first pub. 1832), p. 22.

100. Krishna Dutta and Andrew Robinson, *Rabindranath Tagore: The Myriad-Minded Man*, p. 348.

101. Sukanta Chaudhuri, 'Tagore, Nationalism and Imperialism', p. 71.

102. Pankaj Mishra, *From the Ruins of Empire*, p. 224.

103. Sukanta Bhattacharya, '*Rabindranath-er Prati*' ('To Rabindranath'), in *Chharpatra (Passport)*, p. 7.

104. Shoshana Felman and Dori Laub, *Testimony: Crises of Witnessing*, p. 96.

105. Paul Betts, *Ruin and Renewal*, p. 11.

AFTERWORD

1. Michael Ondaatje, *The English Patient* (London: Bloomsbury, 2004; first pub. 1992), p. 304. All references are to this edition of the novel.

2. Samar Sen, '9th August 1945', p. 30.

3. Quoted in the introduction to Raghavan Iyer, ed., *The Moral and Political Writings of Mahatma Gandhi, Vol. 2: Truth and Non-violence* (Oxford: Clarendon Press, 1986), pp. 1–15 (p. 13).

4. The atomic bombs brought the war in Southeast Asia to a sudden end. On 11 August 1945, Subhas Chandra Bose was notified in advance of Japan's intention to surrender. It precipitated his decision to journey in secret to Russia—he had accurately predicted that the wartime Anglo-American alliance with the Soviet Union would not last. Bose, however, was never to complete this journey, succumbing to his injuries in a plane crash in Taipei. See Sugata Bose, *His Majesty's Opponent*, pp. 297–308. In post-war years, Jawaharlal Nehru, appalled by the use of the atomic bomb, became in 1954 the first world leader to advocate universal disarmament. See Katherine Young, 'Hinduism and the Ethics of Weapons of Mass Destruction', in *The Nuclear Shadow over South Asia, 1947 to the Present*, ed. by Kaushik Roy and Scott Gates (London: Routledge, 2011), pp. 337–367 (p. 337).

5. Joanna Bourke, *The Second World War: A People's History* (Oxford: Oxford University Press, 2001), p. 218.

6. Raghu Karnad, 'Soldiers without borders: Fighting didn't stop for Indians after WWII', 8 November 2020, *The Indian Express* <https://indianex-press.com/article/express-sunday-eye/soldiers-without-bor-ders-6999026/> [Accessed 18 July 2022].

7. WO 204–10381, *Appreciation and Censorship Report No. 51*, 16–31 August 1944, National Archives at Kew, Central Mediterranean Forces (CMF), Indian Troops in Italy.

8. Ibid.

9. Ibid.

10. Raghu Karnad, *Farthest Field*, pp. 239–240.

11. Heather Goodall, 'Port Politics: Indian Seamen, Australian Unions and Indonesian Independence, 1945–47', *Labour History*, 94 (2008), 43–68 (p. 43).

12. Yasmin Khan, *The Raj at War*, p. 307.

13. Saumitra Jha and Steven Wilkinson, 'Does Combat Experience Foster Organisational Skill? Evidence from Ethnic Cleansing During the Partition of South Asia', *American Political Science Review*, 106.4 (November 2012), 1–50 (p. 6).

14. Yasmin Khan, *The Great Partition: The Making of India and Pakistan* (New Haven, CT: Yale University Press, 2008), p. 6.

15. Yasmin Khan, *The Raj at War*, p. 321. Compton Mackenzie's book on the history of the Indian Army during the Second World War was published as *Eastern Epic* (London: Chatto & Windus, 1951).

16. Ibid., p. 319. There is now the Commonwealth Gate at the top of Constitution Hill in central London, unveiled by Queen Elizabeth II in 2002, which commemorates the five million men and women from India, Pakistan, Bangladesh, Sri Lanka, Africa and the Caribbean who served the British in both world wars. See <https://collection.nam.ac.uk/detail.php?acc=2008–08-18-22> for more details [Accessed 23 July 2022].

17. Some soldiers, in fact, did not make it back to India even though they survived the war, because they migrated to other places, such as post-war industrial centres in Britain. Yasmin Khan, 'Wars of Displacement: Exile and Uprooting in the 1940s', in *The Cambridge History of the Second World War Part II, The Social Practice of People's War 1939–1945*, ed. by Michael Geyer and Adam Tooze (Cambridge: Cambridge University Press, 2015), pp. 277–297 (p. 284).

18. Raghu Karnad, *Farthest Field*, p. 240.

19. I have adopted this evocative phrase from the title of the book *Calcutta: the Stormy Decades*, ed. by Tanika Sarkar and Sekhar Bandyopadhyay, which discusses life in the city of Calcutta during the 1940s and 1950s.

WORKS CITED

Primary Sources

Archival Material

British Library

India Office Records:

Clement Attlee, 'India and the War', published in *The Times*, 21 October 1939, L/PJ/5706 (1939).

Harijan, November 25, 1939, L/PJ/5706 (1939).

H.N. Brailsford, 'India—the Path to Victory', 22 October 1939, IOR/L/PJ/5706 (1939).

Marquess of Zetland, Secretary of State for India, to the Home Department of the Government of India, 12 November 1939, L/PJ/5706 (1939).

Middle East Military Censorship Reports: Fortnightly Summaries Covering Indian Troops, August 1942–April 1943, L/PJ/12/654.

Middle East Military Censorship Reports: Fortnightly Summaries Covering Indian Troops, April 1943–October 1943, L/PJ/12/655.

Middle East Military Censorship Reports: Fortnightly Summaries Covering Indian Troops, November 1943–March 1944, L/PJ/12/578.

Middle East Military Censorship Reports: Fortnightly Summaries Covering Indian Troops, June 1944–March 1945, L/PJ/12/656.

M.W.M. Yeatts, *Census of India 1941, Volume 1, Part 1—Tables* (Simla: Government of India Press, 1943).

Oral Archives:

'Field Marshall Sir Claude Auchinleck', interviewed by Charles Allen (1972–1974), MSS EUR T3.

'Transcript, Tara Ali Baig interviewed by Charles Allen between 1975 and 1976', MSS EUR/T77–78, pp. 1–62.

WORKS CITED

Imperial War Museum

Film:

'Air Raid Damage, London, Indian Auxiliary Military Pioneer Corps
(AMPC)', War Office Film Unit, IWM AYY 57.
<https://www.iwm.org.uk/collections/item/object/1060033045>
[Accessed 24 July 2022].

Photographs:

Ministry of Information's Second World War Official Collection of
Photographs, K Series.
War Office's Second World War Official Collection of Photographs, IND
Series.

Posters:

'Indians in Civil Defence', IWM Art.IWM PST 16288.

Amrita Bazar Patrika newspaper archives, India

'"Ruled by Criminals": Germany's Regime of Inhuman Brutality—
Soumyen Tagore's Bitter Experience', *Amrita Bazar Patrika*, 2 June
1933.

National Army Museum

Photograph collection by Captain E.B. Mee (later Major), Royal Signals,
81st West African Division, Burma, 1944–1945. 1996–08–382.

National Archives at Kew

Central Mediterranean Forces (CMF), Indian Troops in Italy,
Appreciation and Censorship Reports, December 1943–September
1944, WO 204–10381.

National Archives of India

'Letter to General Cariappa from Jemadar Ganapathy', 28 November
1945, Cariappa Private Papers, (1912–1972).
The Indian (1939–1940), published in Kuala Lumpur, Microfilm No:
2075.

Netaji Research Bureau, Calcutta

Safrani, Abid Hasan, *The Men from Imphal* (Calcutta: Netaji Research
Bureau, 1971).

WORKS CITED

Strachey, C.J., 'How I came to join the Indian National Army', *The Oracle* (Calcutta: Netaji Research Bureau, January 1982), pp. 53–56.

Published Material

Ali, Ahmed, *Twilight in Delhi* (New York, NY: New Directions, 1994; first pub. 1940).

Anand, Mulk Raj, *Letters on India* (London: Routledge, 1942).

————, *The Sword and the Sickle* (Liverpool: Lucas Publications, 1986; first pub. 1942).

Bandyopadhyay, Bibhutibhushan, *Ashani Sanket* (*Intimations of Thunder*) (Calcutta: Mitra and Ghosh, 2015; first published serially between 1944 and 1946 and in novel form in 1959).

Barbusse, Henri, *Under Fire*, trans. by W. Fitzwater Wray (London: Everyman's Library, 1965; first pub. 1916).

Barnard, John, ed., *John Keats: The Complete Poems*, 2nd edn. (London: Penguin Classics, 1977).

Basu, Baren, *Rangrut* (*The Recruit*) (Calcutta: Sandharan Publishers, 1950).

Bax, Clifford, and Meum Stewart, eds, *The Distaff Muse: An Anthology of Poetry written by Women* (London: Hollis and Carter, 1949).

Bhattacharya, Sukanta, *Chharpatra* (*Passport*) (Calcutta: Kamini Prakashalaya, 2008; first pub. 1948).

Bowen, Elizabeth, *The Heat of the Day* (New York, NY: Anchor Press, 2002).

Chattopadhyay, Bankimchandra, *Anandamath* (*The Abbey of Bliss*) (Calcutta: Basumati Sahitya Mandir, 1954; first pub. 1882).

Chaucer, Geoffrey, *The Canterbury Tales*, ed. by Jill Mann (London: Penguin, 2005).

Crasta, John Baptist, *Eaten by the Japanese: The Memoir of an Unknown Indian Prisoner of War* (New York, NY: Invisible Man Press, 2012; first pub. 1997).

Currey, R.N., and R.V. Gibson, eds, *Poems from India by Members of the Forces* (Oxford: Oxford University Press, 1945).

Day-Lewis, Tamasin, ed., *Last Letters Home* (London: Macmillan, 1995).

Deb, Sabyasachi, and Somesh Chattopadhyay, comp., *Sankalita Samar Sen* (*The Selected Writings of Samar Sen*) (Calcutta: Anustup, 2010).

Dutta, Krishna, and Andrew Robinson, eds, *Selected Letters of Rabindranath Tagore* (Cambridge: Cambridge University Press, 1997).

Eliot, T.S., *Four Quartets* (London: Faber & Faber, 2011; first pub. 1943).

————, *The Waste Land* (London: Faber & Faber, 2002; first pub. 1922).

Forster, E.M., *Two Cheers for Democracy* (San Diego, CA: Harcourt, 1951).

Freud, Sigmund, *The Standard Edition of the Complete Psychological Works*, ed. and trans. by James Strachey (London: Hogarth Press, 1953–74).

Gandhi, M.K., *Hind Swaraj: or, Indian Home Rule* (Ahmedabad: Navajivan Pub. House, 1989; first pub. 1909).

————, *The Moral and Political Writings of Mahatma Gandhi, Vol. 2: Truth and Non-violence*, ed. by Raghavan Iyer (Oxford: Clarendon Press, 1986).

Gardner, Brian, ed., *The Terrible Rain: The War Poets 1939–45* (London, Methuen and Co. 1966).

Ghosh, Amitav, *The Glass Palace* (London: Harper Collins, 2000).

India and the War, 1939–1945, The Facts (London: Information Department, India Office, 1946).

Jonson, Will, intro., *Collected Poems: Isaac Rosenberg* (CreateSpace Independent Publishing, 2013).

Keene, Donald, ed., *So Lovely a Country Will Never Perish: Wartime Diaries of Japanese Writers* (New York, NY: Columbia University Press, 2010).

Kendall, Tim, ed., *Poetry of the First World War: An Anthology* (Oxford: Oxford University Press, 2013).

Khan, Shah Nawaz, *My Memories of the INA and Its Netaji* (Delhi: Rajkamal Publications, 1946).

Lomax, Eric, *The Railway Man* (London: Vintage, 2013; first pub. 1995).

Mushtaq, Nawazish Ali, *Jangi Safarnama (Journey Through War)* (Lahore: Qureshi Book Agency, *c*.1944).

Naidu, Sarojini, *The Broken Wing: Songs of Love, Death and Destiny 1915–1916* (London: William Heinemann, 1917).

Nandy, Pritish, trans., *The Complete Poems of Samar Sen* (Calcutta: A Writer's Workshop Publication, 1970).

Omissi, David, *Indian Voices of the Great War: Soldiers' Letters, 1914–18* (London: Palgrave Macmillan, 1999).

Ondaatje, Michael, *The English Patient* (London: Bloomsbury, 2004; first pub. 1992).

Orwell, George, *All Propaganda is Lies, 1941–1942*, vol. 13 of *The Complete Works of George Orwell*, ed. by Peter Davison (London: Secker and Warburg, 1998).

Poet to Poet: Full text of correspondence between Yone Noguchi and Rabindranath

WORKS CITED

Tagore on the Sino-Japanese Conflict (Calcutta: Reprinted from the *Viswa-Bharati Quarterly*, Volume IV, Part 3, January 1939).

Ray, Shantilal, *Arakan Fronte* (*On the Frontlines at Arakan*) (Calcutta: Bengal Publishers, 1946).

Remarque, Erich Maria, *All Quiet on the Western Front* (London: Vintage, 1996; first pub. 1928).

Robson, Walter, *Letters from a Soldier* (London: Faber and Faber, 1960).

Salvi, R.G., *Whom Enemies Sheltered: A Saga of Human Love in the Midst of World War II* (Mumbai: Bharatiya Vidya Bhavan, 1983).

Spender, Stephen and John Lehmann, eds, *Poems for Spain* (London: Hogarth Press, 1939).

Stallworthy, Jon, ed., *The Oxford Book of War Poetry* (Oxford: Oxford University Press, 1984).

Tagore, Rabindranath, *The English Writings of Rabindranath Tagore, Vol. II: Essays*, ed. by Sisir Kumar Das (Calcutta: Sahitya Akademi, 1996).

——, *The English Writings of Rabindranath Tagore, Vol. III: A Miscellany*, ed. by Sisir Kumar Das (Calcutta: Sahitya Akademi, 1996).

——, *Nationalism*, with an introduction by Ramachandra Guha (London: Penguin, 2009).

——, *Rabindra Rachanabali* [*The Collected Works of Rabindranath Tagore*] (Calcutta: Viswa Bharati, Ashwin 1346–Baishakh 1372 [September 1939–May 1965]), 26 volumes.

——, *Sabhyatar Sankat* (*Crisis in Civilisation*) (Calcutta: Viswabharati, 1941).

Tambimuttu, M.J., 'Fitzrovia', in *Tambimuttu: Bridge Between Two Worlds*, ed. by Jane Williams (London: Peter Owen, 1989), pp. 223–235.

——, *Out of This War* (London: Fortune Press, 1940).

——, 'Swami Rock, Raga Rock', in *Tambimuttu: Bridge Between Two Worlds*, ed. by Jane Williams (London: Peter Owen, 1989), pp. 28–45.

Tennyson, Alfred, *In Memoriam A.H.H.* (Charleston, SC: BiblioLife, 2009; first pub. 1850).

Together: The Contribution made in the Second World War by African, Asian and Caribbean Men and Women (London: Imperial War Museum, 1995).

Wasi, Muriel, *The Narrow Corridor: Moments in A Woman's Life* (New Delhi: Promilla and Co., 2005).

Woolf, Virginia, *Moments of Being*, ed. by Jeanne Schulkind and intro. by Hermione Lee (London: Pimlico, 2002).

WORKS CITED

Secondary Material

Books

Adorno, Theodore W., *Prisms*, trans. by Samuel and Shierry Weber (Cambridge, MA: MIT Press, 1983).

Ahmed, Sara, *The Cultural Politics of Emotion* (Edinburgh: Edinburgh University Press, 2004).

Arendt, Hannah, *The Origins of Totalitarianism* (London: Penguin, 2017; first pub. 1951).

Aydin, Cemil, *The Politics of Anti-Westernism in Asia: Visions of World Order in Pan-Islamic and Pan-Asian Thought* (New York, NY: Columbia University Press, 2007).

Azoulay, Ariella, *The Civil Contract of Photography* (New York, NY: Zone Books, 2008).

Bachelard, Gaston, *The Poetics of Space* (Boston, MA: Beacon Press, 1958).

Barrier, N. Gerald, *Banned: Controversial Literature and Political Control in British India, 1907–1947* (Columbia, MO: University of Missouri Press, 1974).

Barthes, Roland, *Image Music Text*, trans. by Stephen Heath (London: Fontana Press, 1977).

————, *Mythologies*, trans. by Annette Lavers (London: Vintage, 2009; first pub. 1957).

Basu, Shrabani, *Spy Princess: The Life of Noor Inayat Khan* (Cheltenham: The History Press, 2008).

Bayly, Christopher, and Timothy Harper, *Forgotten Armies: The Fall of British Asia, 1941–1945* (London: Penguin, 2005).

Beaumont, Roger, *Sword of the Raj: The British Army in India, 1747–1947* (New York, NY: Bobbs-Merrill, 1977).

Benjamin, Walter, *Illuminations*, ed. by Hannah Arendt (New York, NY: Schoken Books, 1968).

Betts, Paul, *Ruin and Renewal: Civilising Europe after the Second World War* (London: Profile Books, 2020).

Bhagavan, Manu, *India and the Quest for One World: The Peacemakers* (London: Palgrave Macmillan, 2013).

Bharucha, Rustom, *Another Asia: Rabindranath Tagore and Okakura Tenshin* (Delhi: Oxford University Press, 2009).

Bhattacharya, Amiyo, *Kabi Sukanta Bhattacharya O Shei Samay* (*The Poet Sukanta Bhattacharya and Those Days*) (Calcutta: Charu Press, 2008).

Bhattacharya, Sanjoy, *Propaganda and Information in Eastern India, 1939–45: A Necessary Weapon of War* (London: Curzon, 2001).

Bhaumik, Parthasarathi, *Bengalis in Burma: A Colonial Encounter (1886–1948)* (Delhi: Routledge India, 2022).

Blom, Amélie and Stéphanie Tawa Lama-Rewal, *Emotions, Mobilisations and South Asian Politics* (London: Routledge India, 2019).

Bluemel, Kristin, *George Orwell and the Radical Eccentrics: Intermodernism in Literary London* (New York, NY: Palgrave Macmillan, 2004).

Boehmer, Elleke, *Indian Arrivals, 1870–1915: Networks of British Empire* (Oxford: Oxford University Press, 2015).

Bose, Sugata, *His Majesty's Opponent: Subhas Chandra Bose and India's Struggle Against Empire* (Cambridge, MA: Harvard University Press, 2011).

————, and Ayesha Jalal, *Modern South Asia: History, Culture, Political Economy* (Delhi: Routledge, 2011; first pub. 1997).

Bourke, Joanna, *An Intimate History of Killing: Face-to-Face Killing in Twentieth-Century Warfare* (New York, NY: Basic Books, 2000).

————, *The Second World War: A People's History* (Oxford, Oxford University Press, 2001).

Bowman, Ghee, *The Indian Contingent: The Forgotten Muslim Soldiers of Dunkirk* (Cheltenham: History Press, 2020).

Butler, Judith, *Precarious Life: The Powers of Mourning and Violence* (New York, NY: Verso, 2006).

Chakrabarty, Dipesh, *Provincializing Europe: Postcolonial Thought and Historical Difference* (Princeton, NJ: Princeton University Press, 2000).

Chakravarty, Shachi, *Quit India Movement: A Study* (Delhi: New Century Publications, 2002).

Clausewitz, Claude von, *On War* (Princeton, NJ: Princeton University Press, 1993; first pub. 1832).

Cloughley, Brian, *A History of the Pakistan Army: Wars and Insurrections*, 5th edn, (Oxford: Oxford University Press, 2016).

Cohen, Stephen, *The Indian Army: Its Contribution to the Development of a Nation* (Berkeley, CA: University of California Press, 1971).

Collingham, Lizzie, *The Taste of War: World War Two and the Battle for Food* (London: Allen Lane, 2011).

Copland, Ian, *The Princes of India in the Endgame of Empire, 1919–1947* (Cambridge: Cambridge University Press, 1997).

Cowasjee, Saros, *So Many Freedoms: A Study of the Major Fiction of Mulk Raj Anand* (Delhi: Oxford University Press, 1977).

Dalmia, Vasudha, *Fiction as History: The Novel and the City in Modern North India* (Albany, NY: State University of New York Press, 2019).

Das, Santanu, *India, Empire and First World War Culture* (Cambridge: Cambridge University Press, 2018).

———, *Touch and Intimacy in First World War Literature* (Cambridge: Cambridge University Press, 2008).

———, ed., *Race, Empire and First World War Writing* (Cambridge: Cambridge University Press, 2011).

———, Anna Maguire and Daniel Steinbach, eds, *Colonial Encounters in a Time of Global Conflict, 1914–1918* (Abington: Routledge, 2021).

Das, Sisir Kumar, *A History of Indian Literature, 1911–1956, Struggle for Freedom: Triumph and Tragedy* (Calcutta: Sahitya Akademi, 2005).

Daws, Gavan, *Prisoners of the Japanese* (London: Simon and Schuster, 2006).

Deshpande, Anirudh, *Hope and Despair: Mutiny, Rebellion and Death in India* (Delhi: Primus, 2016).

Dutta, Krishna, and Andrew Robinson, *Rabindranath Tagore: The Myriad-Minded Man* (London: Bloomsbury, 1995).

Duus, Masayo, *The Life of Isamu Noguchi: Journey Without Borders*, trans. by Peter Duus (Princeton, NJ: Princeton University Press, 2004).

Edwards, Elizabeth, *Raw Histories: Photographs, Anthropology and Museums* (Oxford: Berg, 2001).

Elliott, Katherine, ed., *The Family and Its Future* (London: Wiley, 1970).

Ellmann, Maud, *The Hunger Artists: Starvation, Writing and Imprisonment* (London: Virago, 1993).

Fanon, Frantz, *The Wretched of the Earth* (London: Penguin, 2001; first pub. 1961).

Fay, Peter Ward, *The Forgotten Army: India's Armed Struggle for Independence 1942–1945* (Delhi: Rupa, 1994).

Feigel, Lara, *The Love-charm of Bombs: Restless Lives in the Second World War* (New York, NY: Bloomsbury, 2013).

Felman, Shoshana, and Dori Laub, *Testimony: Crises of Witnessing in Literature, Psychoanalysis and History* (New York, NY: Routledge: 1992).

Fennell, Jonathan, *Fighting the People's War: The British Commonwealth Armies and the Second World War* (Cambridge: Cambridge University Press, 2019).

Ferguson, Niall, *The War of the World: History's Age of Hatred* (London: Allen Lane, 2006).

Fussell, Paul, *The Great War and Modern Memory* (Oxford: Oxford University Press, 2000; first pub. 1975).

Gandhi, Leela, *Affective Communities: Anticolonial Thought, Fin-de-Siecle Radicalism and the Politics of Friendship* (London: Duke University Press, 2006).

Ghosh, Amitav, *The Great Derangement: Climate Change and the Unthinkable* (Chicago, IL: University of Chicago Press, 2016).

Ghosh, Nityapriya, *Makers of Indian Literature: Samar Sen* (Calcutta: Sahitya Academy, 2001).

Gilbert, Martin, *The Second World War: A Complete History* (London: Phoenix, 2009; first pub. 1989).

Gilroy, Paul, *Postcolonial Melancholia* (New York, NY: Columbia University Press, 2005).

Gopal, Priyamvada, *Insurgent Empire: Anticolonial Resistance and British Dissent* (London: Verso, 2020).

Grazel, Susan R., *At Home and under Fire: Air Raids and Culture in Britain from the Great War to the Blitz* (Cambridge: Cambridge University Press, 2012).

Gupta, Amit Kumar, *Crises and Creativities: Middle-Class Bhadralok in Bengal, c.1939–52* (Hyderabad: Orient Black Swan, 2009).

Hashmi, Taj ul-Islam, *Pakistan as a Peasant Utopia: The Communalisation of Class Politics in East Bengal, 1920–1947* (Delhi: Routledge, 1992).

Hicks, Dan, *The Brutish Museums: The Benin Bronzes, Colonial Violence and Cultural Restitution* (London: Pluto Press, 2020).

Hinton, James, *Nine Wartime Lives: Mass-Observation and the Making of the Modern Self* (Oxford: Oxford University Press, 2010).

Horne, John, ed., *State, Society and Mobilization in Europe during the First World War* (Cambridge: Cambridge University Press, 1997).

Iqbal, Iftekar, *The Bengal Delta: Ecology, State and Social Change, 1840–1943* (London: Palgrave Macmillan, 2010).

Ishikawa, Eisei and David Swain, trans., The Committee for the Compilation of Materials on Damage caused by the Atomic Bombs in Hiroshima and Nagasaki's *Hiroshima and Nagasaki: The Physical, Medical and Social Effects of the Atomic Bombings* (London: Hutchinson, 1981).

Jackson, Ashley, *The British Empire and the Second World War* (London: Hambledon Continuum, 2006).

————, Yasmin Khan and Gajendra Singh, eds, *An Imperial World at War: The British Empire, 1939–45* (London: Routledge, 2016).

Jeffreys, Alan, *The British Army in the Far East 1941–1945* (Oxford: Osprey Publishing, 2005).

Kakar, Sudhir, ed., *Death and Dying* (Delhi: Penguin, 2014).

Karnad, Raghu, *Farthest Field: An Indian Story of the Second World War* (London: William Collins, 2015).

Khan, Yasmin, *The Great Partition: The Making of India and Pakistan* (New Haven, CT: Yale University Press, 2008).

————, *The Raj at War: A People's History of India's Second World War* (London: Bodley Head, 2015).

Killingray, David, *Fighting for Britain: African Soldiers in the Second World War* (Woodbridge: James Currey, 2012).

————, and Richard Rathbone, eds, *Africa and the Second World War* (London: Palgrave Macmillan, 1986).

Kochavi, Arieh J., *Confronting Captivity: Britain and the United States and their Prisoners of War in Nazi Germany* (Chapel Hill, NC: University of North Carolina Press, 2005).

Kristeva, Julia, and Leon S. Roudiez, *Powers of Horror: An Essay on Abjection* (New York, NY: Columbia University Press, 1982).

Lebra, Joyce, *Women Against the Raj: The Rani of Jhansi Regiment* (Singapore: Institute of Southeast Asian Studies, 2008).

Lee, Hermione, *Body Parts: Essays in Life-Writing* (London: Chatto & Windus, 2005).

Louro, Michele, *Comrades against Imperialism: Nehru, India, and Interwar Internationalism* (Cambridge: Cambridge University Press, 2018).

MacKay, Marina, *Modernism and World War II* (Cambridge, Cambridge University Press, 2007).

Maguire, Anna, *Contact Zones of the First World War: Cultural Encounters across the British Empire* (Cambridge: Cambridge University Press, 2021).

Maikap, Satis Chandra, *Netaji Subhas Chandra Bose and Indian War of Independence* (Calcutta: Punaschya, 1998).

Manjapra, Kris, *M.N. Roy: Marxism and Colonial Cosmopolitanism* (New Delhi: Routledge, 2010).

Mazumdar, Rajit, *The Indian Army and the Making of Punjab* (Hyderabad: Orient Blackswan, 2003).

McGlade, Fred, *The History of the British Army Film & Photographic Unit in the Second World War* (Solihull: Helion, 2010).

Mellor, Leo, *Reading the Ruins: Modernism, Bombsites and British Culture* (Cambridge: Cambridge University Press, 2011).

Mishra, Pankaj, *From the Ruins of Empire: The Revolt against the West and the Remaking of Asia* (London: Allen Lane, 2012).

Morse, Daniel, *Radio Empire: The BBC's Eastern Service and the Emergence of the Global Anglophone Novel* (New York, NY: Columbia University Press, 2020).

Mukerjee, Madhusree, *Churchill's Secret War: The British Empire and the Ravaging of India during World War II* (New York, NY: Basic Books, 2011).

Mukherjee, Janam, *Hungry Bengal: War, Famine and the End of Empire* (London: Hurst & Company, 2015).

Nandy, Ashis, *The Intimate Enemy: Loss and Recovery of Self Under Colonialism* (Oxford: Oxford University Press, 1989).

Nasta, Susheila, *Home Truths: Fictions of the South Asian Diaspora in Britain* (London: Palgrave, 2001).

Natarajan, J., *History of Indian Journalism* (Delhi: Publications Division, Ministry of Information and Broadcasting, Government of India, 1955).

Overy, Richard, *The Inter-War Crisis, 1919–1939* (London: Longman, 1994).

Perry, Frederick, *The Commonwealth Armies: Manpower and Organisation in Two World Wars* (Manchester: Manchester University Press, 1990).

Pinney, Christopher, *Camera Indica: The Social Life of Indian Photographs* (London: Reaktion Books, 1997).

Pong, Beryl, *British Literature and Culture in Second World Wartime* (Oxford: Oxford University Press, 2020).

Poologasingham, P., *Poet Tambimuttu: A Profile* (Colombo: Associated Newspapers of Ceylon Ltd, 1993).

Prasad, Bisheshwar, ed., *Official History of the Indian Armed Forces in the Second World War, 1939–1945* (Combined Inter-Services Historical Section, India and Pakistan, 1956).

Rabinow, Paul, *The Foucault Reader* (London: Penguin, 1991; first pub. 1984).

Raghavan, Srinath, *India's War: The Making of Modern South Asia, 1939–1945* (London, Penguin: 2016).

Ranasinha, Ruvani, *South Asian Writers in Twentieth-Century Britain* (Oxford: Oxford University Press, 2007).

Rawlinson, Mark, *British Writing of the Second World War* (Oxford: Oxford University Press, 2000).

Ray, Rajat Kanta, *The Felt Community: Commonalty and Mentality Before the Emergence of Indian Nationalism* (New Delhi: Oxford University Press, 2003).

Roper, Michael, *The Secret Battle: Emotional Survival in the Great War* (Manchester: Manchester University Press, 2009).

Rowland, Antony, *Poetry as Testimony: Witnessing and Memory in Twentieth-Century Poems* (Abingdon: Routledge, 2014).

Rushdie, Salman, *Imaginary Homelands: Essays and Criticism 1981–1991* (London: Vintage, 2010).

Saint-Amour, Paul, *Tense Future: Modernism, Total War, Encyclopedic Form* (Oxford: Oxford University Press, 2015).

Sandhu, Sukhdev, *London Calling: How Black and Asian Writers Imagined a City* (London: Harper Collins, 2003).

Scarry, Elaine, *The Body in Pain: The Making and Unmaking of the World* (Oxford: Oxford University Press, 1985).

Sen, Amartya, *Poverty and Famines: An Essay on Entitlement and Deprivation* (Oxford: Clarendon Press, 1981).

Sen, Rushati, *Bibhutibhushan Bandyopadhyay* (Calcutta: Paschimbanga Bangla Academy, 1995).

Sengupta, Amalendu, *Uttal Challish: Asamapta Biplab* [*The Turbulent Forties: An Incomplete Revolution*] (Calcutta: Pearl Publishers, 1989).

Shetti, Devika, *War over Words: Censorship in India, 1930–1960*, (Cambridge: Cambridge University Press, 2019).

Siegel, Benjamin Robert, *Hungry Nation: Food, Famine, and the Making of Modern India* (Cambridge: Cambridge University Press, 2018).

Singh, Gajendra, *The Testimonies of Indian Soldiers in the Two World Wars: Between Self and Sepoy* (London: Bloomsbury, 2014).

Sinha, Mrinalini, *Colonial Masculinity: The 'Manly Englishman' and the 'Effeminate Bengali' in the Late Nineteenth Century* (Manchester: Manchester University Press, 1995).

Sontag, Susan, *Regarding the Pain of Others* (London: Penguin, 2003).

Srimanjari, *Through War and Famine* (Hyderabad: Orient Blackswan, 2009).

Streets, Heather, *Martial Races: The Military, Race and Masculinity in British Imperial Culture, 1857–1914* (Manchester: Manchester University Press, 2004).

Sunderason, Sanjukta, *Partisan Aesthetics: Modern Art and India's Long Decolonisation* (Stanford, CA: Stanford University Press, 2020).

Terracciano, Emilia, *Art and Emergency: Modernism in Twentieth Century India* (London: I.B. Tauris, 2018).

Tett, David, *A Postal History of the Prisoners of War and Civilian Internees in East Asia during World War Two*, Volumes 1, 2 and 3 (Saint Paul, MN: BFA Publishing, 2002, 2003, 2004).

Tolley, A. Trevor, *The Poetry of the Forties* (Manchester: Manchester University Press, 1985).

Toye, Hugh, *The Springing Tiger: A Study of the Indian National Army and of Netaji Subhas Chandra Bose* (Delhi: Allied Publishers, 2009).

Vernon, James, *Hunger: A Modern History* (Cambridge, MA: Harvard University Press, 2007).

Visram, Rozina, *Asians in Britain: 400 Years of History* (London: Pluto Press, 2002).

Voigt, Johannes H., *India in the Second World War* (Amherst, NY: Prometheus Books, 1988).

Wagner, Kim, *Amritsar 1919: An Empire of Fear and the Making of a Massacre* (New Haven, CT: Yale University Press, 2019).

Webster, Wendy, *Mixing It: Diversity in World War Two Britain* (Oxford: Oxford University Press, 2018).

Winter, Jay, *War Beyond Words: Languages of Remembrance from the Great War to the Present* (Cambridge: Cambridge University Press, 2017).

Zim, Rivkah, *The Consolations of Writing: Literary Strategies of Resistance from Boethius to Primo Levi* (Princeton, NJ: Princeton University Press, 2014).

Chapters in Edited Volumes

Anand, Mulk Raj and Jane Williams, 'Talking of Tambi: The Dilemma of the Asian Intellectual', in *Tambimuttu: Bridge Between Two Worlds*, ed. by Jane Williams (London: Peter Owen, 1989), pp. 191–201.

Bessell, Richard, 'Death and Survival in the Second World War', in *The Cambridge History of the Second World War, Part II, The Social Practice of People's War, 1939–1945*, ed. by Michael Geyer and Adam Tooze (Cambridge: Cambridge University Press, 2015), pp. 252–276.

Bose, Brinda and Subhabrata Bhattacharya, 'Introduction', in *The Phobic and the Erotic: The Politics Of Sexualities In Contemporary India*, ed. by Brinda Bose and Subhabrata Bhattacharya (Calcutta: Seagull Books, 2007), pp. ix–xxxii.

Chatterjee, Indrani, 'Introduction', in *Unfamiliar Relations: Family and History in South Asia*, ed. by Indrani Chatterjee (New Brunswick, NJ: Rutgers University Press, 2004), pp. 3–45.

Chaudhuri, Sukanta, 'Tagore, Nationalism and Imperialism,' in *Tagore and Nationalism*, ed. by K.L. Tuteja and Kaustav Chakraborty (Delhi: Springer India, 2017), pp. 67–75.

Chaudhuri, Supriya, 'The Bengali Novel', in *The Cambridge Companion to Modern Indian Culture*, ed. by Vasudha Dalmia and Rashmi Sadana (Cambridge: Cambridge University Press, 2012), pp. 99–123.

Das, Santanu, 'Entangled Emotions: Race, Encounters and Anticolonial Cosmopolitanism', in *The First World War: Literature, Culture, Modernity*, ed. by Santanu Das and Kate McLoughlin (Oxford: Oxford University Press, 2018), pp. 240–261.

Friedman, Jonathan, 'Law and Politics in the Subsequent Nuremberg Trials, 1946–1949', in *Atrocities on Trial: Historical Perspectives on the Politics of Prosecuting War Crimes*, ed. by Patricia Heberer and Jürgen Matthäus (Lincoln, Nebraska: University of Nebraska Press, 2008), pp. 75–101.

Gandhi, Leela, 'Novelists of the 1930s and 1940s', in *A History of Indian Literature in English*, ed. by Arvind Mehrotra (London: Hurst, 2003), pp. 168–92.

Gupta, Avijit, 'Landforms of Southeast Asia', in *The Physical Geography of Southeast Asia*, ed. by Avijit Gupta (Oxford: Oxford University Press, 2005), pp. 38–64.

Kapila, Shruti, 'Preface and Acknowledgments', in *An Intellectual History for India*, ed. by Shruti Kapila (Cambridge: Cambridge University Press, 2010), pp. v–viii.

Kessler, Jeremy K., 'A War for Liberty: on the Law of Conscientious Objection', in *The Cambridge History of the Second World War: Part III— The Moral Economy of War and Peace*, ed. by Michael Geyer and Adam Tooze (Cambridge: Cambridge University Press, 2015), pp. 447–474.

Khan, Yasmin, 'Wars of Displacement: Exile and Uprooting in the 1940s', in *The Cambridge History of the Second World War Part II, The Social*

Practice of People's War 1939–1945, ed. by Michael Geyer and Adam Tooze (Cambridge: Cambridge University Press, 2015), pp. 277–297.

————, and Gajendra Singh, 'Introduction', in *An Imperial World at War: The British Empire, 1939–45*, ed. by Ashley Jackson, Yasmin Khan and Gajendra Singh (London: Routledge, 2016), pp. 1–9.

Mackay, Marina, 'Introduction', in *The Cambridge Companion to the Literature of the Second World War*, ed. by Marina Mackay (Cambridge: Cambridge University Press, 2009), pp. 1–9.

Mbembe, Achille, 'The Power of the Archive and its Limits', in *Refiguring the Archive*, ed. by Caroline Hamilton, Michele Pickover and Verne Harris (Cape Town: New Africa Books, 2002), pp. 19–27.

McKinnon-Croft, Russell, '*Der Erl-König*: A Personal Memory of Meary James Tambimuttu', in *Tambimuttu: Bridge Between Two Worlds*, ed. by Jane Williams (London: Peter Owen, 1989), pp. 52–55.

Mukherjee, Janam, 'Japan Attacks', in *Calcutta: The Stormy Decades*, ed. by Tanika Sarkar and Sekhar Bandyopadhyay (New Delhi: Social Science Press, 2015), pp. 93–120.

Nasta, Susheila, 'Negotiating a 'New World Order': Mulk Raj Anand as Public Intellectual at the Heart of Empire (1924–1945)' in *South Asian Resistances in Britain 1858–1947*, ed. by Rehana Ahmed and Sumita Mukherjee (London: Bloomsbury, 2012), pp. 140–60.

Noakes, Lucy, 'Communities of Feeling', in *Total War: An Emotional History*, ed. by Lucy Noakes, Claire Langhamer and Claudia Siebrecht (Oxford: Oxford University Press, 2020), pp. 116–136.

Parsons, Timothy, 'The Military Experiences of Ordinary Africans in World War II', in *Africa and World War II*, ed. by Judith Byfield, Carolyn Brown, Timothy Parsons and Ahmad Sikainga (Cambridge: Cambridge University Press, 2015), pp. 3–23.

Ramazani, Jahan, '"Cosmopolitan Sympathies": Poetry of the First Global War', in *The First World War: Literature, Culture, Modernity*, ed. by Santanu Das and Kate McLoughlin (Oxford: Oxford University Press, 2018), pp. 175–196.

Ranasinha, Ruvani, 'Textual Culture and Reception (1870–1950)', in *South Asians and the Shaping of Britain, 1870–1950*, ed. by Ruvani Ranasinha, Rehana Ahmed and Sumita Mukherjee (Manchester: Manchester University Press), pp. 147–206.

Robb, Linsey, and Juliette Pattinson, 'Becoming Visible: Gendering the

Study of Men at War', in *Men, Masculinities and Male Culture in the Second World War*, ed. by Linsey Robb and Juliette Pattinson (London: Palgrave Macmillan, 2017), pp. 1–24.

Sarkar, Tanika, 'Time in Place: Urban Culture in Decades of Crisis', in *Calcutta: The Stormy Decades*, ed. by Tanika Sarkar and Sekhar Bandyopadhyay (New Delhi: Social Science Press, 2015), pp. 461–474.

Siebrecht, Claudia, 'The Tears of 1939: German Women and the Emotional Archive of the First World War', in *Total War: An Emotional History*, ed. by Lucy Noakes, Claire Langhamer and Claudia Siebrecht (Oxford: Oxford University Press, 2020), pp. 78–97.

Snaith, Anna, 'Conversations in Bloomsbury: Colonial Writers and the Hogarth Press', in *Virginia Woolf's Bloomsbury, Volume 2: International Influence and Politics*, ed. by L. Shahriari and G. Potts (London: Palgrave Macmillan, 2010), pp. 138–157.

Spivak, Gayatri Chakravorty, 'Can the Subaltern Speak?', in *Marxism and the Interpretation of Culture*, ed. by Cary Nelson and Lawrence Grossberg (London: Macmillan, 1988), pp. 271–313.

Srimanjari, 'War, Famine and Popular Perceptions in Bengali Literature, 1939–1945', in *Issues in Modern Indian History: For Sumit Sarkar*, ed. by Biswamoy Pati (Mumbai: Popular Prakashan, 2000), pp. 258–290.

Srivastava, Sanjay, '"Sane Sex": the Five-Year Plan Hero and Men on Footpaths and in Gated Communities: On the Cultures of Twentieth-Century Masculinity', in *Masculinity and Its Challenges in India: Essays on Changing Perceptions*, ed. by Rohit K. Dasgupta and K. Moti Gokulsing (Jefferson, NC: McFarland & Company, 2014), pp. 27–53.

Stadtler, Florian, 'Britain's Forgotten Volunteers: South Asian Contributions to the Two World Wars', in *South Asians and the Shaping of Britain, 1870–1950: A Sourcebook*, ed. by Ruvani Ranasinha, Rehana Ahmed, Sumita Mukherjee and Florian Stadtler (Manchester: Manchester University Press, 2013), pp. 80–135.

———, '"Home" front: Indian soldiers and civilians in Britain, 1939–45', in *Culture, Conflict and the Military in Colonial South Asia*, ed. by Kaushik Roy and Gavin Rand (Abington: Routledge, 2018), pp. 258–276.

Sunder Rajan, Rajeswari, 'Death and the Subaltern', in *Can the Subaltern Speak? Reflections on the History of an Idea*, ed. by Rosalind Morris (New York, NY: Columbia University Press, 2010), pp. 117–138.

WORKS CITED

Wachsmann, Nikolaus, 'The Dynamics of Destruction: the Development of the Concentration Camps, 1933–1945', in *Concentration Camps in Nazi Germany: The New Histories*, ed. by Nikolaus Wachsmann and Jane Caplan (New York, NY: Routledge, 2009), pp. 17–43.

Young, Katherine, 'Hinduism and the Ethics of Weapons of Mass Destruction', in *The Nuclear Shadow over South Asia, 1947 to the Present*, ed. by Kaushik Roy and Scott Gates (London: Routledge, 2011), pp. 337–367.

Zachariah, Benjamin, 'The Creativity of Destruction: Wartime Imaginings of Development and Social Policy, *c*.1942–1946', in *The World in World Wars: Experiences, Perceptions and Perspectives from Africa and Asia*, ed. by Heike Liebau, Katrin Bromber, Katharina Lange, Dyala Hamzah and Ravi Ahuja (Leiden: Brill, 2010), pp. 547–579.

Journal Articles

Appadurai, Arjun, 'Patriotism and Its Futures', *Public Culture*, 5.3 (September 1993), 411–429.

Appiah, Kwame Anthony, 'Cosmopolitan Patriots', *Critical Inquiry*, 23:3 (1997), 617–639.

Barkawi, Tarak, 'Culture and Combat in the Colonies: The Indian Army in the Second World War', *Journal of Contemporary History*, 41. 2 (2006), 325–355.

Bhattacharya, Sanjoy, 'British Military Information Management Techniques and the South Asian Soldier: Eastern India during the Second World War', *Modern Asian Studies*, 34.2 (April 2000), 483–510.

Bhattacharya, Sourit, 'Writing famine, writing empire: food crisis and anticolonial aesthetics in Liam O'Flaherty's *Famine* and Bhabani Bhattacharya's *So Many Hungers!*', *Irish University Review*, 49.1 (2019), 54–73.

Campbell, James, 'Combat Gnosticism: The Ideology of First World War Poetry Criticism', *New Literary History*, 30 (1999), 203–15.

Chakrabarty, Dipesh, 'The Climate of History: Four Theses', *Critical Inquiry*, 35.2 (2009), 197–222.

Chatterjee, Partha, 'Book Review: Bricks and Mortar for Educational Reform', *India International Centre Quarterly*, 48.1 (Summer 2021), 132–135.

Das, Santanu, 'Reframing life/war "writing": objects, letters and songs of Indian soldiers, 1914–1918', *Textual Practice*, 29.7 (2015), 1–23.

Douds, G.J., 'The Men Who Never Were: Indian POWs in the Second World War', *South Asia: Journal of South Asian Studies*, 27. 2 (2010), 183–216.

Eyre, Angela, 'Organised Peasant Resistance in Fiction: *The Sword and The Sickle* and *The Lives of Others*', *South Asia Multidisciplinary Academic Journal*, 21 (2019), 1–18.

Fernandes, A.G., and K. Someswara Rao, 'Nutrition Work in the Indian Army', *Special Report Series—Indian Council of Medical Research*, 36.36 (1961), 73–96.

Ford, Douglas, '"A Conquerable Yet Resilient Foe": British Perceptions of the Imperial Japanese Army's Tactics on the India-Burma Front, September 1942 to Summer 1944', *Intelligence and National Security*, 18.1 (2003), 65–90.

Gerwarth, Robert, and Erez Manela, 'The Great War as a Global War: Imperial Conflict and the Reconfiguration of World Order, 1911–1923', *Diplomatic History*, 38.4 (September 2014), 786–800.

Ghosh, Devleena, 'Burma–Bengal Crossings: Intercolonial Connections in Pre-Independence India', *Asian Studies Review*, 40:2 (2016), 156–172.

Goodall, Heather, 'Port Politics: Indian Seamen, Australian Unions and Indonesian Independence, 1945–47', *Labour History*, 94 (2008), 43–68.

Goswami, Omkar, 'The Bengal Famine of 1943: Re-examining the Data', *Indian Economic and Social History Review*, 27.4 (December 1990), 445–463.

Green, L.C., 'The Indian National Army Trials', *The Modern Law Review*, 11.1 (1948), 47–69.

Habib, Irfan, 'The Left and the National Movement', *Social Scientist*, 26, 5/6 (May–June 1998), 3–33.

Harfield, Alan, 'The Women's Auxiliary Corps (India)', *Journal of the Society for Army Historical Research*, 83.335 (Autumn 2005), 243–254.

Heath, Deanna, 'Torture, the State, and Sexual Violence against Men in Colonial India', *Radical History Review*, 126 (2016), 122–133.

Jha, Saumitra and Steven Wilkinson, 'Does Combat Experience Foster Organisational Skill? Evidence from Ethnic Cleansing During the Partition of South Asia', *American Political Science Review*, 106.4 (November 2012), 1–50.

Joshi, Vandana, 'Between Erasure and Remembrance: Shreds from the Lives of South Asian Prisoners of War in Stammlagers, Arbeitskommandos, Lazaretts and Graves During World War II (1939–45)', *Südasien-Chronik—South Asia Chronicle*, 5 (2015), 144–168.

Kamtekar, Indivar, 'A Different War Dance: State and Class in India 1939–1945', *Past and Present*, 176.1 (2002), 187–221.

Kerr, Ian J., 'Representation and Representations of the Railways of Colonial and Post-colonial South Asia', *Modern Asian Studies*, 37 (May 2003), 287–326.

Khaitan, Urvi, 'The Shiver of 1942', *Studies in History*, 18.1 (2002), 81–102.

———, 'Women beneath the Surface: Coal and the Colonial State in India during the Second World War', *War and Society*, 39.3 (August 2020), 171–188.

Levine, Philippa, 'Naked Truths: Bodies, Knowledge, and the Erotics of Colonial Power', *Journal of British Studies* (January 2013) 52.1, 5–25.

Mahmud, Shabana, '*Angare* and the Founding of the Progressive Writers' Association', *Modern Asian Studies*, 30.2 (May 1996), 447–467.

Manela, Erez, 'Imagining Woodrow Wilson in Asia: Dreams of East-West Harmony and the Revolt against Empire in 1919', *The American Historical Review*, 111.5 (December 2006), 1327–1351.

Manjapra, Kris, 'From Imperial to International Horizons: a Hermeneutic Study of Bengali Modernism', *Modern Intellectual History*, 8.2 (2011), 327–359.

Morse, Daniel, 'An Impatient Modernist: Mulk Raj Anand at the BBC', *Modernist Cultures*, 10.1 (Spring 2015), 83–98.

Nandy, Pritish, 'The Poets', *Journal of South Asian Literature: Bengali Poetry Issue*, 9.4 (1974), 177–181.

Noon, Firozkhan, 'Resettlement of Soldiers', *The Asiatic Review* (July 1944), 287–295.

O'Hanlon, Rosalind, 'Issues of Masculinity in North Indian History: The Bangash Nawabs of Farrukhabad', *Bulletin (Centre for Women's Development Studies)*, 4.1 (March 1997), 1–19.

Ortiz, Michael P., 'Spain! Why? Jawaharlal Nehru, Non-Intervention, and the Spanish Civil War', *European History Quarterly*, 2019, 49(3), 445–466.

Priya, P., 'Malabar Famine of 1943: A Critique of War Situation in Malabar (1939–45)', *Proceedings of the Indian History Congress*, 75, Platinum Jubilee (2014), 628–638.

Ranasinha, Ruvani, 'South Asian broadcasters in Britain and the BBC: talking to India (1941–1943)', *South Asian Diaspora*, 2.1 (2010), 57–71.

Raychaudhuri, Tapan, 'Indian Nationalism as Animal Politics', *The Historical Journal*, 22.3 (September 1979), 747–763.

Rettig, Tobias, 'Recruiting the All-female Rani of Jhansi Regiment: Subhas Chandra Bose and Dr. Lakshmi Swaminadhan [*sic*]', *South East Asia Research*, 21.4 (2013), 627–638.

Sahni, Bhisham, 'The Progressive Writers' Movement', *Indian Literature*, 29.6 (116) (November–December 1986), 178–183.

Sarkar, Tanika, 'Birth of a Goddess: "Vande Mataram", "Anandamath", and Hindu Nationhood', *Economic and Political Weekly*, 41.37 (September 16–22, 2006), 3959–3969.

Sen, Amartya, 'Is Nationalism a Boon or a Curse?', *Economic and Political Weekly*, 43.7 (February 2008), 39–44.

Singh, Gajendra, 'The Anatomy of Dissent in the Military of Colonial India during the First and Second World Wars', *Edinburgh Papers in South Asian Studies*, 20 (2006), 1–45.

Snaith, Anna 'Introducing Mulk Raj Anand: the colonial politics of collaboration', *Literature & History*, 28.1 (May 2019), 10–26.

Tauger, Mark B., 'The Indian Famine Crises of World War II', *British Scholar*, 1.2 (2009), 166–196.

Trivedi, Madhu, 'Appropriating an Iranian Literary Tradition: Marsiya in the Indian Context', *Journal of the Indian Musicological Society*, 36–37 (2005/2006), 149–172.

Wilcox, Vanda, '"Weeping tears of blood": Exploring Italian soldiers' emotions in the First World War', *Modern Italy*, 17:2 (May 2012), 171–184.

Woods, Philip, 'From Shaw to Shantaram: The Film Advisory Board and the Making of British Propaganda Films in India, 1940–1943', *Historical Journal of Film, Radio and Television*, 21.3 (2001), 293–308.

Žižek, Slavoj, 'A Permanent Economic Emergency', *New Left Review*, 64 (August 2010), 85–95.

Online Sources

'Arnhem Hero Who Flicked V-sign at The Germans Dies at 97', <https://www.warhistoryonline.com/war-articles/wwii-3.html?safari=1&Exc_D_LessThanPoint002_p1=1> [Accessed 30 July 2022].

Ahmed Ullah, Ansar, 'The South Asian seaman's role during the wars' (Imperial War Museum, 2012) <https://www.iwm.org.uk/sites/default/files/transcripts/2018–04/The%20South%20Asian%

WORKS CITED

20seaman's%20role%20during%20the%20wars %2C%20Ansar%20 Ahmed%20Ullah%20.pdf> [Accessed 25 March 2022].

Bichitra: Online Tagore Variorum, <http://bichitra.jdvu.ac.in> [Accessed 30 July 2022].

Indian propaganda leaflets <http://stampomania.blogspot.com> [Accessed 31 May 2022].

Karnad, Raghu, 'Soldiers without borders: Fighting didn't stop for Indians after WWII', 8 November 2020, *The Indian Express* <https:// indianexpress.com/article/express-sunday-eye/soldiers-without-borders-6999026/> [Accessed 18 July 2022].

Khaitan, Urvi, ''The Women had saved the Situation': Indian Women's Work in War and Famine', <https://blog.royalhistsoc.org/2021/ 05/04/the-women-had-saved-the-situation-indian-womens-work-in-war-and-famine/> [Accessed 16 March 2022].

Matribhumi (*Motherland*, vol. 5 Magh—Chaitra, 1349; 1943 in the English calendar) <https://archive.org/details/dli.bengal.10689.3186/page/ n51/mode/2up> [Accessed 23 July 2022].

'Memorial Gates, Constitution Hill, 2008', National Army Museum's Online Collection <https://collection.nam.ac.uk/detail.php?acc= 2008–08–18–22> [Accessed 23 July 2022].

Progressive Writers' Association, The Open University's 'Making Britain' project, <https://www.open.ac.uk/researchprojects/makingbritain/content/progressive-writers-association> [Accessed 7 February 2022].

Regimental Association of the Queen's Own Highlanders (Seaforth and Cameron): <http://www.qohldrs.co.uk/html/camerons_history. htm> [Accessed 30 July 2022].

Sarkar, Jayita, 'How WWII shaped the crisis in Myanmar', <https:// www.washingtonpost.com/outlook/2019/03/10/how-wwii-shaped-crisis-myanmar/> [Accessed 30 July 2022].

Sartre, Jean-Paul, Preface to Frantz Fanon's *The Wretched of the Earth*, <https://www.marxists.org/reference/archive/sartre/1961/preface.htm> [Accessed 25 April 2022].

'Tara Ali Baig' <http://www.worldcat.org/wcidentities/lccn-n500 17949> [Accessed 15 February 2022].

'Where does "V" for Victory come from?', <https://www.iwm.org.uk/ history/where-does-v-for-victory-come-from> [Accessed 30 July 2022].

WORKS CITED

Unpublished Sources

Bass, Eleanor, "'A Threat to One's Skin": Representing the Human Body in Second World War Writing' (doctoral thesis, King's College London, 2015).

INDEX

Note: Page numbers followed by "*n*" refer to notes and "*f*" refer to figures.

Crasta, John Baptist, 24, 30,
    120–1, 125–6, 129–31
Crisis in Civilisation (Tagore), 31,
    218–19, 226–7
Cultural Politics of Emotion, The
    (Ahmed), 22
Currey, R.N., 176–7, 189
Cyprus, 39
Cyrenaica, 39, 86
Czechoslovakia, 217

Dacca, 79
Dachau concentration camp
    (1944), 10
Dalmia, Vasudha, 25
Das, Kamala, 182–3
Das, Santanu, 41, 66, 119, 164,
    210, 220
De, Bishnu, 27
Defence of India Act and Rules,
    40
Delhi, 164–5
Deshpande, Anirudh, 15–16, 18
Dhillon, Gurbaksh Singh, 13
Diamond Harbour, 79
Dimapur, 148
Douds, G.J., 126–7
'Dulce Et Decorum Est' (Owen),
    183
Dunkirk evacuation (1940), 123
Dunkirk, 229
'durbhikhher kobi', 108, 115
Dutch empire, 233
Dyer, Reginald, 8

Ealing, 197
East Africa, 14
East Asian communities, 127

East Bengal, 79, 184
Eaten by the Japanese (Crasta), 30,
    121, 125
Edwards, Elizabeth, 20
Egypt, 9, 14, 39, 86
Einstein, Albert, 218
Eliot, T.S., 109, 165, 195
Ellmann, Maud, 94, 99, 101–2
Empson, William, 165
England, 161–2, 221
English Patient, The (Ondaatje),
    231
Ethiopia
    Italy's invasion of, 217
Europe, 210, 220
    rise of fascism in, 217
European civilisation, 193, 222–3
European imperialism, 209, 220
Europeans, 124, 220
Ezra, N.E.B., 218

Fanon, Frantz, 210
Faridpur, 79
Farthest Field: An Indian Story of the
    Second World War (Karnad), 11,
    19
Fascibad O Nazibad (*Fascism and*
    Nazism), 27
Fay, Peter Ward, 66
Felman, Shoshana, 84–5, 184,
    190, 228
Finsbury, 197
Forgotten Armies, 149
Forster, E.M., 139–40
French empire, 233
French imperialism, 3
Frontier (newspaper), 109
Frontier Force Rifles, 48

impact on India, 8–9, 22, 79,
189
India's conflicted involvement
in, 25
Indian Army during, 15, 154
Indian army recruitment
during, 45
Indian PoW experience, 123
Indian women participation in,
160
Indian women's responses to,
174–5

letters written during, 40, 122
recruitment rise in Bengal,
147
Tambimuttu and Tagore views
on, 31

Yeats, W.B., 223
Yone Noguchi, 31, 195, 223–4

Zachariah, Benjamin, 16
Zahir, Sajjad, 26
zamindars, 7